Virgil's *Georgics*

# Virgil's *Georgics*

## A New Interpretation

Gary B. Miles

UNIVERSITY OF CALIFORNIA PRESS
BERKELEY · LOS ANGELES · LONDON

University of California Press
Berkeley and Los Angeles, California

University of California Press, Ltd.
London, England

© 1980 by The Regents of the University of California

Printed in the United States of America

1 2 3 4 5 6 7 8 9

**Library of Congress Cataloging in Publication Data**

Miles, Gary B
    Virgil's Georgics.

    Bibliography: p.
    1. Vergilius, Maro, Publicus. Georgica. I. Title.
PA6804.G4M5      871'.01      78-64460
ISBN 0-520-03789-8

*for Peggy*

# Contents

| | | |
|---|---|---|
| Abbreviations and Short Titles | | ix |
| Preface | | xi |
| CHAPTER I | The Roman Context | 1 |
| CHAPTER II | *Georgic* 1 | 64 |
| CHAPTER III | *Georgic* 2 | 111 |
| CHAPTER IV | *Georgic* 3 | 166 |
| CHAPTER V | *Georgic* 4 | 226 |
| A Bibliographical Note | | 295 |

# Abbreviations and Short Titles

Titles of ancient works are abbreviated as in the *Oxford Classical Dictionary*, with slight modifications. Journals and other frequently cited works are abbreviated as follows:

| | |
|---|---|
| *AJPh* | *American Journal of Philology* |
| *Bul. Inst. Cl. Stud.* | *Bulletin of the Institute of Classical Studies of the University of London* |
| *CSCA* | *California Studies in Classical Antiquity* |
| *CW* | *Classical World* |
| Frazer | J. G. Frazer, ed. and comm., *The Fasti of Ovid* (London 1929, reprinted Hildesheim 1973) |
| *GRBS* | *Greek, Roman and Byzantine Studies* |
| Grimal | Pierre Grimal, *Les Jardins Romains à la fin de la République aux deux premiers siècles de l'Empire: Essai sur le naturalisme romain* = *Bibliothèque des Écoles Françaises d'Athènes et de Rome*, 155 (1943), second ed. with revisions, Paris 1969 |
| *HSCPh* | *Harvard Studies in Classical Philology* |
| *JHS* | *Journal of Hellenic Studies* |
| *JRS* | *Journal of Roman Studies* |
| *MDAI(R)* | *Mitteilungen des Deutschen Archäologischen Instituts (Römische Abteilung)* |
| *RE* | A. Pauly, G. Wissowa, and W. Kroll, *Real-Encyclopädie der klassischen Altertumswissenschaft* (Stuttgart 1893–) |

| | |
|---|---|
| *REL* | *Revue des Études Latines* |
| Roscher | W. H. Roscher, ed. *Ausführliches Lexikon der Greichischen und Römischen Mythologie* (Leipzig 1884–, reprinted Hildesheim 1965) |
| *RPh* | *Revue Philologique* |
| Servius | *Servii Grammatici qui feruntur in Vergilii Bucolica et Georgica commentarii*, ed. Georgius Thilo (Leipzig 1927) |
| *Sitz. Berl. Akad.* | *Sitzungsberichte der preussischen Akademie der Wissenschaften zu Berlin* |
| *YCS* | *Yale Classical Studies* |

# Preface

Modern criticisms of Virgil's *Georgics* have generally proceeded on the basis of two assumptions, whether stated or implied. The first is that, notwithstanding the dramatic addresses to the new Caesar and other prominent references to contemporary social and political conditions, the poem is an exposition or, more recently, an idealization of rustic life. The second is that, despite the shifts of tone, emphasis, and perspective which casual readers and critics alike often find bewildering and disorienting, the various parts of the poem all contribute to the elaboration of a single vision of rustic life—that is, that the poem is coherent only if the separate descriptions of rustic life can all be shown to be consistent with each other, complementary aspects of a single vision. My own approach to the *Georgics* is different on both counts.

As I argue in my introductory chapter, changing life-styles, the influence of Hellenistic culture, and the disruptions of the Roman civil wars all contributed to the elaboration not of a single myth, but of several quite different myths about rustic life. Rustic life might variously be associated with the origins of Roman civilization and evoked as the source of those austere yet essentially public-spirited virtues by which the governing aristocracy of Rome characterized themselves, or, to the contrary, it might be seen as offering one or another alternative to the chaos of the city and of politics. The countryside seemed to promise the opportunities both for enjoyment of unprecedented luxury and, equally, for the return to a life of simple tastes and simple virtues. By the time of the *Georgics* representations of rustic life had become a major literary mode of commentary on contemporary events and the larger speculations they provoked about the nature of civilization and the human condition. Therefore, even though Virgil's primary concerns in the *Georgics* were political and philosophical, not agricultural, his choice of a treatise on agriculture as a vehicle for communicating them to the new ruler of the civilized world was neither particularly idiosyncratic nor oblique, but rather fully appropriate to the times.

Appreciation of the diverse, often conflicting interpretations of rustic life in contemporary Roman literature provides an insight into the structure of the *Georgics*. Successive books of the poem may be seen as elaborating and critically examining quite different versions of rustic life, each with its own implications for understanding the nature of civilization and the task of reconstruction that faced the new leader of Rome. Recurrent motifs help to provide a common background against which the distinctive qualities of the different points of view in the poem stand out clearly. Those same recurrent motifs define the irreduceable realities with which all efforts to characterize rustic life or to define the nature of civilization must come to terms. They emerge gradually as the underlying basis for a view of the human condition that cannot be identified with any one description or combination of descriptions of the farmer's world in the *Georgics*—a view of the human condition that is only developed directly and fully in the concluding myth of Aristaeus.

Several considerations have prompted me to keep my references to scholarly interpretations of the *Georgics* to an absolute minimum. My own discussion, although it follows the sequence of the poem, is primarily concerned with what I see as the interplay of different perspectives in the poem and how they effectively comment on one another. Thus, inasmuch as I am concerned with concatenations of passages and their resonances throughout the poem, it has seemed to me that it would be largely superfluous and distracting to become embroiled in controversies about the interpretation of specific passages. My hope is that my readings of individual passages will be confirmed by their consistency with the larger thematic developments of the poem as I elaborate them. I do define the place of my interpretation of the *Georgics* in relation to previous modern criticism in the final section of my introductory chapter, "The Roman Context." I also include a short bibliographical essay at the end of the book. For the rest, I have attempted to present my interpretation in as straightforward a way as possible.

A second reason for minimizing discussions of contemporary scholarship is that I have tried in organization and style to make my argument broadly accessible. To that end I have not only avoided footnotes where I could, but also have translated all Greek and Latin quotations and have tried to make as explicit as possible all references to the literature, events, or thoughts that defined the context of the *Georgics* for its Roman audience. My hope and intention was to have something of interest and value to say to specialists in my field, but I have also tried to be intelligible to scholars in related fields, to undergraduates, and to all who may have some interest in Virgil and the intellectual history of classical Rome. Because the greater part of this book is devoted to an interpretation that focuses quite narrowly on the *Georgics* and because my own arguments tend generally to follow the sequential development of the poem, I have felt that an index would serve little purpose and accordingly have not supplied one.

Since the preparation of this book has extended intermittently over a period of some nine years, it now reflects the generous advice, assistance, and stimulation of several friends and colleagues. Adam Parry, late Professor of Classics at Yale University, introduced me to the *Georgics* in a course devoted to that poem and subsequently both encouraged and challenged me in my first imperfect efforts to come to terms with the *Georgics* in my Ph.D. dissertation. It was from him that I learned to think of the poem as a profoundly ambitious work of philosophical speculation; and without his unusual literary sophistication and his sympathy for my determination, more often than not unsuccessful in those years, to develop an approach to the poem that might begin to make sense of its elusive and bewildering shifts of tone and perspective, the interpretation I have since elaborated would have been unthinkable. When I arrived in California, still not satisfied with my efforts to understand the *Georgics*, conversations with Harry Berger, Jr. and Thomas Vogler, friends and colleagues in Cowell College, University of California, Santa Cruz, stimulated new approaches to the problem. With their encouragement I began to think of the *Georgics* more as structurally and conceptually analogous with the *Eclogues*. More recently, my friend

John Lynch, also a colleague in Cowell College, commented on the first chapter of the manuscript with a perceptiveness and candor for which I am most grateful. His suggestions not only improved that chapter but were of considerable assistance to me in the revision of subsequent chapters as well. To the editors and readers of the University of California Press I am indebted both for their encouragement and for their constructive criticisms. I have been extremely fortunate in being able to call upon typists of the University of California, Santa Cruz, most notably Charlotte Cassidy, Elaine Dilts, and Phyllis Halpin of the Cowell College Steno Pool, and Judy Burton, manuscript typist for the Division of Social Sciences. Their conscientiousness, good judgment, and impeccable professionalism have been an inspiration and a real cause for pleasure. It is perhaps fitting that I should have to thank at the end of this project the man who introduced me to Greek and Latin and by his excellence as a teacher induced me to become a classicist, Archibald W. Allen. He read the final typescript version with great care and thoughtfulness, saved me from innumerable small embarrassments—as well as a few not so small—and made patient suggestions for the improvement of my style. In light of the very generous assistance I received, it must be clear that whatever errors or shortcomings remain can only be due to the oversights, misjudgments, or obstinacy of the author himself.

I would like also to express my appreciation of the Public Library of Santa Cruz, California, for the attractive and peaceful setting in which I drafted the greater part of this book.

I regret that I did not have the benefit of Michael Putnam's new book, *Virgil's Poem of the Earth: Studies in the Georgics* (Princeton 1979) before my own book was already at press. However, I am much encouraged to find that we are in basic agreement on the larger design of the poem and in our new readings of several specific passages, even though our approaches and styles of interpretation are quite different.

Above all I am indebted to my wife Peggy, who has borne with me in the frustrations and has shared with me the joys of this labor. It is as a small token of my gratitude and love that I have dedicated this book to her.

CHAPTER I

# The Roman Context

I

We can be quite confident of the kind of audience Virgil had in mind when he composed the *Georgics*. His *Eclogues*, written earlier, contain many references to historical personages, so many, in fact, that scholars have been encouraged to regard even some of the fictitious characters of these pastorals as representations of still other historical figures, including the poet himself.[1] The Fourth *Eclogue* is addressed to a consul, Pollio, and to a newborn child whose birth and growth to maturity will usher in a new Golden Age. In addition to being an influential politician, Pollio was a man of letters and an important patron of literature, responsible for the first library and first public recitations of poetry at Rome.[2] The identity of the child and his parents is disputed; but if they are, in fact, historical and not symbolic figures, then in the absence of external evidence to the contrary the context suggests that we regard them as social equals of the distinguished statesman to whom the poem is dedicated. The principal figure of the Tenth *Eclogue* is Gaius Cornelius Gallus. Although not of an aristocratic Roman family, he rose under Octavian to the rank

---

1. A list of all the works that include speculations about the identity of the herdsmen of the *Eclogues* would have to include almost the entire corpus of commentary on the poems. The process began very early in antiquity, very likely with the *Eclogues*' first publication. The oldest known attempt of this sort occurs in Servius' identification of Tityrus with Virgil in his commentary on the first line of the first *Eclogue*.
2. Pliny, *HN* 7.30.115; 35.2.10.

*1*

of Eques and after the young Caesar's defeat of Cleopatra was honored with the prefecture of Egypt, a position of special trust which he held until he fell from favor in 29 B.C. Gallus was also one of the distinguished young poets who were introducing new forms and attitudes into Roman literature under the stimulus of the Hellenistic poetry of Alexandria. Other poets who seem to have shared Gallus' tastes are also named in the *Eclogues*, Varius Rufus and Gaius Helvius Cinna in *Eclogue* 9, for example.[3] Virgil's own poetry reveals clearly that he shared many, if not all, of their aesthetic predilections.[4]

The *Georgics* itself offers evidence that, although perhaps less varied than that of the *Eclogues*, points no less emphatically to the same kind of audience. The poem is dedicated to Maecenas, a dilettante rather than a distinguished poet, but the most important patron of the arts in his age, the center of an important group of poets, friend and confidant of the young Caesar, and a man whose ancestry was aristocratic, no less so for being Etruscan rather than Roman.[5] But pride of place in the *Georgics* is reserved for the young Caesar himself. He is the subject of two extraordinarily enthusiastic invocations, of which one introduces the poem and looks ahead to the young hero's deification; the other introduces the third *Georgic*

---

3. In addition to being a distinguished elegiac, epic, and tragic poet, Varius is said to have been one of those who edited the *Aeneid* after Virgil died (Donat., *Vita Verg.* 37). Gallus was a leader among those called neoterics, or "new poets," by Cicero (*at Att.* 7.2.1). Those innovators should not be thought of as forming a specific school, but rather more loosely as sharing common interests, particularly in certain aspects of Alexandrian and especially Callimachean poetics. A. Traglia, *Poetarum Latinorum Reliquiae* vol. 8, *Novi Poetae* (Rome 1962), offers convenient access to the "new poets" in that it collects the extant fragments of their work in a single volume, provides a biographical sketch and a select bibliography for each author, and is a good general introduction to the neoterics and their predecessors. The work is marred by numerous errors of detail, however. The subsequent publication of the second edition of W. Morel's *Fragmenta Poetarum Latinorum* (Stuttgart 1963), in the Teubner series, offers a more reliable text and apparatus, although without the kind of supplementary commentary that Traglia provides.

4. Much has been written on Virgil as a neoteric and on his indebtedness to Alexandrianism and Callimachus. The most significant general discussions are: Wendel Clausen's short but important "Callimachus and Latin Poetry," *GRBS* 5 (1964) 181-196; Brooks Otis, *Virgil: A Study in Civilized Poetry* (Oxford 1964, reprinted with corrections 1966), esp. chs. 2 and 3; J. K Newman, *Augustus and the New Poetry* (Brussels 1967) = *Collection Latomus* 88; Walter Wimmel, *Kallimachos in Rom* (Wiesbaden 1960) = *Hermes* Einzelschriften Heft 16.

5. Horace's celebration of Maecenas' noble ancestry is famous as the first line of the first poem of his first book of *Odes: Maecenas atavis edite regibus* ("Maecenas, descended from ancestral kings").

(and, thus, the second half of the poem) and contemplates the prospect of Caesar as conqueror of the entire world. The poem concludes with yet another address to Caesar and a reference to his triumphant progress. However mundane the subject of the *Georgics* may at first appear, the poem was written for the political, social, and intellectual aristocracy of Virgil's day.

Examination of the *Georgics* itself, of course, offers the most obvious means of coming to terms with the paradox of a poem that purports to offer instruction in the practical technicalities of farming to such an audience. But before turning to the poem, it is essential to consider the relationship of Rome's aristocracy to the countryside, since their attitudes as much as or perhaps even more than the actual practice of agriculture defined the context within which Virgil wrote the *Georgics*. The intensity of interest in the countryside and the possibilities of country life was never greater in any period of Roman history than in the years preceding and during Virgil's composition of his poem on rustic life. It would have been impossible for anyone of his age to read the poem except in the context of the varied attitudes toward country life that were current among the contemporary Roman and Italian aristocracy. Inevitably, the distinctive vision offered in the *Georgics* would have had interest not only in its own right but also as a commentary on other contemporary attitudes.

## II

A number of quite different, often conflicting, circumstances contributed to the making of those attitudes. To begin with, Rome was a traditional or archaic society. The concept of social progress was not important among Romans. Rather, they looked back to an ideal past, the era of Rome's founding and early rise to power. Efforts to recreate the past or to retrieve the spirit of the past were more urgent than efforts to realize a utopia in the future.[6] *Res novae*

---

6. The best general discussion of the glorification of the past in antiquity is E. R. Dodds, "The Ancient Concept of Progress," first delivered as the Frazer Lecture at the University of Glasgow, 1969, a revised version of which appears as the first chapter (pp. 1-25) in a collection of essays by Dodds published under the title *The Ancient Concept of Progress* (Oxford 1973). For a compilation and analysis of relevant texts, see A. O. Lovejoy and George Boas, *Primitivism and Related Ideas in Antiquity*, vol. I of *A Documentary History of Primitivism and Related Ideas*, ed. A. O. Lovejoy (Baltimore 1935), reprinted as vol. I of the series, "Contributions to the History of Primitivism" (New York 1965).

("new things") referred to seditious attacks on established ways and institutions.[7] However much Romans may have changed their ways in fact, they continued to justify their own actions and to judge those of others by the examples of the past. The highest sanction— the standard to which Cicero, for example, appealed repeatedly in his orations—was the *mos maiorum* ("the way of our ancestors"). The oldest examples were the most venerated. Writing at the beginning of the second century B.C., the poet Ennius asserted that *moribus antiquis res stat Romana virisque* ("the Roman state is what she is because of her ancient customs and her men").[8]

As a consequence, Romans never forgot their rustic origins. Rather, they glorified and idealized them. Vitruvius (2.15) tells of old-fashioned huts including "the hut of Romulus," which were kept as reminders of the past. In a description of the huts that the earliest Latins inhabited, Dionysius of Halicarnassus also refers to Romulus' hut and its preservation as a kind of national monument (1.79):

> There remained even to my day [c. 30 B.C.] on the flank of the Palatine Hill that faces toward the Circus a certain [hut] said to be that of Romulus. Those who are charged with such matters guard it as holy. They add nothing to make it more stately, but if any of it should fall into disrepair on account of a storm or time, they restore the damage completely and make it as much like it was before as they are able.

A report in Cassius Dio (54, 29) indicates that the hut was maintained at least until 12 B.C. when, allegedly, crows dropped burning meat from an altar on its roof and set it ablaze.

Central to worship of the past was a tradition that the source of Roman greatness as a nation lay in the virtues of ancestors whose chief occupation was either to work the land themselves or to supervise the management of their own farms. Livy's story of L. Quinctius Cincinnatus, the farmer-statesman who was called from his plow to save the Republic and returned to his plow again after the crisis had passed, is but one of several versions involving different Quinctii.[9] It may reflect Livy's own biases; but the ideal of the

---

7. In this sense it is attested in the historical works of Sallust and both the orations and private correspondence of Cicero.

8. *Annales* fr. 500 in the edition of J. Vahlen, *Ennianae Poesis Reliquiae*³ (Leipzig 1928).

9. For discussion of the story of Cincinnatus at the plow and its legendary origins, see R. M. Ogilvie, *A Commentary on Livy, Books I-V* (Oxford 1965) 441. Cf. also the story in

farmer-statesman was a matter of legend, not Livy's own creation, and reflects a tradition that must have been maintained orally for generations before it was first committed to writing.[10]

Such traditions had considerable force, especially for the ruling aristocracy who identified themselves most closely with Roman tradition and were expected to be worthy of it in their own lives. The classic assertion of the privileged position of agriculture in Roman tradition occurs about 150 B.C. in the preface to Cato the Elder's *De Agricultura*:

> Et virum bonum quom laudabant, ita laudabant, bonum agricolam bonumque colonum. Amplissime laudari existimabatur qui ita laudabatur. Mercatorem autem strenuum studiosumque rei quaerendae existimo, verum, ut supra dixi, periculosum et calamitosum. At ex agricolis et viri fortissimi et milites strenuissimi gignuntur, maximeque pius quaestus stabilissimusque consequitur minimeque invidiosus, minimeque male cogitantes sunt qui in eo studio occupati sunt.
>
> And when [our ancestors] praised a man, they praised him thus: good farmer and good settler. One so praised was thought to be very fully praised. The merchant I regard as energetic and eager to acquire wealth; but, as I said above, he is exposed to danger and disaster. It is from farmers, however, that both the bravest men and the most energetic soldiers come, there follows from them the most pious livelihood, one least likely to provoke envy; and those engaged in that pursuit are least dissatisfied.

One may be inclined to regard Cato's enthusiasm with some reserve. He was distinguished among his contemporaries and later Romans alike for his almost fanatical harping on the value of traditional ways, an insistence inspired, in part, perhaps, because he was himself a newcomer to Rome's ruling aristocracy. Eccentric he may have been, but he struck a responsive chord among his peers. A hundred years later Cicero recalled (*De Off.* 2.25.89)

> illud est Catonis senis; a quo cum quaereretur, quid maxime in re familiari expediret, respondit: "bene pascere"; quid secondum: "satis bene pascere"; quid tertium: "male pascere"; quid

---

Valerius Maximus 4.4.5 of C. Atilius Regulus Serranus (Cos. 257 B.C.) found at work at his plow by a deputation of senators.

10. Ogilvie, ibid. 441, observes, moreover, that "the story was . . . firmly established by the first century B.C., for it is cited by Cicero (*de Domo* 86)."

quartum: "arare." et cum ille, qui quaesierat, dixisset "quid faenerari?" tum Cato: "quid hominem, inquit, occidere?"

that famous saying of Cato when he was an old man. When he was asked by someone what was most profitable in managing property, he replied, "Raising livestock well." What was next best? "Raising livestock satisfactorily." What was third best? "Raising them poorly." What was forth? "Plowing." And when the person who questioned him said, "How about lending money at interest?" then Cato said, "How about killing someone?"

Cicero did not quote Cato merely because he was colorful. He made his own clear and revealing statement on the subject (*De Off.* 1.42,151):

Mercatura autem, si tenuis est, sordida putanda est; sin magna et copiosa, multa undique apportans multisque sine vanitate impertiens, non est admodum vituperanda, atque etiam, si satiata quaestu vel contenta potius, ut saepe ex alto in portum, ex ipso portu se in agros possessionesque contulit, videtur iure optimo posse laudari. Omnium autem rerum, ex quibus aliquid acquiritur, nihil est agri cultura melius, nihil uberius, nihil dulcius, nihil homine libero dignius.

Commerce, moreover, if on a small scale, is to be regarded as sordid. But if it is great and on a large scale, importing many things from many places, and serving many without dishonesty, then it is not so objectionable. Indeed, if the merchant turns from the port to lands and possessions satisfied or, better, content with his profit, just as he often turns from the sea to port, then he seems really to deserve praise. However, of all things from which there is some profit, nothing is better than agriculture, nothing more fruitful, nothing more satisfying, nothing more worthy of a free man.

The Roman sense of identification with and indebtedness to rustic life received particular impetus from exposure to Hellenistic civilization during the second century B.C. Romans were aware that their own culture was rather narrow by the standards of the Hellenistic world. At the same time, they were able to contrast the stability of their own society and their martial preeminence with the political confusion and military weakness of the Hellenistic nations whom they conquered. One important consequence of their ambivalence about their relation to the Hellenistic world was that it encouraged them to make virtues of the very characteristics that caused them to appear backward by Hellenistic standards. They had come to regard the refinement and luxury that were so impressive in the East as both symptoms and causes of its weakness, effeminacy, degeneration.[11] By contrast, in mastering the world Romans felt that they had proved their superiority in the qualities that mattered. They attributed those qualities to the very simplicity and hardiness of their ancestors' way of life.

It is probably no coincidence that the same Cato who affirmed the values of Rome's agrarian traditions in *De Agricultura* wrote at the time when the influence of Hellenistic culture was first beginning to permeate Roman life. And although he undoubtedly took an interest in it and learned from it,[12] he was staunchly and volubly opposed to the general adoption of Hellenistic ways. Cicero's introduction to the *Tusculanae Disputationes* (45/44 B.C.) offers one of the clearest examples of the way in which Romans came to define themselves by contrast to Hellenistic culture (*TD* 1.13):

> hoc mihi Latinis litteris inlustrandum putavi, non quia philosophia Graecis et litteris et doctoribus percipi non posset, sed meum semper iudicium fuit omnia nostros aut invenisse per se sapientius quam Graecos aut accepta ab illis fecisse meliora, quae quidem digna statuissent, in quibus elaborarent. Nam mores et instituta vitae resque domesticas ac familiaris nos profecto et melius tuemur et lautius, rem vero publicam nostri maiores certe melioribus temperaverunt et institutis et legibus.

---

11. Comments on the effeminacy and moral degeneration of Easterners are common in the literature of the Augustan Age. Direct and explicit commentary to that effect is rare in Roman literature before the *Georgics*. Modern commentators most often cite Catullus 11.5, but the very un-Roman characterization of Greeks in the comedies of Plautus and Terrence, and the notion of *pergraecare*, "to act the Greek," which Plautus exploits also deserve notice. See Erich Segal, *Roman Laughter* (Cambridge, Mass. 1968) 33-41 et passim. In the *Georgics* see the extended contrast between Italy and the East, *Georgic* 2.136-172. Roman concern (expressed as early as the second century B.C.) that Eastern influence was undermining Roman society provides ample indirect evidence for the Romans' critical assessment of Easterners' character and morals. That evidence is discussed by A. W. Lintott, "Imperial Expansion and Moral Decline in the Roman Republic," *Historia* 21 (1972) 626-638.

12. See A. D. Leeman's analysis of the introduction to *De Agricultura* in *Orationis Ratio* (Amsterdam 1963), vol. 1, pp. 21-25.

Quid loquar de re militari? in qua cum virtute nostri multum valuerunt, tum plus etiam disciplina. Iam illa, quae natura, non litteris adsecuti sunt, neque cum Graecia neque ulla cum gente sunt conferenda. Quae enim tanta gravitas, quae tanta constantia, magnitudo animi, probitas, fides, quae tam excellens in omni genere virtus in ullis fuit, ut sit cum maioribus nostris comparanda? Doctrina Graecia nos et omni litterarum genere superabat, in quo erat facile vincere non repugnantes . . . Sero igitur a nostris poëtae vel cogniti vel recepti. Quamquam est in Originibus solitos esse in epulis canere convivas ad tibicinem de clarorum hominum virtutibus.

I thought that I ought to elucidate [philosophy] in Latin, not because [it] can't be learned from Greek literature and teachers, but my judgment has always been that our people on their own have discovered all things more wisely than the Greeks or, on receiving discoveries from the Greeks, have improved on them —at least those things that they regarded as worth the effort. As to customs, ways of life, and domestic and economic affairs, surely we see to them better and with more distinction; and our ancestors without a doubt organized the state with better institutions and laws. What need I say about military activity, in which our people are strong not only in courage but also in discipline? Now, those things that are achieved by nature, not by literary theory, are beyond compare either with the Greeks or with any other people. What dignity, what constancy, breadth of vision, honesty, loyalty, what virtue in every area has been so outstanding that it could be compared with that of our ancestors? Greece surpassed us in learning and in every branch of literature where it was easy to conquer those who did not resist. . . . Therefore, among us, poets were either received or acknowledged late. And yet according to [Cato's] *Origines* guests at banquets used to sing to the flute about the virtues of famous men.

Inevitably, the vision of Rome's unique excellence that emerged from such contrasts with the Hellenistic world was projected back upon Rome's past and influenced the interpretation of it.

Rome's backwardness and her rustic origins need not be causes for embarrassment or apology. Far from it, they were, paradoxically, the very basis of her greatness. That idea became a major theme of Augustan literature during and shortly after the time that Virgil was composing the *Georgics*. Cicero himself seems rarely to miss an opportunity to insist on the wisdom of the early Romans at the expense of the Greeks. Even in his earliest orations he contrasted Greek and Roman responses to the crime of parricide (*Pro S. Roscio Am.* 70):

> prudentissima civitas Atheniensium, dum ea rerum potita est, fuisse traditur; eius porro civitatis sapientissimum Solonem dicunt fuisse, eum, qui leges, quibus hodie quoque utuntur, scripsit: is cum interrogaretur cur nullum supplicium constituisset in eum, qui parentem necasset, respondit se id neminem facturum putasse. Sapienter fecisse dicitur, cum de eo nihil sanxerit, quod antea commissum non erat, ne non tam prohibere quam admonere videretur. Quanto nostri maiores sapientius? Qui cum intellegerent nihil esse tam sanctum, quod non aliquando violaret audacia, supplicium in parricidas singulare excogitaverunt.
>
> The state of Athens is said to have been very clear-sighted so long as it was independent. They say, moreover, that Solon was its wisest man: he wrote the laws which they still use today. When he was asked why he had set up no punishment for the person who had killed a parent, he replied that he thought no one would do that. He is said to have acted wisely since he created no sanction against a crime that had not previously been committed, not wanting to seem as though he were suggesting the crime rather than prohibiting it. How much wiser were our ancestors. Since they understood that nothing is so sacred that audacity does not at some time or other violate it, they thought up a special punishment against parricides.

Here, the wisest of the Athenians, the man who by his laws could almost be regarded as the father of the state, is shown to be inferior to his Roman counterparts, men who, unlike Solon, were so undistinguished that their names are unknown.

The paradoxical idea that the wisdom of the *maiores* was due to the rustic simplicity of their lives underlies Cicero's celebration of Rome's founders in *De Republica*. Cicero has the interlocutors of that dialogue express their fulsome admiration for the extraordinary perspicacity of Romulus, who founded Rome on such principles that it endured and became great beyond any other nation. Romulus is shown to be worthy of comparison with the most distinguished lawgivers and philosophers of Greece (2.1-12). In comparing Romulus and the Greeks, moreover, Cicero places great emphasis on the relative antiquity and development of Greek civilization and on how young and primitive the society was from which Romulus came. He makes that comparison not to illustrate Roman dependence on Greek models or to apologize for the inadequacies of Roman civilization, but rather to insist on the extraordinary wisdom of Rome's humble founders, men whose only schooling was their way of life. The eulogy of Romulus begins with a brief summary of the myth of his exposure, suckling by a wolf, and rustic upbringing (*De Republica* 2.4):

> quo in loco cum esset silvestris beluae sustentatus uberibus pastoresque eum sustulissent et in agresti cultu laboreque aluissent, perhibetur, ut adoleverit, et corporis viribus et animi ferocitate tantum ceteris praestitisse, ut omnes, qui tum eos agros, ubi hodie est haec urbs, incolebant, aequo animo illi libenterque parerent.

> There, when he had been suckled at the udder of a wild beast, and shepherds had rescued him and brought him up in the way of life and work of the fields, he so far surpassed others in strength of body and fierceness of spirit as he grew up, that all people who then inhabited the fields where this city is today willingly and gladly obeyed him.

Romulus' anonymous followers shared something of his wisdom (*De Republica* 2.24):

> quo quidem tempore novus ille populus vidit tamen id, quod fugit Lacedaemonium Lycurgum, . . . nostri illi etiam tum agrestes viderunt virtutem et sapientiam regalem, non progeniem quaeri oportere.

> Even then [during the royal period], that new people nonetheless perceived what escaped the Lacedaemonian, Lycurgus. . . . Our distinguished ancestors, rustics even at that late date, perceived that regal manliness and wisdom, not royal ancestry, were what ought to be sought after.

The founders of Rome were exceptional by any standards. Although their way of life was not enough in itself to explain their character or achievements, the repeated emphasis on it suggests that it was not incidental either. If rustic life did not make such men inevitable, we are left with a sense that it served to reinforce their distinctive virtues—their manliness, their prudence, their unerring common sense.[13]

In the oration in defense of Sextus Roscius of Ameria, delivered some years before publication of the *De Republica*, Cicero had explicitly ascribed Roman greatness to rustic life (*Pro Sext. Rosc. Am.* 50):

> At hercule maiores nostri longe aliter et de illo [the farmer-statesman, Atilius] et de ceteris talibus viris existimabant; itaque ex minima tenuissimaque re publica maximam et florentissimam nobis reliquerunt; suos enim agros studiose colebant, non alienos cupide appetebant: quibus rebus et agris et urbibus et nationibus rem publicam atque hoc imperium et populi Romani nomen auxerunt.

> Certainly our ancestors thought quite differently of that man [the farmer-statesman Atilius] and others like him; and so instead of a very small and insignificant nation, they left us one that was great and prosperous. For they busily worked their own land and did not push for that of others. In this way they augmented with territory and cities and nations this republic, this empire, and the fame of the Roman people.

Such an explicit statement of the value of Rome's agrarian past, however, reveals a striking dilemma: the highest value of rustic virtues lies in their contribution to the rise of Roman civilization, the city of Rome, and her empire. That dilemma cannot be explained away by reducing rustic virtues to the status of means to a higher end, since the end they make possible is that very society which now alienates Romans from the rustic source of their virtues. We must, therefore, see their attitudes toward their rustic origins as ambivalent.

---

13. Cf. Livy's assessment of Numa (1.18): *Suopte igitur ingenio temperatum animum uirtutibus fuisse opinor magis instructumque non tam peregrinis artibus quam disciplina tetrica ac tristi ueterum Sabinorum, quo genere nullum quondam incorruptius fuit* ("Therefore, I believe that his spirit was tempered with virtues by his native character and was instructed not so much by foreign techniques as by the fearsome and dour discipline of the ancient Sabines: no people were ever more upright than they").

Likewise, even though the sophistication and grandeur of the Hellenistic world provoked Romans to an aggressive glorification of their own past, those qualities exercised a considerable, ultimately irresistible, attraction. Romans were particularly receptive to new relationships to the countryside that were exemplified in Hellenistic culture, because exposure to them coincided with significant social and economic changes in their own traditional way of life. As the business of governing Rome and her dependencies became more demanding and complex, the ruling elite were drawn more and more from the countryside to the City. During his year as governor of Cilicia, Cicero's longing for Rome, his anxiety that his term of office might be extended, and his dependence on correspondence for all the major news of the day reveal clearly how frustrating and politically inconvenient absence from Rome had become for someone who was committed to a political career.[14] Since the *nobiles* were among the wealthiest of Romans and stood at the pinnacle of Roman society, their move to the City made it the center of social as well as political life.

The tremendous influx of wealth into Rome as a consequence of military conquests during the second century and an escalating standard of living created new economic possibilities which greatly exacerbated the separation of Rome's elite from the countryside. Moneylending and various forms of speculation provided the means to quick and sometimes immense personal fortunes. Even more directly relevant to the character of rustic life was the availability of capital and of cheap slaves, which led to the acquisition of larger and increasing numbers of farming properties by private individuals. The time when an important Roman would actually contribute to the physical work of his farm had largely passed by the second century B.C., as slaves became an increasingly important part of the agrarian economy. By the first half of that century, in fact, many prominent Romans had even given up the gentlemanly task of managing their estates and utilized the services of a slave or freedman *vilicus* ("steward"). It was for such absentee proprietors that

---

14. *Ad Att.* 5.1; 5.10, 1–3; *ad Fam.* 2.2; 2.12, et passim in his correspondence for 51–50 B.C. For Cicero the expression *res urbanae* essentially meant "politics." In *de Off.* 1.84 he urges his son not to put personal glory before the public welfare; he supports his argument with an example from the realm of warfare and then adds: *Quod genus peccandi vitandum est etiam in rebus urbanis* ("This sort of offense must be avoided in politics as well").

Cato wrote his *De Agricultura* in the middle of the century. Surveying the most fundamental aspects of husbandry, Cato's treatise is a dramatic indicator of how far removed from rustic life the Roman aristocracy had become. The City was now their home; rustic life and the countryside were no longer integral parts of their lives.

That separation of country and city paved the way for new relationships between the two and for new attitudes toward the countryside and country life. For the first time the countryside could be conceived as offering refuge from the political and social life of the City. It is indicative of the aristocracy's increasingly single-minded insistence on the importance of a military and political career that the first historical figures who are reported to have retired from public life to country estates did so under the pressure of circumstances not altogether of their own choice.[15] In 184 B.C. Publius Cornelius Scipio Africanus Maior was indicted on a charge of bribery by his political rival, Cato. Rather than stand trial, he retired to his villa at Liternum on the Campanian coast. In 164 B.C. Lucius Aemilius Paullus Macedonicus was incapacitated by a serious illness and left Rome for his estate at Velia on the Lucanian coast, where he stayed for most of the remainder of his life.

Scipio's villa seems pretty clearly to have been a traditional working estate. More than 200 years later the Younger Seneca comments on the austerity of Scipio's rustic existence (*Epistulae* 86.4,8, 12):

> uidi uillam exstructam lapide quadrato, murum circumdatum siluae, turres quoque in propugnaculum uillae utrimque subrectas, cisternam aedificiis ac uiridibus subditam, quae sufficere in usum uel exercitus posset, balneolum angustum, tenebricosum ex consuetudine antiqua . . . minimae sunt rimae magis quam fenestrae muro lapideo exsectae, ut sine iniuria munimenti lumen admitterent . . . quas nunc quorundam uoces futuras credis? "non inuideo Scipioni: uere in exilio uixit, qui sic lauabatur." immo, si scias, non cotidie lauabatur. nam, ut aiunt qui priscos mores urbis tradiderunt, brachia et crura cotidie abluebant, quae scilicet sordes opere collegerant, ceterum toti nundinis lauabantur.

---

15. I use the evidence collected by John D'Arms, *Romans on the Bay of Naples* (Cambridge, Mass. 1970) 1-17.

I have seen his villa. It is constructed of squared masonry; a wall encloses a grove; there are turrets buttressed on both sides to provide protection for the house; there is a reservoir concealed by buildings and shrubbery, large enough to satisfy the needs of an army, and a cramped bath building, totally without illumination, in the old-fashioned style. . . . There are no windows, only chinks cut into the masonry to provide light and yet not weaken the structure. . . . What sort of reaction will this provoke? "I certainly don't envy Scipio; a man who had such bathing habits really was living in exile." Well, if you must know, he didn't bathe every day. Writers who have recorded the conduct of our ancestors tell us that they washed their arms and legs daily, because they dirtied these at their work, but only washed completely once a week.

Perhaps influenced by the farmer-statesman tradition, Seneca asserts in passing that the great Scipio devoted himself willingly to the rigors of farming (*Epistulae* 86.5):

in hoc angulo ille Carthaginis horror, cui Roma debet quod tantum semel capta est, abluebat corpus laboribus rusticis fessum. exercebat enim opere se, terramque (ut mos fuit priscis) ipse subigebat.

In this nook that terror of Carthage used to wash his body when it was worn out with rustic labors, for he disciplined himself with work and, as was customary with the ancients, tilled the earth himself.

Scipio and Lucius Aemilius were not the last of the distinguished Romans who were compelled to find solace in country life. Perhaps the most notable example from Virgil's lifetime was Cicero's self-imposed banishment to his villas during the dictatorship of Julius Caesar. But the kind of life that Cicero passed at Tusculum was quite different from that of Scipio at Liternum. If Cicero exhausted himself on his country estates, it was in the research and writing of philosophical treatises, in friendly conversation, and in anxiety over the state of the Republic, not in hard physical labor.

More and more the countryside came to be viewed as offering not only an acceptable refuge, but even a desirable alternative to politics and the turbulent restlessness of an increasingly congested city. By

Cicero's day it was usual for wealthy Romans to possess several country villas, often widely separated. They visited them according to the season. For men in public life, this meant the political season, according to whether the Senate was in session or in recess.[16] Cicero himself owned six villas: at Cumae, Pompei, and Puteoli on the fashionable Bay of Naples; at Formiae on the border between Latium and Campania; and at Tusculum and Arpinum (the latter, his family estate) both in Latium. In addition to those and his residence at Rome, he also owned a number of small lodges (*deversoria*) along the Appian Way which provided places to stop over on the long journeys to his more distant villas.

By Cicero's age rural estates were not only more numerous than before, they also reflected, both in form and decoration, changing economic conditions and changing attitudes toward the countryside. The dramatic increases in the wealth and power of private individuals, which followed Roman conquests during the second century, and the example of Hellenistic potentates encouraged conspicuous display and the pursuit of luxury on an unprecedented scale. Seneca the Younger emphasized the quaintness of Scipio's life-style at Liternum by contrasting it with that of his own day (*Epistulae* 86.6–8):

> pauper sibi uidetur ac sordidus nisi parietes magnis et pretiosis orbibus refulserunt, nisi Alexandrina marmora Numidicis crustis distincta sunt, nisi illis undique operosa et in picturae modum uariata circumlitio praetexitur, nisi uitro absconditur camera, nisi Thasius lapis, quondam rarum in aliquo spectaculum templo, piscinas nostras circumdedit (in quas multa sudatione corpora exsaniata demittimus), nisi aquam argentea epitonia fuderunt. et adhuc plebeias fistulas loquor: quid cum ad balnea libertinorum peruenero? quantum statuarum, quantum columnarum est nihil sustinentium sed in ornamentum positarum, impensae causa! quantum aquarum per gradus cum fragore labentium! eo deliciarum peruenimus, ut nisi gemmas calcare nolimus . . . nunc blattaria uocant balnea, si qua non ita aptata sunt ut totius diei solem fenestris amplissimis recipiant, nisi et lauantur simul et colorantur, nisi ex solio agros ac maria prospiciunt.

16. Ibid. 48–49, and see references to *peregrinatio* in his index.

> [A man] regards himself as a poor and squalid thing if his walls do not gleam with great expensive mirrors, if Alexandrian marbles are not surrounded by Numidian mosaics, if they are not painstakingly finished with a variegated luster in the manner of paintings, if the vaulted roof is not hidden under glass, if Thasian marble, once a rare sight in a temple, does not line our pools (in which we dunk our bodies, sweat wrung from every pore), if our water does not pour from silver pipes—and I'm only talking about plebeian pipes. What can I say when I come to the baths of freedmen? How many statues there are, how many columns—columns that don't hold anything up but are set up for ornaments, just for the expense! How many streams pour down terraced courses with a clatter! We have come to such a point of luxury that we want to tread only on gems. . . . Nowadays they call baths "closets" unless they are appointed so that bathers get the sun all day through broad windows, unless they tan and bathe at the same time, unless they look out on the fields and seas from their throne.

Of course, the day when freedmen indulged in such luxury as Seneca describes was post-Virgilian, but the tendency toward more extensive, elaborate, and ostentatious dwellings was well under way by Virgil's own age.

Writing under Augustus,[17] Vitruvius describes the accommodations required by men in public life (*De Architectura* 6.5.2):

> nobilibus vero, qui honores magistratusque gerundo praestare debent officia civibus, faciunda sunt vestibula regalia alta, atria et peristylia amplissima, silvae ambulationesque laxiores ad decorem maiestatis perfectae; praeterea bibliothecas, basilicas non dissimili modo quam publicorum operum magnificentia comparatas, quod in domibus eorum saepius et publica consilia et privata iudicia arbitriaque conficiuntur.

> But nobles, who by virtue of their honors and magistracies ought to perform services for citizens, should make their vestibules regal, tall; their landscapes and walks rather spaciously set out as becomes their dignity. In addition, they should have libraries,

---

17. For the dating of Vitruvius' *De Architectura*, see Z. Yavetz, "The Living Conditions of the Urban Plebs," *Latomus* 17 (1958) 500–517 (esp. 501–502), reprinted in Robin Seager, ed., *The Crisis of the Roman Republic* (New York 1969) 162–179 (esp. 162–163).

basilicas appointed not unlike the grandeur of public buildings, because public councils and private judgments and arbitrations very often take place in the homes of these people.

Such styles no doubt began in the City, but they set the standard for country villas also. Vitruvius observes (*De Architectura* 6.5.3):

> Earum autem rerum non solum erunt in urbe aedificiorum rationes, sed etiam ruri.
>
> The plans of buildings, moreover, will be in keeping with these matters not only in the city but even in the country.

Of particular relevance to an appreciation of changing attitudes toward the countryside is the introduction of the peristyle courtyard and interior pleasure gardens. Whatever their precise origins (which are complex and not altogether clear), they became highly stylized creations: plants formally arranged with statuary and fountains interspersed.[18] Often the decoration of these gardens borrowed from the symbolism of popular Hellenistic cults, but in the context of the garden that symbolism performed more of an aesthetic than a religious function. As Peter von Blanckenhagen has observed with reference to the role of cult statues and shrines in landscaping and landscape paintings: "Priapus and Bacchus, Fortuna and Isis may be the guardians, undemanding and not quite serious and therefore all the more charming."[19] A. G. McKay says of courtyard gardens that they became "the focus for art galleries (*pinacothecae*), libraries (*bibliothecae*), lecture halls, meeting rooms, basilicas, and *conclavia* (dining rooms, bedrooms). All were equipped with doors or awnings which could be closed in the forenoon and reopened later to take full advantage of the cool air and the garden's amenities."[20] Such arrangements were common to both villa and town house. The villa differed, however, in that its interior was designed to open to the

---

18. *Grimal* remains the authority on Roman gardens, interior and landscape. On the character of interior pleasure gardens, see ch. III sec. IV, "Théorie et technique des jardins," pp. 72–104, esp. pp. 95–96. For his account of the garden in connection with the evolution of the peristyle courtyard, see pp. 217–228, an account followed by Axel Boëthius and J. B. Warde-Perkins, *Etruscan and Roman Architecture* (Baltimore 1970) 154–158. For an enumeration of some other possibilities see Alexander G. McKay, *Houses, Villas, and Palaces in the Roman World* (Ithaca 1975) 34–35, 44, 46.

19. Peter H. von Blanckenhagen and Christine Alexander, "The Paintings from the Boscotrecase," *MDAI(R)* Sechstes Ergänzungsheft (Heidelberg 1962) 61.

20. A. G. McKay (above n. 18) 61.

outdoors as well as to bring nature inside. The disposition of rooms to take advantage of views and of the light, as well as the addition of colonnades, terraces, and *ambulationes*, complemented the effect of interior gardens and courtyards.[21] Only in that respect did Vitruvius qualify his assertion that the same rules hold for town houses as for country villas (*De Architectura* 6.5.3):

> In urbe atria proxima ianuis solent esse, ruri ab pseudourbanis statim peristylia, deinde tunc atria habentia circum porticus pavimentatas spectantes ad palaestras et ambulationes.
>
> In the city atria are usually next to the entrance, in the country in pseudo-urban style right away there are peristyles and then, after them, atria surrounded by tiled porticos overlooking palaestras and walkways.

Closely related to the development of such fashions in domestic architecture was the introduction of landscape gardening.[22] The Romans called it *ars topiaria* from the word for "gardener," *topiarius*. That term, the compound of a Greek root and a Latin suffix, is clearly indicative of Hellenistic influence. Pierre Grimal argues that the essential object of *ars topiaria* was the composition of tableaux through the creation and disposition of *topia*, that is, aspects of the landscape in their most typical manifestations. He argues further that such a concept of landscape gardening evolved from principles of landscape painting as they, in turn, were influenced by Stoic emphasis on the "distinctive particularity" (*particularité propre*) of phenomena.[23]

Whatever the theoretical origins of Roman landscaping, it is clear that in practice it involved attempts to arrange plants, trees, Hellenistic statuary, and architectural motifs into harmonious unities that were inescapably artificial. The earliest reference to *ars topiaria* occurs in a letter of 54 B.C. written by Cicero (*ad Q. fr.* 3.1.55):

> Topiarium laudavi: ita omnia convestivit hedera, qua basim villae, qua intercolumnia ambulationis ut denique illi palliati topiariam facere videantur et hederam vendere.

21. See H. Drerup, "Bildraum und Realraum in der römischen Architektur," *MDAI(R)* 66 (1959) 147-174.
22. The following brief survey of the topic is based largely on *Grimal* 93-104.
23. *Grimal* 98.

> I praised the gardener: he has covered everything with ivy, here the foundation of the villa, there the spaces between the columns of the walk, so that in the end those statues of Greeks with their *palla* seem to be engaged in gardening and selling ivy.

The tone of that passage betrays a certain self-consciousness on Cicero's part and suggests perhaps that *ars topiaria* was sufficiently novel or pretentious that he was not quite sure what others might think of it and not yet fully at ease with it himself. But since *topiarius* came in time to serve as the most general Latin term for "gardener," we may assume that the domestication and idealization of nature associated with it likewise gained broad acceptance. By the end of the Republic many wealthy Romans would have been able to look out from "sheltered terraces propitiously built for selected vistas," where "A lost world of Theocritean shepherds and nymphs, of simple people in simple worship, of distant shores and romantic isles is blended with familiar views of handsome buildings, votive gifts, statuettes, goats, and sheep into an image of a fairyland where nothing is quite real or even determinable, where nature has lost its threatening powers but has kept its indefinable vastness and beauty."[24]

The "reciprocal penetration of interior and exterior,"[25] which Grimal has identified as a major principle underlying the evolution of domestic architecture during the Late Republic and which was bound up with the new styles of landscaping, was artificially extended by contemporary developments in wall painting. Murals of the so-called Second Style[26] employed trompe l'oeil effects to give the impression that walls were not solid but were, rather, doorways, colonnades, or windows which either implied or actually seemed to open onto a "world beyond the wall."[27] One effect of such decoration,

---

24. Von Blanckenhagen (above n. 19) 60–61.
25. *Grimal* 259.
26. Classification of Romano-Campanian wall paintings into four successive styles was originally made by A. Mau, *Geschichte der decorativen Wandmalerei in Pompeii* (Berlin 1907). A precise chronology for the development of Second Style paintings has been elaborated by H. Beyen, *Die Pompejanische Wanddekoration vom zweiten bis zum vierten Stil*, I (The Hague 1938), II.1 (The Hague 1960). Christine Alexander (above n. 19) 24–25 provides a very helpful list of Second Style landscape paintings with their conjectural dates of execution.
27. I use the phrase of Gilbert Picard, *Roman Painting* (Greenwich, Connecticut 1968) 92 et passim, which seems particularly apt, although I do not subscribe to his argument that the "world beyond the wall" is the world of the dead and that Second Style wall paintings have a particular religious significance connected with worship of the dead.

and very likely an important reason for its popularity, was that it enhanced a sense of spaciousness and grandeur.

That was not its only effect or raison d'être. Another important innovation of the Second Style was the introduction of landscape painting. While the exact relation of the painted landscapes to the trompe l'oeil architectural motifs is sometimes uncertain, the landscapes themselves expressed distinctive and significant attitudes toward the natural environment and inevitably contributed to a vision of what the outside world, the world beyond the wall, was or might ideally be. Sometimes the landscapes seem actually to be a part of the architectural illusion attempted by the painter and to give the appearance of scenes viewed through a niche or window in the wall. Occasionally, entire walls were given over to the depiction of garden scenes which gave the illusion of extending beyond an interior peristyle, separated from it only by a low wall or fence. Landscapes of the Second Style depicted in the villas of Pompeii and Herculaneum can for the most part be divided into four broad categories: Nilotic scenes that emphasize the exotica of Egypt; the backgrounds of mythological scenes whose landscapes have been noted for their imposing sense of atmosphere;[28] depictions of luxury villas in their settings around the Bay of Naples; and, finally, sacral-idyllic paintings,[29] evocative scenes that emphasize suggestions of pastoral serenity and religious solemnity in the Italian countryside.

The exact origins of Romano-Campanian landscape painting and the nature of its evolution are still uncertain.[30] It is clear that Hellenistic influence played an important role and that the paintings themselves were often, if not always, the work of Greek artisans. On the other hand, some scholars have stressed the role of characteristically Roman attitudes and traditions. Whatever the exact relation of Hellenistic and indigenous influences, Romano-Campanian landscape paintings reflected and contributed to a transformation of Roman attitudes toward the countryside. Realistic portrayals of rustic life, no less than of urban life, are conspicuous only

---

28. See the description of George M. Hanfmann, *Roman Art* (Greenwich, Connecticut 1964), in his commentary on plates XXVII-XXIX.

29. The term was coined by M. I. Rostovtzeff, "Die hellenistisch-römische Architektur-Landschaft," *MDAI(R)* 26 (1911) 1-185.

30. For a clear survey of the major attempts to interpret the significance of the Second Style and the basis of its appeal, see Gilbert Picard (above n. 27) 96-99. An additional point of view, the one I favor, is stated by von Blanckenhagen (above n. 19) 61 and esp. nn. 116, 117.

by their almost total absence among the paintings that decorate the villas of Pompeii and Herculaneum.

The paintings that depict Italian scenes reflect the same tendencies to domesticate or idealize the natural environment that characterized contemporary architecture and landscaping. In painting, those tendencies led to that stylization which Vitruvius was to attack in the seventh book of his treatise (*De Architectura* 7.5.3-4):

> Sed . . . ex veris rebus exempla sumebantur, nunc iniquis moribus inprobantur. Nam pinguntur tectoriis monstra potius quam ex rebus finitis imagines certae: pro columnis enim struuntur calami striati, pro fastigiis appagineculi cum crispis foliis et volutis, item candelabra aedicularum sustinentia figuras, supra fastigia eorum surgentes ex radicibus cum volutis teneri plures habentes in se sine ratione sedentia sigilla, non minus coliculi dimidiata habentes sigilla alia humanis, alia bestiarum capitibus. . . . At haec falsa videntes homines non reprehendunt sed delectantur, neque animadvertunt, si quid eorum fieri potest necne.

> But [subjects] that used to be taken from real objects are now disdained because of current bad taste. Monsters are painted in frescoes rather than specific images of specific things: indeed, fluted stalks are put up in place of columns, little appendages with delicately curled leaves and volutes instead of pediments; likewise candelabra supporting pictures of shrines and above their roofs, sprouting from roots in spirals, many fine stalks with little figures seated among them at random, and also little shoots with truncated little figures, some with human, others with animal, heads. But when they see these false images rather than finding fault, men are delighted; they don't care whether any of these things is possible or not.

What all the landscapes have in common in the most general sense is that they direct the viewer's attention and thoughts away from the everyday realities both of the city and of rustic life. The natural environment is represented as a place of escape from traditional ways of life to new possibilities, whether they be the exotica of the East, the worlds of greater than human possibilities depicted in the mythological scenes, the glory and opulence evoked by magnificent villas, or the serenity and sanctity of an idealized Italian countryside.

Such trends in Romano-Campanian landscape painting and the new urbanized style of country life in general have been described as symptomatic of escapist tendencies in the Late Republic.[31] Indeed, it is striking that the new opulence and new styles of domestic architecture, gardening, and landscape painting along with other expressions of new attitudes toward the countryside and rural life seem to culminate in a period of intense innovation in the decades immediately prior to the composition of the *Georgics*, that is, in the years when the Republic was deteriorating most rapidly and violently. Second Style wall painting with its landscapes and trompe l'oeil settings is thought to have been introduced in the first quarter of the first century B.C.[32] Pliny the Elder observed that the house of Lepidus was the most elegant in Rome in 78 B.C. but that within thirty-five years there were a hundred even grander.[33] It is to be expected that new styles in rural architecture were pretty contemporaneous. We know with certainty, for example, that it was Cicero's father who, in his old age, remodeled the family estate and added a library. Likewise, although Scipio Aemilianus was responsible for the first Roman pleasure garden as early as 129 B.C., Pierre Grimal has argued convincingly that gardens landscaped in accordance with Hellenistic fashion were still regarded as new and unfamiliar as late as 54 B.C.[34] and that the "Amaltheum" of Cicero's friend, Atticus, at his country residence in Greece (Buthrotum) seems to be the first of its kind created by a Roman.[35] In addition, he cites the house of Clodia as the first "triumph of architecture dominated by gardens."[36] To Clodia's generation belong also the first public parks at Rome.

In literature, Virgil is supposed to have begun work on his *Eclogues*, the first Roman pastorals, in 42 B.C. Although the pastoral was not a very productive genre at Rome, interest in the possibility of a simple and innocent existence in the countryside was continued in the elegies of Tibullus. It is with the *Eclogues*, too, that the Greek idea of a Golden Age of natural fruitfulness and harmony first seems

31. Karl Schefold, "The Origins of Roman Landscape Painting," *Art Bulletin* 42 (1960) 92; and more fully, von Blanckenhagen (above n. 19), esp. nn. 116–117.

32. On dating see above n. 26, and see also the cautionary argument of Christopher Dawson, "Romano-Campanian Mythological Landscape Painting," *YCS* 9 (1944), reprinted *L'Erma di Bretschneider* (Rome 1965) 80, 94, 104–105, 126, 127n.26, against treating the evolution of wall painting styles too schematically.

33. *HN* 36.109.

34. *Grimal* 95–96.

35. *Grimal* 321.

36. *Grimal* 457, and see also 237.

to emerge as a dominant theme in Latin, sometimes in conjunction with, sometimes displacing, the indigenous Roman tradition of an ideal age under the rule of King Saturnus. Both traditions enjoy their greatest currency and centrality in the literature of the Augustan Age. Finally, all the developments I have surveyed culminate in a work I will consider in some detail below, the *Res Rusticae* of Varro —a work of particular interest in the present context because it was published in 37 B.C., two years before Virgil is thought to have begun writing the *Georgics*.[37]

It cannot be pure coincidence that such widespread interest in country life complements clear signs of disillusionment and rejection of Republican institutions and traditions. The years that saw unprecedented interest in new styles of country life were the years of Lucretius and of the phenomenal rise to popularity of Epicureanism at Rome. While some Romans managed to combine a public career with an interest in Epicureanism,[38] for others the ideal of "the garden" provided an attractive rationale for abandoning public life and thus, in effect, Rome itself. Atticus is only the most well-known representative of that increasing number of Equites who might have entered politics but chose instead a private career. Atticus abandoned Italy entirely. For many others, as for retired politicians of an earlier generation, private villas and gardens must have provided an attractive alternative to public life, just as they were soon to provide a measure of status to ambitious freedmen during the Empire.

But it would be a mistake to see the new styles of country life and the new attitudes toward the countryside only as symptomatic of escapism or to assume that new relations to the countryside meant the end of traditional attitudes toward it. Thus far I have sketched the history not of one idea, but of two parallel developments. On the one hand, we have seen that increased demands of public life, growing wealth, exposure to Hellenistic culture, and the desire to escape the confusion of the Roman civil conflicts all led to new relationships

---

37. The dates for Virgil's composition and publication of his works are reckoned from assertions of the ancient biographers and commentators. The most important passages for dating the *Georgics* are Donatus, *Vita Verg.* 25; Servius, *Praef. Aen.* (Thilo I, p. 2, lines 7ff.); and Pseudo-Probus, *In Verg. Comm.* (Hagen, *App. Serv.* 329.5ff. and 323.13). For a careful assessment of the reliability or, rather, unreliability of the ancient biographical material, see G. S. Bowersock, "A Date in the Eighth *Eclogue*," *HSCPh* 75 (1971) 73–80.

38. There is evidence, for example, that Calpurnius Piso, consul of 58, had been patron of an important Epicurean teacher, Philodemus of Gadara. See Cicero *in Pis.* 68ff.; *Anth. Pal.* 4.349.

to the countryside and to a correspondingly new sense that it offered alternatives to the traditional values, which emphasized the importance of involvement in public life. At the same time another movement sought to consolidate and, in fact, to elaborate an increasingly idealized vision of Rome's agrarian past, the *mos maiorum*, as the basis for the distinctive virtues of the Roman people and their nation. Those two responses to change were associated, as we have seen, explicitly as well as implicitly, with equally antithetical attitudes toward the city, public life, and the Roman state. Thus, attitudes toward country life might be felt to involve questions of considerable political and social consequence. They gave rise to disagreements, sometimes urgently felt, and to genuine dilemmas.

It is in no way surprising, then, that much of what we know about the life that wealthy Romans enjoyed in the country during the Late Republic comes from contemporary critics. As early as mid-second century B.C. Cato is said to have boasted that *villas suas inexcultas et rudes ne tectorio quidem praelitas* ("his own villas were unornamented and crude and unplastered"),[39] implying that villas which were more grand ought to reflect badly on their owners. He seems also to have regarded as one reason for opposing second consulships the fact that there were those

> quibus villae atque aedes aedificatae atque expolitae maximo opere citro atque ebore atque pavimento Poenicis sient.[40]
>
> whose villas and homes were constructed and finished at great expense with citron wood and ivory and Punic tiles.

D'Arms has observed[41] that

> to denouncers of *luxuria* in the Ciceronian age, it was the villas—in the suburbs, in the country, and especially at the seaside—which furnished congenial material. *Aedificare* now first acquires a pejorative sense. Nepos says of Atticus: *nemo illo minus fuit emax, minus aedificator* ["no one was less a buyer, less a builder

---

39. My survey of ancient reaction to rural luxury is indebted to John D'Arms's collection and analysis of evidence (above n. 15), 10–13, 16–17, 26, 30, 39, 40–43, et passim. The quotation of Cato is preserved by Aulus Gellius 13.24.1 ( = H. Malcovati, *Oratorum Romanorum Fragmenta*² [Turin] 1955, M. Porcius Cato fr. 174, p. 71).

40. Quoted in Festus, p. 282. 4 ( = H. Malcovati, ibid. fr. 185, p. 75).

41. D'Arms (above n. 15) 40.

than he"], for he owned *nullam suburbanam aut maritimam sumptuosam villam* ["no sumptuous suburban or maritime villa"].⁴²

Cicero, who, as was observed above, owned six country villas himself, nonetheless shared the view that lavish country villas and retreat to the country for the enjoyment of leisure were signs of degeneracy. In the introduction of *De Legibus* 2, for example, he has the ever-temperate Atticus remark with appreciation on the simplicity of Cicero's family estate at Arpinum and express contempt for magnificent villas with their tiled floors, paneled ceilings, and ridiculous "Niles" or "Euripuses."⁴³ For Cicero, such criticism is of a kind with his attacks on Epicureanism, a philosophy repugnant to him because it also seemed to encourage public irresponsibility and self-indulgence.⁴⁴

But the critics of rural luxury and escapism were caught in something of a dilemma. Even for them, the simple life of the farmer-statesman celebrated in tradition had become virtually unthinkable as an alternative. For all of his criticisms, Cicero *did* own six country villas plus assorted *deversoria*; he *did* employ Greek gardeners; and he *did* send to Greece for well covers and other such adornments for his villas.⁴⁵ The inescapable fact was that even the most reactionary of Cicero's peers lived a fundamentally new kind of country life, one influenced by the examples of Hellenistic civilization as well as by changes in Roman politics and economy. Atticus may have scorned lavish villas; he may have been known "neither as a buyer nor a builder," but his "Amaltheum" seems to have been in the avant-garde of gardens landscaped in Hellenistic style.⁴⁶

On the other hand, whether measured against the ease and luxury that wealthy Romans had come to expect in the country or against the idealized life of the farmer-statesman of tradition, the existence of the small farmer during the Late Republic was conspicuously disappointing. Indeed, the lot of the small landholder had

42. Nep., *Atticus* 14, 3.
43. *De Legibus* 2.1.
44. For a full discussion of this aspect of Cicero's hostility to Epicureanism, see Jean-Marie André, *L'otium dans la vie morale et intellectuelle romaine des origines à l'époque augustéenne* (Paris 1966) = *Publications de la faculté des lettres et sciences humaines de Paris: Série "Recherches"* 30, ch. IV, "*Otium* épicurien et essor du lyrisme: L'*Otium* et la crise de la cité: Cicéron contre l'otium épicurien," 205–277.
45. *Ad Att.* 1.10.3.
46. Grimal 321–323.

26   Virgil's *Georgics*

never been an enviable one. In his book *Roman Social Relations*, Ramsay MacMullen has surveyed the timeless miseries of the peasant throughout the ancient world: poverty, harassment and intimidation by rivals and powerful neighbors, robbery.[47] Those dangers were compounded by the virtually complete impossibility of obtaining any effective recourse against them, since the agents of the law were uninterested, remote, and approachable only at an expense of time and money which the peasant did not have.

But Romans of the Late Republic had more than the peasants' timeless miseries to give them pause. In their own day the condition of the small independent farmer was deteriorating conspicuously. The protracted series of wars that enriched some Romans and Italians took many husbands and sons from their fields. In their absence many small farms ran into disrepair and debt. These were often bought up by the wealthy to become the possessions of absentee landlords, managed by overseers, and worked by slaves.[48] Or they might be converted into pastureland, the *solitudinem Italiae* which Cicero lamented in a letter of 63 B.C.[49] The plight of the small farmer was brought dramatically to the attention of Romans and Italians alike by the Gracchan land reform measures and the accompanying civil strife.[50] Thereafter, continuing controversies surrounding land reform assured that Romans would not altogether deceive themselves about realities of rustic life.[51] Although individ-

47. (New Haven 1974), esp. chs. 1 and 2, pp. 1–56.
48. W. E. Heitland, *Agricola* (Cambridge 1921, reprinted Westport, Connecticut 1970), esp. the section entitled "Rome: Middle Period," 151–202, remains an important discussion of changes in the agrarian economy and labor. The important changes that took place prior to the Gracchan attempts at land reform are admirably summarized by A. E. Astin, *Scipio Aemilianus* (Oxford 1967) 161–165, with notes to major primary and secondary sources. The whole question of changing land use is a major focus of Arnold J. Toynbee, *Hannibal's Legacy* (Oxford 1965), esp. sections I–III, VI–VIII of vol. 2. K. D. White, "Latifundia: A Critical Review of the Evidence on Large Estates in Italy and Sicily up to the End of the First Century A.D.," *Bul. Inst. Cl. Stud.* no. 14 (1967) 62–79, assembles the literary evidence for a central aspect of change in agrarian economy and labor.
49. *Ad Att.* 1.19.
50. See especially the famous speech attributed to T. Gracchus by Plutarch, *Tiberius Gracchus* 9.5–6.
51. After the protracted controversies surrounding the reform efforts of the Gracchi, the issue of land reform was kept alive in controversies and dislocations occasioned by demands of land for veterans. In 63 Cicero felt able to argue against the agrarian bill of Servilius Rullus on the grounds that the urban plebs enjoyed a better life at Rome than they would in the country (*Leg. Agr.* 2.71 and cf. 2.9; 102). That the urban plebs in fact shared Cicero's view is suggested by P. A. Brunt's conclusion, "The Army and the Land and the Roman Revolu-

uals might seek to reassure themselves that they were not trapped in a life they did not enjoy by imagining the pleasures of rustic life, they were hardly prepared to act on such fantasies.

Horace ridicules just such escapism in his second *Epode*. He begins the poem as though he were expressing his own enthusiasm for rustic life (*Epode* 2.1-8):

> Beatus ille qui procul negotiis,
>   ut prisca gens mortalium,
> paterna rura bobus exercet suis
>   solutus omni faenore
> neque excitatur classico miles truci
>   neque horret iratum mare
> forumque vitat et superba civium
>   potentiorum limina.

> Blessed is that man who, far from business affairs as the ancient race of mortals was, works his ancestral lands with his own oxen. Safe from all usury he is neither roused by the harsh bugle like a soldier nor does he shudder at an angry sea; he shuns the forum and the haughty thresholds of powerful citizens.

Only after we have been drawn into that fantasy does Horace destroy the illusion (*Epode* 2.67-70):

> haec ubi locutus faenerator Alfius,
>   iam iam futurus rusticus,
> omnem redegit idibus pecuniam,
>   quaerit kalendis ponere.

> When he has said all this, the moneylender, Alfius, always just about to become a rustic, calls in all his money on the Ides—and on the Kalends seeks to lend it out again.

It is not until that last line, when we find that Alfius calls in his money, not because he plans to quit his business but only to continue it, that we become fully aware of Alfius' self-delusion and, to the extent that we have been induced to share his fantasy, our own.

---

tion," *JRS* 52 (1962) 69-86, that "for the urban proletariat an agrarian agitation was not serious; or rather, it did not seriously desire to receive land so much as to blackmail the Senate into other concessions. The agrarian agitation of 63 was followed by Cato's law . . . greatly increasing the number of recipients of cheap corn" (72). See also A. W. Lintott, *Violence in Republican Rome* (Oxford 1968) 178-181.

Most wealthy Romans knew well enough, with Horace, that a life of ease on a small farm, no matter how attractive or dignified by tradition, was no more than an illusion. Varro, writing an agricultural treatise in 37 B.C., could advise quite matter-of-factly (*Res Rusticae* 1.17.2-3):

> Omnes agri coluntur hominibus servis aut liberis aut utrisque: liberis, aut cum ipsi colunt, ut plerique pauperculi cum sua progenie, aut mercennariis, cum conductiis liberorum operis res maiores, ut vendemias ac faenisicia, administrant . . . de quibus universis hoc dico, gravia loca utilius esse mercennariis colere quam servis, et in salubribus quoque locis opera rustica maiora, ut sunt in condendis fructibus vindemiae aut messis.
>
> All crops are cultivated either by slaves or by freemen or both: by freemen either when they do the work themselves, as many very poor farmers do with the help of their own children; or by paid laborers when farmers employ hired freemen for the larger operations such as the vintage and reaping. . . . With regard to all these [laborers who work to pay off debts] I advise the following: It is more profitable to use hired hands than slaves for the cultivation of unhealthy locations and even in healthy locations for the heavier farm work such as is involved in storing the products of vintage or harvest.

Cicero might praise the hardy life of Rome's founders and he might evoke Cato's memory and pronouncements with approval, but he and his friends used *rusticus* occasionally and *agrestis* regularly as pejorative epithets, just as they used *urbanus* to indicate approval and a sense of shared values.[52]

---

52. On Cicero's use of *agrestis* see for example, Gustav Landgraf, *Kommentar zu Ciceros Rede Pro Sex Roscio Amerino*[2] (Berlin 1914) 158: "agrestem bauerisch, cf. Orat. § 148 quis se tam durum agrestem *praeberat*, So stehen nicht selten die *agrestes* = Ungebildeten den *docti* = den Gebildeten gegenüber, zB, leg. 1 § 41 fin: o rem dignam, in qua non modo *docti* sed etiam *agrestes* erubescant!" In *de Off.* 1.130 Cicero characterizes poor personal hygiene as an *agrestem et inhumanam neglegentiam* ("a rustic and inhuman neglect") that is to be avoided. Likewise, in a general discussion of deportment, *de Off.* 1.128-129, Cicero uses *rusticus* in a pejorative sense: *status, incessus, sessio, accubitio, vultus, oculi, manuum motus teneat illud decorum. Quibus in rebus duo maxime sunt fugienda, ne quid effeminatum aut molle et ne quid durum aut rusticum sit* ("In standing, walking, sitting, reclining, in expression, look, gesture one should maintain this propriety. In these matters two things especially are to be avoided, anything effeminate or soft and anything tough or rustic"). The opposition between *rusticus* and *urbanus* is seen most frequently in Cicero's remarks on propriety of style. In *De Oratore* 3.42-47, for example, Cicero argues that

It was not only the lot of the peasant farmer that was in disrepute. As we learn from Cicero, the plaintiffs in a murder case, the *Pro Sexto Roscio Amerino*, adduced as one evidence of the defendant's bad relations with his father (whom he was accused of murdering) that the father never brought his son with him on trips to Rome, but left him behind on the family estate. Clearly, the prosecution expected that to be at least a plausible argument. We know of it only because Cicero took the trouble to refute it, and it is perhaps significant that to do so he said not one word about contemporary practice but appealed rather to the authority of Caecilius' comedies, written a century earlier, and to legend.[53]

That the plaintiff's argument was not an act of rhetorical desperation but was based solidly on contemporary attitudes is confirmed by Livy. Despite his glorification of Cincinnatus, Livy, too, sees that a father's decision to make his son responsible for the family farming estate could be regarded as evidence of parental disapproval and harshness. He has a tribune say of Lucius Manlius (*Ab Urbe Condita* 7.4.6-7) that

> malum malo augere filii et tarditatem ingenii insuper premere, et, si quid in eo exiguum naturalis vigoris sit, id exstinguere vita agresti et rustico cultu inter pecudes habendo.

> [he] augmented his son's inherent badness by bad treatment and repressed his sluggish nature, and, if there was any small element of natural energy in him, he crushed it by confining him to a country life and a rustic upbringing amid the herds.[54]

---

affecting a rustic pronunciation is a fault and that urban pronunciation should provide the correct standard for the orator. The importance of *urbanitas* may further be judged from *Brutus* 285 where Cicero has Brutus admit that the *ieiunitas, siccitas,* and *inopia* of the Attic style may be acceptable *dum modo sit polita, dum urbana, dum elegans*. It is not only in matters of oratorical style that *urbanitas* is the assumed standard. Cicero's son, in a letter to Tiro, his father's freedman personal secretary, congratulated him teasingly on the purchase of a country villa, saying that now Tiro would have to give up his city ways. Instead, the young Cicero imagines him busy with buying rustic supplies, chatting with his steward—and storing up pips left over from dessert in the folds of his cloak! (*ad Fam.* 16.21.7). Gaius Cassius, the tyrannicide, in a letter to Cicero remarks: *scis Gnaeus quam sit fatuus; scis quo modo crudelitatem virtutem putet; scis quam se semper a nobis derisum putet; vereor ne nos* **rustice** *gladio velit* ἀντιμηκηρίσαι ("You know what a fool Gnaeus is, how he thinks cruelty a virtue; you know how he always thinks we're laughing at him. I'm afraid that *like a bumpkin* he may want to sneer back at us with his sword," Cicero, *ad Fam.* 15.19.4).

53. *Pro S. Rosc. Am.* 40-51.

54. In fact, Livy's attitude toward Manlius and his treatment of his son is complex, for the son kills the tribune who attacked his father, thus, perhaps, putting the lie to the tribune's

We have, also, the even more personal testimony of Sallust. Having left politics because of its corruption, he explains his decision to take up the writing of history (*Catilinae Coniuratio* 4.1.2):

> Igitur, ubi animus ex multis miseriis atque periculis requievit, et mihi reliquam aetatem a republica procul habendam decrevi, non fuit consilium socordia atque desidia bonum otium conterere, neque vero agrum colendo aut venando, servilibus officiis, intentum aetatem agere. sed a quo incepto studio me ambitio mala detinuerat, eodem regressus statui res gestas populi Romani carptim, ut quaeque memoria digna videbantur, perscribere.

> Therefore, once my mind was at rest from many miseries and dangers and I decided that the rest of my life should be spent far from public affairs, my plan was not to waste my good leisure with dull-witted sloth or, indeed, to pass my life intent on cultivation of crops and hunting, servile occupations. Rather, I decided to return to a previous interest from which unfortunate ambition had kept me and to write out the deeds of the Roman people, selectively, as they seemed worthy of memory.

Sallust's particular antipathy to rustic life has been explained in part by the fact that his rejection of a political career made it impossible for him to adopt the respectable pose "as a Cincinnatus or a Cato, looking on the farm life as an interlude in public service or as the final regimen of a well-ordered career."[55] It reflects a genuine devaluation of farming as an actual way of life among Sallust's peers. To say that farming can only be valued as an adornment or a pendant to a political career is to say that it has ceased to exercise any real attraction of its own. Those Romans who felt bound by the tradition that Rome's greatness rested on the rustic virtues of her peasant soldiery and her farmer-statesmen were actually excluded, both by their own tastes and by the knowledge of contemporary realities, from realizing the ideal to which they subscribed and which they preached.

---

charges. The passage nonetheless confirms that to City people rustic life might not seem at all desirable.

55. Eleanor Winsor Leach, *Vergil's Eclogues: Landscapes of Experience* (Ithaca 1974) 68–69.

## III

The question how to reconcile their tastes with their respect for tradition was an important and often very difficult one for the kinds of Romans who made up Virgil's audience. It was the more difficult because, as we have seen, the conditions that gave rise to it were just beginning to have their full impact on Roman consciousness in the quarter of a century or so before Virgil began the *Georgics*. In a few cases we can actually see wealthy and aristocratic Romans attempting to define some sort of compromise between the luxury country life offered them and the comparatively austere and public-spirited country life that tradition demanded.

We have already observed that Cicero found fault with those Romans who fled from their public responsibilities to luxurious self-indulgence in country villas. At the same time he took the opportunity to stress the modesty of his own family estate at Arpinum and to suggest that his father had added libraries only because failing health had kept him from a more active life.[56] In the introduction to the *Academica*, one of the philosophical treatises with which he occupied himself during his self-imposed exile from public life in 45/44 B.C., Cicero could find little justification for the studies he pursued at such length in his country villas:

> Ego autem (dicam enim ut res est), dum me ambitio, dum honores, dum causae, dum rei publicae non solum cura sed quaedam etiam procuratio multis officiis implicatum et constrictum tenebat, haec inclusa habebam, et ne obsolescerent renovabam cum licebat legendo; nunc vero et fortunae gravissimo percussus vulnere et administratione rei publicae liberatus doloris medicinam a philosophia peto et oti oblectationem hanc honestissimam iudico. Aut enim huic aetati hoc maxime aptum est, aut iis rebus si quas dignas laude gessimus hoc in primis consentaneum, aut etiam ad nostros cives erudiendos nihil utilius, aut si haec ita non sunt, nihil aliud video quod agere possimus.

> For my own part, however (for I will speak as the situation warrants), as long as political campaigns, public office, law cases, care for the Republic, and even a certain guardianship for it kept

---

56. *De Legibus* 2.3.

me tied up and hindered with many obligations, I held these [studies] in check, and I renewed them by reading when I could, so that they wouldn't grow dull. But now that I have been struck by a most serious blow of fortune and have been freed from the administration of the Republic, I seek a salve for my pain in philosophy and I judge this to be the most honorable amusement for my leisure time. For either this is particularly suited to my age or it is especially consistent with whatever I may have done worthy of praise, or there is nothing more useful for educating our fellow citizens, or if these are not the case, I see nothing else that I can do.

In other works, however, and especially in more active periods of his life, he did feel able to defend his interest in letters and, by implication, the country retirement which the cultivation of that interest required: literature is valuable because it teaches moral lessons, presents heroes of the past as models for imitation, and disciplines the orator's mind and supplies him with the varied material that adorns his arguments.[57]

Such arguments may seem to be based on an excessively literal and narrow kind of utilitarianism, but they are calculated to win support by association with two important and closely related Roman traditions. One is that leisure is justified if it prepares for a return to public life.[58] The other and more venerable of the two is that Roman public virtues have their origins in country life. Cicero reinterprets those two ideals to suit the contemporary realities. Instead of emphasizing the austerity and discipline of country life— qualities out of keeping even with his own allegedly modest estates— Cicero made a virtue of the opportunity for relaxation which the

---

57. *Pro Archia* 12-14.

58. The standard discussion of changing concepts of leisure and its role in Roman thought is Jean-Marie André (above n. 44). On the idea that leisure can be justified as a preparation for return to public life (although intellectual activity was not originally included among acceptable leisure occupations), see esp. 45-49, 57-58. Also particularly relevant are chs. III, "L'*otium* et la vie intellectuelle" (135-201) and V, "Cicéron et le drame de la retraite impossible" (279-334). Cicero sums up his own view in his admiring quotation of the elder Scipio's epigrammatic pronouncement on the subject (*de Off.* 3.1): *numquam se minus otiosum esse, quam cum otiosus, nec minus solum, quam cum solus esset. Magnifica vero vox et magno viro ac sapiente digna; quae declarat illum . . . in otio de negotiis cogitare* ("[Scipio said that] he was never less retired from public business than when in retirement and never less lonely than when he was alone—a magnificent sentiment indeed, worthy of a great and wise man inasmuch as it demonstrates that even in retirement he was preoccupied with public business").

villas of his age offered to wealthy Romans. In periods of country retirement prominent Romans could indulge a growing need to rationalize conventional morality and to satisfy a corresponding interest in Hellenistic philosophies.

The nature of Cicero's new ideal may perhaps be seen most clearly in his philosophical dialogues. Typically, they are set in the garden of a country villa. There, distinguished public figures discuss subjects of concern to the well-being of society. It is significant that the models of civic virtue who engage in those discussions are not drawn from among the rustic founders of Rome (although, as we have seen, they are referred to with respect), but rather from the Hellenized statesmen of the second century B.C. or of Cicero's own day. *De Republica* is a notable example. The dramatic date of the dialogue is the Latin holidays of 129 B.C. The setting is the garden of Publius Cornelius Scipio Aemilianus, the younger Africanus, phil-Hellene, the first Roman famous as a patron of philosophers and literati, conqueror of Carthage and Numantia, and a statesman who held the high office of censor. The companions with whom he is pictured are inevitably less distinguished than he, but only slightly so.[59] These men gather in the garden of Scipio's villa outside of Rome where they occupy their leisure by discussing the nature of the ideal commonwealth and its needs. Their interest in philosophy, far from being self-indulgent, is shown to reaffirm the value of public service.[60] Their discussion culminates with the famous Dream of Scipio, a vision of the unparalleled rewards that await the true statesman. In this manner Cicero unites the traditional concept of the proper country retirement with new Hellenized life-styles in such a way that the former is revitalized and the latter are sanctioned.

Another notable effort to come to terms with the conflict between the traditional ideal and contemporary realities of country life is *Res Rusticae* by the antiquarian Marcus Terentius Varro. The work is of particular interest for several reasons. It was published in 37 B.C.,

---

59. Biographical sketches of the interlocutors of this work may be found in George H. Sabine and Stanley B. Smith, trans., *On the Commonwealth* (Columbus, Ohio 1929) 4–6. The standard biography of Publius Cornelius Scipio Africanus Minor, the major figure in the dialogue, is that of Astin (above n. 48).

60. Cicero is explicit about this function of philosophy and its value in *de Off.* 1.155: *nosque ipsi, quicquid ad rem publicam attulimus, si modo aliquid attulimus, a doctoribus atque doctrina instructi ad eam et ornati accessimus* ("as for myself, whatever I have contributed to the Republic, if indeed I have contributed anything, I have come to it trained and prepared by teachers and their instruction").

not long before Virgil is believed to have begun the *Georgics*, and it has been demonstrated that Virgil drew upon *Res Rusticae* extensively both for specific content and for general organization.[61] It is not my object, however, to remark on those aspects of his relationship to Varro since they have already received much attention from scholars. I find more immediate significance in the fact that in a work of his old age, a work he admits may be his last,[62] Varro touches on virtually all the conditions that influenced the character of country life in his day in an effort to reconcile them in a new concept of the proper role of country life in the career of the distinguished Roman.

Varro's treatise is based on a clear understanding of contemporary conditions in the countryside. It takes for granted the depressed circumstances of the small farmer who was available to be hired for work that endangered the health of slaves. Of more immediate concern to Varro and his audience was the question of rural luxury and its relation to the tradition that combined rustic austerity and civic responsibility. Varro emphasizes repeatedly the extremes that self-indulgent luxury had reached in the countryside. Axius, one of the speakers in *Res Rusticae* (which is presented as a conversation), observes (3.17.5-6):

> Quintus Hortensius, familiaris noster, cum piscinas haberet magna pecunia aedificatas ad Baulos, ita saepe cum eo ad villam fui, ut illum sciam semper in cenam pisces Puteolos mittere emptum solitum. neque satis erat eum non pasci e piscinis, nisi etiam ipse eos pasceret ultro.

> Although my friend Quintus Hortensius had expensive fishponds built near Bauli, I have been with him at his villa often enough to know that he was always in the habit of sending to Puteoli for fish for dinner. And it wasn't enough not to eat from his ponds, he even fed [the fish] himself.

---

61. In the first decade of this century, J. Jahn published a series of articles attempting to assess Virgil's indebtedness to Varro. The references have been conveniently collected by L. P. Wilkinson, *The Georgics of Virgil: A Critical Survey* (Cambridge 1969, reprinted 1978). See his bibliography, p. 346 and Appendix VI: "Literature on Agricultural Lore in the *Georgics*," p. 329. Erich Burck, *De Vergilii Georgicon partibus iussivis* (diss. Leipzig 1926), shifted emphasis to Virgil's reworking of his sources. Most recent in that tradition is M. Sodja, *Virgil's Poetic Art in the Georgics: The Poetic Recasting of Prose Material in Varro's 'Res Rusticae'* (diss. Madison, Wisconsin 1973).

62. Varro, *RR* 1.1.

Similarly, aviaries in the Greek style, and called by the Greek name, *ornithones*, now dwarf whole villas of an earlier age.⁶³ It is particularly notable, moreover, that such extravagant indulgence in Hellenistic styles is not only recent but even exemplified by the author himself. One of the characters in the treatise is made to ask Varro (*RR* 3.5.8):

> tu dic illud alterum genus ornithonis, qui animi causa constitutus a te sub Casino fertur, in quo diceris longe vicisse non modo archetypon inventoris nostri ornithotrophion M. Laeni Strabonis, qui Brundisii hospes noster primus in peristylo habuit exhedra conclusas aves, quas pasceret obiecto rete, sed etiam in Tusculano magna aedificia Luculli.

> Describe that other kind of ornithon [one constructed for pleasure rather than profit] which you are said to have constructed near Casinum for your amusement. With it you are reported to have far surpassed the archetypical bird house of our friend, its inventor, M. Laenius Strabo. He was our host at Brundisium and was the first to have birds penned up in the recess of a peristyle where he fed them through a net. Your aviary is even supposed to surpass Lucullus' great buildings at Tusculum.

Varro responds by describing a most elaborate and extensive ornithon. It features among its many attractions canals for fish, a small artificial island, and a tholos-temple under whose dome (*RR* 3.5.17)

> Stella lucifer interdiu, noctu hesperus, ita circumeunt ad infimum hemisphaerium ac moventur, ut indicent, quot sint horae. in eodem hemisphaerio medio circum cardinem est orbis ventorum octo, ut Athenis in horologio, quod fecit Cyrrestes; ibique eminens radius a cardine ad orbem ita movetur, ut eum tangat ventum, qui flet, ut intus scire possis.

> the morning star by day and at night the evening star circle at the bottom of the hemisphere and move in such a way as to indicate the time. In the middle of the same hemisphere around the axis is a circle of the eight winds as in the horologium that Cyrrestes made at Athens. There is an arm extending from the axis toward the rim—it moves in such a way that it touches the wind that is blowing, so that you may know it even inside.

---

63. Varro, *RR* 3.3.7.

The propriety of such luxury is explicitly called into question by comparison with the practice of earlier, more respected generations (*RR* 1.13.7):

> Nunc contra villam urbanam quam maximam ac politissimam habeant dant operam ac cum Metelli ac Luculli villis pessimo publico aedificatis certant.

> Nowadays, however, [wealthy Romans] are at pains to see that they have a villa in the urban style, as large and fine a villa as possible, and they vie with those villas of Metellus and Lucullus which were constructed to the great detriment of the state.

That criticism is developed, perhaps most fully in an exchange between Appius and Axius. Appius chides Axius for his opulent villa and contrasts it unfavorably with the actual scene of their discussion, the Villa Publica in the Campus Martius (*RR* 3.2.3–6):

> Sed non haec, inquit, villa, quam aedificarunt maiores nostri, frugalior ac melior est quam tua illa perpolita in Reatino? Nuncubi hic vides citrum aut aurum? Num minium aut armenium? Num quod emblema aut lithostrotum? Quae illic omnia contra. Et cum haec sit communis universi populi, illa solius tua; haec quo succedant e campo cives et reliqui homines, illa quo equae et asini; praeterea cum ad rem publicam administrandam haec sit utilis, ubi cohortes ad dilectum consuli adductae considant, ubi arma ostendant, ubi censores censu admittant populum. Tua scilicet, inquit Axius, haec in Campo Martio extremo utilis et non deliciis sumptuosior quam omnes omnium universae Reatinae? . . . Denique quid tua habet simile villae illius, quam tuus avos ac proavos habebat? . . . Nam quod extra urbem est aedificium, nihilo magis ideo est villa.

> "Isn't this villa . . . that our ancestors built more frugal and better than that fine villa of yours at Reate? You don't see citrus wood or gold here, do you? You don't see vermilion or azure, patterned or mosaic work? Everything at your place is the opposite. And, while this villa is shared by the entire people, yours is for you alone. This one provides a place to which citizens and other people can come from the Campus; yours is a place for mares and asses. Moreover, this is useful for official activities,

since the cohorts are summoned here by the consul for the levy, since they parade here in review; since the censors gather the people here for the census." Axius replies, "Surely this useful villa of yours on the edge of the Campus Martius is more sumptuous in pleasures than all the villas owned by anybody in Reate? . . . In short, what has your villa in common with that villa which your grandfather and great-grandfather had? . . . For the fact that a building is outside the city doesn't make it a villa."

Those contrasts of the old and the new styles are particularly revealing in two respects. First, they reflect how recent rural opulence and the introduction of Hellenistic styles of country architecture were. Second, they suggest a significant degree of confusion, uncertainty, and disagreement about the proper character and function of country villas, a natural consequence of the newness of the innovations transforming country life in Italy. Even as Varro himself has his characters express respect for traditional practices and the virtues with which they were associated, he dwells on the extraordinary opulence of his own pleasure garden with its ornithon. In fact the dialogue between Appius and Axius leads Appius to say, *subridens, Quoniam ego ignoro . . . quid sit villa, velim me doceas* ("with a smile, 'Since I don't know . . . what a villa is, I would like you to teach me'") (*RR* 3.2.7). Appius is, of course, being playful. Nonetheless, it is clear that the question was a real one. In a very important sense, Varro's treatise may be regarded as an effort to answer that question and thus, more generally, to arrive at a definition of what should be the proper relation of country and city, retired and public life.

Central to that effort is a reassertion of the dignity of rustic life and its place in Roman culture. Varro's treatise begins with a famous passage in which the author contrasts the virtues of the Italian soil and climate with those of Asia and the North (*RR* 1.2.3–7). Being more northern than Asia (according to Varro), Italy is cooler, therefore more healthful and more fruitful. Still, it does not suffer the "continual winters" (*sempiternae hiemes*) of the more distant North. In contrast to the North (*RR* 1.2.6),

> quid in Italia utensile non modo non nascitur, sed etiam non egregium fit?

What useful product is there that does not both grow in Italy and indeed grow exceptionally well here?

Later, the speaker compares Italy favorably even with the lands celebrated for their fruitfulness in Homer's epics (*RR* 1.2.7):

> an Phrygia magis vitibus cooperta, quam Homerus appellat ἀμπελόεσσαν quam haec? aut tritico Argos, quod idem poeta πολύπυρον?

> Is Phrygia more covered in vines, that Phrygia which Homer calls "vine-clad," than Italy? Or Argos, which the same poet calls "abundant with grain," more rich than Italy in grain?

Behind that praise it is not difficult to detect a certain self-consciousness about Italy's standing in the Hellenistic world. It is significant that, by making Italy's fruitfulness and the productiveness of Italian agriculture the basis for comparison with other nations, Varro is acting within the tradition that makes rustic life a particular source of Roman excellence.

He returns explicitly to that theme later in the introduction to *Res Rusticae* 2:

> Viri magni nostri maiores non sine causa praeponebant rusticos Romanos urbanis. ut ruri enim qui in villa vivunt ignaviores, quam qui in agro versantur in aliquo opere faciendo, sic qui in oppido sederent, quam qui rura colerent, desidiosiores putabant. . . . Quod dum servaverunt institutum, utrumque sunt consecuti, ut et cultura agros fecundissimos haberent et ipsi valetudine firmiores essent, ac ne Graecorum urbana desiderarent gymnasia.

> Those great men, our ancestors, not without reason preferred Romans who lived in the countryside to those who lived in the city. For, just as in the countryside those who live in a villa are lazier than those who are involved in performing some task in the field, so they thought that those who sat in town were lazier than those who cultivated the land. . . . As long as they preserved that practice, they achieved two ends: by cultivating their fields they made them most fertile, and they themselves were healthier and did not need the Greeks' city gymnasia.

Having established the special contributions of rustic life to Roman culture, Varro goes on to affirm its dignity in more general terms (*RR* 2.1.6):

> Origo, quam dixi; dignitas, quam dicam. de antiquis inlustrissimus quisque pastor erat, ut ostendit et Graeca et Latina lingua et veteres poetae.

> The origin [of rustic life] is as I have described. I will now describe its dignity. Of the ancients the most illustrious were shepherds, as the Greek and Latin languages and the old poets show.

In the introduction to Book 3 Varro claims that rustic preceded urban life. He supports his assertion by reference not only to the Roman past, but especially to the more ancient past recorded in Greek myth.

Against that background his picture of rustic life is built around elements that recall the distinctive place of farming and farmers in Roman culture. The names of the characters in his dialogue are virtually all obvious puns based on the particular branch of agriculture with which each character is associated. Appius, for example, discourses on bees; Vaccius, on cattle; Fundanus and Agrasius, on the cultivation of fruit and cereal crops. In part, this is simply a playful expression of Varro's interest in words and etymologies. But it is more than that, for it calls attention to the fact that a memory of Rome's agrarian origins was preserved in many Roman names, such as Cicero ("chickpea"), Fabius ("bean"), or Catulus ("cub"). In 2.1.10 Varro explicitly remarks on that phenomenon:

> nomina multa habemus ab utroque pecore, a maiore et a minore —a minore Porcius, Ovinius, Caprilius; sic a maiore Equitius, Taurius, Asinius—et idem cognomina adsignificare quod dicuntur, ut Anni Caprae, Statili Tauri, Pomponi Vituli, sic a pecudibus alia multa.

> We have many names from each category of livestock, both the larger and smaller. From the smaller we have Porcius, Ovinus, Caprilius; likewise from the larger, Equitius, Taurius, Asinius. Cognomina (so-called) point up the same thing, for example, the Anni Caprae, the Statili Tauri, the Pomponi Vituli are named from livestock, as are many others.

Varro's puns, then, precisely because they are blatant, direct his audience's attention forcefully to the fact that many prominent families had origins in rustic life.

The characters in *Res Rusticae* recall Rome's agrarian past in yet another and more significant way. Typically, they combine high social position, in some cases a political career, with actual participation in the agricultural work of their estates. In Book 2.4.2–3 Scrofa asserts:

> nec minus septimus sum deinceps praetorius in gente nostra. Nec tamen defugio quin dicam quae scio de suillo pecore. Agri enim culturae ab initio fui studiosus, . . . Quis enim fundum colit nostrum, quin sues habeat?

> I am no less than the seventh man of praetorian rank in a row in our family. Just the same, I don't hesitate to say what I know about pigs, for I have always been interested in farming, . . . and which of us who manages a farm does not have pigs?

The chief interlocutors of the third book are Varro (who himself had achieved praetorian rank); Quintus Axius, a senator; and Appius Claudius, the augur. Among the others is Cornelius Merula, a member of a consular family. Each of these men, like the others in the conversation, discourses on specific agricultural topics in which he is personally experienced. They all speak not only as theoreticians but as practitioners as well. In presenting such figures, Varro is reverting to the type of the farmer-statesman. He is archaizing, for he is recalling a tradition that was already fading in the mid-second century: Cato, it must be remembered, wrote his agricultural treatise for the absentee landlord.

Yet Varro is not by any means proposing an unqualified return to the practices of that earlier age. His vision of rustic life also has a strong intellectual-aesthetic appeal that reflects very much the tastes of his own day. At the outset he surveys the previous authorities on the subject and establishes a scientific or scholarly context for his own treatise. The subject matter of each of the three books is dealt with very much in the manner of the philosophical and rhetorical treatises of Cicero: several prominent Romans put their leisure time to good use by discussing informally subjects of general interest and some social consequence. In contrast to Cato's rather rambling presentation in *De Agricultura*, Varro's characters impose a rigorous organization upon their subject. Scrofa, for example, introduces his exposition (*RR* 1.5.3-4):

> Agri culturae, . . . quattuor sunt partes summae: e quis prima cognitio fundi, solum partesque eius quales sint; secunda, quae in eo fundo opus sint ac debeant esse culturae causa; tertia, quae in eo praedio colendi causa sint facienda; quarta, quo quicque tempore in eo fundo fieri conveniat. De his quattuor generalibus partibus singulae minimum in binas dividuntur species.
>
> Of agriculture . . . there are four main categories: the first is knowledge of the farm, the character of the soil and its constituents; second, what means [men, animals, tools] are needed and ought to be available on the estate for farming it; third, what should be produced on this property; fourth, at what time it is appropriate for everything to be done on the farm. Each of these four general divisions is divided at least into two sub-categories.

At times, this kind of categorizing is carried to almost ridiculous extremes (*RR* 1.17.1):

> Nunc dicam, agri quibus rebus colantur. Quas res alii dividunt in duas partes, in homines et adminicula hominum, sine quibus rebus colere non possunt; alii in tres partes, instrumenti genus vocale et semivocale et mutum, vocale, in quo sunt servi, semivocale, in quo sunt boves, mutum, in quo sunt plaustra.
>
> Now I will discuss the means by which the land is cultivated. Some divide these into two categories, into men and aids without which men cannot cultivate. Others divide the subject into three categories: the articulate class of instrument, the semiarticulate, and the mute—the articulate to which belong slaves, the semiarticulate to which belong oxen, the mute to which belong farm wagons.

Like Varro's blatant play on the names of his characters, such insistence on the orderliness of his subject matter is significant. For one thing, it supports his efforts to elevate agriculture to the level of philosophy and science.

Perhaps even more important, the elaborate organization of the subject matter contributes to a general sense of orderliness and control, which enhances the attractiveness of rustic life and contrasts it sharply with the disorder of the City. Thus, in the first book, conversation begins while several friends await the return of a temple curator from the City. The conversation is interrupted, however, when (*RR* 1.69.2)

> venit libertus aeditumi ad nos flens et rogat ut ignoscamus, quod simus retenti, et ut ei in funus postridie prodeamus. Omnes consurgimus ac simul exclamamus, "Quid? in funus? quod funus? quid est factum?" Ille flens narrat ab nescio quo percussum cultello concidisse, quem qui esset animadvertere in turba non potuisse, sed tantum modo exaudisse vocem, perperam fecisse.
>
> the temple curator's freedman arrives in tears and asks us to forgive him for keeping us waiting, and to attend the funeral on the next day. We all spring up and cry out together: "What? To a funeral? What funeral? What has happened?" Tearfully he explains that [his master] has been stabbed by someone with a knife and has fallen dead, that he was unable to see who it was in the crowd, but that he only heard a voice saying that a mistake had been made.

Not only the violence but the turbulence and anonymity of the City are completely antithetical to the orderly but nonetheless informal society of the waiting friends. Similarly, the exposition of Book 3 is momentarily interrupted by a commotion in the nearby Campus Martius while a ballot watcher caught cheating is dragged off to the consul by supporters of the other candidates (*RR* 3.5.18).

Some indication of Varro's own way of reconciling the various styles of rustic life is provided by the character of the little society comprised by the interlocutors of *Res Rusticae*, urbane yet orderly, leisured yet purposeful, private yet socially responsible. The focus and embodiment of that reconciliation for Varro is the villa itself. In Book 1.4.1 Varro has Agrasius assert: *agricolae ad duas metas dirigere debent, ad utilitatem et voluptatem* ("farmers ought to aim at two goals, utility and pleasure"). Thus, two major themes of Varro's work are brought together, for in each book there is a separate emphasis on the profitability of villas and the pleasure they afford. While calculation of the profits to be had from certain crops is a recurrent motif, so also is elaboration of the opulence of country life. We have seen clear disapproval of the latter when excessive and self-indulgent, but Varro by no means rejects it entirely. In answer to Appius' question, "What is a villa?" Axius replies (*RR* 3.2.11):

> Quid enim refert, utrum propter oves, an propter aves fructus capias? Anne dulcior est fructus apud te ex bubulo pecore, unde apes nascuntur, quam ex apibus, quae ad villam Sei in alvariis opus faciunt?

> What difference does it make whether you make a profit on account of sheep or on account of birds? Is the profit sweeter from oxen—from which bees are born—than from bees which perform their work in hives at Seius' villa?

The making of profit is more important than the manner in which it is made. There is no reason, therefore, not to combine business with pleasure.

In several passages Varro indicates that rustic luxury should be appropriate to the location; it should reflect the wealth of the countryside, not of the City. Perhaps the most explicit of those passages occurs in *Res Rusticae* 1.59.1–3:

> Et ideo oporothecas qui faciunt, ad aquilonem fenestras habeant atque ut eae perflentur curant, . . . ideoque in iis camaras marmorato et parietes pavimentaque faciunt, quo frigidius sit. In quo etiam quidam triclinium sternere solent cenandi causa. Etenim in quibus luxuria concesserit ut in pinacothece faciant, quod spectaculum datur ab arte, cur non quod natura datum utantur in venustate disposita pomorum? Praesertim cum id non sit faciendum, quod quidam fecerunt, ut Romae coempta poma rus intulerint in oporothecen instruendam convivi causa.

> And so, those who build oporothecas [greenhouses] see that they have windows facing north and that they let in the breeze. . . . And, thus, they face the ceilings, walls, and floors with marble, to make them cooler. Some people are even accustomed to placing a table in it so they may dine there. Since luxury makes it possible for them to do this in a picture gallery, an impressive setting which is provided by art, why should they not employ what has been given by nature in a lovely arrangement of fruits? Especially if you don't do as some and import fruits bought at

Rome into the country in order to arrange the greenhouse for a banquet.

Varro dedicates the third book of his treatise to Pinnius with the following explanation (*RR* 3.1.10):

> Cum enim villam haberes opere tectorio et intestino ac pavimentis nobilibus lithostrotis spectandam et parum putasses esse, ni tuis quoque litteris exornati parietes essent, ego quoque, quo ornatior ea esse posset fructu, quod facere possem, haec ad te misi.

> Since you had a villa worth seeing for its frescoes, inlays, and pavements of splendid mosaics and you regarded it as inadequate unless the walls were made illustrious by your writings, I too, in order that it might be enhanced by produce to the extent that I can make it so, have sent these writings to you.

The products of the villa, then, are regarded in a double light: they enhance the villa aesthetically as well as materially.

The most dramatic, if not the final, vision of the ideal villa is presented in the description (*RR* 3.5.9–17), from which I quoted above, of Varro's own extraordinary ornithon. Although it is specifically designated as an aviary designed for pleasure rather than profit, the larger context of Varro's argument demands, I believe, that we regard it as part of a productive villa. In its elaborate architectural design, in its careful attention to the care of the birds and the pleasure of the guests, in its arrangement of weather vanes and hour hands, Varro's ornithon epitomizes the perfectly ordered villa. More than that, it represents a kind of sanctuary within the villa which is itself semi-independent from the larger society. The villa and the ornithon within it, then, offer a protected world within which the small society of Varro's friends may retire, undisturbed by the disorder of the City. Varro perhaps meant to suggest as much when not long before the description of his ornithon he has Axius say jokingly to Appius—whose companions are named after birds—*Recipis nos . . . in tuum ornithona, ubi sedes inter aves?* ("Will you welcome us . . . into your aviary where you sit with the birds?") (*RR* 3.2.2). Thus, the villa becomes a retreat from the world outside.

But it is a retreat for men who will appreciate its pleasures, its order, and its profits, equally. Above all, it is a retreat for men who have been engaged in the larger world and will return to it. Appius responds to Axius' playful greeting (*RR* 3.2.3):

> Te praesertium, quoius aves hospitales etiam nunc ructor, quas mihi apposuisti paucis ante diebus in Villa Reatina ad lacum Velini eunti de controversiis Interamnatium et Reatinorum.
>
> Welcome. Especially you. I still haven't gotten over those hospitable birds you served me a few days ago in your villa at Reate, that time I was on my way to Lake Velinus on the matter of disagreements between the people of Interamna and Reate.

For Varro as for Cicero, the countryside is primarily an adjunct to the City, but in a different way. Varro makes no apology for the fact that it offers both an escape from the confusion of the City and an opportunity for unparalleled indulgence in luxury. Nonetheless, the countryside is also supposed to recall prominent Romans to their responsibilities as proprietors who must take a personal interest in the management and productivity of their estates and who as public figures must be prepared to offer their services to the Republic.[64]

Although Varro brings those varied ideals together within his treatise, their relationship remains loosely defined. What, really, do the enjoyment of luxury, a sense of civic responsibility, and the careful management of a rustic estate have to do with one another? One might think of several plausible responses to that question, but Varro's treatise itself reveals no clear answer. Ultimately, however, that lack of clarity and definition is not the most significant aspect of his work. More revealing is the simple fact that he perceived confusion about the role of country life and was sufficiently concerned to address it in what he thought might be his last public act before departing life.

### IV

Discussions of country life were not all narrowly focused on the role of the countryside in the life of the responsible Roman citizen. The very associations and traditions which made that question important to Romans also made visions of country life particularly suitable vehicles for the most general responses to the collapse of the

---

64. For the idea, implicit here, that management of the commonwealth and of an estate are analogous, see also Cicero, *De Republica* 4.7, 5.3-4.

Republic and to the fundamental questions it raised about the nature and possibility of return to a civilized existence. In his *Eclogues*, for example, Virgil examines critically the desire for escape to an ideal primitive innocence. He sees the limits of that ideal both in the irresistible impingement of external realities on the pastoral world and in fundamental aspects of human nature that first created the very realities from which escape is sought.[65] Thus, the collection of *Eclogues* begins and concludes with poignant references to the confiscations that disrupted life in the Roman countryside during the conflicts of the Late Republic.[66] At the same time, Virgil demonstrates—whether in Silenus' stories of sexual perversion (and in the naive shepherds' obvious delight in them), in the crazed passions of Alphesiboeus, or in Gallus' ultimate inability to find solace in the countryside for his private griefs or a sufficient counterpoise to his own *Amor Martis*[67]—an inherent human restlessness that cannot be contained within the narrow bounds of an idealized pastoral existence.

Within that context he considers, tentatively, in *Eclogue* 4 the possibility of return to a Golden Age of universal harmony and abundance in nature. The return to that age must begin with a new moral order and the reconstitution of the Roman state (*Eclogue* 4.11-14):

> teque adeo decus hoc aeui, te consule, inibit,
> Pollio, et incipient magni procedere menses;
> te duce, si qua manent sceleris uestigia nostri,
> inrita perpetua soluent formidine terras.

> With you the glory of the age shall go forth, with you as consul, Pollio, and the great months will begin to advance. Under your leadership if any traces of our crimes remain, they will be rendered of no account and so free the earth from constant fear.

Attention at the conclusion of the poem to the newborn infant, and exhortations that he ensure a successful career by smiling propitiously upon his parents, put the expansive expectations expressed

---

65. Those sets of limits are concerns of two recent books on the *Eclogues*, that of Michael C. T. Putnam, *Virgil's Pastoral Art: Studies in the Eclogues* (Princeton 1970), and Eleanor Winsor Leach (above n. 55).

66. *Ecls.* 1 and 9.

67. One meaning of the ambiguous line (*Ecl.* 10.44): *nunc insanus amor duri me Martis in armis / . . . detinet.*

earlier in the poem in a new perspective. They introduce a note of reserve and suggest that Virgil offers the vision of a new Golden Age more as the exploration of a possibility than as the assertion of a certainty.[68] He has made his pastoral an occasion to enunciate a vision that, even if acknowledged as ultimately unrealistic, reveals the important assumption that improvement of the human condition will be realized within the framework of Roman government, under the political and moral leadership of its official ruler.

In his sixteenth *Epode*, Horace organizes very similar images of a Golden Age to support an antithetical point of view. His poem begins with a statement of despair (*Epode* 16.1-2):

> Altera iam teritur bellis civilibus aetas,
>     suis et ipsa Roma viribus ruit.

> Now another generation is worn down by civil wars, and Rome herself, by her own might, plunges into ruin.

In *Eclogue* 4 Virgil had looked forward to a kind of chaos, but it was to be a fruitful chaos: *omnis feret omnia tellus* ("all lands will bear all things," *Ecl.* 4.39). The coming age would see the end of strife and violence: oxen will not fear great lions (*Ecl.* 4.22), snakes and treacherous poisonous plants will perish (*Ecl.* 4.24-25). It is a measure of Horace's pessimism that he envisions a return to the violent disorder of barbarism. Rome once withstood the most violent foes, but soon (*Epode* 16.10-11)

> ferisque rursus occupabitur solum;
> barbarus heu cineres insistet victor

> wild beasts will once again take over her soil, the barbarian, alas, will tread on her ashes, victorious.

For Horace there is no prospect of a restored order at Rome. He advises abandonment and a determination to return only when (*Epode* 16.28-33)

> Padus Matina laverit cacumina,
>   in mare seu celsus procurrerit Appenninus
>     novaque monstra iunxerit libidine
> mirus amor, iuvet ut tigris subsidere cervis,
>   adulteretur et columba miluo,
> credula nec ravos timeant armenta leones

68. Leach (above n. 55) 229-231.

the Po washes the mountain peaks near Matinus or the lofty Apennines thrust out into the sea and a strange love brings together monsters with a new desire, so that tigers delight to lie down with stags, the dove commits adultery with the kite, and trusting oxen do not fear tawny lions.

The vision of oxen safely intermingling with the king of predators was a hopeful symbol of possibility for Virgil, but is here another impossibility that emphasizes Horace's conviction that civilization can never be restored at Rome.

Horace introduces other images of a Golden Age only to reinforce that conviction (*Epode* 16.41-43, 49, 51-54):

> nos manet Oceanus circumvagus: arva beata
>     petamus, arva divites et insulas,
> reddit ubi cererem tellus inarata quotannis
> . . . . . . . . . . . . .
> illic iniussae veniunt ad mulctra capellae
> . . . . . . . . . . . . .
> nec vespertinus circumgemit ursus ovile
>     nec intumescit alta viperis humus;
> nulla nocent pecori contagia, nullius astri
>     gregem aestuosa torret inpotentia.

There remains to us the circling Ocean: let us seek blessed fields and rich islands where the earth, unplowed, yields grain each year. . . . There, unsummoned, she-goats come for milking . . . and in the evening bears do not growl about the sheepfolds, nor deep down does the earth swell with vipers. No contagions harm the flocks, nor does the seething power of any star burn down upon the herd.

By urging his audience to escape to "blessed fields and rich islands" where Golden Age conditions prevail, Horace is clearly enough directing them to an *Ou topia* ("No-place"),[69] a place that is no more

---

69. On the ambiguity of More's term and concept of "utopia," see M. I. Finley, "Utopianism Ancient and Modern," originally presented to the Congressus Internationalis: Antiquitas Graeco-Romana ac Tempora Nostra in Brno 14 April 1966, revised and published in *The Critical Spirit: Essays in Honor of Herbert Marcuse*, ed. K. H. Wolff and B. Moore Jr. (Boston 1967) 3-20, and subsequently in M. I. Finley, *The Use and Abuse of History* (New York 1975) 178-192.

real and accessible than an Italy where rivers wash mountain peaks and tigers lie down with stags.

Despite its obvious pessimism, the final lines of the *Epode* make it impossible to interpret the poem simply as a message of despair (*Epode* 16.63-66):

> Iuppiter illa piae secrevit litora genti,
>     ut inquinavit aere tempus aureum,
> aere, dehinc ferro duravit saecula, quorum
>     piis secunda vate me datur fuga.

> Jupiter set those shores apart for a pious race when he mingled bronze with the Golden Age, bronze, and then he hardened the ages with iron. To the pious of those ages there is granted, with me their priest, a favorable escape.

While Horace concludes with the assertion that escape *is* possible, his emphasis on piety and his designation of himself as a *vates*, a priest,[70] suggest the kind of escape and regeneration he intends. It is not a literal escape to some specific place, but rather a spiritual escape, a rededication to the obligations of piety, so that for Horace as for Virgil in the fourth *Eclogue*, the landscape symbolizes "undefined goods and abundance belonging to a state where man has learned to live in harmony with man."[71]

Still, the two poets conceive of that ideal state quite differently. For Virgil it is public, formal, and inclusive. It is "the state," Rome under the leadership of a worthy consul. For Horace, on the other hand, the "state" can only be something essentially abstract, no place, a state of mind. Insofar as the "blessed isles" to which Horace refers can have any concrete reality, we should perhaps think of them as comparable to the garden of Epicurus or the small circle of friends Horace presents in the *Satires* as a model of society, an island of prosperity created within a chaotic world by the serenity and moral integrity of its inhabitants. The fact that Horace and Virgil should employ the same imagery of natural abundance and harmony to two such different ends has led to the general assumption

---

70. On the special use of *vates* in Latin poetry, particularly in the Augustan age, see J. K. Newman, *The Concept of* Vates *in Augustan Poetry* (Brussels 1967) = *Collection Latomas* 89, and his *Augustus and the New Poetry* (above n. 4), ch. 4, pp. 99-206.

71. Leach (above n. 55) 225.

that one of the two poems (it is impossible to be sure which) was provoked by the other. Whichever of the poems came first, however, together they demonstrate clearly how conflicting visions of the countryside and its potential could provide the basis for a lively debate on issues of pressing concern and genuine substance.

Between the extremes offered by *Epode* 16 and *Eclogue* 4, less fantastic visions of the country and rustic life conveyed less radical solutions to the crises of contemporary Rome. The *Elegies* of Tibullus, for example, combine pastoral and traditional Roman ideas about rustic life to create a new ideal. Tibullus offers no vision of a spontaneously fruitful countryside pouring out a superabundance of goods. He envisions an adequate, yet modest livelihood won by his own labor (1.1.1–8):

> Divitias alius fuluo sibi congerat auro
> et teneat culti iugera multa soli,
> quem labor adsiduus uicino terreat hoste,
> Martia cui somnos classica pulsa fugent:
> me mea paupertas uita traducat inerti,
> dum meus adsiduo luceat igne focus.
> ipse seram teneras maturo tempore uites
> rusticus et facili grandia poma manu

Let another pile up wealth in shining gold for himself and possess many acres of cultivated land, one who is terrified by the constant toil of battle with the enemy nearby, one whose sleep is broken by the sounding of martial trumpets. May my poverty carry me through an unambitious life, so long as my hearth shines with a constant fire. I myself will sow tender vines when the season is right; I will live in the countryside and will sow great fruit trees with skillful hands.

Nor does Tibullus imagine himself in this setting as a partner of the gods, but rather as their humble worshipper (1.1.11–12):

> nam ueneror, seu stipes habet desertus in agris
> seu uetus in triuio florida serta lapis

For I stand in awe, whether it is a tree trunk, alone in the fields with a garland of flowers, or an old stone at the crossroads.

Ultimately, his sense of the simple integrity of rustic life derives from the example of his Roman ancestors (1.1.37-40):

> adsitis, diui, neu uos e paupere mensa
>   dona nec e puris spernite fictilibus.—
> fictilia antiquus primum sibi fecit agrestis
>   pocula, de facili composuitque luto.

> Attend me, gods, do not spurn gifts from a poor table and from pure earthenware. Of earthenware the farmer of old made his first cups; he shaped them from soft clay.

Nonetheless, the rustic life Tibullus envisions is characterized by a certainty that he will always have enough, even if not more than enough, and by a pervasive sense of ease in spite of the necessity for labor (1.1.25-32):

> iam mihi, iam possim contentus uiuere paruo
>   nec semper longae deditus esse uiae,
> sed Canis aestiuos ortus uitare sub umbra
>   arboris ad riuos praetereuntis aquae.
> nec tamen interdum pudeat tenuisse bidentem
>   aut stimulo tardos increpuisse boues;
> non agnamue sinu pigeat fetumue capellae
>   desertum oblita matre refere domum.

> Now, if only now I might live content with a little, not always be committed to a long journey, but avoid the hot risings of the Dog Star beneath the shade of a tree with a stream passing by its foot. Still, I would not be ashamed from time to time to take up the hoe or poke lagging cattle with a goad. I would not find it distasteful to carry back home in my arms a lamb or a kid abandoned by its forgetful mother.

Clearly, Tibullus imagines the work of farming as involving no more than occasional interruptions in an otherwise peaceful existence. His list of chores reads more like a series of diversions than of difficult responsibilities.

Whatever his longings, however, Tibullus is no simple-minded idealist. He intends that this attractive picture be taken no more literally than the Golden Age or blessed isles of Virgil and Horace.

His vision takes its meaning in conjunction with his attitude toward certain important aspects of the City and what it stands for.[72] His rejection of luxury is, of course, a major theme, as is his rejection of the pursuit of glory through public life. His statements to his patron, Messalla, are tactful but clear on this point (1.1.53-54):

> te bellare decet terra, Messalla, marique,
>     ut domus hostiles praeferat exuuias.

> For you it is becoming to do battle on land, Messalla, and on sea, so that your house may display the spoils of the enemy.

Messalla, then, cannot enjoy the pleasures of the rustic idyll Tibullus contemplates.

On the other hand, Tibullus' own allegiance to country life is not unqualified (1.1.55-58):

> me retinent uinctum formosae uincla puellae,
>     et sedeo duras ianitor ante fores.
> non ego laudari curo, mea Delia: tecum
>     dum modo sim, quaeso segnis inersque uocer.

> As for me, I am held back, bound by the bonds of a beautiful girl and I sit, a doorkeeper before a hard door. I do not care to win praise, my Delia: so long as I can be with you, I strive to be called lazy and without ambition.

Although Tibullus does make up fantasies in which his mistress shares his rustic idyll (*Elegy* 1.5), we know that she is not at all a rustic herself, either in fact or in spirit. She is inaccessible to him because she values the very luxury he rejects: he laments that *donis vincitur omnis amor* ("gifts conquer every love," 1.5.60). And yet Tibullus' rustic idyll is impossible without her. He cannot simply reject his urban mistress any more than he can forget his dream of rustic life. He can be satisfied, therefore, neither with country life nor with his mistress as they are. Each represents an element of a larger ideal. What Tibullus' poetry suggests is that the poet wants somehow to combine the virtues of simplicity and innocence with the attractions of urbane sophistication. With his Delia in the countryside he can imagine entertaining Messalla, the statesman (1.5.31-34).

---

72. See the analysis of F. Solmsen, "Tibullus as an Augustan Poet," *Hermes* 90 (1962) 295-325, esp. 297-312.

Tibullus knows well enough that he is caught in an impossible dilemma, that neither his mistress nor the countryside can ever be as he would like them to be.[73] He acknowledges as much when he asserts that he is kept from the countryside by the bonds of love, even as Messalla is by the demands of his public career (1.1.53–58). He repeats that point when he asserts that he is a *dux* and *miles* of love (1.1.75), even as Messalla is a soldier in war. If Tibullus feels compelled to endure his dilemma in the city, where he must confront his mistress's infidelity and indifference, rather than in the countryside, where he might enjoy the ease and pleasant distractions of rustic life, it is only partly because of Delia's magnetic charm. It is also because the countryside as he imagines it, even without his mistress, is not a real place. It is rather an accumulation of images and associations by which he can articulate an ideal for which there is no other model in Roman thought.

In time, Horace made images of rustic life the vehicle for yet another response to the needs of his society, a response that modified significantly but did not altogether reject the fundamental impulse expressed in the sixteenth *Epode*. That poem was almost certainly written early in Horace's career, while his Republican sympathies were still strong—he had fought on the losing side at Philippi—and before he had come under the reassuring patronage of Maecenas. The desire for escape which was the motive force of that poem never entirely disappeared in his later works, but it was radically transformed in them. For Horace, rustic life came to combine possibilities for escape from the City and its vices and, simultaneously, for a contribution to the restoration of public morality.

After he had received the patronage of Maecenas and his early pessimism was abated, Horace's interest in the countryside shifted from the blessed isles to the traditional embodiment of Roman virtue, the peasant farmer. He acknowledged the oppressive effect of contemporary events on the small landholder. In *Satire* 2.2, Horace argues that those who are habitually satisfied with the simple pleasures sufficient for a good life can best endure adversity, and he cites a rustic, Ofellus, as an example (112–115):

---

73. Solmsen, ibid., observes that Tibullus celebrates two not altogether consistent kinds of experiences in his poems. Gilbert Lawall, "The Green Cabinet and the Pastoral Design: Theocritus, Euripides, and Tibullus," *Ramus* 4 (1975) 87–100, suggests that that duality of vision expresses a tension between the poet's conflicting attractions to "a world of activity in which he cannot participate and a world of dreams that cannot be fulfilled" (p. 98).

> . . . puer hunc ego parvus Ofellum
> integris opibus novi non latius usum
> quam nunc accisis. videas metato in agello
> cum pecore et gnatis fortem mercede colonum.

When I was a small boy I knew this Ofellus and he drew on his resources no more heavily then, when they were whole, than he does now that they have been cut back. You might see him on a confiscated little plot with his flock and his children, a hardy farmer, working for hire.

Ofellus seems to have been one of those farmers who lost their holdings during the turmoil of the Late Republic and had been reduced to the most unenviable of lots, working as hired help. He is, consequently, an excellent example of one forced to live in straitened circumstances.

Horace chose him as a subject because he epitomized certain essential virtues that reveal themselves most clearly in adversity. *Satire* 2 concludes with the self-assured and satisfied reflections of the stalwart old farmer. He begins by surveying the simple but hardy fare and the spontaneous fellowship he has always enjoyed (116–122):

> non ego . . . temere edi luce profesta
> quicquam praeter holus fumosae cum pede pernae.
> ac mihi seu longum post tempus venerat hospes
> sive operum vacuo gratus conviva per imbrem
> vicinus, bene erat non piscibus urbe petitis,
> sed pullo atque haedo; tum pensilis uva secundas
> et nux ornabat mensas cum duplice ficu.

I was never one to eat rashly on work days anything except cabbage and a slice of smoked ham. And if a guest arrived, someone I hadn't seen for a long time, or if, on a day when there was nothing to do because of the rain, a welcome neighbor joined me for dinner, I got along well without fish sent for from the City, just a chicken and a kid. For the rest, raisins and nuts and split figs adorned my table.

Theoretically, such simple fare is available to anyone but it seems to belong more naturally to the countryside than to the City, from which delicacies like fish may be imported. Ofellus belongs among those heroes of Rome's venerable past whom Horace had cited with approval earlier in the poem (89–93):

> rancidum aprum antiqui laudabant, non quia nasus
> illis nullus erat, sed, credo, hac mente, quod hospes
> tardius adveniens vitiatum commodius quam
> integrum edax dominus consumeret. hos utinam inter
> heroas natum tellus me prima tulisset.

The ancients used to praise rancid boar not because they lacked noses but rather, I believe, because they were of the mind that it was better for a guest arriving late to eat spoiled meat than for a greedy host to eat the whole thing. Would that I had been born among the heroes when the earth was still new.

The example of the farmer also suits Horace's argument particularly well for another reason. It suggests a kind of independence and self-sufficiency, which was at once central to the Roman idea of economy and in dramatic contrast with the anxious dependence on the approval of others by which Horace characterized life in the City (94–99). For in the final and most striking part of his reflections, Ofellus asserts his own independence despite the fact that he is now only a hired laborer on someone else's property. He distinguishes sharply between possession of the land and use of it. The new owner possesses it now, just as Ofellus himself did before and as yet another person will possess it in the future. But it is still Ofellus himself who works it (134–135). Implicit in that assertion of dignity and independence is a strong sense that the virtues Ofellus exemplifies, even if not exclusive to the farmer's way of life, are inherent in it: they are available to anyone who works the land.

Although Maecenas' gift to Horace of a villa in the Sabine hills provided the poet with an opportunity to actualize the rustic virtues that he celebrated in his poems, Horace had no illusions about himself as a farmer. Not only was he aware of the realities of peasant life, he was also untroubled by the gentle condescension with which his rustic neighbors viewed his own recreational gardening.[74] His object was not to confine himself to the necessities of rustic life, but rather to realize its virtues. In *Satire* 2.6 he writes of enjoying the same

---

74. *Epist.* 1, 14.39, and cf. Heitland (above n. 48) 234–237 on Horace's "realism" in contrast to Virgil's.

simple fare, the same informal hospitality as the rustic Ofellus. Looking forward in the City to a return to his farm, Horace exclaims (63-69):

> o quando faba Pythagorae cognata simulque
> uncta satis pingui ponentur holuscula lardo?
> o noctes cenaeque deum, quibus ipse meique
> ante Larem proprium vescor vernasque procacis
> pasco libatis dapibus. prout cuique libido est,
> siccat inaequalis calices conviva solutus
> legibus insanis.

> O when will beans, Pythagoras' relative, and simple greens seasoned just enough with rich lard be laid before me? O nights and banquets of the gods which my friends and I enjoy before my own Lar and with which I feed my perhaps too familiar home-bred slaves after thanks to the gods. And just as each guest desires, he drains cups of different measures, not bound by crazy drinking rules.

But such pleasures and the leisurely country routine are not the whole of Horace's rustic experience. They are, rather, the context for other activities.

Like Cicero, he regards country life at its best as an opportunity for the pursuit of those activities that require leisure and repose (60-62):

> o rus, quando ego te adspiciam quandoque licebit
> nunc veterum libris, nunc somno et inertibus horis
> ducere sollicitae iucunda oblivia vitae?

> O countryside, when may I see you, when may I enjoy pleasant forgetfulness of life's troubles, now with books of the ancients, now with sleep and hours of relaxation?

More specifically, rustic life provides the proper ambience for certain kinds of reflection. The simple fare Horace shares with his friends is presented as actually determining the nature of those reflections (71-76): *ergo*, he says,

> sermo oritur, non de villis domibusve alienis,
> nec male necne Lepos saltet; sed, quod magis ad nos
> pertinet et nescire malum est, agitamus, utrumne

divitiis homines an sint virtute beati,
quidve ad amicitias, usus rectumne, trahat nos
et quae sit natura boni summumque quid eius.

there is conversation not about villas and other people's houses nor whether or not Grace dances well; but we discuss what is closer to ourselves and what it is bad not to know: whether wealth or virtue makes men happy, or what leads us to friendship—custom or uprightness—what is the nature of the good and what its highest form is.

For Horace, unlike Cicero, not only the subjects of his discourse but even their manner is influenced by the rustic setting. The countryside offers him something more than leisure, something different from the inspiring examples of philosophical gardens and the dignified rustic pastimes of earlier Roman statesmen. Horace does not withdraw to his Sabine villa in order to engage in "Socratic" dialogues.[75] His rustic companions include actual farmers as well as statesmen (77-79):

Cervius haec inter vicinus garrit anilis
ex re fabellas. siquis nam laudat Arelli
sollicitas ignarus opes, sic incipit. . . .

In the midst of such discussions, Cervius, a neighbor of mine, reels off old people's stories on the subject. For example, if someone praises Arellius' wealth, unaware of the troubles it brings, he begins like this. . . .

What follows is the famous allegory of the city mouse and the country mouse. However lofty the themes of Horace's discussions, they are colored by the unassuming style of rustic discourse. What distinguishes them even more from Cicero's dialogues is that we are encouraged to regard them as informed by a certain rustic wisdom. The discussions at Horace's villa offer penetrating insights into the essential values not in spite of their rustic flavor and their homely common sense but because of those qualities.

Related to Horace's confidence in the virtues of country life is another major difference between his view of the countryside and

75. Cf. Cicero, *Tusculanae Disputationes* 1.8.

that of Cicero. For Cicero, retreat to the countryside was valuable only as preparation for a return to the City and public life. Horace makes it abundantly clear that life in the City holds no attractions for him. He ends each day there longing for the time when he can return to his Sabine villa (59). Cicero apologizes for his attention to literature and philosophy on the grounds that he has nothing better to do during his periods of enforced retirement. The thrust of Horace's poetry, especially his *Satires*, is that there really *is* nothing better to do than to enjoy the kind of life he leads in the countryside. And it is partly for that reason that his country retirement is not, in his eyes, self-indulgent.

But there is yet another, more important reason. Through his poetry Horace makes his life public. More than that, he invites his audience to join him in his world. One commentator has astutely pointed, for example, to the significance of the way in which *Satire* 2.6 is organized.[76] Horace begins with an essentially straightforward assertion of how much his Sabine villa means to him (1–23). He then proceeds to explain the reasons for his enthusiasm. First, there are the obligations and harassments of the City from which he gladly escapes (23–59). Then there are the positive attractions of his country life. It is in the midst of this last section (line 77), that the story of the country mouse and the city mouse is introduced, modestly, as no more than an example of the kind of plain conversation that Horace enjoys at his villa. The story itself is engaging, and it is of some length—longer, in fact, than any of the previous sections of the poem. As Cervius tells his story we become fellow listeners with Horace and the rest of his guests. And that is precisely where we are left at the conclusion of the poem. Horace does not resume his own commentary. We are not invited to look back on the scene again as outsiders; we are left rather with an experience of it. For Horace, the rustic life is not simply valuable as a private escape from the chaos of his times. Through his poetry it becomes available to others as an example of a kind of alternative they too may share. For already implicit in Horace's version of country life is a sense that for him the countryside is "An Isle of the Blessed located not at Sirmio or Virgil's rural Italy, nor even in the famous Sabine farm itself, but

---

76. Michael O'Loughlin, *The Garlands of Repose: The Literary Celebration of Civic and Retired Leisure* (Chicago 1978) 106–107.

within the mind of the genius of the place."⁷⁷ In his *Odes* and *Epistles*, published after the *Georgics*, Horace goes on to articulate more fully and emphatically the idea that rustic life provides, above all, a model for the qualities of integrity and self-sufficiency which transcend place.

V

This survey of changing attitudes toward country life has important implications for a reading of the *Georgics*. It suggests, first of all, that among Virgil's audience there was no single, generally accepted vision of what country life was or should be, or of what truths were to be learned from it. Appreciation of that diversity of viewpoint offers an invaluable perspective from which to approach the vexed problem of the unity and purpose of the *Georgics*. Wilhelm Kroll defined the terms of modern controversy about the *Georgics* by questioning the poem's fundamental coherence.⁷⁸ He argued that the poem is a technical treatise on agriculture relieved by purple passages that bear no thematic relationship to the main body of the work. Erich Burck countered by arguing for the essential unity of the poem on two grounds.⁷⁹ Structurally, he pointed out that the transitions

---

77. Michael O'Loughlin, *The Garlands of Repose: Studies in the Literary Representations of Civic and Retired Leisure* (diss. Yale 1966) 295.

78. W. Kroll, *Studien zum Verständnis der römische Literatur* (Stuttgart 1924), esp. 185–197. For helpful summaries of scholarship on the composition of the *Georgics*, see L. P. Wilkinson, *The Georgics of Virgil* (Cambridge 1969, reprinted 1978), Appendix I, 314–315; and K. Büchner's article on Virgil in *RE* VIII A 2, (2. Reihe) 1955 ( = *P. Vergilius Maro: Der Dichter der Römer* [Stuttgart 1956], cols. 1265–1266 et passim). A full bibliography of scholarship on the *Georgics* from 1940 to 1973 is available in three publications: George E. Duckworth, "Recent Work on Vergil (1940–1956)," *CW* 51 (1958) 89–92, 116–117, 123–128, 151–159, 185–193, 228–235, reprinted in 1964 by the Vergilian Society of America under the title, *Recent Work on Vergil: A Bibliographical Survey, 1940-1956*; George E. Duckworth, "Recent Work on Vergil (1957–1963)," *CW* 57 (1964) 193–228, reprinted by the Vergilian Society of America in 1964 under the title, *Recent Work on Vergil: A Bibliographical Survey, 1957-1963*; Alexander G. McKay, "Recent Work on Vergil: A Bibliographical Survey, 1964–1973," *CW* 68 (1974) 1–92, reprinted in 1974 by the Vergilian Society of America under the same title. More recently those bibliographies have been collected with other material in Walter Donlan, ed., *The Classical World Bibliography of Vergil* (The Classical World Bibliographies, Garland Reference Library of the Humanities, Vol. 96) (New York, London, 1978). They are supplemented and updated annually in "Vergilian Bibliography" published by Alexander G. McKay in *Vergilius*.

79. E. Burck (above n. 61) and "Die Komposition von Vergils Georgica," *Hermes* 64 (1929) 279–321, and esp. p. 317 is also helpful for a summary of his two main conclusions about Virgil's method of composition.

between the technical and mythological or political sections of the poem are carefully arranged. In addition, he demonstrated a thematic relation between mythological and political passages, on the one hand, and technical passages, on the other, inasmuch as the former often appear to generalize or universalize the latter. The most important subsequent contribution in this direction was Friedrich Klingner's sensitive commentary in his *Virgils Georgica*.[80] Those works succeeded in revealing relationships between the apparently incompatible subjects in the poem: technical instruction, myth, politics, and other topics earlier regarded as digressive.

In the process they called attention to another equally troubling problem. For, if the reader is to approach the poem as a unity, then it is necessary to come to terms with dramatic, sometimes violent contrasts in perspective and tone. The poem, in fact, is organized in such a way as to emphasize those contrasts. Thus, while the first and third *Georgics* depict the harshness of rustic life and the limitations of the human condition, the intervening *Georgic* stresses the spontaneous fruitfulness of nature and the ease of rustic life and suggests the attractions of a contemplative, as opposed to active, existence. Similarly, the conclusion of *Georgic* 2 contrasts the virtues of rustic retirement to the corruption of contemporary urban society and civic life, but immediately afterward the introduction to *Georgic* 3 transforms the very symbols of urban and civic corruption of *Georgic* 2 into symbols of the ultimate victory of Roman civilization under the military generalship of Caesar and the artistic leadership of Virgil himself.

The focus of Burck and Klingner is generally too narrow to address those larger problems, since it is primarily on individual passages in their relationship to the passages that proceed or follow them directly. Consequently, while the works of those critics are often most illuminating as regards associative or thematic connections between immediately adjacent passages, they are less helpful in explaining the thematic relationships between passages that are not immediately adjacent. When Burck and Klingner do broaden their scope, they tend mostly to call attention to relationships or patterns

---

80. Friedrich Klingner, *Virgils Georgica* (Zürich 1963), reprinted as the second part of his *Virgil: Bucolica, Georgica, Aeneis* (Zürich 1967), is also helpful. In the same tradition is Büchner (above n. 78).

of development among passages that seem prima facie to share a common perspective, but they do not relate those passages to others within the poem that seem to present different perspectives.

Brooks Otis's discussion of the *Georgics* in his book, *Virgil: A Study in Civilized Poetry*,[81] made an important critical advance by viewing the poem from a broad perspective that acknowledges the larger thematic contrasts within the poem. Otis's attempt to deal with the problems they raise, however, while very illuminating, is not completely satisfying for several reasons. His approach is overly schematic. While he emphasizes the distinctive thematic character of different sections of the poem, he pays considerably less attention to the recurrence of motifs that both heighten contrasts between sections and provide essential elements of continuity in the poem. When he does discuss the interrelationships of discrete passages, he tends to do so less in thematic than in narrowly structural terms, emphasizing parallelism, contiguity, or antithesis.[82] Finally, I find his ultimate synthesis to be marred by a tendency, which I have discussed elsewhere,[83] to Christianize the poem—that is, to discuss it anachronistically in terms of such Christian concepts as the Fall, sin, atonement, and resurrection.

Most recently, several critics have attempted to give a thematic value to the alternations of perspective and tone to which earlier analyses had called attention. According to these critics, a major theme of the *Georgics* is the universal pattern of degeneration and renewal.[84] The structure of the poem is itself determined by that pattern and is the vehicle for communicating it to the reader. I agree that such a pattern emerges as one of the central and underlying concerns of the poem, but it does not come close to exhausting the

---

81. Above n. 4, ch. 5, "The *Georgics*" 144-214 and Appendixes 6 and 7 (407-413).

82. Otis (above n. 4), esp. 151-154, 189-190. L. P. Wilkinson, *The Georgics of Virgil: A Critical Survey* (Cambridge 1969, reprinted 1978), does not bring any fundamentally new perspectives to bear on the poem but does, as his title promises, provide a very useful survey of important questions and scholarship relating to interpretation of the *Georgics*. His work also contains helpful readings of specific passages.

83. G. B. Miles, "*Georgics* 3.209-294: *Amor* and Civilization," *CSCA* 8 (1975) 177-197.

84. Smith Palmer Bovie, "The Imagery of Ascent-Descent in Vergil's *Georgics*," *AJPh* 78 (1956) 337-358; Michael O'Loughlin (above n. 76), "The Public Context: Vergil's *Georgics*: Rural Work and Civic Leisure," 59-75; Charles Paul Segal, "Orpheus and the Fourth *Georgic*: On Nature and Civilization," *AJPh* 87 (1966) 307-325; Dorothea Wender, "Resurrection in the Fourth *Georgic*," *AJPh* 90 (1969) 424-436.

full range of meaning that the poem presents. It does little to account for the specifc elements of the overall pattern or for their particular deployment. More important, while it accounts satisfactorily for alternation of tone, it does not come to terms with the contradictory visions of rustic life within the poem. If regarded as a fully adequate account of the contrasts in the poem, it would imply that when Virgil says, in one passage, that the earth can only be made fruitful by constant hard labor[85] and, in another, that the earth pours out her fruits with bounteous spontaneity,[86] then the only value we can rightly attribute to his words is that of rhetorical hyperbole intended to emphasize the contrasting realities of rebirth and degeneration.

Elsewhere I have argued that the apparent contradictions in the poem are so forcefully drawn, sharply contrasted, and fundamental that they cannot be dismissed simply as part of a rhetorical strategy.[87] In the following chapters, I shall attempt to demonstrate that in successive sections Virgil considers a series of radically different visions of rustic life,[88] each one responding to or growing out of the limitations of the previous one. The unity of the poem, then, will be shown not to lie in the elaboration of a single vision, however complex, of rustic life but rather to emerge gradually, out of critical explorations of successive possibilities, as a growing appreciation of the fundamental conditions of human existence.

In addition to emphasizing the variety of perspectives at Virgil's disposal, the material I have reviewed in this chapter has other important implications for a reading of the *Georgics*. We have seen that in country life two polar opposites of Roman experience were embodied and symbolized: on the one hand austerity, discipline, and a tradition of civic responsibility; on the other, luxury, self-indulgence, and the rejection of traditional values and customs. Consequently, it should not be surprising that in the Late Republic and early Augustan Age interpretations of country life became the primary literary vehicles for expressing different responses to the

85. E.g., *Georgic* 1.121-159, 197-203.
86. E.g., *Georgic* 2.9-12, 458-460.
87. *Virgil's* Georgics *on the Nature of Civilization* (diss. New Haven 1971), esp. ch. 1, pp. 1-57.
88. Here I am greatly indebted to my friend and colleague, Harry Berger, Jr. Some idea of how much my ideas have been shaped by conversations with him may be gained by a reading of his brief discussion of the *Georgics* in "Archaism, Vision, and Revision: Studies in Virgil, Plato, and Milton," *Centennial Review* 11 (1967) 24-52, esp. 30-33.

crisis and final collapse of the Republic and for considering the nature of possible or ideal reconstructions of society. In reflecting on diverse visions of country life, then, the *Georgics* offers a commentary on different notions of the human condition.[89] It is a profoundly ambitious poem, a philosophically speculative attempt to find some comfort and guidance for the future by subjecting both Roman traditions and the actualities of Roman experience to critical examination.

89. My reading of the *Georgics* as a philosophical-political statement has been much influenced by my readings of English Augustan literature, most notably Pope's *Windsor Forest* and its predecessor, Denham's *Cooper's Hill*. Also, most suggestive have been two modern studies of English neoclassic poetry: John Chalker, *The English Georgic* (Baltimore 1969), and Earl R. Wasserman, *The Subtler Language* (Baltimore 1959, reprinted 1964).

CHAPTER II

# Georgic 1

## I

The *Georgics* begins with deceptive modesty. The first two lines—"What makes crops fruitful, under what star to turn the earth, Maecenas, and to join vines to elms"—suggest an agricultural manual, technical instruction embodied in a series of precepts. The following lines, however, promise something more. *Cura, cultus, experientia* ("care," "cultivation," "knowledge gained from experience") urge that agriculture be viewed as a civilized and civilizing activity. The implicit relationship between "cultivation" and "civilization"—which we acknowledge in the ambiguities of "cultivation" and "cultivated," "culture" and "cultured"—the Romans expressed similarly in the ambiguity of *cultus* (the ordinary term both for "cultivation" and for what we usually mean by "civilization"). How closely the concepts were associated in the Roman mind may be judged, for example, from Cicero's use of the term *cultus* in his treatise *De Republica*. Cicero traces the uniqueness of the Roman state to its origins in the agrarian society that fostered Romulus: "shepherds took him up and nourished him in rustic *cultu* and work" (2.2). What Cicero refers to here is more than a specific kind of work: it is a way of life. Similarly, in his *Commentary on the Gallic War* (1.1), Julius Caesar explains the exceptional toughness of the Belgae by observing that "they are the most far removed from the *cultu* and *humanitate* of the province." By his choice of terms, Virgil has defined farming as a way of life that is reflective, ordered, active, and rational. That is his point of departure: "from this point I begin my poem" (*hinc canere incipiam*, 1.5).

The list of divinities whose blessings Virgil evokes (1.5-23) further substantiates his concern with the characteristically civilized aspects of the farmer's world. Although some of the divinities attest to the spontaneous vitality of the countryside (the Fauns, for example, or the Dryads), more often the gods and goddesses are praised for specific discoveries or inventions that distinguish civilized from barbarian society. Liber added wine to water. Ceres taught men to cultivate grains rather than gather acorns. Pan is a "shepherd" (*custos*) who "cares" (*curae*) for his domain. Minerva is "inventress" of the olive. Two figures in the invocation are identified only by their contributions to human technology, not by name at all. They are the heroes Aristaeus, "cultivator [*cultor*] of groves," and Triptolemus, who demonstrated the use of the curved plough (*unci . . . puer monstrator aratri*). The "brilliant lights of the universe" refer to the heavenly bodies which allow the farmer to dispose his work according to the appropriate seasonal and climatic conditions. If a conjecture in Servius is to be trusted,[1] Silvanus' attribute, "slender cypress roots and all," may symbolize the propagation of plants by transplanting and related arts. Likewise, divinities who nurture crops without seed may be regarded as tutelaries of grafting and, thus, contrasted with the divinities who irrigate crops that have been sown. But whatever the specific role of each divinity, Virgil's particular interest in rustic life is clear. Marcus Terentius Varro provides a useful basis for comparison. In *Res Rusticae*, published, as we have seen, just about the time Virgil was begining the *Georgics*, Varro invoked the *di consentes*, a pantheon of twelve divinities which, although modeled on the pantheon of the twelve Olympian gods, was nonetheless dominated by characteristically Roman and Italian gods of agriculture.[2] Virgil's own pantheon is unique, and the prominence in it of Greek divinities of discovery and invention creates a strong orientation toward the remote mythic origins of civilization within agriculture.

At line 24 Virgil unexpectedly introduces an entirely new dimension to his poem. The address to Caesar, a god just beginning his divine career, brings the poet and his audience to the very center

1. *Servius auctus* ad *G.* 1.20.
2. *RR* 1.1.5-6.

of contemporary political life and raises the most pressing issue of the moment, the restoration of a world shattered by civil war. For more than a quarter of a century Rome, her allies and dependencies throughout the Mediterranean, and, above all, Italy had experienced tremendous drains on human resources, extraordinary taxation, confiscation of property (often attended by wholesale displacement of local populations), pillage, and proscriptions. The transport of grain supplies vital to Rome was periodically blockaded. Agriculture (particularly the work of the small independent landholder) was undermined. In addition, there were the horrors and losses of the civil battles themselves. A brief aside in Plutarch's biography of Mark Antony gives some sense of the extent to which daily life was disrupted throughout the Mediterranean:

> My great-grandfather Nicarchus used to relate that the whole body of the people of our city were put in requisition to carry each one a certain measure of corn upon their shoulders to the sea-side near Anticyra, men standing by to quicken them with the lash. They had made one journey of the kind, but when they had just measured out the corn and were putting it on their backs for a second, news came of Antony's defeat, and so saved Chaeronea, for all Antony's purveyors and soldiers fled upon the news, and left them to divide the corn among themselves.[3]

Moreover, bewildering shifts of alliances and loyalties, years of living in anxious uncertainty, the barrage of political propaganda which sullied the reputations of the most distinguished public figures, and conflicting appeals to Liberty, the Republic, Pietas, and the gods—all combined to undermine Roman morale. Disillusionment with the Roman state and public morals and a sense of greatness betrayed are common themes in the contemporary literature. They inform the political treatises of Sallust, the introduction to Livy's history of Rome, and Horace's *Epodes* and *Satires*.

Reckoning from ancient biographies, Virgil began the *Georgics* around 35 B.C. and published it in 29 B.C.—that is, he began composition during an interval of precarious détente between the remaining contenders for supremacy. He published the poem shortly after the adopted son of Julius Caesar had established undisputed

---

3. Plutarch, *Mark Antony* 68.4–5. The translation is that of John Dryden.

claim to rule, but before the young Caesar had publicly articulated his political aspirations and policies. The fourth century A.D. Donatus-Suetonius biography of Virgil gives the following report of the first presentation to the public of the *Georgics* (27[42]):

> Georgica reverso post Actiacam victoriam Augusto atque Atellae reficiendarum faucium causa commoranti per continuum quadriduum legit, suscipiente Maecenate legendi vicem, quotiens interpellaretur ipse vocis offensione.
>
> While Augustus was stopping over at Atella to cure a throat ailment on his return from the victory of Actium, [Virgil] recited the *Georgics* in the course of four consecutive days. Whenever trouble with his voice forced him to stop, Maecenas took turns reciting.

Although that story may be apocryphal (it is not substantiated in other sources), it reflects, nonetheless, a keen sense of the *Georgics*' relation to its times. The appeal to the new Caesar in the poem's introduction acknowledges the full extent of his newly won powers and implies a moment of decision. Caesar may choose to oversee the cities of the world, to safeguard the farmer's work, to share a place in the heavenly constellations, or to exercise dominion of the seas: earth, air, fire, and water—the destiny of the universe is at Caesar's disposal.

Extravagant as the glorification of Caesar's powers may seem, it serves a higher purpose than mere flattery. Hyperbole suggests the extent to which world order actually does depend on the new ruler, and thus provides the context for the poet's repeated and increasingly emphatic exhortations that Caesar accept the responsibilities that his powers entail. A few lines later, for example, Virgil says (36-37):

> . . . te nec sperant Tartara regem,
> nec tibi regnandi ueniat tam dira cupido.
>
> Do not let Tartarus hope for you to be its king; may no such terrible desire to rule possess you.

That graceful prayer for long life is the vehicle for a more urgent plea: of all the alternatives available to him, Caesar must not consider retirement from public life. Virgil acknowledges the attractiveness of such retirement. He recalls the Greeks' admiration for Elysium (38); for in an apparently unprecedented departure from tradition, he asserts that Proserpina, whom Hades had abducted, is actually reluctant to make her annual reunion with her mother (39). Nonetheless, references to Proserpina also contain a warning that has relevance to Virgil's specific theme, since according to myth it is only during the periods of Proserpina's return to the upper world that the earth is fertile. Similarly, Virgil's plea for a generous audience—*da facilem cursum atque audacibus adnue coeptis* ("grant a propitious course and assent to bold undertakings," 40)—is couched in general terms that apply as much to the challenges before the statesman as to those before the poet. We are prepared, then, for the blunt and forceful command with which the poet concludes his address to Caesar: *ingredere et uotis iam nunc adsuesce uocari* ("come forward and accustom yourself even now to be addressed as a god," 42).

Other details in Virgil's account of the alternatives available to Caesar suggest more specific responsibilities that he must fulfill. He may choose to oversee the world, as he binds his temples with a crown of the myrtle sacred to his mother (*cingens materna tempora myrto*, 28). That is, he must be a champion of peace, for his ancestral mother is Venus and her myrtle is a symbol of peace.[4] Similarly, Virgil says that a place is already being prepared for Caesar among the heavenly constellations, between Virgo (identified here as Erigone) and Scorpio, who even now is drawing back his claws from the excessive space they had occupied (32–35). The place thus designated for Caesar is that of the constellation Libra. It is a fitting location for several reasons.[5] According to one reading of his horoscope, Libra was his natal sign. Moreover, it was Caesar's own adoptive father who, in his revision of the calendar, followed the Egyptian practice of recognizing a constellation between Virgo and Scorpio in the place that had been occupied by Scorpio's claws in the zodiacs of the Chaldean and Greek astrologers. For Caesar to occupy that position in the zodiac was to confirm as his birthright

---

4. On the myrtle as a symbol of peace see, for example, Tib. 1.10.27–32. At Rome it accompanied the return of a general from a bloodless victory. See Pliny, *HN* 15.125, and Aulus Gellius, *NA* 6, 20ff.

5. On the role of Libra in Augustus' horoscope and in Julius Caesar's version of the calendar, see Robert J. Getty, "*Liber et Alma Ceres* in Vergil's *Georgics* 1.7," *Phoenix* 5 (1951) 96–107.

succession to the elder Caesar's extraordinary sovereignty of the Roman world. Finally, Libra, as the Latin name signifies, represents scales and was regarded as a symbol for the scales of justice: Caesar must champion justice as well as peace.[6]

General references to the statesman's responsibilities aside, the explicit relationship between Virgil's announced subject and the unprecedented glorification of Caesar that follows is contained in a single ambiguous line (36-43):

> quidquid eris . . .
> . . . . . . . . . . . . . . . . .
> da facilem cursum atque audacibus adnue coeptis,
> ignarosque uiae mecum miseratus agrestis
> ingredere et uotis iam nunc adsuesce uocari.
>
> Whatever you will be, . . . grant a propitious course and assent to bold undertakings and pitying, with me, the farmers who are ignorant of the way, come forward and accustom yourself even now to be addressed as a god.

Any simple interpretation of line 42 is precluded by the syntactic ambiguity of *mecum*. Most modern commentators and translators take *mecum* as an adverbial phrase modifying the following participle and, consequently, interpret the line, "pitying as I do (*mecum*) the farmers who are ignorant of the way." Now, as a request that Caesar patronize a poem offering technical instruction to the farmer, the phrase is conspicuously inadequate to support Virgil's commands to bless "bold undertakings" and to accept the role of a divinity. Taken in context, therefore, urgent appeals to share the poet's concern for the farmer reinforce suggestions in the first half of the introduction that Virgil's treatment of his subject will not be narrowly technical. Indeed, insofar as agriculture was seen to embody the origins of civilization, the helpless confusion of the farmer is symptomatic of the complete deterioration of society. Virgil seeks to enlist Caesar's aid in restoring the farmer's way of life because it is the cornerstone of civilized existence. He presents his own patronage of the farmer as an example for Caesar to follow. As a consequence his poem must be prescriptive in a special sense: it must look

---

6. On the association of the constellation Libra with the scales of justice, see Manilius, *Astronomica* 4.547-552.

to the broader responsibilities of the statesman as well as to the more limited work of the farmer.

Servius records a second possible reading of the line—one that complements the previous reading and further characterizes the poet's complex relationship to his subject. Servius observes that *mecum* may be taken to modify the participial phrase that precedes it rather than that which follows it.[7] Dryden seems to have followed such an interpretation of the line in his elegant translation, "Pity the ploughman's and the poet's cares." Contrast with the reading discussed in the previous paragraph may perhaps be expressed with greater sharpness, although with less elegance, by translating, "Pitying the farmers who are ignorant of the way, as I am" (*mecum*). Utterly inappropriate to the purveyor of technical instruction, the lack of confidence this statement expresses is nonetheless meaningful in the complex context Virgil has created. For one thing, by reaffirming the poet's respectful deference to Caesar's unequaled status and power, it mitigates the boldness of the commands with which Virgil concludes this introduction. But the request is more than an example of artful diplomacy. It implies that the questions the farmer must face, from whatever quarters they arise, may be fundamentally so challenging as to preclude clear and direct responses even from the poet who has undertaken to guide the farmer and to represent his interests to the statesman. By calling attention to the potential magnitude of his task, Virgil has explained the inclusion of his poetic efforts among the "bold undertakings" that he asked Caesar to bless in the previous line. More important still, he has given a further indication concerning the nature of his poem: exposition will be presented in a broader context of reflection and speculation. Underlying the climactic imperative (really, it is true, a prayer) that Caesar accept the role of a divinity is the sobering thought that the challenges epitomized in the disruption of rustic life may exceed mortal capacities.

## II

An eloquent evocation of spring provides an effective transition between Virgil's prayer to Caesar and his exposition of rustic life (43-49):

7. *Servius* ad *G.* 1.41.

Vere nouo, gelidus canis cum montibus umor
liquitur et Zephyro putris se glaeba resoluit,
depresso incipiat iam tum mihi taurus aratro
ingemere et sulco attritus splendescere uomer.
illa seges demum uotis respondet auari
agricolae, bis quae solem, bis frigora sensit;
illius immensae ruperunt horrea messes.

In early spring, when the frozen waters of hoary mountains melt, and the loose clod is softened by the west wind, that is when my bull should begin to groan under the heavy plow and my plowshare be worn to a smooth shine in the furrow. That crop which has twice felt the sun, twice felt cold will respond in time to the prayers of the greedy farmer; his, the granaries that huge harvests have burst.

For the farmer as for the statesman there is a time of fruitful renewal when old obstacles give way to new beginnings and the prospect of hard work is immediate and inviting. And just as Virgil had asked Caesar to reflect on the nature of his task in the introduction to the poem, so here he adds that the farmer must learn "the character" (*morem*) of the climate (1.51), *patrios cultusque habitusque locorum* ("the ancestral cultivation and disposition of places," 52), and *et quid quaeque ferat regio et quid quaeque recuset* ("both what each region bears and what it rejects," 53). By personifying the objects of the farmer's inquiries, Virgil suggests the broader application of his injunction to precede action with deliberation. The moment of promise and challenge demands of the statesman as of the farmer the assessment of possibilities, the definition of goals, and the acceptance of the necessity of hard work.

Virgil also makes his initial instructions to the farmer an occasion to sketch one view of the human character and the fundamental conditions of human action according to which they both share their origins with the universal laws of nature. Man lives in a world of limited possibilities. In the Fourth *Eclogue* Virgil described the full return of the Golden Age as a time when *omnis feret omnia tellus* ("all the earth will bear all things," *Ecl.* 4.39). In *Georgic* 1 he emphasizes rather the restrictiveness of specific regions. The examples by which he supports his argument do not apply to the farmer alone. It is true that the localities suitable to cereal crops, grapes, trees, or hay are of particular concern to the farmer (54–56); but dye from Tmolus, iron from the Chalybes, beaver oil from Pontus, and race horses from Elis (56–59) reflect the aspirations of a more sophisticated society and demonstrate that it, too, is subject to the restrictiveness of natural order.

The farmer's character complements the harsh conditions of his existence. His goal here, and throughout the *Georgics*, is a livelihood that offers satisfactions beyond mere survival. He is, Virgil asserts, *auarus* ("greedy," 47); his ambition is to burst his granary with *immensae messes* ("huge harvests," 49). Inasmuch as the conditions of the farmer's existence are universal, his character reflects that of all humankind (60–63):

> Continuo has leges aeternaque foedera certis
> imposuit natura locis, quo tempore primum
> Deucalion uacuum lapides iactauit in orbem,
> unde homines nati, durum genus.

> Nature immediately imposed these laws and eternal covenants on specific places when Deucalion first cast stones upon the empty earth whence men were born, a hard race.

By proceeding swiftly from the actual work of the farmer to the mythic origins of civilization, Virgil has confirmed his intention, implicit in the poem's introduction, to view agriculture in a broad perspective; and he has exemplified his bold contention that its apparently limited and mundane concerns deserve the statesman's serious attention. Seen as a continual reenactment of the origins of civilization, the farmer's work becomes a link between what is unique and ephemeral in human experience and what is universal and eternal. The spring of the farmer's year calls attention to fundamental aspects of the human character and of natural law, which are as relevant to the statesman's efforts to create an ordered and prosperous environment as they are to the farmer's.

Equally important, the passage we have been examining helps to orient the audience toward the complex interrelation of style and content that is characteristic of the *Georgics* and essential to its import. Although the opening lines of the introduction established the fiction that the poem will address itself to the technical instruction of the farmer, Virgil omits numerous subjects of practical value

—often critical steps in the specific procedures he describes. In other passages he expands on themes that do not advance our knowledge of agricultural technology. Nor does he confine himself narrowly to a technical language, but makes generous use of poetic archaisms, metaphors, and other resources of a literary tradition. Throughout the poem, vagueness, ambiguity, and seemingly gratuitous complexity compromise lucidity and directness of exposition. In that respect lines 43–63 are typical of the whole: the promise of a direct and orderly introduction to the farmer's work is disappointed almost immediately by the unexpected revelation that it is not, after all, the hard physical labor of early spring plowing, but observation, analysis, and deliberation that are the farmer's first responsibility; metaphor emphasizes the almost human qualities of the landscape; Virgil intrudes his own judgments that farmers are greedy and competitive; the constraints imposed by the natural environment are acknowledged with conspicuous elegance in the balanced antithesis between "what each region will bear and what each will refuse;" analogies extend the farmer's experience to the realm of commerce; appeal to myth expands the poet's frame of reference still further. Disparity between the manner of presentation and even the minimum requirements of technical exposition, then, is thrust upon the reader's attention from the outset.

The particular value of the Deucalion myth, however, is not that it relieves an otherwise bleak didacticism or that it merely extends the farmer's experience by analogy as the examples of dye and iron do. Rather, it elaborates and explains the very aspects of the foregoing exposition, which would have been most out of place in a purely technical treatise. The conspicuous integrity of the relationship between the Deucalion myth and its context, then, is an assurance that we may look for significance in the apparent anomalies of Virgil's style. The repeated definition and subsequent frustration of formal expectations throughout the poem must be taken as a stimulus to regard the unique and private concerns of the farmer as invitations to reflect on the conditions and character of civilized activity. Indeed, it is by its promise of a return to the essentials of civilization that rustic life recommends itself, whether as the object of uncritical admiration or of searching contemplation, to audiences who are more concerned with rescuing society from barbarism than with the details of growing millet or spelt. The effect of Virgil's style in the

*Georgics* is not to make a discussion of agriculture *seem* more important than it is, but to demonstrate to an urbane audience that it *is* more important than it seems.

Just as the initial exposition of the poem led to a consideration of the fundamental conditions that determine the nature of civilization, so line 71 introduces a series of passages that emphasize the magnitude of the claims agriculture makes, not only on brawn but also on the human intellect and spirit. In so doing the passages prepare for a teleological account of the world that designates man's capacity for work and invention as his highest and most essential qualities. Thus, lines 71–83 treat the two subjects of fallow land and crop rotation in such a way as to emphasize the sheer complexity of the conditions that the farmer has to master. The passage is arranged in a chiasmus, instead of sequentially; that is, it begins and ends with one of the two topics and devotes the intervening lines to the second. The consequent shifting back and forth and the attendant repetition compound the complexity of the subject matter. Virgil first calls attention to the value of leaving land fallow in alternate seasons (*alternis*, 71–72), only to turn directly to the related technique of crop rotation with specific instructions that spelt should be rotated with beans, vetch, and lupine (73–76). He next describes the deleterious effect of certain other crops: flax, wild oats, and poppies (77–78). Here, too, "alternation" (*alternis*) is beneficial, although now "alternation" seems to refer to the practice of rotating crops rather than to the use of fallow land, and Virgil adds the proviso that fertilization (either with manure or with ashes) is also necessary (79–81). He then reasserts the value of crop rotation (82) and concludes that leaving land fallow, while effective, is a less desirable procedure: *nec nulla interea est inaratae gratia terrae* ("In the meantime unplowed land is not ungrateful," 83). A simple review of the ways in which Virgil connects his argument within these thirteen lines is revealing: *et . . . aut ibi . . . unde . . . aut . . . -que . . . enim . . .* asyndeton (*urit, urit, urunt*) *. . . sed tamen . . . tantum ne . . . neve . . . sic quoque . . . nec. . . .* Directness and simplicity do not seem to have been his first concern nor, in my judgment, was mere poetic variation or ornament. Rather, the effect of the organization here has been to suggest something of the bewilderingly complex world in which humans find themselves and to impress the consequent necessity, even in such a comparatively simple environment as the farmer's, for knowledge, reflectiveness, and organization.

In the next passage (84-93) Virgil actually suggests an affinity between the farmer's work and pure philosophical speculation. He remarks that yet another technique at the farmer's disposal is the burning over (*incendere*) of unproductive fields (84-85). He then considers several ways in which burning over may be effective (86-93):

> siue inde occultas uiris et pabula terrae
> pinguia concipiunt, siue illis omne per ignem
> excoquitur uitium atque exsudat inutilis umor,
> seu pluris calor ille uias et caeca relaxat
> spiramenta, nouas ueniat qua sucus in herbas,
> seu durat magis et uenas astringit hiantis,
> ne tenues pluuiae rapidiue potentia solis
> acrior aut Boreae penetrabile frigus adurat.

> whether thereby the earth receives hidden strength and rich nourishment, or because of the fire its faults are cooked out and useless moisture is evaporated, or the heat opens up more ways and blocked pores by which nourishing sap may reach the young plants, or it makes harder and tightens gaping veins in order that fine rains or the excessive strength of the hot sun or the permeating cold of the north wind not burn the earth.

It is not immediately clear how many distinct alternatives Virgil is offering here—whether the later alternatives (89-93) are to be taken as new possibilities or as elaborations of earlier statements. The conjunctions (*sive* and its varient form *seu*) that connect the four major explanations in the list are not strongly disjunctive (in contrast to the conjunction, *aut*) and may connect alternatives that are not mutually exclusive. Consequently, it is also unclear whether Virgil means to present alternatives that are opposed—one burns either because there is too much moisture or too little—or whether he has in mind different conditions (unspecified) that respond to heat in opposite ways. Altogether the passage seems to have as much to do with scientific-philosophical speculation about the intermingling of fire, water, and air with earth, the four elements of Sicilian philosophers, as it does with the communication of practical information about agriculture. Virgil has reaffirmed the direct relationship between the concerns of rustic life and the fundamental laws of nature, this time to suggest that the mundane practice of agriculture may confront the farmer with a task that is not only complex but even worthy of a philosopher. Or, seen from another perspective, the passage looks forward to the rise of civilization, for it sees even the evolution of philosophy in the farmer's humble occupations.

Still, Virgil has not yet taken the full measure of the demands rustic life makes on the farmer. With each additional task (harrowing and cross-plowing), the burden of his work is felt more strongly. And against the promise of abundance if the weather is right (100–103), Virgil holds the prospect of even more work (104–117). He expresses his admiration for the man who accepts that challenge in a passage that approximates the elevated tone of epic. An initial rhetorical question becomes more urgent with successive repetitions: *quid dicam . . . qui . . .* ("What shall I say of the one who . . . ," 104), *quid qui . . . quique . . .* ("What of the one who," 111, ". . . and who," 113). As he does not infrequently elsewhere, Virgil concludes the passage with a conspicuously elaborate line. Here, after an initial conjunction, he arranges two adjectives, a verb, and two nouns in a chiasmus: *unde cavae* (a) *tepido* (b) *sudant umore* (b) *lacunae* (a) (117).

Essential to the passage and to its elevated tone is the military metaphor of the first lines (104–105):

> quid dicam, iacto qui semine comminus arua
> insequitur cumulosque ruit male pinguis harenae

> What shall I say of the one who, after he has cast the seed, hand-to-hand, attacks the fields and levels mounds of sterile sand?

That metaphor looks ahead to a description of irrigation noteworthy both for its deployment of sound and rhythm and for its origins in epic poetry (107–110):

> et, cum exustus ager morientibus aestuat herbis,
> ecce supercilio cliuosi tramitis undam
> elicit? illa cadens raucum per leuia murmur
> saxa ciet, scatebrisque arentia temperat arua.

> and, when the field is parched and burning, its crops dying, behold! from the lip of a steep channel [the farmer] leads off a

wave of water; as it clatters over worn rocks it raises a hoarse murmuring and, splashing, tempers the parched plow land.

Those lines recall a memorable scene in the *Iliad*, Achilles' battle with the Scamander River. In a simile, also noted for its effective combination of sound and sense, Homer compares the onslaught of the Scamander to the sudden rush of a stream which a farmer has undammed to irrigate his crops (*Iliad* 21.257–264):

ὡς δ' ὅτ' ἀνὴρ ὀχετηγὸς ἀπὸ κρήνης μελανύδρου
ἂμ φυτὰ καὶ κήπους ὕδατι ῥόον ἡγεμονεύῃ,
χερσὶ μάκελλαν ἔχων ἀμάρης ἐξ ἔχματα βάλλων·
τοῦ μέν τε προρέοντος ὑπὸ ψηφῖδες ἅπασαι
ὀχλεῦνται· τὸ δέ τ' ὦκα κατειβόμενον κελαρύζει
χώρῳ ἔνι προαλεῖ, φθάνει δέ τε καὶ τὸν ἄγοντα·
ὣς αἰεὶ Ἀχιλῆα κιχήσατο κῦμα ῥόοιο
καὶ λαιψηρὸν ἐόντα·

As when a man draws water off from a black spring and guides it in a stream among his plants and crops, holding a hoe in his hands, striking obstacles from the trench, when the water rushes ahead all the pebbles beneath it are rolled along and in a sudden flood it burbles down a sloping place and even gets ahead of its guide, so always the wave of the running water overtook Achilles, even as swift as he was.

Virgil's reminiscence of epic reaffirms his earlier use of military metaphor and his admiration for the farmer's achievements: there are heroic dimensions to rustic life. The physical and spiritual toughness that characterized the farmer in Virgil's first description of him has been elevated, almost transformed. Just as the farmer shares something of the philosopher's comprehension of nature and its workings, so he shares also something of the heroic warrior's resourcefulness, determination, and aggressiveness. Once again we are confronted with the suggestion that agriculture itself contains the seeds of other more glorious expressions of the human character, that mankind's own cultivation is somehow implicit in his cultivation of the earth.

That same idea is reinforced by the use of metaphor. In the struggle for a satisfying livelihood the farmer must sometimes, for example, allow a "lazy" (*segnem*) field to "become hard" (*durescere*,

72), just as he is "hard"; plow lands "repose" (*requiescunt*) when crops are rotated (82); unplowed land returns "thanks" (*gratia*, 83); the farmer must shatter "sluggish" (*inertis*) clods (94); he must break the "backs" (*terga*) of ridges (97). Such personification of the earth works two ways. It makes description of agriculture vivid by making nature accessible in terms of human experience. It also transforms nature into a virtual metaphor for man. Man, too, may be cultivated. Indeed, only by cultivation will he become fruitful, will he realize his potential for energy and resourcefulness as fields realize theirs for abundant harvests.

An obvious extension of the metaphor, or perhaps conceit, of the earth for man is that the statesman's responsibility is to cultivate his people as the farmer cultivates his fields. In line 99 Virgil observes that the farmer: *exercetque tellurem atque imperat aruis* ("trains the earth and commands the fields"). The metaphor is an effective evocation of the demanding combination of effort and discipline that characterizes rustic life. The term "command" (*impero*), however, carried a special force for Virgil's contemporaries. Its technical function was to express the formal authority of the heads of state, the consuls, over Roman citizens; and in the years of civil war the most conspicuous aspect of that authority was military command. The significance of Virgil's insistence that the farmer exercise a political-military discipline over his fields is unlikely to have escaped the attention of his audience. In elevating agriculture to the level of epic achievement (and that just after observing that the farmer "commands" his fields), Virgil offers cultivation as a fitting object of the statesman's attention. In exploiting parallels between the farmer's and the statesman's roles, he has not addressed Caesar directly, much less laid down a specific program. Nonetheless, he has effectively conveyed a sense of the complexity, the difficulty, and the urgency of the task confronting Caesar, and he has sketched the substantial rewards awaiting him.

It is, however, less with the statesman's responsibilities in mind than with a sense of the development of a greater civilization which is implicit in agriculture that Virgil proceeds to a teleological account of the necessity for work. The first passage of exposition in the *Georgics* (43–70) interpreted agriculture according to its origins in the laws of nature and in the character of the human race. The account of Jupiter's theodicy that follows (118-146) expands that argument and further defines the conditions governing civilization and its development. Although Virgil acknowledges the hardships and limitations those conditions impose on man, for the first time in the poem he explicitly asserts their value as stimulants to the realization of human potential. His attitude toward civilization, just as toward the conditions that necessitate it, is ambivalent. Admiration for man's capacity to respond to the challenges of his environment is balanced by an implicit warning against the excesses to which human energy and resourcefulness, admirable as they are, may lead.

The alternation of tone in the account of the theodicy reflects the ambivalence inherent in the relationships both between man and nature and between the possibilities and limitations of civilization. The account begins as a commentary on the difficulty of the farmer's life. Even after he has applied his knowledge to the proper care of the soil and his crops and after he has set methodically to work, the farmer is beset with new challenges (118-121):

> Nec tamen, haec cum sint hominumque boumque labores
> uersando terram experti, nihil improbus anser
> Strymoniaeque grues et amaris intiba fibris
> officiunt aut umbra nocet.

> Nonetheless, despite the toil of man and beast skilled in turning the earth, the ruinous goose and Strymonian cranes and endive with its bitter fibers hinder their work or shade harms it.

That discouraging report is balanced by an account of the divine origins of the harshness of man's environment and its positive consequences for him (121-124):

> . . . pater ipse colendi
> haud facilem esse uiam uoluit, primusque per artem
> mouit agros, curis acuens mortalia corda
> nec torpere graui passus sua regna ueterno.

> The father of cultivation himself did not want its way to be easy and was first to change the fields by design, sharpening mortal wits with cares, not allowing his kingdoms to become sluggish with heavy old age.

The hardships imposed by Jupiter and his order have their compensations: they give to human existence its vitality. But we are not allowed to think that their blessings are unmixed (125-132):

> ante Iouem nulli subigebant arua coloni:
> ne signare quidem aut partiri limite campum
> fas erat; in medium quaerebant, ipsaque tellus
> omnia liberius nullo poscente ferebat.
> ille malum uirus serpentibus addidit atris
> praedarique lupos iussit pontumque moueri,
> mellaque decussit foliis ignemque remouit
> et passim riuis currentia uina repressit.

Before Jupiter no farmers plowed the fields; it was not even right to set up property markers or to divide a field with a boundary line; men used to seek for the common good and earth herself, uncommanded, bore all things only too generously. He is the one who gave venom to foul snakes and commanded wolves to prey, stirred up the sea, shook honey from the leaves, took back fire, and everywhere checked the wine flowing in streams.

With the dissolution of the Golden Age man has lost something more than physical leisure and a carefree relationship with the land. At a time when *terrae ferre omnes omnia possunt* ("all lands can bear all things"), private property and personal competition are pointless. As always, the character of the environment is reflected in the character of man. The changes that force man to become civilized in the best sense also force him to become civilized in the worst. They lead to competition among men—competition which is *nefas*. Virgil has sounded the first muted warning in the *Georgics* that civilization brings with it danger as well as advantages.

The perspective shifts once again. Our attention is recalled to Jupiter's purpose and to the rewards of struggle. Jupiter introduced conflict (133-146)

> ut uarias usus meditando extunderet artis
> paulatim, et sulcis frumenti quaereret herbam,
> ut silicis uenis abstrusum excuderet ignem.
> tunc alnos primum fluuii sensere cauatas;
> nauita tum stellis numeros et nomina fecit

Pleiadas, Hyadas, claramque Lycaonis Arcton.
tum laqueis captare feras et fallere uisco
inuentum et magnos canibus circumdare saltus;
atque alius latum funda iam uerberat amnem
alta petens, pelagoque alius trahit umida lina.
tum ferri rigor atque argutae lammina serrae
(nam primi cuneis scindebant fissile lignum),
tum uariae uenere artes. labor omnia uicit
improbus et duris urgens in rebus egestas.

in order that experience and reflection should beat out skills little by little and seek grain stalks in the furrows, that they should strike out fire hidden in the veins of flint. Then for the first time rivers felt hollowed trunks, then the sailor named and numbered the stars: the Pleiades, the Hyades, Arctos, the shining daughter of Lycaon. Then men discovered how to hunt wild beasts in snares, to trap them with birdlime, and to surround great glades with hounds; and now one beats a broad river with a casting net seeking its depths and another draws his sodden line from the sea; then came the unyielding iron and the blade of the shrill saw [for the first men split brittle wood with wedges]; then all kinds of skills came into being. Toil has overcome all things, ruinous toil and need, pressing in harsh circumstances.

That catalogue, culminating as it does in the victory of human effort, is an impressive tribute to man's abilities and to the scope of his accomplishments. The examples of human achievements go beyond the immediate subject of farming to include the discovery of fire, hunting, navigation, and carpentry. Jupiter's innovations did more than lay the foundation for farming. Indeed, Virgil pointedly changes tense at line 141, "*now one beats*" (*iam uerberat*) and brings his narrative from distant accomplishments of the past to those vividly manifest in the present. Jupiter has set in motion the continuing process of evolution which leads civilization to ever higher stages of development. Man first learns to cut wood by splitting it with wedges; then he finds a more efficient means in the saw. The pace of invention seems to accelerate from its slow and laborious beginnings, *extunderet artis / paulatim* ("he should beat out skills / little by little") through successive triumphs, "then . . . then . . .

then . . . then . . ." to the final, brief, and inclusive "then all kinds of skills came into being," with its suggestion of endless and ever-quickening progress. That breathless survey of mankind's great technological advancement is followed directly by the statement that *labor omnia uicit* ("toil has overcome all"). In context we are virtually compelled to take such a pointed assertion of *labor's* victory as an epigrammatic tribute to human initiative and resourcefulness in overcoming the obstacles Jupiter has set in man's way.

But such a victory was ambiguous at best by the general standards of ancient thought. Indeed, by moving beyond the immediate skills of agrarian technology in his survey of human achievement, Virgil calls to mind a tradition, central to the works of his literary predecessors and widely current among his contemporaries, that associated the development of civilization with the corruption of man.[8] The dangers of civilization, first touched on by reference to the division of property, now reappear in association with the evolution of technology. Thus, conquest of the sea and navigation occur in the lists of man's various achievements. In Roman thought, particularly of this period, they were identified with commerce and were conspicuous symbols both of the passing of the Golden Age and of man's propensity to excess and folly. One has only to think of Horace's propempticon to Virgil (*Odes* 1.3), where the discovery of fire (also prominent in Virgil's list) and man's conquest of the sea are portrayed more as irrefutable evidence of the baseness of the age and the boundless audacity of man, than as tributes to human inventiveness and initiative (*Odes* 1.3.21-40):

> nequiquam deus abscidit
> > prudens oceano dissociabili
> terras, si tamen inpiae
> > non tangenda rates transiliunt vada.
>
> audax omnia perpeti
> > gens humana ruit per vetitum nefas,
> audax Iapeti genus
> > ignem fraude mala gentibus intulit.

---

8. For a list of specific symbols of degeneration associated with the vice of technology and for their distribution in ancient literature, see Kirby Flower Smith, *The Elegies of Albius Tibullus* (New York 1913, reprinted Darmstadt 1971), ad 1.3.35-48; 1.10.1; and 2.3.71.

post ignem aetheria domo
    subductum macies et nova febrium
terris incubuit cohors
    semotique prius tarda necessitas
leti corripuit gradum.
    expertus vacuum Daedalus aera
pinnis non homini datis;
    perrupit Acheronta Herculeus labor.
nil mortalibus ardui est:
    caelum ipsum petimus stultitia neque
per nostrum patimur scelus
    iracunda Iovem ponere fulmina.

In vain did a wise God place the prohibitive ocean between lands, if nonetheless impious rafts speed over forbidden crossings. Bold to try all, the human race rushes through forbidden crime; bold, the clan of Iapetus carried fire to men in wicked deceit. After fire was brought down from its heavenly home, wasting sickness and a new troop of fevers settled upon the lands; the inevitability of death, remote before and slow, stepped up its pace; Daedalus tried the open sky with wings not meant for man; Hercules' toil burst through Hades. Nothing is steep for mortals: in our folly we seek heaven itself; our wickedness forbids Jupiter to lay aside his wrathful lightning.

Comparison with Hesiod and Aratus further clarifies the sinister undertones in Virgil's account of the theodicy. Virgil was unquestionably familiar with Aratus' *Phaenomena* and with the passage in it where Aratus modified the Hesiodic conception of the Golden Age. In Hesiod the Golden Age was a time of ease and leisure, clearly mythological and beyond the aspirations of contemporary mankind.[9] For Aratus, the Golden Age was less remote from contemporary reality. It was a time when mankind supported itself by farming, but a time, nonetheless, of peace, undisturbed by the complications of more sophisticated civilization. It was a time when the goddess Astraea still associated with men and bestowed her special blessings among them (*Phaenomena* 105-113):

9. Hesiod, *WD* 109-201.

84  Virgil's *Georgics*

καί ἑ Δίκην καλέεσκον· ἀγειρομένη δὲ γέροντας,
ἠέ που εἰν ἀγορῇ ἢ εὐρυχόρῳ ἐν ἀγυιῇ,
δημοτέρας ἤειδεν ἐπισπέρχουσα θέμιστας.
οὔπω λευγαλέου τότε νείκεος ἠπίοταντο
οὐδὲ διακρίσιος πολυμεμφέος οὐδὲ κυδοιμοῦ,
αὔτως δ' ἔζωον· χαλεπὴ δ' ἀπέκειτο θάλασσα,
καὶ βίον οὔπω νῆες ἀπόπροθεν ἠγίνεσκον,
ἀλλὰ βόες καὶ ἄροτρα καὶ αὐτή, πότνια λαῶν,
μυρία πάντα παρεῖχε Δίκη, δώτειρα δικαίων.

And men called her Justice, and assembling the elders either somewhere in a marketplace or in a broad street she spoke and disseminated popular laws. Not yet did men of that time know baneful strife or constant litigation or the din of battle, but they lived as before: the harsh sea lay at a distance and ships did not yet bring their livelihood from afar, but oxen and plows and the goddess herself, queen of peoples, Justice, bestower of just things, provided everything in abundance.

The men of the Bronze Age, more degenerate than their predecessors (*Phaenomena* 131-134),

... πρῶτοι κακόεργον ἐχαλκεύσαντο μάχαιραν
εἰνοδίην, πρῶτοι δὲ βοῶν ἐπάσαντ' ἀροτήρων,
καὶ τότε μισήσασα Δίκη κείνων γένος ἀνδρῶν
ἔπταθ' ὑπουρανίη·

first forged from bronze the destructive sword of the traveler and first fed on plow oxen. Then, too, did Justice, hating that race of men, fly to heaven.

Litigation, commerce, and warfare mark the distinction between the societies of the Golden and of the Iron Ages. And each of those conditions may be found in the survey of the new world Jupiter has created: litigation, in the division of property; commerce, in the discovery of navigation; warfare, in the smelting of *ferri rigor* ("unyielding iron").

Virgil confirms his own reservations about the value of mankind's technical achievements through his sudden and wholly unexpected qualification of *labor omnia uicit* by the striking adjective, *improbus*, at the beginning of the next line. Although the use of *improbus* to modify *labor* may, indirectly, comment on the magnitude of the challenge that man faces, *improbus* was used by Virgil's contemporaries almost without exception as a term of moral disapprobation to characterize people. Its use here suggests not only that human toil may be burdensome, but more importantly that it may be positively destructive.[10] Such a reading is further encouraged by the use of *improbus* only twenty-seven lines earlier in the very introduction to the account of Jupiter's theodicy. There it characterized the goose whose relentless pecking threatened the farmer's crops even after it seemed that he had laboriously provided all the conditions necesary for their fruitful growth. The description of man's toil as *improbus* recalls us to the essential qualities of man that were first signaled in this book by Virgil's characterization of the farmer as *auarus* ("greedy") and of mankind as a *durum genus* (a "hard race"). Man's *labor improbus* (his "ruinous toil") is therefore appropriately coupled with *duris urgens in rebus egestas* ("need, pressing in hard circumstances"): both are threats to a civilized existence.

In contrast to Hesiod and Aratus, Virgil has found no true Golden Age. Hesiod's Golden Age offered leisure, freedom from care, an abundance of nature's fruits, and fellowship with the gods. But in Virgil's view, it also stifled human initiative and growth; in the "Golden Age" the earth poured out her bounty "too freely" (*liberius*). Virgil's attitude toward rustic life is, likewise, more complex than that of Aratus, who saw in it the full realization of an ideal existence. For Virgil, rustic life belongs to the age of iron: Ceres taught men to turn the earth with "iron" (*ferro*, 147). It is difficult and confining—conspicuously so. When measured against mankind's inspiring capacity for invention, the farmer's busy plodding with rake and hoe seems grimly oppressive. Contrasted, however, with the unexpected danger and the terrible violence that civilization was to unleash in Virgil's own age, the comparative simplicity of rustic life is reassuring, even attractive. Virgil has suggested in the theodicy that civilization may be threatened by the forces of nature and man alike. The first danger is that the environment—with its

10. On the unequivocally negative connotations of *improbus* throughout Virgil's works, see *G.* 1.119, 388; 3.431; *A.* 2.80, 356; 4.386, 412 et passim. Also of particular interest is Lucr., *DRN* 5.1006 (although the line is the object of controversy), where the phrase *improba navigii ratio* ("the ruinous science of navigation") suggests as in *G.* 1.146 an association of the term with a critical view of the evolution of technology.

complexity, its harshness, its violence—may defy cultivation, that unless man exercises all his powers, he may have to eke out his existence on acorns (155–159). The other danger to civilization lies in man himself. His restless energies, his inventiveness, his insatiable appetite, and his hard insensitivity may transform civilization from a means for creation and growth into a means for self-destruction. That danger is only hinted at in the theodicy; it was manifest in the devastation of the Roman civil wars and in the degeneration of Roman society that preoccupied Virgil's contemporaries. The collapse of civilization whether from the harsh conditions of nature or from the avarice, hardness, and restless energy of man is equally disastrous. The best that can be hoped for is an unstable balance between the magnitude of the challenges man faces and his ability to meet them.

The account of the theodicy began as a comment on rustic life. When Virgil returns to that subject in line 147, Jupiter's motives, his actions and mankind's response provide a perspective from which to judge it and its relationship to other forms of civilization. Agriculture now appears as the first stage of a larger historical process. Attention shifts from Jupiter, "father of cultivation" in the broadest sense, and from the continuing series of changes he initiated, to the past and to a characteristically agricultural deity (147–149):

> prima Ceres ferro mortalis uertere terram
> instituit, cum iam glandes atque arbuta sacrae
> deficerent siluae et uictum Dodona negaret.

> Ceres first taught men to turn the earth with iron when the sacred forests were beginning to run short of acorns and berries, and Dodona to deny sustenance.

But plowing alone is not enough. Fresh problems arise so that civilization evolves through the continual interplay between man and his circumstances (155–159):

> quod nisi et adsiduis herbam insectabere rastris
> et sonitu terrebis auis et ruris opaci
> falce premes umbras uotisque uocaueris imbrem,
> heu magnum alterius frustra spectabis aceruum
> concussaque famem in siluis solabere quercu.

So, unless you will keep after the weeds with constant raking and scare birds away with noise, and pare back the dark field's shade with a pruning hook and pray for rain, alas, in vain you will look upon another's great harvest and you will appease your hunger by shaking oaks in the forest.

Successive challenges elicit successive skills. From plowing to raking, pruning, and ritual, man finds ever more ways to respond to the demands of nature and his own needs.

In that context, the metaphor with which Virgil introduces a discussion of agricultural implements is particularly suggestive: "Now I must discuss the farmer's *weapons*" (*arma*, 160). It acknowledges the continuing development of civilization which is implicit at each stage. Making plowshares is not far removed from making weapons: both imply a similar resourcefulness and a similar aggressiveness. Nonetheless, the farmer's "weapons" are still characteristically rustic. They are unwieldy, heavy, and cheap (162). They are dedicated to Ceres and her Eleusinian mysteries (163). The "glory" (*gloria*) they make possible is not the recognition won in politics and warfare that Romans normally associated with that term,[11] but a sense of achievement that is almost paradoxical by conventional standards, the *diuini gloria ruris* ("glory of the divine countryside," 168).

### III

With that important sense of the inevitable imperfection of civilization in mind, Virgil continues to elaborate his vision of rustic life, to explore its unique qualities and to reveal through it universal truths about the relationship between man and his environment and the cosmos, but always now with a clear understanding that agriculture is not only a paradigm for all civilized activity but also has its own distinctive character and its own place in the larger history of civilization. Thus Virgil defends the mundane details his subject imposes on him (176–177). Although there are many precepts he can report, they are not familiar matters from everyday life, but precepts of "the ancients" (*ueterum*) and they require indulgence, for they are

---

11. On the role of the concept of *gloria* in traditional Roman values, see Donald C. Earl, *The Moral and Political Tradition of Rome* (London 1967) 52.

"slight concerns" (*tenues curas*). The poet has again intruded and offered himself as a mediator between the sophisticated interests of his audience and the apparent insignificance of the details of rustic life. From the perspective of his audience, above all of Caesar, inspecting a threshing floor for cracks, observing the number of blossoms in a nut tree, or sorting seeds may seem trivial, but to the farmer they are everything: whether or not he will be able to preserve his harvest from the attacks of pests which can lay waste (*populat*) a huge pile, whether or not he can look forward to an abundance of nuts, whether or not he will be able to plant vigorous crops next season. In short, it is in just such details that the issue of survival is decided (197–203):

> uidi lecta diu et multo spectata labore
> degenerare tamen, ni uis humana quotannis
> maxima quaeque manu legeret: sic omnia fatis
> in peius ruere ac retro sublapsa referri,
> non aliter quam qui aduerso uix flumine lembum
> remigiis subigit, si bracchia forte remisit,
> atque illum in praeceps prono rapit alueus amni.

> I have seen seeds selected over a long period and with great pains nonetheless degenerate, if human effort each year does not pick out all the biggest ones by hand: so, as it is destined, everything degenerates, slips back and is carried away, just as one who can barely row his frail craft upstream, if for a moment he rests his arms, the headlong current sweeps him down the river course.

The generalizing force of the simile, "so all things (*omnia*) are destined to decline," enforces the paradox that the details for which Virgil apologized earlier reveal a universal truth. Even so it does not diminish the uniqueness of rustic life. For it is precisely in the urgent attendance to numberless and inglorious details that the farmer realizes a way of life that, however unassuming, can make a legitimate claim to its own kind of glory.

A particularly significant characteristic of the farmer's life is its direct responsiveness to the fundamental processes and patterns of nature. In the farmer's work the necessity for attention to even the finest details and for unceasing vigilance is manifest in consequences that threaten his livelihood directly and significantly. For example, Virgil describes the danger of mice in the storage bin with a humorous appreciation of the disproportion between the frail animal and the havoc he can wreak with the farmer's harvest. He places the monosyllabic "mouse" (*mus*) after its comparatively grandiose adjective, *exiguus* ("tiny") and at the very end of its line (181). Because of the infrequency of monosyllabic words in that position and because of the jarring conflict between the anticipated falling off of stress there and the monosyllable's own emphatic accent, *mus* achieves a rather comical pomposity. In a roughly contemporary passage Horace made similar fun of the mouse (*Ars Poetica*, 139): *Parturient montes, nascetur ridiculus mus* ("The mountains will give birth, and there will be born a ridiculous mouse"). In the *Georgics* emphasis on the tiny mouse, however mocking, is nonetheless apt, for mice are capable of destroying a harvest for the farmer. The law that all things decline unless constantly and energetically cultivated is a clear and ever-present reality.

Similarly, the farmer must arrange his work in strict accordance with the natural cycles of change governing his environment. There is only one time to sow barley, flax, and poppies, from the summer solstice to the first rains of winter (210–214); beans, clover, and millet must be sown in the spring (215–218). The farmer adapts to those conditions because the consequences of failure are unequivocal. Virgil's arrangement of his material, moreover, leads to an increasing awareness of the fineness and the extent of the conditions around which the farmer shapes his life. The survey of natural cycles progresses from the demands of each season (204–275), to each day (276–286), to a passage that begins, at least, by suggesting the importance of observing specific times of day (287–310). As is often the case in the *Georgics* the development of the passage is not strictly logical and depends for its effect more on the juxtaposition of related ideas than on systematic analysis. Virgil introduces the passage by asserting that certain tasks are best done in the chill of night or of early dawn (287–290). That leads to an enumeration of tasks for which the long nights of winter are especially suited (291–296). The passage concludes with examples of work that should be done in the winter season, "when snow lies deep" (*cum nix alta iacet*, 305–310). We have passed from night to winter. The transition is associative rather than chronological: from the chill of night to the cold of winter. But between the focus on night and that on winter come puzzling lines about heat: grain must be harvested and threshed "in the middle of the heat" (*medio aestu*); one must strip (*nudus*) to plow and to sow (297–299). The expressions are ambiguous. Does *medio aestu* signify the middle of the day, in opposition to the chill of night in the previous lines? Or does it signify the middle of summer, in opposition to the cold of winter in the following lines? Commentators are not in agreement. Perhaps it is not really important. The thrust of the argument is clear. Day and night, summer and winter, heat and cold—all play a part in the organization of rustic life.

So ubiquitous are the demands on the farmer, so pervasive is the order to which he must conform, that the distinction between work and leisure ceases to be meaningful. Winter may be a "lazy time" for the farmer, as for the sailor; but in contrast to the sailor, the farmer has responsibilities even in his season of rest (299–310):

> . . . hiems ignaua colono:
> . . . . . . . . . . . . . . . .
> ceu pressae cum iam portum tetigere carinae,
> puppibus et laeti nautae imposuere coronas.
> sed tamen et quernas glandes tum stringere tempus
> et lauri bacas oleamque cruentaque myrta,
> tum gruibus pedicas et retia ponere ceruis
> auritosque sequi lepores, tum figere dammas
> stuppea torquentem Balearis uerbera fundae,
> cum nix alta iacet, glaciem cum flumina trudunt.

> Winter is a lazy time for the farmer, . . . just as when laden keels at last reach harbor and the joyful sailors place garlands of thanksgiving on the sterns. But nonetheless, that is a time to gather acorns, laurel berries, the olive, and the blood-red myrtle. Then is the time to set traps for cranes and snares for deer, to chase long-eared hares, and to catch fawns by hurling the hempen thongs of the Balearic sling, when snow lies deep, when rivers thrust up ice.

The fact that there is always work to do represents only one-half of the integration of work and leisure in the farmer's life. The other half is that work itself may be the occasion for recreation and relaxation. In a rare and moving glimpse of the farmer's domestic life, we see husband and wife working side by side late into a winter's evening (291–296):

> et quidam seros hiberni ad luminis ignis
> peruigilat ferroque faces inspicat acuto.
> interea longum cantu solata laborem
> arguto coniunx percurrit pectine telas,
> aut dulcis musti Volcano decoquit umorem
> et foliis undam trepidi despumat aëni.

> and a certain farmer stays up late by the winter firelight and splits firebrands with sharp iron. In the meantime his wife relieves her long toil with song while she runs the chattering comb through her loom or cooks out the moisture of sweet must over a fire and with leaves skims the ripples in her shimmering bronze kettle.

Work has become an occasion for companionship and song. Similarly, Virgil observes that *inuitat genialis hiems curasque resoluit* ("genial winter is inviting and resolves cares," 302). But he makes rustic conviviality itself an object of care: *mutuaque inter se laeti conuiuia curant* ("The joyful farmers care for banquets which they share among themselves," 301). The juxtaposition of the "cares" which the farmer frees himself of in winter and the other "care" which he devotes to recreation suggests the essential similarity of those two apparently different activities of rustic life.

The integration of work and recreation in rustic life is expressed perhaps most strikingly in a later passage. Virgil warns against disastrous storms and advises precautions. The farmer should watch for weather signs, but, especially, he should perform the appropriate rituals (338–347):

> in primis uenerare deos, atque annua magnae
> sacra refer Cereri laetis operatus in herbis
> extremae sub casum hiemis, iam uere sereno.
> tum pingues agni et tum mollissima uina,
> tum somni dulces densaeque in montibus umbrae.
> cuncta tibi Cererem pubes agrestis adoret:
> cui tu lacte fauos et miti dilue Baccho,
> terque nouas circum felix eat hostia fruges,

omnis quam chorus et socii comitentur ouantes
et Cererem clamore uocent in tecta.

Above all, worship the gods and pay to great Ceres her annual rites: sacrifice on the burgeoning grass at the very end of winter, as soon as it is calm spring. Then lambs are fat; then wine is sweetest; then sleep is sweet and there are dense shadows on the hills. Let all your rustic youth pray to Ceres; mix honeycomb with milk and gentle wine; let a propitious victim three times circle the new crops; let the whole chorus of your neighbors accompany it in prayer and let them call Ceres into their homes with their voices.

The attractive spring setting, the conspicuous fertility of the land, images of honey-sweetened wine, neighboring farmers uniting in song, the sacrificial animal—all convey indirectly a sense of joyfulness and release. At the same time, the practical function of the celebration is never lost sight of. The designation of the season, or rather the moment when winter ends and spring begins, the country youth, the wine, the sacrificial victim, and the chorus are all specific requirements of a ritual to ensure the fertility of crops and to protect against the devastation of storms. The interplay of work and celebration is captured neatly in the final lines of the passage (347–350):

. . . neque ante
falcem maturis quisquam supponat aristis
quam Cereri torta redimitus tempora quercu
det motus incompositos et carmina dicat.

and let no one touch his sickle to the ripe crops before he binds his temples with twisted oak and performs impromptu dances and hymns to Ceres.

The controlling order of the ritual provides an occasion for the farmer's spontaneous expression of joyful release, and both serve the higher order of natural law.

The picture of rustic life Virgil has elaborated thus far corresponds to traditional idealizations of that agrarian life which was felt to have been responsible for the Romans' distinctive virtues and successes. It is a way of life that serves man's own need to be cultivated as the fields are cultivated. The first third of *Georgic* 1 argued that the earth is most fruitful, for example, when it has been left fallow or when crops are rotated. Just so, we now find, the farmer's own life is varied. Seasons of demanding work alternate with seasons of comparative leisure that is re-creative in the fullest sense and that prepares for renewed commitment to toil. The varied tasks of rustic life not only serve the goal of a generous livelihood; equally important, they are attractive ends in themselves. They are occasions for meaningful occupation, for fellowship, even for joyful abandon. But underlying all those attractions are the traditional Roman virtues of industry and discipline, and a sense that rustic life is good precisely because it is confining. Not only does it demand the fulfillment of human potential, it also leaves no opportunity for luxury, idleness, or self-indulgence in any of its forms. If it requires and encourages ambition, it also contains that vice. Or, at least, it seems to, as long as our attention is focused on rustic life itself and not on the larger history of civilization.

Virgil has placed that characteristically Roman view of rustic life in the context of the most Roman of the Hellenistic popular philosophies, Stoicism. The view that hard work and stern discipline were the most important of virtues and not necessary evils was utterly inconsistent with the powerful tradition extending down from Hesiod, according to which the deterioration of the human condition was measured by the necessity for work. It did, however, fit well with the Stoic conviction that the universe was informed by a divine intelligence whose benevolence toward mankind is everywhere manifest in the workings of the universe as well as in the nature of man himself. A Stoic view of the human condition was implicit in the *Georgics* as early as the theodicy passage. There, we saw, a benevolent deity—"the divine father himself," the *pater ipse* as Stoics for convenience sometimes named the divine principle[12]—transformed

---

12. Allegorizing allowed the Stoics to accept identification of the divine intelligence that informs the universe with the traditional anthropomorphic concept of deity. Stoics could regard the latter as a convenient metaphor for the true divinity. Identification of the Stoic divinity with the supreme god of the Greek pantheon, Zeus, is celebrated movingly in *The Hymn to Zeus* of Cleanthes (331-232 B.C.). Traditionally, Zeus' preeminence found one expression in his designation as "father of men and gods." In Cleanthes' *Hymn* that aspect of Zeus becomes a convenient means of affirming the beneficence and creative power of the Stoic god. Thus, Cleanthes addresses his Stoic Zeus as πάτερ (v. 34) and asserts that all mortals are of his race (vv. 4, 5). That idea is repeated by Aratus of Soli in the invocation to the Stoic Zeus that introduces his *Phaenomena* (v. 5). Particularly notable is that in his *De Natura Deorum* (2.4)

a too generous world of ease into one that would challenge mortals and thus not allow his kingdoms to grow sluggish with oppressive old age.

Some critics of the *Georgics* have seen a Lucretian influence in the celebration of technological progress that follows the divine father's intervention, but the entire passage is undoubtedly Stoic in its outlook. The leading idea, that the world in its present form is the direct result of a beneficent divinity, is utterly contrary to Lucretius' insistence on the mechanistic operation of the universe. Moreover, the idea of technological progress was by no means exclusively Epicurean. It had a place in Stoic philosophy as well, despite that philosophy's doctrine that civilization is ultimately corrupting. In fact, the closest parallel in Latin literature to Virgil's celebration of technology in *Georgic* 1 is to be found not in Lucretius, but in the exposition of the Stoic, Lucilius Balbus, in Cicero's *De Natura Deorum*. One of his proofs that the universe is shaped by a divine purpose benevolent toward man is the marvelous usefulness of the human hand. He begins (*DND* 2.150-152):

> Quam vero aptas quamque multarum artium ministras manus natura homini dedit. . . . ex quo intellegitur ad inventa animo, percepta sensibus adhibitis opificum manibus omnia nos consecutos, ut tecti ut vestiti ut salvi esse possemus, urbes muros domicilia delubra haberemus. . . . nos e terrae cavernis ferrum eligimus rem ad colendos agros necessariam, nos aeris argenti auri venas penitus abditas invenimus et ad usum aptas et ad ornatum decoras. Arborum autem consectione omnique materia et culta et silvestri . . . ad aedificandum ut tectis saepti frigora caloresque pellamus; magnos vero usus adfert ad navigia faci-

---

Cicero has the Stoic Lucilius Balbus begin his proof of the existence of divinity as follows: "*Ne egere quidem videtur*" *inquit* "*oratione prima pars. Quid enim potest esse tam apertum tamque perspicuum, cum caelum suspeximus caelestiaque contemplati sumus, quam esse aliquod numen praestantissimae mentis quo haec regantur? Quod ni ita esset, qui potuisset adsensu omnium dicere Ennius: 'Aspice hoc sublime candens, quem invocant omnes Iovem,' illum vero et Iovem et dominatorem rerum et omnia nutu regentem et, ut idem Ennius, 'patrem divumque hominumque,' et praesentem ac praepotentem deum?*" ("'The first part,' he said, 'doesn't even seem to need discussion. For what could be so obvious and clear when we look up at the sky and contemplate the heavenly bodies as that they are governed by some exceedingly intelligent divinity? If this weren't the case, how could Ennius have said with universal approval: "Behold this brilliance on high which everyone calls Jupiter." Indeed, not just Jupiter, but the master of the universe, and the one who rules all at his nod and, as that same Ennius said, "*father of gods and men,*" and eminent and preeminent god?'").

enda, quorum cursibus subpeditantur omnes undique ad vitam copiae.

Indeed, what servants, and well-suited to how many skills are the hands that nature gave to man. . . . Thus, we understand that when the hands of the artificer are applied to the inventions of thought and the perceptions of the senses, we accomplish everything, so that we can be housed, clothed, and safe, so that we may have cities, walls, homes, shrines. . . . From the caves of the earth we gather iron, a necessity for tilling the land; we discover deep hidden veins of copper, silver, gold, materials both suited for use and beautiful for adornment. Moreover, by felling trees of every kind, cultivated and wild, [we use them] for construction so that protected by our buildings we drive off cold and heat. Indeed, [timber] is of great use in making ships by whose voyages all goods from everywhere are provided for our livelihood.

Balbus concludes his survey of the achievements made possible because the Stoic divinity provided us with hands with a sweeping climax that celebrates the same triumphant progress Virgil suggests at the end of his survey of technology: *nostris denique manibus in rerum natura quasi alteram naturam efficere conamur* ("by means of our hands, then, we try to construct, as it were, a second nature within the nature of things," *DND* 2.152).

In the description of the farmer's round of work following the theodicy passage, Virgil reasserts a Stoic context. The explanation of the reliability of the constellations as seasonal signs expands beyond the immediate concern with the cultivation of cereals, beyond the role of the constellations, to consider man's relationship to the cosmos in the broadest possible terms. The farmer must plant each crop in the correct season. "Therefore" (*idcirco*), Virgil asserted, the sun governs the earth's orb and the constellations (231). But instead of describing further the celestial bodies and their immediate relationship either to agriculture or to any other specific human activity, Virgil proceeds to elaborate the idea (implicit in the connective *idcirco*) of a cosmos that has been designed for man's benefit. He orients the zodiac according to the arctic, temperate, and tropical zones dividing the earth. The account is not altogether clear and appears to conflate several views. In any event, Virgil does not claim absolute confidence in all details and offers, for example, alternative theories of the location and disposition of the South Pole (247-251):

> illic, ut perhibent, aut intempesta silet nox
> semper et obtenta densentur nocte tenebrae;
> aut redit a nobis Aurora diemque reducit,
> nosque ubi primus equis Oriens adflauit anhelis
> illic sera rubens accendit lumina Vesper.

> There, it is said, either the dead of night is silent always, and shadows thicken under the covering night; or dawn returns from us and brings back day, and when the panting horses of the sun's first rising breathe on us, there the glowing evening star ignites its late gleam.

Virgil is not speculating idly about the earth's geography. Rather, he is pointing out that what is important about his argument is not the precise disposition of the earth's zones, but the fact that man can only exist in the moderate climate of the temperate zone, dramatic evidence of both man's comparative frailty and, its corollary, the beneficence of the gods who designed the cosmos. Between the two arctic regions and the tropics (237-239),

> has inter mediamque duae mortalibus aegris
> munere concessae diuum, et uia secta per ambas,
> obliquus qua se signorum uerteret ordo.

> two zones have been granted to sickly mortals as a gift of the gods, and a path has been cut through both where the slanting succession of constellations moves.

When the argument returns, after speculation about the poles, to the reliability of the heavenly signs (252-258), the logical development, "consequently" (*hinc*), depends as much on the appreciation of man's relationship to the gods as it does on the physical plan Virgil has sketched.

Once again, Virgil's argument belongs clearly to the Stoic tradition. The meaning of the arrangement of climatic zones on the earth was a specific area in which differences between Stoics and Epicureans were most sharply defined. In his *De Rerum Natura* Lucretius argues that the fact that only one-third of the earth is habitable is a sure proof of the gods' indifference to mankind.[13] Stoics argued just the reverse. The fact that the gods should have provided a habitable region for mankind demonstrates their active good will.[14] By appealing to Stoic cosmology, Virgil does two things. He suggests that the vision of rustic life he is elaborating here is confirmed by the actual design of the cosmos. In so doing, he calls attention to a far more basic truth: any attempt to elaborate a vision of rustic life, of man's relation to his environment, must inevitably rest on important assumptions about the nature of the cosmos and man's place in it.

The effectiveness of the farmer's regimen and of the larger Stoic cosmos with which Virgil has associated it is contingent on man's acceptance of his place in nature and in the cosmic order. As I have already observed, the possibility that mankind might overcome the challenges set by the divine father, that he might seek to free himself from the constraints of the natural order, has already been hinted at in the theodicy passage. Virgil reintroduces that possibility again and warns against it in his survey of the farmer's calendar (276–286). It acknowledges the characteristic ambition of mankind and warns against its consequences. The fifth day of the lunar month, for example, is a day of ill omen and requires caution (277). On that day "pale Orcus" (god of the underworld) and the Eumenides (protectors of the unwritten laws of human behavior) were conceived (277–278). The fifth, then, commemorates human mortality and the obligations of flesh and blood to the gods. Moreover, Iapetus and his brothers were born on this day. Like man, they were born from the earth and, according to one myth, are ancestors of the human race: Iapetus begot Prometheus who, in turn, fashioned men from clay. Their relation to Prometheus is also relevant, because he brought fire to mortals and thus introduced the civilized arts. The fact that their births, like the conception of Orcus and the Eumenides, are a sign of ill omen reaffirms the sinister possibilities Virgil hinted at in the theodicy passage.

The fate of Otus and Ephialtes, who conspired to overthrow Jupiter, is even more revealing. Usually regarded as sons of the giants Aloeus and Iphimedeia, Virgil makes them children of Earth. His alteration of tradition reinforces their symbolic relationship to

13. Lucr., *DRN* 5.195–205.
14. This is the major argument Cicero has the Stoic Lucilius Balbus advance in defense of his belief in divinity in *DND* 2, esp. 73–133.

the "hard human race" which sprang from Deucalian's stones. Their undertaking was prodigious (281-283):

> ter sunt conati imponere Pelio Ossam
> scilicet atque Ossae frondosum inuoluere Olympum;
> ter pater exstructos disiecit fulmine montis.

> Three times they tried to pile Ossa on Pelion and, what is more, to roll leafy Olympus onto Ossa; three times father Jupiter dislodged the piled-up mountains with his lightning.

A series of spondees, and hiatus, unusual for Virgil, between the *i*'s of *conati* and *imponere* and between the *o*'s of *Pelio* and *Ossam* retard the movement of the line and suggest the ponderous magnitude of the giants' labor and their determination. Although the myths are introduced in the context of rustic life, they speak to characteristics of the human spirit and of civilization that are rooted in the origins of mankind. The brief calendar of days concludes with a few apparently miscellaneous observations that concern rustic life in particular and reflect the influence of Hesiod. But typically, Virgil has transformed Hesiod's material. In the context of the foregoing myths and their broad warning to mankind, the final enumeration of days and their omens transcends the immediate concerns of the farmer. It exemplifies and symbolizes man's larger responsibility to accept his limitations and to obey the divine order of the cosmos. Virgil has placed the virtues of industry and discipline within the context of the most comprehensive Roman virtue, *pietas*.

## IV

Virgil's own attitude toward that vision of rustic life and the Stoic concept of the universe with which he has associated it is not unequivocal. The alternation of emphasis on human limitation (warnings to accept the consequences of mortality) and on divine benevolence (two climatic zones that the gods provided for mankind) re-creates the ambivalence of Jupiter's theodicy on a large scale. The insistence that his dispensations are at once oppressive and liberating is sustained in the discussion of storms and weather signs which begins at line 311. Autumn is a season of storms of terrifying intensity (316-327). But more fearsome than the storms themselves is the potential magnitude of divine wrath and destructiveness that they reveal (328–334):

> ipse pater media nimborum in nocte corusca
> fulmina molitur dextra, quo maxima motu
> terra tremit, fugere ferae et mortalia corda
> per gentis humilis strauit pauor; ille flagranti
> aut Atho aut Rhodopen aut alta Ceraunia telo
> deicit; ingeminant Austri et densissimus imber;
> nunc nemora ingenti uento, nunc litora plangunt.

> The father himself in a midnight of clouds brandishes lightning in his flashing right hand; at its movement the entire earth shudders; wild beasts have fled and fear has laid low mortal hearts through the races. He with burning spear dislodges Mt. Athos or Rhodope or tall Ceraunia. The south winds redouble their force along with the heaviest rains. They strike, now groves, now the shores, with a great blast.

For all its destructiveness, the fury of god and storm is nonetheless subsumed within a divine order. The farmer is advised to observe the seasons and the constellations, and, above all, to worship the gods (335–338).

The introduction of weather signs also reasserts divine benevolence and expresses confidence in a divine order and purpose (351–354):

> Atque haec ut certis possemus discere signis,
> aestusque pluuiasque et agentis frigora uentos,
> ipse pater statuit quid menstrua luna moneret,
> quo signo caderent Austri.

> And that we may learn these things by reliable signs—periods of heat, rain, and winds that bring cold—the father himself decreed what the moon reveals in its monthly cycles, under what sign the west wind descends.

The repetition of *ipse pater* ("the father himself") in lines 328 and 353 joins the two passages with their contrasting views of Jupiter's authority. At the same time it echoes the *pater ipse* of the theodicy passage and calls attention to continuity with the complex relationship presented there between mankind and god.

The discussion of storms and weather signs beginning in line 311 adds a further dimension to Virgil's argument. It leads toward a growing sense of discontinuity between the microcosm and divine order. This development is particularly clear in light of Aratus' *Phaenomena* 733-1154. Similarities of content and organization indicate that Virgil relied heavily on Aratus' influential poem for his discussion of weather signs. His indebtedness to Aratus renders the unique and salient features of his own treatment of the subject particularly conspicuous. Virgil adds elements that have no place in Aratus. Like Aratus, although at less length, he describes numerous signs and the weather they portend. Unlike Aratus he devotes a substantial portion of his account to describing in vivid and dramatic detail the destructive consequences of storms. For Aratus, who was largely concerned with demonstrating the beneficence of the Stoic universe in the orderly disposition of the heavens, it was enough to demonstrate the existence of reliable weather signs which assist humans in planning their activities.

Virgil introduces his discussion of weather signs by evoking impressions of particularly violent storms. In addition, his use of military metaphor suggests a redefinition or at least a new dimension of the farmer's relation to his environment. Previously, it had been the farmer who acted the part of the warrior, commanding the fields or attacking them with his weapons. Now it is the environment that assumes a martial character. An imposing "army" of ravens may warn of impending bad weather (381-382):

... et e pastu decedens agmine magno
coruorum increpuit densis exercitus alis.

and retreating from its pasturage in a great column, an army of crows has clashed its innumerable wings.

Storms themselves may be battles of epic proportion (316-327):

saepe ego, cum flauis messorem induceret aruis
agricola et fragili iam stringeret hordea culmo,
omnia uentorum concurrere proelia uidi,
quae grauidam late segetem ab radicibus imis
sublimem expulsam eruerent: ita turbine nigro
ferret hiems culmumque leuem stipulasque uolantis.
saepe etiam immensum caelo uenit agmen aquarum

et foedam glomerant tempestatem imbribus atris
collectae ex alto nubes; ruit arduus aether
et pluuia ingenti sata laeta boumque labores
diluit; implentur fossae et caua flumina crescunt
cum sonitu feruetque fretis spirantibus aequor.

Often, when the farmer was leading the reaper onto the tawny fields and was already stripping barley from its fragile stock, I have seen all the winds rush together in battles that ripped the heavy crop everywhere from its very roots and tossed it high: so in a black whirlwind the storm would carry off both light stubble and whirling stalks. Often, too, an immense column of water has come from the sky and clouds gathered from on high whip up a foul storm with black rain: the sheer heavens collapse and with huge rains wash out fruitful crops and the bulls' labors; ditches are filled; sunken rivers grow with a roar and water seethes in hissing channels.

The devastations such meteorological battles wreak upon the farmer's existence have their only real parallels in this book in the literal battles, the civil wars, that Virgil describes at its conclusion.

The farmer's vulnerability is further underscored by comparisons with sailors and their condition. During thunderstorms *omnia plenis / rura natant fossis atque omnis navita ponto / umida uela legit* ("the entire countryside swims, ditches are flooded, and every sailor at sea furls his drenched sails," 371–373). When the horns of the moon's crescent are obscured by black clouds, then *maximus agricolis pelagoque parabitur imber* ("the greatest rains are in store for farmers and at sea," 429). At the sign that good weather will hold to the month's end, *uotaque seruati soluent in litore nautae* ("on shore sailors who have been saved will make good their promised offerings," 436). If the sun's orb is blotched, *non illa quisquam me nocte per altum / ire neque a terra moneat conuellere funem* ("let no one advise me to go abroad on the deep sea that night or to detach my stern hawser from land," 456–457). The combined effect of such comparisons and of the environment's martial aspect is to impart to the farmer's experience a meaning that extends beyond his immediate circumstances. Just as rustic life achieved epic stature earlier in the book, so it does in the latter sections; but now Odysseus, not Achilles, defines the epic norm. Resourcefulness and toughness continue to be among the farmer's cardinal virtues, but they manifest themselves in new ways. Awareness of the disproportion between man and the forces of the cosmos urges the value of adaptation and endurance. Overriding the unique attractions of rustic life is a broader appreciation of human limitation. That is not to deny the possibility of human achievement, but to qualify it. Civilization requires not only steadfast opposition to the natural processes of degeneration; it also requires repeated acts of regeneration and renewal. Virgil's earlier comparison between the farmer and the rower of a small boat urged the necessity of unremitting labor by dramatizing the suddenness with which catastrophe descends on those who are remiss. The violence of storms represents a more oppressive aspect of the environment: they are quite simply beyond human control.

Paradoxically, this heightened emphasis on the imminence and magnitude of destructive forces to which mankind is subject occurs within the context of repeated and ever more confident assertions that the cosmos is divinely ordered. Aratus began his account of weather signs by describing the indications given by the heavenly bodies, especially the sun (*Phaenomena* 773-908), and then proceeded to an enumeration of a wide miscellany of diverse heavenly and terrestrial signs (*Phaenomena* 909-1043). That arrangement is well suited to a logical explication of the religious-philosophical viewpoint implicit in the opening lines of his poem. It was a commonplace of Stoic allegorizing to identify the sun as a symbol of Stoic divinity.[15] Aratus reminds his audience of the divine benevolence that both validates and is validated by the reliability of the signs he is going to describe. Virgil reverses Aratus' order with important consequences for our perception of the relationship between the macrocosmic scale on which divine purpose operates and the microcosm in which humans experience their lives.

For example, assurance that *numquam imprudentibus imber / obfuit* ("rain has never overtaken anyone unawares," 373-374) is not altogether satisfying in light of the terrible damage floods may cause. Nor is the warning, *caeli mensis et sidera serua* ("observe the months and the constellations of the heavens," 335), fully convincing when

---

15. Identification of the sun with the informing intelligence that pervades the universe in Stoic thought is first attested in the philosopher Cleanthes; see J. von Arnim, *Stoicorum Veterum Fragmenta* (Leipzig 1921) I.499. That identification quickly became widespread with the growing popularity of astrology throughout the Mediterranean.

it is clear that nothing can actually abate the storms' fury. Likewise, the sun is accompanied by "the surest signs" (439), but the only recourse against the storms it announces may be to hide indoors (456-457). In fact, Virgil, on his own authority, urges skepticism about the efficacy of divine purpose in the microcosm. In a striking departure from the Stoic teleology that provided the basis for much of his argument in *Georgic* 1, he offers the following account of why certain birds' behavior forecasts storms reliably (415-423):

> haud equidem credo, quia sit diuinitus illis
> ingenium aut rerum fato prudentia maior;
> uerum ubi tempestas et caeli mobilis umor
> mutauere uias et Iuppiter umidus Austris
> denset erant quae rara modo, et quae densa relaxat,
> uertuntur species animorum, et pectora motus
> nunc alios, alios dum nubila uentus agebat,
> concipiunt: hinc ille auium concentus in agris
> et laetae pecudes et ouantes gutture corui.

> Not, I myself believe, because they possess a nature bestowed by the gods or a greater foresight granted by fate; but when the weather and the changeable humidity of the sky have altered their courses and moist Jupiter with the wet south wind condenses what was scattered before and rarefies what was dense, the dispositions of the birds' spirits are changed and their breasts experience now one set of movements, and another when the wind was driving on the clouds: that is the reason for that gathering of birds in the fields, for joyful flocks and for ravens' guttural rejoicing.

The foregoing explanation is unequivocally mechanistic rather than theological. In this context the "moist Jupiter" who gathers and disperses storm clouds is not the Stoic god who embodies and creates cosmic order; he is, rather, the archaic sky god, little more than a symbolic equivalent for wind and rain. Virgil has not with this one expression wiped out the Stoic teleology that informs his concept of the universe in *Georgic* 1, but he has effectively distinguished the cosmic scale on which that teleology operates from the full range of vicissitudes that affect human experience. Jupiter's theodicy defines the broad limits within which mankind acts; it is manifest in the macrocosm, in the celestial bodies, and in the larger course of history, but it does not account for the details of individual experience or for every moment of history. It defines an ideal and theoretical order whose realization is neither inevitable nor even always possible within the scope of individual human experience or of specific historical moments. The truth of that viewpoint is brought home dramatically in the next and final section of *Georgic* 1.

With a defiant question, "Who would dare to call the sun false?" Virgil introduces by far the greatest storm to break over the heads of the beleaguered farmers, the Roman civil wars (463-514). In answer to his question, he asserts that the sun warns that disturbances are at hand, even when they are unseen (*ille etiam caecos instare tumultus / saepe monet*, 464-465). The full force of his assertion does not depend on the obvious emphasis of "even unseen" (*etiam caecos*) so much as it does on the less immediately obvious ambiguity of the term *tumultus* ("disturbances"). Among Virgil's contemporaries the term could mean natural disturbances, that is, storms. Horace often used it in this sense.[16] In the context of the foregoing discussion of weather signs, this interpretation would seem, on first sight, to be natural here. However, *tumultus* also regularly meant manmade disturbances—that is, civil disturbances, uprisings[17]— and, in the next line of his argument, Virgil continues, "often warns that treachery and open wars are brewing." The unexpected turn from the discussion of natural disorders to an interest in political and military disorders requires reinterpretation of the meaning of *tumultus*. The ambiguity of the term, emphasized by the necessity of reinterpreting it, suggests a parallel between natural and political disorders, and that their relationship to the divine cosmic order represented by the sun is comparable. The use of the sun to introduce the following discussion of the Roman civil wars, therefore, is more than a simple matter of poetic convenience or cleverness.

Like storms, the civil war concerns the macrocosm of divine will and the microcosm of human existence in different ways. The assassination of Julius Caesar is the immediate cause of disorder in the

16. For *tumultus* as "storm" in Horace, see *C.* 1.16.12; 3.27.17; 3.29.63.

17. In this sense *tumultus* could have a technical meaning, referring to immediate threats to the City of Rome itself which required a general mobilization of its people. On this use of the term, see A. W. Lintott, *Violence in Republican Rome* (Oxford 1968, reprinted 1972) 91-92, 153-155.

cosmos. It is registered by a dimming of the sun, an act of mourning that attests to the seriousness of the crime and forebodes its dire consequences. The personification of the sun is significant in that its grief symbolizes the violation not only of the political but of the divine order as well (466-468):

> ille etiam exstincto miseratus Caesare Romam,
> cum caput obscura nitidum ferrugine texit
> impiaque aeternam timuerunt saecula noctem.

> Even when Caesar was killed it pitied Rome, when it covered its shining head with a dull rust and the impious ages feared eternal night.

Other portents also suggest the theme of impiety. The eruptions of Aetna, for example, overflowing onto the fields of the Cyclopes (471-473), recall Virgil's earlier warning about the giants' attempts to overthrow Jupiter; for it was beneath Aetna, according to a well-known version of the myth, that Jupiter buried the defeated Typhoeus. The assassination of Caesar, thus, becomes a reenactment of the archetypical struggle of the creatures of Earth to destroy the Olympian forces of order and justice. Appropriately, then, the entrails of sacrificial victims reveal only threatening omens (483-485).

Earlier in this book, Virgil made the efficacy of the cosmic order and of rustic discipline contingent on man's acceptance of his place and of the limitations which that implies. In addition, he revealed that the history of man—whether one looks back to the mythical example, the Titans, or ahead to the evolution of technology—suggests that he will not, in fact, accept his limitations. The assassination of Caesar confirms that possibility. As a consequence, the extent to which Stoicism, or the vision of rustic life that Virgil has elaborated in conjunction with it, may offer effective responses or alternatives to the chaos of contemporary society has been thrown into question.

The traditional Roman models of rustic life and Stoicism are shown to be of uncertain value in other ways as well. Just as the physical and spiritual dimensions of the civil wars are cosmic, so their temporal dimensions call for a perspective that dwarfs the lifetime of an individual or even the history of an age. Virgil assigns the problems of contemporary Rome a specific origin, but it exists outside the scope of history in the remote past of myth (501–504):

> . . . satis iam pridem sanguine nostro
> Laomedonteae luimus periuria Troiae;
> iam pridem nobis caeli te regia, Caesar,
> inuidet atque hominum queritur curare triumphos.

> Long enough have we paid for Laomedon's perjury at Troy with our blood; long enough, Caesar, have the kingdoms of heaven begrudged you to us and complained of your care for mortal triumphs.

The new Caesar's as yet unsuccessful efforts to bring order to the Roman world are subordinate to a larger process of divine retribution which began with Rome's Trojan ancestors when Laomedon cheated Apollo and Neptune of the wages he promised them for their help in building Troy's defenses.

Similarly, seen within the context of the enduring order of the cosmos, one may look forward to a time when rustic life will be restored (493–497):

> scilicet et tempus ueniet, cum finibus illis
> agricola incuruo terram molitus aratro
> exesa inueniet scabra robigine pila,
> aut grauibus rastris galeas pulsabit inanis
> grandiaque effossis mirabitur ossa sepulcris.

> No doubt, too, a time will come when a farmer, in those fields as he works the earth with his curved plow, will come upon a javelin, eaten with clotted rust, or with his heavy harrows he will strike helmets, empty ones, and will marvel at great bones dug up from their graves.

That expectation is hardly reassuring. It is no more immediate or real to Virgil than his own age will be to those distant farmers who will plow up the remnants of the civil wars and, all uncomprehending, attribute them to an age of great-boned giants.

Within the present there is only disorder, and the very signs that mark Caesar's assassination (earthquakes, volcanic eruptions, floods) are themselves a part of the chaos they portend. They reveal a world not only out of control, but even beyond comprehension:

*pecudesque locutae / (infandum!)* ("livestock talked—unspeakable!" 478-479). More important still, the Romans' punishments are their own crimes. Because of the assassination of Caesar and the disorder it introduced into the cosmos (489-492),

> ergo inter sese paribus concurrere telis
> Romanas acies iterum uidere Philippi;
> nec fuit indignum superis bis sanguine nostro
> Emathiam et latos Haemi pinguescere campos.

> therefore, Philippi saw Roman battle lines a second time engage one another, both sides armed alike. Nor did the gods deem it unfitting a second time to enrich Emathia and the plains of Haemus with our blood.

The Stoic vision of man's relation to the cosmos makes such helplessness as the Romans now experience inescapable. The divine father's beneficent order encourages man to develop his potential precisely because nonconformity to the requirements of his order leads to instant and irrevocable downfall. Like the rower whose boat is carried headlong downstream, the Roman people have been helpless victims of their own vices ever since Laomedon's treachery. Virgil himself expresses both despair and exasperation in his repeated cry that Romans have suffered *satis iam pridem . . . iam pridem* ("long enough . . . long enough," 501-503). In his prayer for deliverance, therefore, he ignores Jupiter, the divine father of the Stoic cosmos, and turns instead to the more intimate divinities of the Roman people (498-499):

> di patrii Indigetes et Romule Vestaque mater,
> quae Tuscum Tiberim et Romana Palatia seruas.

> ancestral gods of our people, Romulus and you, mother Vesta, who preserve the Tuscan Tiber and the Roman Palatine.

The macrocosmic order of the Stoic divinity may account for the helpless confusion Virgil's contemporaries experienced, but it offers the Roman people no way out of their dilemma.

Neither does the traditional Roman vision of rustic life provide an alternative to contemporary chaos. Indeed, the farmer has been driven from the field: *non ullus aratro / dignus honos* ("there is no fitting honor given to the plow," 506-507). More important still, rustic life as it has been pictured in *Georgic* 1 seems in retrospect to have cultivated in man the very qualities that have caused the Roman civil wars. If rustic life, as idealized in Roman tradition, required strict discipline, it also required toughness and ambition. The farmer was from the time of Deucalion *duras* and *avarus*. The struggle for a livelihood reinforced those qualities and stimulated man's energies. The civil war reveals the full meaning of the assertion that man's *labor omnia uicit / improbus* ("toil has overcome all things / ruinous toil"). With the assassination of Caesar and the civil wars man's toil has finally transformed the very cosmos. The final lines of *Georgic* 1 evoke the centrifugal thrust of human energy as it spirals aimlessly outward: first the farmer is drawn away from his fields (506-508); then the very borders of civilization (the Euphrates to the east and Germany to the north) join the growing chaos (509); then cities everywhere break the bonds of law and take up arms (510); until, finally (511-514),

> . . . saeuit toto Mars impius orbe,
> ut cum carceribus sese effudere quadrigae,
> addunt in spatia, et frustra retinacula tendens
> fertur equis auriga neque audit currus habenas.

> impious Mars rages over the entire globe, just as when chariots burst from the starting gates. They pick up speed and, uselessly holding the reins, the driver is carried along by his horses; the chariot does not respond to his commands.

Like the *labor* of the theodicy passage, the forces unleashed here have no goal, know no bounds. The simile of the chariot speaks not only to the disintegration of Virgil's Rome, but to every age which feels that civilization has grown out of hand: the chariot that carries its driver off to destruction is itself a creation of man's own ingenuity and ambition.

There is yet another way in which the civil wars appear to be the fulfillment of potentialities inherent in the farmer's way of life. Virgil dramatized the difficulty of the farmer's existence and at the same time glorified it, as we have seen, by suggesting that his struggle for survival is like that of the heroic warrior of epic. He called attention specifically to the martial quality of rustic life. The farmer was a warrior who attacked his fields in hand-to-hand combat or commanded them with martial discipline. In using those metaphors

Virgil was recalling the Roman tradition according to which her military excellence rested on the virtues of the hardy Italian peasantry. In one sense the civil wars as they are evoked in *Georgic* 1 may be seen as nothing more than a realization of the metaphors that had earlier characterized the farmer. His "weapons" (*arma*) have become by the slightest of metamorphoses the literal implements of warfare: *curuae rigidum falces conflantur in ensem* ("curved pruning hooks are molded into the unyielding sword," 508). In that context, even the farmer's name takes on a new meaning. *Coloni* (507) was a regular term for "farmer" in the Late Republic. Virgil himself used it earlier in the poem without any hint of a double meaning. In contemporary usage, however, *coloni* also designated settlers, "colonists," who were almost always veterans given land as a kind of severance pay.[18] Often the land they received had been forcibly confiscated from its previous owners as punishment for their opposition in the social or civil wars. Virgil himself has left us the most poignant memories of such settlements in his first and ninth *Eclogues*. Insofar as the civil wars may be seen as a consequence of traditional values, then, they offer a criticism of those values. In the introduction to his treatise on agriculture, Cato observed that farmers make the best soldiers. In *Georgic* 1 Virgil suggests that such a vision of rustic life may not offer a secure alternative to the violent competitiveness of contemporary society.

The brief evocation of the civil wars and the challenges they posed to contemporary Roman society and its leader brings the poem back to the concerns implicit in the introduction. The relationships between poet, farmer, and statesman announced there have continued to determine the argument of the poem to the conclusion of the book. Although the poet has not offered a specific program, he has defined the challenge that confronts the statesman. Images of rustic life at its best identify the quality of individual experience as the ultimate concern of civilization and suggest that the rewards of civilization are to be measured not so much by the accumulation of power or luxuries (Virgil does not mention them) as by opportunities for meaningful occupation, for the exploitation of human potential, and by a happy adaptation to the larger order of which man is a part.

18. E. T. Salmon, *Roman Colonization Under the Republic* (Ithaca 1970) 129, observes that "it was not until 100 [B.C.] and later that provision for veterans became the principal, as distinct from an incidental, aim of colonization." On the character of Republican colonies from Sulla on, see Salmon's ch. 7, "Coloniae Militares" 128-144.

In addition, Virgil has urged an appreciation of the inevitable imperfection of civilization, of the limits to the control that man is capable of exercising over his environment or over himself. In light of the magnitude of the forces with which he must cope, Caesar's heir appears at the end of the book not as a god incarnate, but as a mere youth. The change of attitude toward him need not be explained by speculation about the order of the *Georgics'* composition, by arguing that the conclusion of *Georgic* 1 was written while the civil wars were still in doubt, but that the introduction was written after their end and Caesar's emergence as victor.[19] That change follows from the gradual alteration of perspective that evolves in the course of the book: within the microcosm of human affairs, compared with the helpless rustic, Caesar's powers are indeed of divine magnitude. In light of the cosmic design that comes increasingly to the fore as the argument of the book progresses, the meagerness of Caesar's power becomes more and more apparent. The final prayer that the gods *hunc saltem everso iuuenem succurrere saeclo / ne prohibete* ("not prevent at least this youth from coming to the aid of an age in turmoil," 500-501) is a reminder that Caesar is a mortal and must accept the limitations of mortality.

Within the sphere of his competence, however, another warning applies. According to the analogy between man and the environment, man requires discipline as do the farmer's crops. The statesman must exercise his energy and resourcefulness to order his people as the farmer must exercise his to make his crops fruitful. But Virgil's examination of this aggressive approach to the problem of civilization-cultivation exposed the danger that the exercise of power and resourcefulness may become an end in itself and exceed its immediate goal. The civil wars dramatize the consquences of such excess. The examination of rustic life in *Georgic* 1 exposes the paradox that, just as the struggle to achieve an ordered and productive existence demands the full exertion of human power, it simultaneously demands restraint. That is not to say that energy and resourcefulness are to be abjured—Virgil has demonstrated that they are essential to the work of cultivation—but they are not in themselves sufficient to the challenge facing contemporary society and its young leader. The first need of the new age is a vision of civilization that includes values other than those that led to the present chaos.

19. The argument of Jacques Bayet, "Les premiers *Georgiques* de Virgile," *RPh* 56 (1930) 128-150, 227-247.

CHAPTER III

# Georgic 2

### I

Hactenus aruorum cultus et sidera caeli;
nunc te, Bacche, canam.

So much for cultivation of fields and the heavenly constellations. Now Bacchus, I will sing of you.

At the very outset of *Georgic* 2, Virgil dissociates it vigorously from the previous book and directs attention toward its differences. In the following lines he presents Bacchus as the emblem of a new vision of rustic life, and in his prayer exemplifies the poetic perspective that makes that vision possible. Bacchus embodies the principle of fruitful vitality, and thus abundance, in nature. Images of fullness are prominent in Virgil's brief evocation (4-7):

huc, pater o Lenaee: tuis hic omnia plena
muneribus, tibi pampineo grauidus autumno
floret ager, spumat plenis uindemia labris;
huc, pater o Lenaee, ueni.

Come hither, O Father Lenaeus; here everything is full of your gifts; for you the field is flourishing, heavy with autumn's vines; vats foam, filled to their brims. Come hither, O Father Lenaeus.

In man a further consequence of natural vitality is an exuberance, an overflowing of spirit that expresses itself in the intensity of immediate experience. With his emphatic insistence on the here-and-now,

Virgil acknowledges that experience and accepts the perspective it implies. The introduction to *Georgic* 2 betrays none of *Georgic* 1's expansive concern either with the disorders of contemporary society or with mankind's place in the cosmic order. The comparative brevity of the passage (eight lines as opposed to the forty-two lines of the introduction to *Georgic* 1) gives concrete embodiment to the narrowness of its focus. The poet who invoked a pantheon of divinities and urged Caesar to join him in pity for the farmer now calls on one god, Bacchus, to join him in spontaneous celebration (7-8):

> . . . nudataque musto
> tinge nouo mecum dereptis crura coturnis.

> . . . tear off your buskins and stain your naked calves in the new vintage with me.

Within the narrower limits to which Virgil confines himself here he has achieved a vision of material abundance and spiritual exuberance that escaped him in the larger view of the human condition in the previous book.

In the following passage Virgil turns to the exposition of his subject and begins confidently to elaborate on the theme of vitality and abundance that Bacchus represents (9-12):

> Principio arboribus uaria est natura creandis.
> namque aliae nullis hominum cogentibus ipsae
> sponte sua ueniunt camposque et flumina late
> curua tenet.

> To begin with, nature has varied ways of creating trees. For some, themselves, without human coercion, of their own accord come into being and occupy fields and the winding riverbanks far and wide.

Examples of the spontaneous growth of trees are everywhere. The variety of ways in which they propagate themselves is equally impressive. The great stature and the sanctity of certain trees also provide a measure of nature's power and of the poet's admiration for it: tall chestnut trees and the sacred oak of Jupiter, which Greeks regard as oracular, grow from seed; even the Parnassian bay of Apollo, which furnishes the garlands of poetic and athletic victors, grows from insignificant beginnings to the impressive size of its parent. In *Georgic* 1, Virgil dignified rustic life by appeal to the great divine plan of which it was a part; in *Georgic* 2, divinity seems rather to emerge from the immanent creativity of nature itself.

Still, there is room for human ingenuity: *sunt alii, quos ipse via sibi repperit usus* ("There are other means that experience itself finds out along the way," 22). The variety of human invention is not less than nature's own, and the responsiveness of nature offers ample encouragement to human effort (28-31):

> . . . summumque putator
> haud dubitat terrae referens mandare cacumen.
> quin et caudicibus sectis (mirabile dictu)
> truditur e sicco radix oleagina ligno.

> The pruner does not hesitate to take cuttings from the very tops of trees and entrust them to the earth. Indeed, if he cuts into the trunk of an olive tree (miraculous to tell) an olive root thrusts itself from the dry wood.

Human inventiveness not only augments but actually transforms nature (32-34):

> et saepe alterius ramos impune uidemus
> uertere in alterius, mutatamque insita mala
> ferre pirum et prunis lapidosa rubescere corna.

> and often we see the branches of one tree, without injury, turn into those of another and a pear tree, transformed, bear grafted apples, and hard cornel berries redden on plum trees.

Virgil concludes with enthusiasm (35-37):

> Quare agite o proprios generatim discite cultus,
> agricolae, fructusque feros mollite colendo,
> neu segnes iaceant terrae.

> Wherefore, come, learn the methods of cultivation suitable to each kind, farmers, and soften wild fruits by cultivating them, so that the earth will not lie idle.

Although that exhortation recalls his charge to the plowman in *Georgic* 1—"Therefore, come, let stout bulls turn the eath's rich soil immediately, in the very first months of the year" (1.63-64)—the tone of the two passages contrasts sharply. The urgency of the earlier command is informed by a sense of necessity. It reflects an appreciation of the hard work required to adapt the environment to the restrictive laws of nature. The urgency of the command in *Georgic* 2 is born rather of the confidence that man can do more than adapt to nature; he can improve on it. The tone of the passage expresses a sense of possibility, a spirit of exaltation: *iuuat Ismara Baccho / conserere atque olea magnum uestire Taburnum* ("It is a delight to sow Ismara with Bacchus and to clothe great Taburnus with the olive," 37-38).

Virgil interrupts his exposition briefly to ask for the sympathetic attention of his patron, Maecenas. His appeal is based not so much on the actual character of the subject matter as on the manner in which he intends to approach it. Like the prayer to Bacchus this passage invites comparison with the introduction to the previous book. The address to Maecenas, *tuque ades* (39), is reminiscent of his address to Caesar, *tuque adeo* (1.24). Both men are addressed as superiors by the poet who solicits their support for his efforts. In the context of those similarities, differences between the two passages emerge clearly. The shift from statesman to patron is in keeping with the less ambitious focus of *Georgic* 2. Virgil's undertaking is admittedly difficult (an *inceptum laborem*), but he no longer calls it "audacious." Although he acknowledges Maecenas' contribution to his public reputation, he does not ask him, as he had Caesar, to share a common concern of public importance. The tenor of his remarks is personal rather than political. Within the narrower and more intimate bounds of his relationship with Maecenas, Virgil sustains the spiritual exuberance that characterized the opening passages of the book: *o decus, o famae merito pars maxima nostrae* ("O glory, o greatest part of my fame," 40). The address to Maecenas is an invitation, which is implicitly extended to the wider audience of the poem, to share the poet's enthusiasm, to accept his attitude toward the subject matter of the poem: *pelagoque uolans da uela patenti* ("as you speed on, spread your sails to the open seas," 41).

Although the initial force of Virgil's invitation comes from his own enthusiasm, he offers other encouragement as well (42-44):

> non ego cuncta meis amplecti uersibus opto,
> non, mihi si linguae centum sint oraque centum,
> ferrea uox.

> I do not propose to embrace everything in my verses, no, even if
> I had a hundred tongues and a hundred mouths, an iron voice.

The expression originates in epic. In the *Iliad*, Homer introduced the catalogue of ships that joined the Greek expedition against Troy as follows (*Iliad* 2.488-492):

πληθὺν δ' οὐκ ἂν ἐγὼ μυθήσομαι οὐδ' ὀνομήνω,
οὐδ' εἴ μοι δέκα μὲν γλῶσσαι, δέκα δὲ στόματ' εἶεν,
φωνὴ δ' ἄρρηκτος, χάλκεον δέ μοι ἦτορ ἐνείη,
εἰ μὴ 'Ολυμπιάδες μοῦσαι, Διὸς αἰγιόχοιο
θυγατέρες, μνησαίαθ' ὅσοι ὑπὸ "Ιλιον ἦλθον.

Their number I could neither tell nor name—not even if I had ten tongues and ten mouths and an unbreakable voice and a heart of bronze within, unless the Olympian Muses, daughters of Zeus the aegis bearer, should recall how many came to Ilion.

Homer's statement glorifies his subject by emphasizing its sheer magnitude, which, in conformity to epic norms, he dramatizes in terms suited to the battlefield: numbers and bronze. A variation is found among the fragmentary remains of Ennius' epic, *The Annales*, and presumably fulfills the same function there as it does in the *Iliad*.[1] Virgil deviates from Homer in two significant respects. He resorts to hyperbole, a hundred tongues and mouths instead of ten. Thus he insists on the heroic magnitude of his unheroic subject. In addition, while Homer claims that he can only treat his subject fully because of the Muses' help, Virgil asserts that he will not try to be exhaustive and even suggests that such an effort would be undesirable: it would require a voice of iron, the metal symbolizing mankind's most degenerate age. Whereas Homer welcomed divine assistance toward the fulfillment of his goal, Virgil makes a virtue of his limitations (44-46):

. . . ades et primi lege litoris oram;
in manibus terrae. non hic te carmine ficto
atque per ambages et longa exorsa tenebo.

Join me and skirt the very edge of the shore in the hands of the earth. I will not hold you with fictions and through digressions and long exordia.

---

1. Ennius, *Ann.* 561-562. For a good discussion of the probable history of this image in Latin literature before Virgil and for a careful assessment of the complex evidence for Virgil's own most likely model, see Michael Wigodsky, *Vergil and Early Latin Poetry* (Wiesbaden 1972) = *Hermes* Einzelschriften 24, pp. 52, 98.

What gives Virgil's argument its unique force is a subtle interplay between abundance and containment, emotional exuberance and restraint. He indicates that his subject is virtually inexhaustible and argues for Maecenas' attention on the grounds that he will accept his limitations as a poet and treat his subject economically and directly. His poem is worthy of attention not only because of the magnitude of its subject, but even more because the author will attempt no more than what his poem can effectively contain. Virgil's play with nautical metaphors suggests further that he can claim the unrestrained participation of his audience ("set your sails for the open sea") precisely because he has exercised restraint ("skirt the very edge of the shore"). At the heart of his argument is the idea that expansiveness is possible only within limits. Thus, the brief address to Maecenas serves to elaborate and explicate the perspective that characterized the introduction to *Georgic* 2 and that will, in fact, control the exposition of the entire book. We are thereby encouraged from the outset to regard this book not only as an exposition of arboriculture and viticulture but also as an examination of that point of view which promises abundance in exchange for the containment and focus of human energies, freedom in exchange for restraint.

## II

Virgil returns (47-52) to the exposition of arboriculture with an explicit and concise summary of themes introduced thus far in *Georgic* 2. Against that background he prepares for a further elaboration of rustic life and its implications by reconsidering themes important in *Georgic* 1. Despite the assumption of natural vitality, he affirms the environment's incapacity to realize its full potential for fruitfulness without cultivation. He acknowledges the existence of conflicting forces at work within the environment (53-56) and of a related tendency for fruits to degenerate (57-60). As a consequence he places renewed emphasis on the inescapable necessity for hard work (61-62):

> scilicet omnibus est labor impendendus, et omnes
> cogendae in sulcum ac multa mercede domandae.
>
> Indeed, toil must be expended on all kinds of trees; all must be forced into furrows and tamed at considerable expense.

Finally, he reintroduces the idea of nature's restrictiveness. Different trees respond to different techniques (63-72).

The continued prominence of those and other themes from the previous book contributes to the argument of *Georgic* 2 in several ways. It makes clear that the vision of a spontaneously abundant environment is not to be confused with a pastoral fantasy. Virgil's poem is still a georgic concerned with the possibilities of cultivation and human resourcefulness, not with the possibilities of leisure. Nonetheless, familiar themes are adapted to the new context in which they are presented, for the sense of urgency and constraint accompanying them in *Georgic* 1 is here relieved. Instead of impressing the consequences of failure ("unless you do this . . . alas you will . . . solace your hunger in the woods by shaking acorns from oaks," 1.155-159), Virgil directs attention toward the rewards of success. The economic metaphors in which he expresses the necessity for work (*labor impendendus, multa mercede domandae*) describe an investment that will bring returns not in cash but in fruitfulness (69-72):

> inseritur uero et fetu nucis arbutus horrida,
> et steriles platani malos gessere ualentis,
> castaneae fagos; ornusque incanuit albo
> flore piri glandemque sues fregere sub ulmis.

> But the bristling arbute is grafted with the fruit of the walnut and, by grafting, sterile plane trees have borne hearty apples; chestnuts have borne beech-mast and the mountain ash has grown hoary with the white flower of the pear; under elm trees pigs have crunched acorns.

However, it is not through abundance alone, but through abundance coupled with variety that the potentialities of rustic life achieve their full realization. Although Virgil specifies that different trees respond to different techniques, he soon adds that *Nec modus inserere atque oculos imponere simplex* ("there is not just a single means of grafting and inoculation," 73). And his brief survey of the different techniques and their wonderful results opens up the still larger prospect of nature's own variety (83-84):

> Praeterea genus haud unum nec fortibus ulmis
> nec salici lotoque nec Idaeis cyparissis.

Moreover, there is not just one class either of hardy elms or of willow or lotus or Idaean cypress.

Similarly, one kind of grape clusters on vines in Italy, another on Lesbos. One vine is suited to heavy soils, another to light. And there are different kinds for different tastes. Each has its virtues. Such variety, dependent as it is on different conditions and locales, could be restrictive were it not for the virtually limitless number of alternatives available (103–108):

> sed neque quam multae species nec nomina quae sint
> est numerus, neque enim numero comprendere refert;
> quem qui scire uelit, Libyci uelit aequoris idem
> dicere quam multae Zephyro turbentur harenae
> aut, ubi nauigiis uiolentior incidit Eurus,
> nosse quot Ionii ucniant ad litora fluctus.

But there is no number for their many kinds or names, for there is no profit in comprehending them with a number; the one who would want to know it, would also want to tell how many grains of sand are tossed on the Libyan desert or to know how many Ionian swells come ashore when the violent east wind comes down on ships.

Virgil has returned to the theme of his address to Maecenas and expanded its application. The farmer, like the poet, is faced with a superabundance of material. It would be folly to attempt to master it all. But because of the plethora of alternatives that natural variety offers, such mastery is unnecessary. Thus the assertion, *nec uero terrae ferre omnes omnia possunt* ("nor, to be sure, do all lands bear all things," 109), paradoxically enforces a sense not so much of confinement and limitation as of alternatives and possibilities.

From line 110 Virgil begins to illustrate the regional diversity of the environment. His examples soon lead to an emphasis not simply on the principles of diversity but on its range as well (112–117):

> . . . denique apertos
> Bacchus amat collis, Aquilonem et frigora taxi.
> aspice et extremis domitum cultoribus orbem
> Eoasque domos Arabum pictosque Gelonos:
> diuisae arboribus patriae.

and then Bacchus loves open hills; yew trees love the north wind and cold. And observe the earth's orb subdued by cultivators to its very limits, both the Arabs' houses in the East, and the tatooed Geloni [of the Ukraine]—nations distinguished by their trees.

Almost incidentally a new theme has emerged: the diversity of the civilizations that different regions support. Virgil mentions the tatooed Geloni as if in passing. As his survey of exotic trees progresses, he devotes increasing attention to the people with whom those trees are associated. He remarks upon the groves of India where, he observes, it is impossible to shoot arrows over the tops of the trees, they are so high. And then he adds parenthetically, *et gens illa quidem sumptis non tarda pharetris* ("and indeed that race is not backward when they've picked up their quivers," 125). The citron tree, remarkable for its bitter taste and its deceptive similarity to the bay tree, is closely associated with the Romans' stereotype of the Persians as both treacherous and effeminate; but its fruit serves as an antidote to poison, to bad breath, and to the shortness of breath that accompanies old age (134-135).

There is little here pertaining to the practical concerns of the orchard grower. Rather, Virgil is exploring the implications of abundance and variety for civilization. His attention has shifted from the specific circumstances of the farmer, who is confronted by more possibilities than he can take advantage of, to mankind in general, which is faced with alternative ways of life. In first introducing the general question of how to cope with abundant variety in terms of the poet's or the farmer's specific relationship to his material, Virgil reasserted his position as intermediary between the limited realm of the farmer and the larger concerns of his own audience. In addition, he took the bold step of offering his poem as a concrete embodiment of the very question he is exploring. In the section of the book immediately following (136-176), he restates his response to that question in spatial and nationalistic terms.

Virgil's praise of Italy is more than just a continuation of the demonstration of the earth's diversity, for it asserts not only the uniqueness but also the superiority of this one particular region. The opening lines of the passage define the terms by which Italy will be compared to Eastern nations and her excellence be proven (136-139):

> Sed neque Medorum siluae, ditissima terra,
> nec pulcher Ganges atque auro turbidus Hermus
> laudibus Italiae certent, non Bactra neque Indi
> totaque turiferis Panchaia pinguis harenis.

> But neither the trees of Persia, an exceedingly rich land, nor the beautiful Ganges and the Hermus turbid with gold can compare with Italy's claims to praise, no, not Bactra and all Panchaia, rich in incense-bearing sands.

Later in the passage Virgil will celebrate Italy's fruitfulness (150-154) and her mineral wealth (165-166). Here he merely asserts her superiority with a vague appeal to her *laudibus* ("claims to praise"). In contrast, he acknowledges the East's wealth fully and explicitly: it is, after all, *ditissima terra* ("an exceedingly rich land"). The vagueness of Italy's claims, consequently, seems to suggest that Virgil intends not to advance the hyperbolic argument that Italy has even taller trees and greater riches but rather to urge that her superiority is based on other attributes. Unlike his contemporary, Varro,[2] Virgil, while not belittling the abundance of Italy's fruits and minerals, will base his claims more on differences of quality than on degrees of quantity.

This is borne out in the succeeding lines. Although not yet characterizing Italy in positive terms, Virgil does call attention to specific shortcomings of the East (140-142):

> haec loca non tauri spirantes naribus ignem
> inuertere satis immanis dentibus hydri.
> nec galeis densisque uirum seges horruit hastis.

> These places are not plowed by bulls that breathe fire from their nostrils or sown with the teeth of a huge dragon, nor have their crops bristled with men's helmets and densely packed lances.

As an implicit criticism of the natural environment of the East, of course, those assertions cannot be taken literally, although they do express a general distaste for a world that Romans regarded as bi-

---

2. Cf. *Res Rusticae* 1.2-7 and for later eulogies of Italy in the same tradition, see Dionysius of Halicarnassus, *Ant. Rom.* 1.36-37, and Strabo, *Geography* 6.4.1, p. 286.

zarre and in some way sinister. As metaphorical comments on Eastern peoples and their civilization, they have specific and compelling implications for Virgil's attitude toward Italy and her unique claims to excellence.

The full force of the passage depends on a familiarity with the mythical narrative to which it alludes. The myth is that of Jason's quest for the Golden Fleece, and the relevant portions of it are best preserved to us in Apollonius Rhodius' *Argonautica*. Similarities of imagery suggest that Virgil had Apollonius' account in mind. In any event, the myth was popular and had recently been recalled to the attention of his Roman audience in a Latin version by Varro. Unfortunately, we cannot judge Varro's influence on Virgil because his poem has not survived. According to Apollonius, King Aeetes of Colchis (located on the eastern coast of the Black Sea) possessed the Golden Fleece, but promised it to Jason if he could fulfill certain conditions. Using a pair of bronze bulls that breathed fire, Jason was to plow a field and then sow it with dragon's teeth. The ultimate challenge lay in the fact that armed men, whom Apollonius refers to both as "giants" and as "earthborn," would spring up from the sown teeth and attack Jason. However, with the aid of Aeetes' daughter, the sorceress Medea, Jason prevails. Medea instructs him in rituals, provides him with magic ointments, and tells him how to overcome the giants (*Argonautica* 3.1025-1062). The climactic moment of his struggle comes after he has sown the dragon's teeth (*Argonautica* 3.1354-1363):

οἱ δ' ἤδη κατὰ πᾶσαν ἀνασταχύεσκον ἄρουραν
γηγενέες· φρίξεν δὲ περὶ στιβαροῖς σακέεσσιν
δούρασί τ' ἀμφιγύοις κορύθεσσί τε λαμπομένῃσιν
"Αρηος τέμενος φθισιμβρότου· ἵκετο δ' αἴγλη
νειόθεν Οὔλυμπόνδε δι' ἠέρος ἀστράπτουσα.
ὡς δ' ὁπότ' ἐς γαῖαν πολέος νιφετοῖο πεσόντος
ἂψ ἀπὸ χειμερίης νεφέλας ἐκέδασσαν ἄελλαι
λυγαίῃ ὑπὸ νυκτί, τὰ δ' ἀθρόα πάντ' ἐφαάνθη
τείρεα λαμπετόωντα διὰ κνέφας· ὣς ἄρα τοίγε
λάμπον ἀναλδήσκοντες ὑπὲρ χθονός.

And now over the entire field the earthborn were springing up like grain and the precinct of Ares who destroys men bristled with stout shields and double-pointed spears and flashing helmets, and the gleam from below flashed up to Olympus through the air. And, as when snow has fallen thick to the earth and storm winds have scattered the wintry clouds under murky night, and all the stars have appeared in a body shining through the gloom; so these shone, springing up above the earth.

Jason is clearly outmatched by his opponents, but quantity alone, their size and numbers, means nothing. Pursuant to Medea's instructions he takes up an immense boulder and throws it among them. Immediately they turn on each other and fight for its possession, as Medea had said they would, "like snarling dogs over food" (*Argonautica* 3.1058). While they are thus distracted and occupied in self-destruction, Jason advances on them one at a time and destroys them utterly.

By referring to this myth Virgil has reiterated his earlier suggestion that the superiority of Italy to other lands cannot be measured in the abundance of material resources alone. More important still, he has implicitly portrayed the Italian people and their civilization in terms that contrast sharply not only with the East, but also with the view of human nature and the vision of the Roman civil wars presented in *Georgic* 1. There, in several passages he identified the farmer and the Romans who participated in the civil wars as members of an earthborn race and suggested an affinity between them and the race of giants in particular. In his praise of Italy, Virgil still regards Italians as earthborn, that is, as mortal, but he will assert that in contrast to other peoples they are not related to the giants; they are born rather of the land of Saturn and, consequently, display a more noble character.

The matter of origins is one of considerable importance for understanding the potentialities of Italian civilization. The weakness of the earthborn giants who opposed Jason was the insatiable and undiscriminating avarice that roused them to internecine strife over a sterile boulder. By insisting that the Italian fields do not bristle with spears and helmets and that the Italian people are not born of dragon's teeth, Virgil is in effect rejecting the Roman civil wars as a valid expression of the Italian character. His praise of Italy, then, must be seen as an idealization of Italy and its people, a portrait of them only at their best. The particular virtue of the myth of Jason and of the men sprung from dragon's teeth is that it focuses attention on the character of the Italian people and their civilization without losing sight of the environmental conditions with which that character is intimately connected.

Virgil's first explicit characterization of Italy parallels that of the East in the opening lines of the passage. He begins with a straightforward account of Italy's natural environment, which he then expands into an implicit comment on her people and civilization so that they and their environment are clearly seen as complementary (143-150):

> sed grauidae fruges et Bacchi Massicus umor
> impleuere; tenent oleae armentaque laeta.
> hinc bellator equus campo sese arduus infert,
> hinc albi, Clitumne, greges et maxima taurus
> uictima, saepe tuo perfusi flumine sacro,
> Romanos ad templa deum duxere triumphos.
> hic uer adsiduum atque alienis mensibus aestas:
> bis grauidae pecudes, bis pomis utilis arbos.

> but heavy crops and Campania's Bacchic drink have filled [these places]; olives and rich flocks hold them. From here the war horse strides tall to the field of battle. From here herds of white bulls, the greatest of sacrificial victims, often anointed with your sacred water, Clitumnus, have led Roman triumphs to the temples of the gods. Here there is continual spring and summer in the months not her own. Twice a year flocks give birth; twice, the tree is useful for its fruits.

Virgil has arranged his material for maximum effect. If he had contrasted his description of Italy with the initial survey of Eastern riches (136-139), his argument for Italian superiority would hardly have seemed compelling. By introducing it directly after references to Aeetes' perverted agriculture, he has defined the contrast as one between the exotic and essentially corrupt riches of the East and the wholesome fruitfulness of Italy. Heavy crops of grain and wine are indisputably preferable to the fruits of dragons' teeth. Similarly, the spirited war horse and the gleaming white bulls of Italy are more noble beasts than the fire-breathing bronze bulls of Colchis. As the account of Aeetes' agriculture implies a judgment on Eastern civilization, so the war horse and the sacrificial bulls which ascend to the gods' temples in celebration of Roman victories reflect the piety, valor, and patriotism of the Italians.

What gives coherence to the vision of Italy Virgil presents here, with its emphasis on both natural fruitfulness and martial excellence, and what integrates it with the rest of this book is a sense of focus and containment. Just as the invocation to Bacchus emphasized the intensity and fullness of experience which is sharply focused, so, too, does the initial description of Italy: "these places" (*haec loca*) . . . "from here" (*hinc*) . . . "from here" (*hinc*) . . . "here" (*hic*). Italy is presented as a physical embodiment of the contracted focus that Virgil introduced in the opening lines of this book and within whose boundaries Bacchus' vitality found expression in natural abundance and spiritual exuberance. Likewise Italy is filled with the fruits of nature, and the virile war horse symbolizes the energy of the Italian people. But the energy here is not centrifugal as that manifest in the civil wars. It does not expand ever outward without direction or purpose. It moves out only to turn back again toward its center, to augment rather than to expend the fullness of its source.

In the latter half of his praise Virgil explores more directly and fully the relationship between the Italian landscape and Italian civilization. The cities, harbors, and canals that characterize Italy's civilized accomplishments are presented as the results of the Italians' strenuous engagement with the landscape. "Toil" (*labor*) once again becomes an explicit concern of the poem (155-157):

> adde tot egregias urbes operumque laborem,
> tot congesta manu praeruptis oppida saxis
> fluminaque antiquos subter labentia muros.

Add so many huge cities and products of toil, so many towns built up by hand on mountains of sheer rock and rivers flowing beneath ancient walls.

The ruggedness of the landscape is a perfect complement to the vitality of the people. One commentator on the *Georgics* remarks of lines 156-157: "Note the sense of effort in one line and that of repose in the other, the contrast between *oppida congesta manu* and *antiquos muros*, and the artistic opposition of *praeruptis saxis* with *flumina subter labentia.*"³ The conflict between man and the landscape has been resolved in a lasting harmony, which is further emphasized by the interlocking word order of line 157: it suggests that the timeless rivers have imparted some of their permanence to the ancient walls.

This process of conflict and resolution also controls the description of the Portus Iulius (161-164). The Portus Iulius was an artificial harbor that Caesar's lieutenant, Agrippa, constructed off the Gulf of Puteoli in the vicinity of Baiae and Cumae. After losses sustained in the course of hostilities with the fleet of Sextus Pompey, the son of Pompey the Great and a Republican holdout against the Caesarian forces, the young Caesar needed a protected harbor in which to rebuild and train his navy. In 39 B.C., Agrippa undertook to construct a suitable harbor. He drove a passage through the mole that supported the Via Herculanea across the Lucrine Lake, thus providing access between the lake and the Gulf of Puteoli. He then dredged out the lake and cut a canal inland to the nearby Lake of Avernus, which had been formed by a volcanic crater. His achievement was one of the marvels of contemporary Roman engineering.⁴ Virgil celebrates it along with the natural wonders of the Italian seas and lakes (158-164):

> an mare quod supra memorem, quodque adluit infra?
> anne lacus tantos? te, Lari maxime, teque,
> fluctibus et fremitu adsurgens Benace marino?
> an memorem portus Lucrinoque addita claustra
> atque indignatum magnis stridoribus aequor,
> Iulia qua ponto longe sonat unda refuso
> Tyrrhenusque fretis immittitur aestus Auernis?

Shall I recall the Upper Sea and the Lower or so many lakes? You, great Larius, and you, Benacus, surging with the flow and roar of the sea? Or shall I recall the port and the moles added to the Lucrine and the raging sea that crashes loudly where it is blocked, where Julian waters reverberate far and wide and the tide of the Tyrrhenian Sea is let in through the Straits of Avernus?

---

3. T. E. Page, *P. Vergili Maronis Bucolica et Georgica* (London 1898, reprinted New York 1965), ad 2.156, p. 258.

4. On the construction and archaeology of the Portus Julius, see R. F. Paget, "Portus Julius," *Vergilius* 15 (1969) 25-32.

Perhaps one measure of Virgil's purpose is that he never mentions the military background of the Portus Julius. To do so would be to acknowledge the existence of the civil wars and thus to compromise the idealized civilization Italy is made to represent here.

Instead, he concentrates on the impressive struggle between the Italians and their environment. Man himself creates harbors and even puts up barriers against the sea. The magnitude of that accomplishment is vividly conveyed in the great crashing of the seas against the moles protecting the exposed side of the harbor. The ponderous spondees of *atque indignatum magnis stridoribus* ("and raging, crashes loudly") further dramatize the massiveness of the force that must be subdued. Once again, however, the description concludes on a note of resolution and accommodation: "and the tide of the Tyrrhenian Sea is let in through the Straits (*freta*) of Avernus." There is no longer a clear distinction between nature and artifice, for the "straits" referred to here are Agrippa's canal. The ambiguity of the one word captures and heightens the sense of close interrelation between the Italian people and their landscape, which is implied by the continued shift of focus from the one to the other throughout the passage. By utilizing the vitality of their environment and by responding to its challenges, the Italian people have created a civilization whose order and stability are manifest in the harmony between the monuments of human engineering and the timeless landscape.

The heroic warriors whom Virgil adduces as further examples of excellence introduce a new aspect of the Italians' relation to their country. They do not engage the Italian landscape as do the founders of cities or the builders of harbors and canals. Each of them achieved his reputation by defending Rome against foreign enemies: the Decii against the Latins, Marius against the Cimbri, Camillus against the Gauls, the Scipios against Carthage. It is significant that those heroes are introduced late in the passage, for the previous lines explain their motivation: Italy, its landscape, and its civilized accomplishments provide a focus for their loyalties. It is also significant in terms of contemporary attitudes that the heroes whom Virgil names are all defenders of Italy who, with the exception of the young Caesar, had gained their reputations by 146 B.C. That was the year in which Rome asserted undisputed dominion over the Mediterranean with the annihilation of Carthage in the western sphere and Corinth in the eastern. Pompey's victories against the pirates and in

Asia, and Caesar's in Gaul, equaled those of the other heroes, but Pompey and Caesar had also been major figures in the civil wars. In fact, it would be difficult, if not impossible, to find great Roman generals after 146 who had not been similarly tainted. As the civil wars intensified, Romans of the Late Republic looked back with increasing nostalgia to Rome's early struggles for survival. And there was a tendency to explain her apparent decline as a consequence of expansion. Two basic theories developed.[5] One was that unscrupulous *ambitio* ("campaigning for election"), associated particularly with bribery, and *avaritia* ("greed")—the exact relation of the two varies and is often vague in the Roman tradition—were consequences of exposure to extravagant wealth, particularly of the East. The second theme was that *metus hostilis* ("fear of a foreign enemy") had contributed to domestic harmony by suppressing factional strife, and that the end of *metus hostilis* with Rome's reduction of all serious rivals, especially Carthage, gave rise to increased factionalism and, finally, civil wars. There is ample evidence in Livy's *History* and in the historical writings of Sallust to indicate that both theories of decline were prominent in the minds of Virgil's contemporaries. Both theories are clearly relevant to Virgil's praise of Italy. The first underlies his contrast between Italian wholesomeness and Eastern wealth, and the second controls his selection of heroes.

Such is the context, then, in which Virgil addresses Caesar and urges him against the Parthians (170-173):

. . . et te, maxime Caesar,
qui nunc extremis Asiae iam uictor in oris
imbellem auertis Romanis arcibus Indum.

and you, greatest Caesar, who now, already victorious on the furthest borders of Asia, turn the unwarlike Indian aside from the citadels of Rome.

In keeping with both the argument of the passage and the tradition that lay behind that argument, Caesar is not advised to acquire Parthian territory, that is, to extend the empire. Quite the contrary, even though the Parthians were in fact at the outermost borders of

---

5. The relevant evidence has been collected and discussed by A. W. Lintott, "Imperial Expansion and Moral Decline in the Roman Republic," *Historia* 21 (1972) 626-638, and by D. C. Earl, *The Political Thought of Sallust* (Amsterdam 1961, repr. 1966) 13-15, 51-52, 104-105, and esp. 41-49.

the Roman Empire, they are pictured as threatening the very citadels of Rome. The use of hyperbole expresses the seriousness with which contemporary Romans took the Parthian threat. They had, after all, killed the Roman general Crassus, routed his troops, and captured his legionary standards in 53 B.C. But Virgil's turn of expression also defines the physical limits of his concern. In asking Caesar to defend the citadels of Rome against a potent foreign enemy, Virgil was asking him to recreate the national unity which, in current thought at least, had gradually deteriorated after Roman domination had spread decisively beyond Italy.

The farmer and agriculture are conspicuous for their virtual absence from Virgil's praise of Italy—an absence that is the more striking since the passage celebrates Italy's fruitfulness and occurs within a poem about agriculture and rustic life. The effect of their omission is to emphasize the close relationship between the landscape and other aspects of Italian civilization and, consequently, to enforce the parallels between the work of the farmer and that of laying the foundations of the Italian nation. Both are presented as struggles to control the environment, to impose order on it and to shape it to man's uses. Both are undertakings of large proportions. Both demand effort and discipline. Moreover, the list of heroes from Rome's past raises again the question of the relationship between the farmer and the soldier. In many ways Virgil has reintroduced those tough, energetic qualities that proved ambiguous, at once necessary and potentially destructive, in *Georgic* 1. Just as the new vision of nature and of rustic life in *Georgic* 2 promised to resolve that ambiguity, so does the new vision of Roman civilization expressed in the praise of Italy—and for similar reasons. Italy offers a focus within which to both concentrate and contain the energies that had burst forth destructively in the Roman civil wars.

In the conclusion to his praise of Italy, Virgil calls attention once more to the formative influence of the Italian countryside and, indirectly, to the rustic traditions that were central to the Romans' experience and their perception of it. From his survey of the works and heroes of the Italian peoples he turns to a final, climactic tribute to the land itself, and adds a description of his own role as poet (173-176):

salue, magna parens frugum, Saturnia tellus,

magna uirum: tibi res antiquae laudis et artem
ingredior sanctos ausus recludere fontis,
Ascraeumque cano Romana per oppida carmen.

Hail, great mother of crops, Saturnus' land, great parent of men: for you I undertake matters and skills of ancient renown, I who have dared to open the sacred springs of poetic inspiration. I sing an Ascraean song through Roman towns.

Once again Virgil has offered himself and his poem as examples of the perspective he is describing in *Georgic* 2. Like the builders of Italian civilization, both the humble laborers and the noble heroes, the poet makes Italy the focus of his loyalties and his energies. He goes beyond her borders only to return with his own contribution to her greatness.

Thus far in *Georgic* 2 rustic life has been founded on a general appreciation of natural vitality, abundance, and variety and, consequently, has encouraged a sense of freedom and a confident attitude toward the realization of a good life. The praise of Italy assigns that vision a specific home and gives it a peculiarly local quality. Hereafter, until late in the book, all the places Virgil mentions by name are in Italy: Etruria (193), Tarentum (197), Mantua (199), Capua, and the vicinity of Vesuvius (224-225). At the conclusion of the praise of Italy, the poem returns to the purely rustic aspects of life within this particular region. The general vision that emerged from the first 135 lines of the book is immediately revalidated: there is a great variety of soils and terrains; even terrain of clay or pebbled soil, although difficult, is nonetheless eminently suitable for the olive and betrays its inherent fruitfulness by an abundance of wild olive trees and ground strewn with olives (177-183). Those lines invite comparison with the opening passage of exposition in *Georgic* 1. There, the ambitious farmer was instructed to become acquainted with "what each region bears and what it rejects" (1.53) and was then urged to the hard task of shaping the land to the conditions necessary for successful cultivation (1.65-70). Here, emphasis is on the usefulness and spontaneous fruitfulness even of terrain that is most discouraging to the uninformed eye. The farmer's work consists not so much in shaping the land to his needs as in the easier task of selecting land that is naturally suited to his crops.

## III

Virgil does not stop with a mere restatement of established themes and attitudes. He further elaborates and defines the possibilities of the vision announced in the opening lines of the book. Within the context of a bounteous and varied environment, it is not surprising to find that the aggressive qualities that characterized mankind in *Georgic* 1 are out of place. In surveying the varieties of terrain Italy offers, Virgil mentions *qualem infelix amisit Mantua campum* ("the kind of field that unfortunate Mantua lost," 198). That brief reference is enough to evoke the horrors of confiscation that were characteristic during the bitter turmoil of the Late Republic. Mantua was close to Virgil's own native Andes. In the *Eclogues* he had dramatized the suffering caused by the confiscations (*Eclogues* 1 and 9) and had evoked Mantua and the music of her swans as a specific example (*Eclogue* 9.27–29):

> Vare, tuum nomen, superet modo Mantua nobis,
> Mantua uae miserae nimium uicina Cremonae,
> cantantes sublime ferent ad sidera cycni.

> Varus, your name, if only we may keep Mantua—Mantua, alas, too close to wretched Cremona—your name, Varus, the musical swans will raise on high to the stars.

In *Georgic* 2 Virgil lingers over his description of Mantua in terms that recall the *Eclogues* (197–202):

> saltus et saturi petito longinqua Tarenti,
> et qualem infelix amisit Mantua campum
> pascentem niueos herboso flumine cycnos:
> non liquidi gregibus fontes, non gramina deerunt,
> et quantum longis carpent armenta diebus
> exigua tantum gelidus ros nocte reponet.

> Seek out glades and the distant plains of rich Tarentum, and a field such as ill-fated Mantua lost, where white swans fed on the lush river banks: there will be no lack of fresh springs or grass for the flocks and, however much the herds graze during long days, the cool dew will restore in even a short night.

The reminiscence of the *Eclogues* and the attractiveness of the scene itself add to the sense of loss and by their poignancy condemn the ruthlessness that caused it.

But Virgil's criticism extends beyond the obvious ravages of civil strife. He is concerned here as in the previous book with the fundamental capacity for violence of which civil war is only the most extreme manifestation. The aggressive qualities that characterized the farmer in *Georgic* 1 are as inimical to the vision of *Georgic* 2 as civil war. The lines that follow the nostalgic description of Mantua comment on violence as an aspect of rustic life itself. The best soil for grain crops is generally black, rich, and crumbly. This soil offers conditions naturally which plowing can only achieve in imitation; it is unsurpassed for productivity (203–205). There follows a memorable comparison with land (207–211),

> . . . unde iratus siluam deuexit arator
> et nemora euertit multos ignaua per annos,
> antiquasque domos auium cum stirpibus imis
> eruit; illae altum nidis petiere relictis,
> at rudis enituit impulso uomere campus.
>
> from which an angry plowman hauled off the forest and upturned glens that were unproductive for many years and ripped up the ancient homes of birds from their deepest roots; the birds flew up, leaving their nests behind, but the virgin field was brought to a shine by the force of the plow.

What those lines have described is simply the difficult but creative task of cultivation, of making an unproductive environment productive. In this particular case, however, the act of cultivation has been exposed as a ruthless violation of the landscape. Just as the farmer of *Georgic* 1 was *avarus* or *durus*, so the plowman here is *iratus*, "angry." The adjective may reflect his outrage at good land gone to waste or his frustration at the tedious work of cultivation, but the fate of the birds extends its application to suggest the fundamental alienation of this plowman from his environment. The proximity of the lament for Mantua suggests a particularly damning parallel: the uprooting of people from their ancestral homes was precisely the loss Mantua suffered. The violation of Mantua for political ends and the violation of the birds' homes for agricultural ends reflect each other.

They emerge from Virgil's exposition as two expressions of a common disposition, a common propensity to ruthless aggression that is disruptive in both situations.

That Virgil can here criticize the very quality that appeared essential to the farmer in his hard struggle for a livelihood in *Georgic* 1 is in part a consequence of the stark revelations of the civil wars which concluded that book; it is also a function of the altered perspective of *Georgic* 2: generous abundance and variety make such ruthlessness on the farmer's part seem unnecessary. The angry plowman does succeed in cultivating his land but only by doing positive violence to it, and what he achieves, finally, is only an imitation of conditions already shown to occur naturally.

As the exposition of *Georgic* 2 advances, sympathy with the environment and restraint become dominant aspects of rustic life. Although careful preparation of the soil, for example, continues to be an important part of the farmer's work, as it had been in *Georgic* 1 (43-99), and Virgil does not minimize its difficulty (259-314), now such work is perceived as a cooperative effort of the farmer and his fields (262-264):

> . . . optima putri
>
> arua solo: id uenti curant gelidaeque pruinae
> et labefacta mouens robustus iugera fossor.
>
> The best plow fields have crumbly soil. The winds take care of this and chill frosts and the sturdy hoer who breaks up and loosens the ridges of earth.

The elements themselves assume responsibility for the work: they "take care of" (*curant*) the treatment of the soil, just as the farmer must "take care" in his work. The hoer himself does no more than contribute to a natural process. The sense of happy cooperation implicit in those lines prepares for an appreciation of the similarities between man and his environment (265-272). Like children, young vines are dependent on their "mother" (*matrem*). Detailed instructions concerning the exact disposition of vines and their props with relation to the points of the compass and the winds reveal a youthful vulnerability that is universal: *adeo in teneris consuescere multum est* ("so great is the force of habit in tender things," 272). The farmer is required to exercise the same paternal care for his young vines as for his own children. The basis of human sympathy with the environment has shifted from the sense of a common toughness in *Georgic* 1 to a sense of a common fragility and a corresponding need not for stern discipline but for gentle protectiveness.

This emerging emphasis on the value of restraint and the containment of energy complements the sense of fragility and vulnerability in nature. Virgil makes his argument in an unexpected but particularly effective way. The disposition of the trees that are to support vines should be like an army drawn up in formation (279-284):

> ut saepe ingenti bello cum longa cohortis
> explicuit legio et campo stetit agmen aperto,
> derectaeque acies ac late fluctuat omnis
> aere renidenti tellus, necdum horrida miscent
> proelia, sed dubius mediis Mars errat in armis.
> omnia sint paribus numeris dimensa uiarum.

> as often in a great war when a long legion has deployed its cohorts and the column is marshaled on the open field and the lines are dressed, and far and wide the whole earth shimmers with glinting bronze, and horrid battle has not yet been joined, but Mars, undecided, wanders between the opposed armies. Let all be measured out in equal numbers of rows.

The epic tone of the passage is established clearly in the opening line by the classic simile and the spondees of *ut saepe ingenti bello cum*, which dramatize the weight and substance of the massed forces. And yet the thrust of the simile is to deny traditional epic standards, for it assigns value to a static order, which is antithetical to the actual turmoil of battle and can only be destroyed by it. Virgil acknowledges and reemphasizes the extent of his departure from the epic tradition in the concluding lines of this brief passage (285-287):

> non animum modo uti pascat prospectus inanem,
> sed quia non aliter uiris dabit omnibus aequas
> terra, neque in uacuum poterunt se extendere rami.

> not merely that the prospect may feed a mind without purpose but because only so will the land give equal strength to all and the branches be able to extend themselves into empty space.

At the heart of the simile is a respect for order, stability, and permanence and a conviction that vitality derives from them. Fruitfulness is a result of energy that is contained rather than expended chaotically.

The same idea is restated almost immediately in another memorable image, that of the great oak tree whose roots extend down as deep into the earth as its peak extends up in the sky (293–297):

> ergo non hiemes illam, non flabra neque imbres
> conuellunt: immota manet multosque nepotes,
> multa uirum uoluens durando saecula uincit,
> tum fortis late ramos et bracchia tendens
> huc illuc media ipsa ingentem sustinet umbram.

> Therefore, no storms, no blasts of wind, no rains tear it up: unmoved it remains and by its toughness outlasts many generations, many ages of man; then stretching its strong branches and arms wide, all around from its center it supports great shade.

Like the simile of the legion drawn up for battle, the image of the great oak recalls epic tradition. In *Iliad* 12.131–134 Homer had compared two stalwart Lapiths before the gates of the Greek camp to durable, deep-rooted oaks upon a mountain. Virgil has put the image to new use. In the *Iliad* the steadfastness of the Lapiths was but a complement to the more active and aggressive qualities of the central heroes. The oak tree in *Georgic* 2 prefigures the redefinition of epic values that Virgil will elaborate in the *Aeneid*, where peace, order, and stability replace personal renown and martial valor as the highest good. Within the context of *Georgic* 2 the oak tree symbolizes an alternative to the aggressiveness of the traditional hero rather than a complement to it. The oak that can extend its protective shade precisely because it is firmly rooted to one place is in complete contrast to the expansive but chaotic energy of the rushing chariots that symbolized the civil wars at the conclusion of *Georgic* 1. It is, rather, a perfect emblem for the ideal nation Virgil envisioned in his praise of Italy.

The virtues of restraint and containment implicit in the image of the ordered legion or the oak tree are urged explicitly in subsequent instructions to the viticulturist and are coupled with renewed emphasis on the vulnerability of his crops. A vivid description of a fire raging through an orchard of olive trees and the vines they support reintroduces the theme of natural degeneration (302–314). The viticulturist must not intergraft wild and domestic strains of the olive, for if there should be a fire the wild strains would survive while the superior, domestic strains, being less hardy, would perish. The general problem of degeneration that underlies those instructions and the sudden uncontrollable rush of the fire after it has caught recall the simile in *Georgic* 1 of the boatman who, once he has let up on his oars, is carried off headlong downstream. That simile, however, occurred in a context of earnest exhortations to strive actively against the obstructive powers of nature itself. The passage in *Georgic* 2 occurs within a connected series of prohibitions: *neve . . . neve . . . neve . . . neu . . . nec . . .* (298–315). The danger confronting the farmer of *Georgic* 1 is that he will not be assertive enough to subdue a recalcitrant, often hostile environment. The farmer of *Georgic* 2 must also act, but the danger Virgil chooses to emphasize here is man's own capacity to violate a comparatively generous and friendly environment. The viticulturist himself will create the conditions for degeneration if he joins wild and domestic olives, and it is the shepherd's fire which, if it is not contained, will bring on the degeneration.

Up to now the exposition has been concerned with the general conditions that define the context of the viticulturist's work (the variety of vines, the different kinds of terrain, the inherent fruitfulness of the environment, and so forth) and with the specific preparations (such as the identification of different soils and the disposition of trees to support the vines) that must precede the cultivation of vines. The introduction of instructions on the actual planting of vines (315–345) offers a particularly suitable opportunity to pause and reflect broadly on the vision of rustic life that has emerged in the course of this book, for the various aspects of that vision are epitomized in the temperate seasons required for the nascent vines to flourish. In his celebration of spring, above all, Virgil presents the conditions of rustic life at their most attractive and in such a way as to raise questions about their place in the larger dimensions of the agricultural year and of human experience in general.

Spring is the best time for sowing the vine, for it is the season that most encourages spontaneous growth. Although the description of spring begins and concludes with particular reference to the vine

(315–319, 335), it acknowledges other life as well: this is the season when birds return to the fields, when groves and forests become verdant, when the earth swells and demands seed, when flocks breed and grass sprouts from the earth. The word "all" (*omnis*) reappears in various forms throughout the description: Jupiter, who impregnates the earth, is *omnipotens*; he nourishes "all young" (*omnis fetus*); there is a superabundance of moisture "for all" (*omnibus*); the vine "thrusts out its buds and unfolds its leaves, all of them" (*et frondes explicat omnis*). This emphasis on the promise of abundance and vitality in the delicate vine, of great things in small, of more in less, continues the perspective that governed the invocations to Bacchus and Maecenas at the opening of *Georgic* 2.

It is presented here as a manifestation of divine powers, a consequence of the *hieros gamos*, the "sacred marriage" between the sky father and the earth mother. Spring is the time when (325–327)

> . . . pater omnipotens fecundis imbribus Aether
> coniugis in gremium laetae descendit, et omnis
> magnus alit magno commixtus corpore fetus.
>
> father omnipotent, the sky, with fruitful showers comes down into the womb of his joyful wife, in his greatness joins with her great body and nourishes all young.

The myth of the sacred marriage had a long and varied tradition among Virgil's literary predecessors, but Virgil's own version of it is specifically suited to the context of *Georgic* 2. The earliest literary allusion to the myth occurs in Homer, *Iliad* 14.346–351. Homer pictures the bed of Zeus and Hera burgeoning with flowers and plants when the two gods have intercourse. The scene preserves Zeus' prehistoric identification with a sky god and reflects the ancient belief that the sky and the earth were divine beings whose literal copulation is the cause of all generation in the natural environment. Such a view was already obsolete, perhaps as early as Homer himself. Nonetheless, the idea of the sacred marriage persisted as a valuable literary resource and was exploited effectively by Aeschylus, for example, to dramatize the powers of the Olympian gods and mankind's dependence on them.[6] Conversely, Lucretius,

---

6. A. Nauck, *Tragicorum Graecorum Fragmenta Supplementum adiecit Bruno Snell* (Hildesheim 1964), fr. *Danaid* 44, p. 16.

whose influence can be traced throughout the *Georgics*, reduced the sacred marriage to a transparent metaphor for the purely mechanistic processes of the universe in *De Rerum Natura* (1.250–253):

postremo pereunt imbres, ubi eos pater aether
in gremium matris terrai praecipitavit;
at nitidae surgunt fruges ramique virescunt
arboribus, crescunt ipsae fetuque gravantur.

Finally, the rains end when father air has precipitated them into the womb of mother earth; but gleaming crops spring up, boughs become green on trees, which themselves grow and become heavy with fruit.

Virgil's account clearly owes something to both extremes of the tradition but cannot be fully identified with either. Instead of Lucretius' perfunctory "father air" (*pater aether*), Virgil introduces the divine father as "omnipotent" and presents "fruitful rains" (*fecundis imbribus*) as an attribute of the god rather than as a distinct entity. Only then does he identify the god with the sky: *pater omnipotens fecundis imbribus Aether* (325). Lucretius undercuts the god's role by describing his action with the harshly impersonal and prosaic "precipitated" (*praecipitavit*). Virgil's god "comes down into the womb" of the earth (*in gremium . . . descendit*), and the actual process of impregnation is presented as a literal joining of bodies in intercourse (*magno commixtus corpore*). However, if Virgil does not reduce the sacred marriage to an intentionally transparent metaphor as Lucretius does, neither does he use it to express the obsolete idea that natural fruitfulness is a product of literal intercourse between two anthropomorphic deities. In Virgil's account the sacred marriage is prefigured in the earth's own swelling and demand for seed: *terrae et genitalia semina poscunt* ("the lands swell and demand generative seeds," 324). Similarly, the natural processes of creation are described in sexual metaphor: the nourishing field *parturit* ("gives birth," 330); plowlands *laxant arua sinus* ("loose their loins," 331). The sacred marriage is not just a metaphor. It does exist, but inseparably from the natural processes of generation. The role of the sacred marriage in this description of spring reaffirms an important aspect of rustic life as it has been presented in *Georgic* 2: mankind lives in a world where divinity is immanent not in a harsh order of nature or a grand cosmic design but in the creative vitality of his immediate environment itself. The special virtue of the sacred marriage theme in Virgil's praise of spring is that it provides a fitting emblem for the vision of a natural environment in which the conditions for awesome creativity are the gentleness and cooperation of the elements.

In fact, Virgil does make the dramatic fruitfulness of spring a consequence as much of the restraint and containment of natural energies as of inherent vitality. He frames his celebration of spring's creativity with descriptions of the extreme conditions that are inimical to nascent life. The passage begins with a prohibition against sowing the vine in winter, when the frozen hardness of the ground makes it impossible for seeds to take root (315-318). Conversely, the ideal times for sowing are characterized at first chiefly by their freedom from destructive conditions. They are the spring when the stork comes to prey on long snakes or *autumni sub frigora, cum rapidus Sol / nondum hiemem contingit equis, iam praeterit aestas* ("at the first chill of fall, when fierce Sun has not yet touched winter with his horses, the heat of summer has already passed," 321-322). Spring itself enjoys *Zephyrique tepentibus auris* ("the tepid breezes of the west wind," 330) and an abundance of *tener umor* ("gentle moisture," 331). Under such conditions the tenderness of new life is safe: *inque nouos soles audent se gramina tuto / credere* ("grasses dare entrust themselves safely to mild suns," 332-333). The assertion that *nec metuit surgentis pampinus Austros / aut actum caelo magnis Aquilonibus imbrem* ("the vine shoot does not fear either rising south winds or rain driven from the sky by great north winds," 333-334) leads back to the beginning of the passage, to the vine and the harsh conditions that it cannot sustain and in spring need not fear (315-322). A final line celebrates the union of vitality and gentleness in the luxuriant growth of the vine's delicate foliage: *sed trudit gemmas et frondes explicat omnis* ("but it thrusts out its buds and unfolds its leaves, all of them," 335).

Virgil has no higher praise for spring than to suggest that it recalls the first burgeoning of life on earth, a comparison that does more than elevate his conception of spring. By attributing the high point of the earth's fruitfulness to the conditions that characterize spring, it suggests the possibility of a basis in nature for a civilization very different from that offered in *Georgic* 1 (2.336-345):

non alios prima crescentis origine mundi
inluxisse dies aliumue habuisse tenorem
crediderim: uer illud erat, uer magnus agebat
orbis et hibernis parcebant flatibus Euri,
cum primae lucem pecudes hausere, uirumque
terrea progenies duris caput extulit aruis,
immissaeque ferae siluis et sidera caelo.
nec res hunc tenerae possent perferre laborem,
si non tanta quies iret frigusque caloremque
inter, et exciperet caeli indulgentia terras.

No different, I should think, were the growing days that dawned at the first beginning of the world, nor did they have any different tenor: *that* was spring; the great globe was living its spring, and the east wind withheld its winter gusts, when the first flocks drank in the light and man, progeny of the earth, raised his head from the hard fields, and wild beasts were released into the forests and stars into the heavens. Tender things would not be able to endure such labor, if there were not such calm between cold and heat, and heaven's indulgence did not greet the lands.

Then, as in the seasonal spring, nascent life was delicate and the extraordinary fruitfulness of the time was the result of the unequaled mildness of the weather.

Virgil's analogy between the mildness of spring and the mildness that made possible the first life on earth, as obvious an idea as it may seem, was quite original and the more striking for that fact. Not all contemporary speculation even regarded life as born from the earth. The most popular philosophy at Rome, Stoicism, taught that life, at least in its highest forms, had descended to the earth from the more rarefied and pure regions of the heavens.[7] The idea that the earth was the "mother" of life, of course, was prevalent in the Greek scientific tradition, but its most prominent Roman exponent was Lucretius, whose version of life's first appearance on earth is significantly different from Virgil's. Lucretius' version was influenced

---

7. Cicero, *DND* 2, 18. The various elements of the Ionian and Eleatic philosophers also continued to hold an important place in men's speculations about the nature of life as can be seen, for example, not only from the passage cited above but also in Vitruvius' discussion of the effects of climate on humans, 6.1.

by his belief in the continual process of birth, decay, and new birth that is caused by the never-ending coming together and separating of atoms throughout the universe. The period of creation is the highest point in that cycle and the fullest expression of nature's great powers.

Describing the first appearance of animal life, for example, he says (*DRN* 5.818–825):

> at novitas mundi nec frigora dura ciebat
> nec nimios aestus nec magnis viribus auras.
> omnia enim pariter crescunt et robora sumunt.
>     Quare etiam atque etiam maternum nomen adepta
> terra tenet merito, quoniam genus ipsa creavit
> humanum atque animal prope certo tempore fudit
> omne quod in magnis bacchatur montibu' passim,
> aeriasque simul volucris variantibu' formis.

But the newness of the world brought forth neither hard cold nor too great heat nor winds of great force, for all things equally grow and take strength. Wherefore again and again having acquired the name "mother," the earth holds it deservedly, since she herself created the race of mankind and almost at a fixed moment poured forth every animal that revels in bacchic frenzy everywhere in the great mountains and simultaneously the birds of the air in their varied shapes.

Lucretius, like Virgil, remarks on the mildness of the weather. For him, however, that mildness is not a condition of the earth's great fruitfulness, but simply a result of the fact that all things, inanimate as well as animate, follow the same cycle of birth, growth, senescence, and, finally, death. For Lucretius the reason for the flourishing of new life is to be found rather in nature's awe-inspiring vitality. The earth itself *creavit*, "created" life, and *fudit*, "poured it forth." Lucretius impresses on us both the intensity and the scope of her creative power: new animals express their energies in bacchic-like revels; they fill the countryside. In contrast, Virgil's emphasis on both the frailty of new life and nature's mildness stand out with striking clarity.

The place of mankind in Virgil's brief description of the origins of life also commands attention. Lucretius, in keeping with his idea of the cycle of birth, decay, and new birth, argues the comparative hardness of the first men (*DRN* 5.925-930):

> At genus humanum multo fuit illud in arvis
> durius, ut decuit, tellus quod dura creasset,
> et maioribus et solidis magis ossibus intus
> fundatum, validis aptum per viscera nervis,
> nec facile ex aestu nec frigore quod caperetur
> nec novitate cibi nec labi corporis ulla.

But that race of men was much harder in the fields, as was fitting, inasmuch as the hard earth created it, and it was constructed on greater and more solid bones within, fastened throughout its viscera with strong sinews, not something easily harmed by heat or cold or the newness of diet or any wasting away of the body.

Virgil, too, when referring to the origins of civilization in *Georgic* 1.60-63, described men as a *durum genus*, a "hard race," equipped with the physical and spiritual toughness to deal with an environment bound by nature's restrictive laws. Now, however, mankind is not likened to the hard earth, but contrasted to it. His emergence from the *duris aruis*, "hard fields," is part of Virgil's tribute to the extraordinarily mild conditions that made such birth possible. Mankind is included among the *res tenerae*, "tender things," that could only have flourished when the winds "spared their wintry gusts" and the heavens extended their "indulgence." Man is thus shown to be dependent on the very restraint with which Virgil has been urging the farmer to treat his environment throughout this book. According to this account of the origins of life, man and nature complement each other in a way that seems to affirm the vision of a civilization based not, as in *Georgic* 1, on the aggressive, potentially chaotic expenditure of energy, but rather on the ideal of containment and restraint that has been developed in *Georgic* 2.

## IV

At the same time that Virgil's praise of spring offers an inspiring affirmation of that ideal, it also undercuts it. For the passage calls attention to the impermanence of spring and of the conditions that distinguish it. The brief description of the "spring of the world" in *Georgic* 1.60–63, when nature imposed her laws and mankind was born from Deucalion's stones, had in common with Lucretius an emphasis on man's hardness, but differed fundamentally from his version in seeing the conditions of that remote past as permanent aspects of reality. Both the complexity and difficulty of the farmer's yearly springtime duties and the toughness he brought to them were conditions that had been fixed for all time. In *Georgic* 2, although Virgil disagrees with Lucretius about the nature of the origins of life on earth, he agrees with him in seeing them as belonging to a remote past. He introduces his description of that epoch with *crediderim*. By using the subjunctive mood he qualifies his belief: "I should have thought," "I am tempted to believe." The tentativeness of his assertion indicates an event about which the poet feels that he can only speculate. Likewise, there is also a suggestion that that remote time was in fact of short duration, for Virgil locates it between extremes of hot and cold whose duration is stressed by the rhetorical disposition of terms in the poetic line. The words *frigusque caloremque* conclude one of Virgil's rare hypermetric lines. Their consequent tendency to spill out into the next line is reinforced not only by the elision of the extra final syllable (*-que*) with the first word of the next line (*inter*) but also by the enjambment of the two lines which the postponement of the preposition, *inter*, requires.

The period of the earth's first fruitfulness, therefore, was little more than a brief respite from the extremes of hot and cold. Because they are dominant, it is their harshness more than the mildness of spring that must determine the nature of civilization. Lucretius' view of nature's cycle and of the earth's place in it led him to the conclusion that mankind along with the rest of creation had become softened and less vigorous with time. The reverse is implicit in Virgil's praise of spring: if conditions were uniquely temperate in the past, now, the inference is, they no longer are so in the same degree. It is true that the period of the earth's first fruitfulness is recalled each spring, but spring itself, like autumn, comprises only the briefest of moments between the cold of winter and the heat of summer.

In making the relation of fruitful abundance to restraint and the containment of energies the distinguishing aspect of the world at its best—in its period of first fruitfulness and in spring—Virgil calls attention to the highly selective view of reality on which the attractive vision of *Georgic* 2 is based. Of course, his choice of subjects and examples has been carefully selected throughout the book, but until now we have not been invited to take note of that fact or to reflect on its implications. Virgil was able to sustain his vision of Italy's unique excellence only by appealing to those moments in the past when Italy was at its best. The struggles between the orders, the Social War, and the civil wars of his own day were all passed over in silence. No effort was made to explain either their occurrence in history or their omission from his description of Italy. Similarly, Italy was described as a land of *uer adsiduum* ("continual spring," 149). In emphasizing the uniqueness of spring, Virgil casts doubt on the universality of the conditions that distinguish it. For the first time in *Georgic* 2 a question has been raised whether the containment of energies that has been made to characterize Italy, rustic life, and nature at their best can be sustained in the world as we know it, a world where even in Italy spring is not really perpetual.

Those implicit reservations are acknowledged and elaborated in the subsequent exposition. An abrupt lowering of tone, *Quod superest* ("For the rest," 346), signals a resumption of instructions to the viticulturist and a dramatic return to the world view of *Georgic* 1. Directly, the viticulturist is ordered to scatter rich dung over his fields, *sparge fimo pingui* (347), just as in the previous book the plowman was instructed not to let a misplaced fastidiousness prevent him from covering his fields with rich dung: *ne saturare fimo pingui pudeat* (1.80). The changing requirements of the vine in progressive stages of its growth lead back to a renewed sense of the toughness of nature and of a corresponding toughness in man. Although the farmer must exercise restraint when vines are young (362-366), he must nonetheless be prepared to impose a ruthless discipline upon them as they reach maturity (367-370):

inde ubi iam ualidis amplexae stirpibus ulmos
exierint, tum stringe comas, tum bracchia tonde
(ante reformidant ferrum), tum denique dura
exerce imperia et ramos compesce fluentis.

When they have embraced the elms with their strong stalks and have sprung up, then trim their hair; then cut back their limbs

144    Virgil's *Georgics*

(before this they fear iron); then, finally, exercise a hard command and check their flowing branches.

The metaphors "hair" and "limbs" are conventional, but they are metaphors, nonetheless, and the comparison with human beings is reinforced by personification elsewhere in the passage. Consequently, the farmer's pruning, however necessary, is made to seem unexpectedly ruthless—the more so as it is in such sharp contrast to the need for gentleness and restraint, which had been urged immediately before.

For the first time, too, we learn that even in the mildest season of the year, when the vine is still young, there are degenerative forces at work that must be opposed. In a passage reminiscent of *Georgic* 1.118–120, where Virgil called attention to the unexpected and troublesome depredations of geese and cranes, he warns against the ravages of wild oxen, goats, and sheep (371–379). Those observations do not lead here, as in the previous book, to an excursus on the purpose of the natural order and its implication for mankind. They lead rather to the description of the rites by which Bacchus is appeased for the damage done to his vine. The sacrifice of a goat is the occasion for relaxation in soft fields, for games and extemporaneous performances which Virgil suggests were the origins not only of Greek drama but of the raucous Italian farces, as well (382–386):

> praemiaque ingeniis pagos et compita circum
> Thesidae posuere, . . .
> . . . . . . . . . . .
> nec non Ausonii, Troia gens missa, coloni
> uersibus incomptis ludunt risuque soluto.

The descendants of Theseus set prizes for the display of talent around the villages and crossroads, . . . so also the Ausonian settlers, a race sent from Troy, make play with unpolished verses and uninhibited laughter.

The last line brings us back to the promise of joyous abandon made in the invitation to Bacchus to join the pressing of the vintage which introduced this book of the *Georgics*. Such carefree release, however, no longer represents the essence of rustic experience as we had initially been led to hope. Its place in the farmer's life is now shown to be the same as that of the ambarvalia which Virgil described in *Georgic* 1.337-350. That rite, also, culminated in spirited celebration, in *motus incompositos* ("unpolished dances"), but it represented only a brief respite from the more burdensome and confining demands of the farmer's occupation.

In fact, immediately after the description of those rites of Bacchus, diction characteristic of the harsh struggle depicted in *Georgic* 1 reemerges, this time in unparalleled concentration (397-399):

> Est etiam ille labor curandis uitibus alter,
> cui numquam exhausti satis est: namque omne quotannis
> terque quaterque solum scindendum.

> There is this additional labor in caring for vines of which there is no end: for every year the soil must be broken three and four times.

And (401):

> . . . redit agricolis labor actus in orbem.

> The farmers' labor comes back to them full circle.

And (405-406):

> iam tum acer curas uenientem extendit in annum
> rusticus.

> Right then the keen rustic extends his care into the coming year.

And (410-412):

> . . . bis uitibus ingruit umbra,
> bis segetem densis obducunt sentibus herbae;
> durus uterque labor.

> twice shade attacks the vines, twice weeds with their thick brush obstruct the crop; each is a hard task.

And (415):

> . . . incultique exercet cura salicti.

> the care of uncultivated willow thickets also exercises a claim.

The discussion of viticulture concludes with an observation, again reminiscent of passages in *Georgic* 1 (416-419):

> iam uinctae uites, iam falcem arbusta reponunt,
> iam canit effectos extremus uinitor antes;
> sollicitanda tamen tellus puluisque mouendus
> et iam maturis metuendus Iuppiter uuis.

> Now the vines have been bound, now the trees put aside the pruning hook, now the last vine dresser sings that his rows are finished; nonetheless, the earth must be stirred up, the dust moved, and now the mature clusters of grapes must look out for Jupiter.

As in *Georgic* 1.118-121 and 299-310, we are advised that even after the farmer has seen to the immediate needs of his crop, there is always more to do and new dangers to anticipate. Viticulture has failed to provide the basis for an alternative to the vision of civilization presented in the first book of the *Georgics*. Despite the initial promise of *Georgic* 2, this aspect of agriculture has, rather, led back to conditions that demand the same relentless, often aggressive, and ultimately uncontrollable energies as those that achieved their fullest realization in the Roman civil wars.

Abruptly, then, our attention is directed back to the other, now apparently more hopeful, alternative of *Georgic* 2, arboriculture. When Virgil does return again to the subject of the vine, it is not to recall its virtues but to reject it as unworthy (454-457):

> quid memorandum aeque Baccheia dona tulerunt?
> Bacchus et ad culpam causas dedit; ille furentis
> Centauros leto domuit, Rhoecumque Pholumque
> et magno Hylaeum Lapithis cratere minantem.

> What have Bacchus' gifts borne so worthy of memory? Bacchus has even given cause for reproach; he tamed the raging Centaurs with death—Rhoecus and Pholus and Hylaeus who threatened the Lapiths with a great wine bowl.

The centaurs—half men, half beasts—were traditionally portrayed in ancient literature as unrefined and violent. Their drunken brawls epitomized the passions and energies that threatened civilization. In particular, the battle that followed their drunken attack on the Lapiths at a wedding celebration was presented as an archetypical conflict between untamed bestiality and civilization.[8] Virgil's reference to that battle here constitutes a final and irrevocable rejection of viticulture both as an alternative to the social chaos of his own day and as the basis for the vision of a civilized existence of easy abundance and order.

Arboriculture, on the other hand, still seems to offer a hopeful alternative and recalls us to the promise of ease and abundance with which *Georgic* 2 began: *Contra non ulla est oleis cultura* ("By contrast [with the vine] olive trees require no cultivation at all," 420); *ipsa . . . tellus* ("the earth itself") provides new-sown crops with moisture (423-424). In fact, the olive does require some work (2.423-424) but very little, and the result is a harvest that is not only rich but consonant with peace: *hoc pinguem et placitam Paci nutritor oliuam* ("therefore, nourish the olive, fertile and pleasing to Peace," 425). As the argument expands to consider other kinds of trees besides the olive (430-453), we are reminded again of nature's spontaneous fruitfulness and her variety. At the beginning of *Georgic* 2, Virgil stressed variety by enumerating different kinds of trees and by emphasizing the dramatic possibilities of such techniques as ingrafting. No longer concerned primarily with fruit trees, he now points out the varied uses of different kinds of wood.

That shift of focus, although slight, is significant, for it places arboriculture in an entirely new perspective. In *Georgic* 1, the exposition looked beyond the immediate topic of cultivating cereal crops to the varied activities of the traditional, largely self-sufficient peasant farmer; but few statements invited us to view the farmer as part of a larger society. Although the exposition of farming revealed potentials, both creative and destructive, that might be realized in the development of civilization, farming itself was contrasted with the society that created Rome's civil wars and drove the farmer from the fields. In *Georgic* 2 Virgil has discussed specific kinds of agricultural work without reference either to a larger society of which the farmer is a part or even to the farmer's life as a whole. The result has been that single specialized activities came to suggest an entire way of life

---

8. Centaurs are cited as exemplars of brutishness and the disastrous effects of too much wine as early as Homer, *Il.* 1.263-268; 2.742; and especially *Od.* 21.293-304. The battle between the Centaurs and Lapiths was thought significant enough to be the subject of the relief on the west pediment of the temple of Zeus at Olympia.

and, even more important, to suggest that relationship between man and nature which determines the essential character of civilization.

In *Georgic* 2.440-453 examples of the usefulness of trees call attention to the whole of which arboriculture is but a part. We find that trees provide fodder and shade for livestock and material for fences, housing, utensils, beehives. They also provide the material for ships, spearshafts, and bows. For the first time in *Georgic* 2 our attention is called to the fact that arboriculture is but one aspect of the farmer's work and, further, that the farmer himself is not entirely independent of a larger society—a society characterized by warfare and navigation, the most suspect of civilized activities. As a result, it is no longer clear to what extent the hopeful vision inspired by the study of arboriculture can in fact be realized or sustained in actual practice. Can we be confident that the farmer's work as arboriculturist, rather than his other activities or his relationship with society, determines the essential character of his way of life? Or, to put it another way, can a perspective that restricts itself narrowly to certain aspects of life provide a reliable guide to the true nature and possibilities of civilization?

## V

That question is addressed indirectly in the dramatic final section of *Georgic* 2. Exposition of specific kinds of farming gives way to a celebration of the excellence of rustic life in general. This passage not only sums up but goes far beyond the themes of ease and abundance which have been central to the development of the exposition thus far. Contrast between urban and rustic life leads to increasing emphasis on spiritual disposition rather than material prosperity. More specifically, disparagement of the frenetically active life in the city leads to an appreciation of the pleasures of a calmly reflective existence and, then, to the suggestion that those pleasures are inherent in rustic life itself. The hopefulness of this passage, however, is first questioned and finally undercut by a growing sense that it represents an ideal that in actuality was never accessible to mankind.

An enthusiastic affirmation of the security, ease, and prosperity that farmers enjoy begins this section of the book (458-460):

O fortunatos nimium, sua si bona norint,
agricolas! quibus ipsa procul discordibus armis
fundit humo facilem uictum iustissima tellus.

O farmers, too fortunate, if they but recognized their own wealth. For them the earth itself, far from the weapons of civil war, pours forth an easy livelihood, the earth most just.

It is indicative of how overpowering the experience of the Roman civil wars was and of how central to Virgil's own interest in the possibilities of rustic life that he should make remoteness from those conflicts the first condition of the farmers' good fortune. The fact that they are physically removed from civil disorders, moreover, is not the result of mere geographical accident. Postponement of *iustissima tellus*, subject of the relative clause of line 459, to the end of the following line emphasizes the idea that the farmers' prosperity reflects an essentially well-ordered existence. From the first it is suggested that ease and prosperity, the most superficial requirements of a good life, are dependent on other more fundamental virtues of rustic life.

Virgil develops that idea further by suggesting that the extravagant luxury to be found in the city is fundamentally unsatisfying. Thus, the conventional assemblage of clients at the home of their wealthy and influential patron becomes an indictment of social corruption: the doors of the patron's house are "haughty" (*superbis*, 461); the crowd of clients, a "fluid mass" (*undam*, 462) which the house "vomits up" (*uomet*, 462). The effect of inlaid doorposts, of gold-embroidered clothing, and of imported statues is offset by the vacuousness of those who "gawk" (*inhiant*) at them (463–464); wool is not dyed but "tainted" (*fucatur*, 465), and Eastern dye is called "poison" (*ueneno*, 465); olive oil is "corrupted" (*corrumpitur*, 466) by the addition of cinnamon. If Virgil did not explain his antipathy to the pursuit and conspicuous display of wealth as practiced in the cities of his age, it is because he did not need to. The belief that luxury was destructive to morals and public order was already well established. As early as the mid-second-century B.C., Cato the Elder had forged a successful political career and a lasting reputation from attacks on competition for wealth and political power, and from appeals for the return to a simpler and more austere past. With growing disillusionment concerning the Republic and with the increasing influence of Hellenistic philosophies, the purely private disadvantages of the pursuit of wealth and status were also stressed. Horace, for example, in his first *Satire* argues that competition for wealth and power is symptomatic of a failure to appreciate the true goods in life and leads only to frustration and anxiety (*Satire* 1.1, 108-119):

> illuc, unde abii, redeo, qui nemo, ut avarus,
> se probet ac potius laudet diversa sequentis,
> quodque aliena capella gerat distentius uber,
> tabescat neque se maiori pauperiorum
> turbae conparet, hunc atque hunc superare laboret.
> sic festinanti semper locupletior obstat,
> ut, cum carceribus missos rapit ungula currus,
> instat equis auriga suos vincentibus, illum
> praeteritum temnens extremos inter euntem.
> inde fit, ut raro, qui se vixisse beatum
> dicat et exacto contentus tempore vita
> cedat uti conviva satur, reperire queamus.

I return to where I began, how no one—no greedy person—approves of himself but praises rather those who pursue different goals, and because someone else's goat has a more bulging udder, wastes away, and because he does not compare himself to the greater crowd of those who are poorer, he labors to surpass first this man, then that one. So as he hurries on, there is always someone richer in his way, just as when horses' hooves wrench the chariots from open starting gates, the driver presses after those who are beating his own team, with no thought for the one that has been left behind at the back of the field. So it happens that rarely are we able to find one who says that he has lived well and when his time is up leaves life content, like a dinner guest who has eaten his fill.

In the context of such criticisms, Virgil's disapproving survey of urban luxury would have been understood as an attack on the perversion of values that leads to the misuse of wealth, as well as on luxury per se. Impatient of the simple pleasures at hand, the ambitious and greedy pass them over or spoil them by the addition of ever more farfetched and artificial effects—just as they spoil the taste of pure olive oil by the addition of cinnamon. Virgil's choice of examples, then, signals a general confusion of values and a consequent restlessness of spirit as the basic weaknesses of urban society.

In contrast, the essential virtue of rustic life appears more clearly to reside not in the wealth but in the serenity available to the farmer. The farmer enjoys *secura quies* ("carefree calm," 467). The earth itself contributes to that condition (467-471):

> . . . et nescia fallere uita,
> diues opum uariarum, at latis otia fundis,
> speluncae uiuique lacus, at frigida tempe
> mugitusque boum mollesque sub arbore somni
> non absunt; illic saltus ac lustra ferarum.

> [But for the farmer] a livelihood that does not know how to deceive, a wealth of varied resources, leisure on broad farmlands, caves, natural lakes, cool vales, the lowing of cattle and light naps beneath a tree—those are not lacking; there are glades there and the haunts of wild animals.

Of course, the farmer's carefree calm would be impossible without the earth's bounty and the assurance of a livelihood. But beyond that, the earth offers immediate and simple pleasures. Its wealth is not contrived but, rather, ubiquitous and inherently satisfying. It does not depend on the envy of others for its value.

Equally important to the farmer's serenity are the values his way of life instills (472-474):

> et patiens operum exiguoque adsueta iuuentus,
> sacra deum sanctique patres; extrema per illos
> Iustitia excedens terris uestigia fecit.

> [In the countryside are] also a youth patient of work and accustomed to little, the sacred rites of the gods, hallowed ancestors; among those people Justice, departing from the earth, left her last traces.

It is because rustics are imbued from youth with a willingness to work that they are beneficiaries of nature's bounty, because they have learned to contain their ambitions and their appetites that they find the simple pleasures of the countryside satisfying. They are embodiments, then, of the distinctive perspective that has been the subject of Virgil's attention throughout this book and whose value they seem to confirm by the attractiveness of their example.

The vision of rustic life that Virgil epitomized in the seventeen lines since his first exclamation at the farmer's good fortune in line 458, inasmuch as it is fundamentally different from that which he elaborated in the theodicy passage of *Georgic* 1 (118-159), leads to a very different judgment about the nature of the good life. In *Georgic* 1 Virgil argued that the difficulty of rustic life is its greatest virtue, that Jupiter made the farmer's work necessary because it requires man to shake off the torpor of idleness and to develop his human capabilities. In the celebration of rustic life that concludes *Georgic* 2, although Virgil places value on the industry of the farmer, he emphasizes, as he has throughout most of this book, the spontaneous fruitfulness of the earth and the bounty of her produce. Rustic life, in fact, seems to approximate that very Golden Age whose shortcomings Jupiter sought to remedy when he introduced the necessity for work.

The two ideals that inform the theodicy passage of *Georgic* 1 and the praise of rustic life in *Georgic* 2 may be characterized in general terms as active and contemplative, respectively. Thus, in *Georgic* 1, Virgil exemplifies the success of Jupiter's theodicy by pointing to the accelerating discovery of the *artes*. The rustic ideal he envisions at the conclusion to *Georgic* 2 inspires him to affirm his own intensely personal attraction to the life of philosophical speculation (475-489):

> Me uero primum dulces ante omnia Musae,
> quarum sacra fero ingenti percussus amore,
> accipiant caelique uias et sidera monstrent,
> defectus solis uarios lunaeque labores;
> unde tremor terris, qua ui maria alta tumescant
> obicibus ruptis rursusque in se ipsa residant,
> quid tantum Oceano properent se tingere soles
> hiberni, vel quae tardis mora noctibus obstet.
> sin has ne possim naturae accedere partis
> frigidus obstiterit circum praecordia sanguis,
> rura mihi et rigui placeant in uallibus amnes,
> flumina amem siluasque inglorius. o ubi campi
> Spercheosque et uirginibus bacchata Lacaenis
> Taygeta! o qui me gelidis conuallibus Haemi
> sistat, et ingenti ramorum protegat umbra!

But for my part, first before all else may the sweet Muses—for smitten with a great love I perform their rites—may they receive me and show the paths of the heavens and the stars, the various eclipses of the suns and the labors of the moon; whence come tremors of the earth, by what power the deep seas swell, breaking their barriers, and then subside of their own accord into themselves again; why the winter suns hasten so to touch the ocean or what delays hinder sluggish nights. But if I should be unable to attain those goals because cold blood surrounds and obstructs my heart, may the countryside and cool streams in valleys please me; may I love rivers and forests—inglorious though I may be. O for the fields, for Spercheus and Taygetus and its Laconian maenads! O to be set in the cool glades of Haemus and to be sheltered by the great shade of branches!

In those initial exclamations, Virgil does not attempt to justify his aspirations by appeal to some larger philosophical system or to a sense of higher ends which his studies may serve. Contemplation is presented as absorbing and satisfying in and of itself—whether it be contemplation of the heavens or of the countryside.

The two kinds of contemplation are not the same. Each offers unique attractions. Although the unveiling of the cosmic order is more glorious than the contemplation of nature as it is expressed in landscapes, Virgil admits to some misgivings about it. Whether because study of the heavens is too demanding or austere an activity, he fears that he may not be equal to it, that his blood may chill and become congested around his heart. If contemplation of the countryside is less exalted than that of the heavens, it has other compensations; for the countryside is less remote than the heavens. It offers experiences that are intimate and sensual without being any the more disruptive to the observer's serenity. Ultimately, however, Virgil seems here to treat the countryside almost as an abstraction. General references to cool streams, rivers, and the like give way to literary allusions, to names of an almost symbolic value. Virgil seems to evoke Thessalian Spercheus, Taygeta, and Thracian Haemus not as specific locales of compelling attraction but rather because of their common associations with Bacchus, who came to the Greeks through Thrace and Thessaly and to whose worship in the Taygetus mountain range of Laconia Virgil specifically calls attention. He treats Taygetus, in fact, as an abstraction, using the name, which normally appears in a masculine singular form, as a neuter plural. Delight in the actual experience of the countryside is superseded by a more general sense of the poet's fascination with Bacchus and his rites: contemplation of the countryside means contemplation of the spontaneity and the vitality that Bacchus and his worshippers signify.

We are prepared, then, for the assertion that the contemplation of rustic life is no less liberating than the truths revealed by scientific study of the cosmos (490-494):

> felix qui potuit rerum cognoscere causas
> atque metus omnis et inexorabile fatum
> subiecit pedibus strepitumque Acherontis auari:
> fortunatus et ille deos qui nouit agrestis
> Panaque Siluanumque senem Nymphasque sorores.

> Happy the man who has been able to learn the causes of things and has trampled beneath his feet all fears, inexorable fate, and the howl of greedy Acheron. Fortunate, too, the one who has come to know the gods of the countryside, Pan, old Silvanus, the sister Nymphs.

In the first of those beatitudes the thought and diction combine to suggest Lucretius' Latin exposition of Epicureanism. According to Lucretius, the greatest cause of misery for mankind is the mistaken view that the gods take an active part in human affairs and, in particular, that they administer rewards and punishments in an afterlife. Men live in fear of the gods and of death, and that fear perverts their entire way of life. While Lucretius does not actually use the phrase *rerum causas* ("the causes of things") as Virgil does, he argues that false belief in the gods results from ignorance of the workings of nature, *rerum natura* (*DRN* 3.1072). Men explained the annual progression of the seasons, for example, by appeal to the gods, because *nec poterant quibus id fieret* **cognoscere causis** ("they were unable to understand by what causes it occurred," *DRN* 5.1185). Lucretius claimed that human understanding revealed that the operation of the universe was purely mechanistic, *quare religio* **pedibus subiecta** *vicissim / obteritur* ("whereby superstition in turn is *cast beneath our feet /* and trampled," *DRN* 1.78-79). His goal was to see that **metus** *ille foras praeceps* **Acheruntis** *agendus* ("*fear of Acheron* be driven out headlong," *DRN* 3.37). Epicureans, of course, were not the only philosophers of antiquity who claimed to free people from an unreasoning fear of death—one thinks of Socrates, for example—but the context of the beatitude in *Georgic* 2 immediately after Virgil's exclamation on the joys of understanding the patterns of the universe—and the obvious affinity between his diction and Lucretius'—suggests that he had Epicureanism particularly in mind here.

Whether Virgil means to affirm or to deny a special commitment to Epicureanism seems to me to be less important than the fact that, as a preeminent example of the contemplative life and its rewards, Epicureanism provides a high and vivid standard by which to confirm the value of rustic life. The inhabitants of the countryside find no less satisfaction in their simple piety and in the assurance of natural vitality (which Pan, Silvanus, and the Nymphs—like Bacchus—embody) than Epicureans find in their philosophy. Indeed, the rustic is characterized by that very aloofness from the turmoil of public life whose advocacy particularly distinguished Epicureanism at Rome. Lucretius, for example, finds the true Sisyphus not in the Underworld, but in Roman politics (*DRN* 3.995-1002):

> Sisyphus in vita quoque nobis ante oculos est
> qui petere a populo fascis saevasque securis
> imbibit et semper victus tristisque recedit.
> nam petere imperium quod inanest nec datur umquam,
> atque in eo semper durum sufferre laborem,
> hoc est adverso nixantem trudere monte
> saxum quod tamen ⟨e⟩ summo iam vertice rursum
> volvitur et plani raptim petit aequora campi.

Sisyphus, too, in the flesh, is before our very eyes, the one who thirsts to seek the *fasces* and the cruel axes from the people and is always defeated and always falls back, disappointed. For to seek after an authority that is empty and never granted, and for that always to suffer hard labor, this is to push a boulder from its resting place up a mountain, a boulder that nonetheless, just at the very top, rolls back again and headlong seeks the level of the flat plain.

Virgil asserts of the one who knows the rustic gods that (495-500)

> illum non populi fasces, non purpura regum
> flexit et infidos agitans discordia fratres,
> aut coniurato descendens Dacus ab Histro,
> non res Romanae perituraque regna; neque ille
> aut doluit miserans inopem aut inuidit habenti.

> he has not been moved by the peoples' *fasces*, nor by the purple of kings and by the discord that drives faithless brothers, not by the Dacians who descend from the Hister, united in conspiracy, not by the Republic and kingdoms that will perish; nor did he either grieve in pity for the poor or envy the rich.

We find that the rustic, like the true Epicurean, is distinguished from the victims of greed and ambition. Lucretius attributes those vices to the fear of death and describes their influence as follows (*DRN* 3.59-72):

> denique avarities et honorum caeca cupido
> quae miseros homines cogunt transcendere finis
> iuris et interdum socios scelerum atque ministros
> noctes atque dies niti praestante labore
> ad summas emergere opes, haec vulnera vitae
> non minimam partem mortis formidine aluntur.
> . . . . . . . . . . . . . . . .
> unde homines dum se falso terrore coacti
> effugisse volunt longe longeque remosse,
> sanguine civili rem conflant divitiasque
> conduplicant avidi, caedem caede accumulantes;
> crudeles gaudent in tristi funere fratris.

Finally, greed and blind desire for honors which compel wretched men to transgress the bounds of law and, sometimes as allies and accomplices in wickedness, day and night to strive with surpassing labor to attain the highest wealth—those wounds to life are nourished not least by fear of death . . . while men who are compelled by false terror and wish to have escaped [the gates of death] and to have removed themselves far, far away, amass wealth with the blood of fellow citizens, redouble their riches, greedily piling slaughter on slaughter, and take a cruel delight in the sorrowful funeral of a brother.

Virgil describes the residents of the city in comparable terms (503–512). In contrast to the farmer,

> sollicitant alii remis freta caeca, ruuntque
> in ferrum, penetrant aulas et limina regum;
> . . . . . . . . . . . . . . . .
> . . . gaudent perfusi sanguine fratrum,
> exsilioque domos et dulcia limina mutant
> atque alio patriam quaerunt sub sole iacentem.

> others churn blind straits with their oars, and rush to the sword, force their way across the thresholds and into the courts of kings; . . . they rejoice, soaked in their brothers' blood, exchange their own sweet thresholds for exile and seek a fatherland under another sun.

In that last passage we have returned again to the chaotic and self-destructive world of the Roman civil wars as they were evoked at the conclusion of *Georgic* 1. The image of men rejoicing in their brother's blood is an obvious and precedented metaphor for civil war.

Images of men as they "churn blind straits with their oars" and flee to exile, like the simile of the charioteer in *Georgic* 1, convey a sense of disorder spinning outward centrifugally from its center, spreading chaos in its aimless, uncontrollable flight. Appropriately, the contrasting orderliness of the farmer's existence is expressed in terms that recall the opening lines of *Georgic* 2 (513–515):

> agricola incuruo terram dimouit aratro:
> hic anni labor, hinc patriam paruosque nepotes
> sustinet, hinc armenta boum meritosque iuuencos.

> The farmer moves the earth with his unyielding plow: here is the year's labor, from here he sustains his country and young grandchildren, from here he sustains his herds of cattle and his deserving bullocks.

The repetition—*hic, hinc, hinc*—emphasizes the limits of the farmer's work, just as the *huc . . . hic . . . huc* of the invocation to Bacchus (4–7) suggested the immediate availability of plenty and joyful release. In contrast to those whose misguided search for satisfaction is never-ending, all the farmer's needs are supplied at home by the mere cultivation of the land. But more is now implicit in that repetition than the farmer's material circumstances. It also calls attention to the farmer's willingness to contain his ambitions, his capacity to recognize the wealth available to him in the countryside.

Contrast between the vision of a harsher environment in *Georgic* 1 and a generous environment in *Georgic* 2, then, has developed not only into a contrast between the ideals of the active life and of the contemplative life, but beyond that to a more general contrast between two different views of the form and possibility of human virtue. In *Georgic* 1 the countryside required hardness, and perhaps even the farmer's greed contributed to his capacity to wrest a livelihood from a hard and recalcitrant earth. In *Georgic* 2 not only does the fruitfulness of the countryside make such aggressiveness unnecessary, but Virgil also suggests that, in the supportive environment of the rustic world at least, man is proof against the vices that corrupt urban society. The farmer is actually capable of the very wisdom toward which philosophers strive.

To understand the unique thrust of Virgil's praise of rustic life, it will be helpful to compare it for a final time to a passage in Lucretius' *De Rerum Natura*. In his introduction to the second book of his poem, Lucretius, like Virgil, contrasts the moral confusion of contemporary urban society to the simple pleasures to be experienced in the countryside (*DRN* 2.23-33):

> gratius interdum neque natura ipsa requirit,
> si non aurea sunt iuvenum simulacra per aedes
> lampadas igniferas manibus retinentia dextris,
> lumina nocturnis epulis ut suppeditentur,
> nec domus argento fulget auroque renidet
> nec citharae reboant laqueata aurataque templa
> cum tamen inter se prostrati in gramine molli
> propter aquae rivum sub ramis arboris altae
> non magnis opibus iucunde corpora curant,
> praesertim cum tempestas arridet et anni
> tempora conspergunt viridantis floribus herbas.

Nature herself seeks nothing more pleasing from time to time—even if there are no golden statues of youths throughout the house holding shining torches in their right hands so that there is light for nocturnal banquets, even if the house does not gleam with silver and glitter with gold, even if the music of lutes does not resound from polished and gilded beams—nature seeks nothing so long as men stretch out together in soft grass next to a flowing river beneath the branches of a tall tree and happily provide for their bodies without great expense, especially when the weather smiles and the seasons of the year mingle flowers among the green grasses.

Lucretius is not interested in the countryside per se. The idyllic scene he describes is meant to be no more than an example of the kinds of simple pleasures available to those who have learned to discard false fears and to recognize the truly good things in life. Its dramatic effect derives in part from the very fact that it depicts a special occasion, something we do *interdum* ("from time to time"), and thus offers the kind of lifting of cares and the relaxation we experience on a vacation from the complications of our daily life as a model for the kind of benefits we may expect to gain from Epicurus' revelations.

Like Lucretius, Virgil also seeks to dramatize his argument by the description of a country holiday (523-531):

> interea dulces pendent circum oscula nati,
> casta pudicitiam seruat domus, ubera uaccae
> lactea demittunt, pinguesque in gramine laeto
> inter se aduersis luctantur cornibus haedi.
> ipse dies agitat festos fususque per herbam,
> ignis ubi in medio et socii cratera coronant,
> te libans, Lenaee, uocat pecorisque magistris
> uelocis iaculi certamina ponit in ulmo,
> corporaque agresti nudant praedura palaestra.

> Meanwhile his darling children hang on his lips; a pure home preserves chastity; cows' udders hang down with milk; on the rich turf fat young goats compete among themselves, horn to horn. The farmer himself enjoys his holidays, stretched out on the grass. While his companions, gathered about a fire, wreath drinking cups, he pours libations to you, Lenaeus; he calls on you and sets up targets for the shepherds; the men bare their hard bodies for wrestling.

What Virgil has described is, to be sure, a special occasion, but one, unlike the scene in Lucretius, that stands for a whole way of life. The celebrants are not visitors to the countryside, but residents of it. Their games are not an escape from their normal way of life but a part of it—every bit as much as their loving families and chaste homes. The presence of goats and the libation to Bacchus might suggest, in fact, that this is the same festival to Bacchus described earlier in the discussion of viticulture (2.380-396). If so, it is literally part of the farmer's work to assure the success of his crops. Even if it is not, the farmers make it an occasion to display the very toughness demanded of them in their daily routines. Their piety and their happy celebration manifest the consequences of a life in which the *iustissima tellus* demands and rewards discipline, in which youth grow up accustomed to endure work and to be satisfied with little. But however hard they may be, these farmers lack the persistent aggressiveness required of the farmer in *Georgic* 1. We see them enjoying instinctively those simple pleasures whose value residents of the city must learn from philosophy. Rustic life, not even the poet's somewhat detached contemplation of it, but rustic life itself is here presented not as a call to philosophy, but as an alternative to it.

Virgil presents an attractive vision of that alternative, however, only to question its accessibility. Despite his emphasis on the countryside as a place where desirable values and spiritual tranquility are engendered, he began his praise with a qualification: *O fortunatos nimium sua si bona norint / agricolas* ("O farmers, too fortunate, if they but knew their own wealth!" 458). The farmer's happiness is contingent on his own recognition of how fortunate in fact he is—that is, on his capacity to resist the temptations that confound the lives of those who reside in the city. In calling attention to that contingency, Virgil raises the possibility at least that the farmer may not be so wise. Similarly, repeated assertions that the farmer is removed from civil discord or that he is unmoved by Roman affairs fly in the face of both historical reality and Virgil's own description at the conclusion of *Georgic* 1 of the disruptive impact of the civil wars upon the farmer. As a consequence, the celebration of rustic life at the conclusion of *Georgic* 2 seems less a description of a present reality than the vision of an uncertain ideal.

Still other aspects of the passage associate that vision with an increasingly remote and inaccessible past. Virgil says that Justice left her last traces in the countryside (474). By that assertion he distinguishes rustics for their unparalleled virtue. But he also recalls an important tradition that looks on the present as a hopelessly degenerate age. In the eighth century B.C. Hesiod described the present as an Iron Age of toil to which we have been condemned by the departure of the goddesses *Aidos* and *Nemesis*, "Shame" and "Retribution." That idea was taken up and modified in Aratus' Stoic poem, *Phaenomena*, whose important influence on *Georgic* 1 we have already noted. According to Aratus, the final arrival of the Iron Age was marked by the departure not of Aidos and Nemesis, but of the goddess Dikē, "Justice," who dissociated herself from a corrupt human race and chose a new home in the heavens as the star Astraea. The reference here to the departure of *Iustitia*, then, implies that, despite the virtues of rustic life, we live in a hopelessly degenerate age in which the very best we can hope for are vestiges of justice, and that the ideal of an uncorrupted rustic life is based on a memory of the past rather than knowledge of the present.

In fact, Virgil's description of an ideal rustic life is marked by a progressive shift from the present to the past. He begins with the present tense (458–474), implying that the life he describes is separated only in space from the chaos of contemporary Roman affairs. The assertion that *extrema per illos / Iustitia excedens terris vestigia* **fecit** ("among those people Justice, departing from earth, *left* her last traces," 473–474) marks a turning point in the passage. Virgil breaks off to affirm his attraction to the contemplative life and to suggest that the countryside offers no less satisfying an object of contemplation than the heavens (475). When he returns to his description of the farmer and his life (495), the verbs are in the past tense (*flexit, doluit, inuidit, carpsit, uidit*), while verbs in the description of city life remain in the present tense (*sollicitant, ruunt, penetrant, petit, incubat, stupet, gaudent, mutant, quaerunt*). Against the vividness of present chaos, the vision of a better life in the countryside recedes into an uncertain past. Virgil does return to the present tense (519 ff.), but then the effect is to express a vague and timeless quality suitable to the idyllic character of the subject rather than a direct description of a present reality (519–522):

uenit hiems: teritur Sicyonia baca trapetis,
glande sues laeti redeunt, dant arbuta siluae;
et uarios ponit fetus autumnus, et alte
mitis in apricis coquitur uindemia saxis.

Winter has come: the Sicyonian berry is crushed in the olive press; pigs return fat with acorns; the forest yields strawberries; autumn produces various fruits; high up on rocky hillsides in the sun the vintage mellows in warmth.

But it is in the final lines of *Georgic* 2 that Virgil relegates his idealized vision of rustic life most clearly to a past that is irretrievable. At first he seeks to confirm the virtues of rustic life by identifying them as the source of the tremendous vitality that was expressed in the growth of the early Latin and Etruscan kingdoms, and especially of Rome itself (532-535):

> hanc olim ueteres uitam coluere Sabini,
> hanc Remus et frater; sic fortis Etruria creuit
> scilicet et rerum facta est pulcherrima Roma,
> septemque una sibi muro circumdedit arces.

> This is the life that once the Sabines of old cultivated, this the life of Remus and his brother; thus, undoubtedly, Etruria grew strong, and of all things Rome became most beautiful and encircled her seven citadels with one wall.

That statement involves a conspicuous contradiction, for a central characteristic of the farmer, a source of his strength, was that he regarded *res Romana perituraque regna* ("the Roman Republic and kingdoms doomed to perish") with equal indifference. Commitment to the founding and glorification of Rome represents a denial of the very containment and focus of energies that are essential to the way of life from which Romulus and Remus supposedly drew their strength.

Within the context of the passage as a whole it is strongly suggested that the founders of Rome lost as much as they gained by that change of perspective. A recurrent theme in Virgil's praise of rustic life is security—especially from the ravages of civil war. The very first of the blessings of rustic life was that the farmer lived *procul discordibus armis* ("far from the weapons of civil strife"). Later, Virgil associated civil war with fratricide, when he contrasted the farmer with those who are moved not only by public ambitions—the *populi fasces* and *purpura regum*—but also by their concomitant, *infidos agitans discordia fratres* ("civil strife driving faithless brothers," 496). Yet again he contrasts the farmer, content with his lot, to the politically ambitious who become embroiled in Rome's fratricidal civil wars: *gaudent perfusi sanguine fratrum* ("they take delight, soaked in their brothers' blood," 510). When we are told that Rome was founded not by Romulus and Remus but by *Remus et frater*, it is difficult not to recall that each of those brothers was determined to found the greater nation, and that their desire for glory led to conflict in which Remus was killed by his brother. Virgil's contemporary, Horace, actually regarded that initial fratricide as both emblem and origin of the disorders that attained their fullest realization in the civil wars of his own days (*Epode* 7.1-4, 17-20):

> Quo, quo scelesti ruitis? aut cur dexteris
>     aptantur enses conditi?
> parumne campis atque Neptuno super
>     fusum est Latini sanguinis,
> . . . . . . . . . . .
> sic est: acerba fata Romanos agunt
>     scelusque fraternae necis,
> ut inmerentis fluxit in terram Remi
>     sacer nepotibus cruor.

Where, where you wicked men are you rushing headlong? Why do your right hands grasp swords that have only just been sheathed? Have fields and Neptune been too little drenched in Latin blood? . . . So it is: harsh fates drive the Romans—the fates and the crime of a brother's murder—ever since the blood of Remus, undeserving, poured onto the earth, a curse to posterity.

Remus and his brother did not realize the potential of their rustic life. Rather, they betrayed it. They cannot, after all, attest to its excellence.

Virgil looks back, then, to yet another age, at once more exalted and more remote than that of the founders of Rome (536-540):

> ante etiam sceptrum Dictaei regis et ante
> impia quam caesis gens est epulata iuuencis,
> aureus hanc uitam in terris Saturnus agebat;

> necdum etiam audierant inflari classica, necdum
> impositos duris crepitare incudibus ensis.
>
> Even before the scepter of Jupiter, the king from Mount Dictē, and before an impious race slaughtered bullocks and dined on them, golden Saturnus used to live this kind of life on earth; war horns had not even been heard to sound yet, nor had swords clattered on the tops of anvils.

We have been brought back to an age in which the promise of rustic life is realized without compromise, but to do so Virgil has taken us beyond even legend to the timeless past of myth. The model for the Golden Age described here comes, once again, from Aratus' *Phaenomena*. In contrast to Hesiod, who envisioned the Golden Age as a time when work was unnecessary and men passed their life in banqueting and companionship with the gods, Aratus, who belonged to a society less familiar with the toil of farming, characterized the Golden Age as a time when civilization was still completely agrarian (*Phaenomena* 100-136). Men did not engage in litigation; trade and navigation were unknown; the sword was not used; men did not slaughter their oxen. According to Aratus the final and decisive event in the transition from that happy age to the degenerate present was, as noted above, the departure of the goddess Dikē, or Justice. Virgil does not mention litigation, trade, or navigation in his description of "golden Saturnus'" reign. His designation of that age as a time before warfare, the slaughter of oxen, the forging of swords, and the departure of Justice is enough to imply the rest. By locating his rustic ideal in a mythical past that precedes the revolutionary intervention of Jupiter described in *Georgic* 1.121-146, Virgil has removed that ideal beyond attainment in this world.

He concludes this book with a brief two-line epilogue (541-542):

> Sed nos immensum spatiis confecimus aequor,
> et iam tempus equum fumantia soluere colla.
>
> But we have covered an immense amount of ground in our courses, and now it is time to release the harnesses from our horses' steaming necks.

The image of horses coming to a halt at the end of their course contrasts sharply with the image of runaway horses that concluded

*Georgic* 1, and it expresses Virgil's own commitment to the ideal of limit and restraint which he developed throughout *Georgic* 2. But it recalls that perspective ironically, only to take leave of it. Despite his initial promises to be brief, the poet has, by his own admission, covered an *immensum aequor*. He unharnesses his horses not because he has found a solution to the problem of disorder and to the failures of contemporary Roman civilization, but because the present line of inquiry (like that of the previous book) has led to a dead end.

CHAPTER IV

# Georgic 3

### I

*Georgic* 3 begins with the assumption that the containment of energy and ambition proposed in *Georgic* 2 is not possible. The introduction to *Georgic* 3 acknowledges instead the expansiveness of human energy, and envisions it set in an appropriate context. As in the conclusion of *Georgic* 1, Romans will move beyond their own frontiers; but now rather than spreading chaos, they will reduce the entire world to order by bringing it under the single coherent command of their own nation and its unequaled leaders. Virgil returns, then, to the hopefully ambitious vision of the introduction to *Georgic* 1, although with some qualifications: his concern is less with the seemingly limitless alternatives available to the new ruler and with his imminent deification than with the more limited and specific prospect of world supremacy, both military and cultural. This prospect seems at first the more vivid and accessible as it is expressed in terms that evoke actual festivities which were planned to commemorate the new ruler's recent victories and to herald the magnificence of his reign. But Virgil's recourse to specific images drawn from contemporary events is ambiguous, for it also provides a concrete measure of the utopianism that informs the introduction to this *Georgic*, and it provides an equally strong contrast to the insistent realism with which he describes the mundane obstacles to human order and control in the subsequent exposition.

While the first two lines of *Georgic* 3 announce the agricultural topic of this book by invoking the tutelary gods of the shepherd—the Italian Pales and Apollo in his bucolic aspect—and by invoking the haunts of Pan, the body of the introduction elaborates a hopeful vision of world order in which the possibilities of civilization are fully realized. It begins with a dramatic assertion of the poet's own ambitions (3-12):

> cetera, quae uacuas tenuissent carmine mentes,
> omnia iam uulgata: quis aut Eurysthea durum
> aut inlaudati nescit Busiridis aras?
> cui non dictus Hylas puer et Latonia Delos
> Hippodameque umeroque Pelops insignis eburno,
> acer equis? temptanda uia est, qua me quoque possim
> tollere humo uictorque uirum uolitare per ora.
> primus ego in patriam mecum, modo uita supersit,
> Aonio rediens deducam uertice Musas;
> primus Idumaeas referam tibi, Mantua, palmas.

The other subjects with which song might have kept the attention of empty minds have long since become trite. Who does not know about hard Eurystheus or about the altars of Busiris—unpraised and unworthy of praise—who has not been told of the boy, Hylas, and Latona's Delos, Hippodame and Pelops, noted for his marble shoulder, a fierce horseman? I must find a way to raise myself from the earth and fly victorious, my name on the lips of men. I will be the first—if only life be long enough—to return to my homeland bringing the Muses down with me from the peak of Mount Aonia. I will be the first, Mantua, to bring back to you palms of victory from Palestine.

Virgil dissociates himself from the poets who repeat myths that had been told and retold, often with increasing emphasis on the exotic and arcane, during the Hellenistic period. In his claim to be an innovator he recalls the boast at the conclusion of his praise of Italy in *Georgic* 2 (174-176):

> ... tibi res antiquae laudis et artem
> ingredior sanctos ausus recludere fontis,
> Ascraeumque cano Romana per oppida carmen.

for you [Saturnian land] I undertake affairs and skills of ancient renown, I who have dared to open the sacred springs of poetic inspiration. I sing an Ascraean song through Roman towns.

Both of those statements recall still earlier assertions by other poets of their originality and supremacy, and they reveal by comparison how extraordinarily ambitious Virgil is being here. Ennius' combination of Roman themes and Greek meters set a precedent that determined the character of subsequent Latin poetry. In an epitaph he is said to have composed himself, he rejected the normal rites for the dead with a bold assertion of his own immortality as a poet (Vahlen, *Epigrammata* II):

> Nemo me lacrimis decoret nec funera fletu
> faxit: cur? Volito vivus per ora virum.
>
> Let no one grace me with tears or make my funeral with lamentation: Why? I fly, alive, on men's lips.

The striking imagery and alliteration in the second line of that couplet is closely matched in *Georgic* 3.9 quoted above, *uictorque uirum uolitare per oram*. Lucretius, also, recalled Ennius, as the one (*DRN* 1.117-119)

> . . . qui primus amoeno
> detulit ex Helicone perenni fronde coronam,
> per gentis Italas hominum quae clara clueret.
>
> who first brought down from lovely Mount Helicon the garland of deathless leaves to win clear fame among the Italian peoples.

He acknowledged that achievement only to dramatize still further his own and that of his master, Epicurus. Lucretius claimed his own originality: *iuvat integros accedere fontis / atque haurire* ("It is a delight to approach untouched fountains and to drink from them," *DRN* 1.927-928). Moreover, he emphasized the importance of Epicurus' philosophical accomplishments by comparing his return from his mental excursions to that of a general from a successful campaign: *unde refert nobis victor quid possit oriri* ("from there the victor reports to us what can come into being," *DRN* 1.75).

In the thought and diction of *Georgic* 3.8-10, Virgil recalls those bold claims of his predecessors and even his own earlier claims in

*Georgic* 2, only to assert his intention of surpassing them. For he now looks forward to a poetic victory so stunning that it will win him recognition not only in Italy but throughout the world and at the very home of the Muses. More than that, he anticipates a success so revolutionary that he will overcome the Muses themselves and, like a victorious general, conduct them back to his homeland to display in the triumphal celebration of his accomplishment. He aspires to nothing less than to be the agent through whom Italy will achieve cultural preeminence over the entire world—including Greece itself. It is fully appropriate, then, that in the following lines he should imagine celebrating that victory by a formal "triumph" such as was traditionally awarded to Roman generals who had rendered outstanding service to their country on the field of battle.

The thought of that ambitious goal leads to reflection on the possibility of an equally impressive achievement by the young Caesar. In fact, Virgil expresses his intention of making his celebration an offering to Caesar himself, just as the conventional triumph was celebrated in honor both of the victor and of Jupiter Feretrius, the god to whom the victor owed his success and to whom he dedicated spoils of victory in gratitude (13-18):

> et uiridi in campo templum de marmore ponam
> propter aquam, tardis ingens ubi flexibus errat
> Mincius et tenera praetexit harundine ripas.
> in medio mihi Caesar erit templumque tenebit:
> illi uictor ego et Tyrio conspectus in ostro
> centum quadriiugos agitabo ad flumina currus.

> and in a green field I will establish a temple of marble, next to the water where the great Mincius meanders in its gentle turnings and has bordered its banks with pliant reeds. I will have Caesar in the middle and the temple will be his: for him, I, the victor, conspicuous in Tyrian purple, will drive a hundred four-horse chariots to the waters.

Henceforth, the triumph Virgil imagines is presented as a celebration of himself and Caesar equally, so that even the various trophies that traditionally represented the triumphator's victories here attest to Caesar's as well as the poet's. Thus, the fact that *cuncta . . . Graecia* ("all Greece," 19-20) will abandon Olympia and Nemea, the cities of the greatest Panhellenic games, to compete in Virgil's triumph is a particularly appropriate way of acknowledging his success in making Italy, not Greece, the center of the civilized arts. Similarly, the construction of a theatre, with a richly embroidered curtain, the working of scenes in gold and ivory inlay on the temple doors, and lifelike statues—all offer a fitting testament to the nature and importance of Virgil's projected accomplishment.

But it is to Caesar, who like a god will possess (*tenebit*) the new temple, that the triumphant poet will dedicate his victory; and the subject of the art that will adorn the temple will be the statesman's achievements, not the poet's. Indeed, the events Virgil will commemorate and the festivities he imaginatively anticipates all bear a striking resemblance to recent exploits in Caesar's career and to the festivities that were planned for 29 and 28 B.C. to celebrate his official entry into Rome and his formal accession to the position he had won for himself in the Roman civil wars. We are brought back to that momentous sense of new beginnings which, I have suggested above, was the context for the introduction to *Georgic* 1 and to the *Georgics* as a whole; however, the spirit of hopeful anticipation, which was evoked very broadly at the beginning of the poem, is now grounded in conspicuous parallels between the triumphant future that the poet envisions and specific historical events that are closely contemporary with the time of the poem's composition and publication.[1]

Chief among those events was the Triple Triumph of 13 to 15 October 29 B.C. whose final preparations Caesar was awaiting when he supposedly listened to a recitation of the *Georgics* by Virgil and Maecenas at Atellae.[2] The first triumph celebrated victories over

---

1. I do not want to become embroiled here in controversy about the date of the completion of the *Georgics*. As far as concerns the interpretation of *Georgic* 3.1-48, it makes no difference whether Virgil's allusions to nearly contemporary events are reminiscences of the recent past or anticipations of the near future. On the whole I can see no good reasons for disputing the testimony of the ancient biographies and commentaries, that the *Georgics* were completed and published in 29 B.C. Speculations about one or more revised editions of the poem ranging anywhere from 34 to 27 B.C. seem to me to raise many more problems than they answer; they tend to originate in a sense of dissatisfaction about the coherence of the poem as we have it and, therefore, tend by their nature to subordinate interpretation of the existing text to unverifiable speculation about the history of the poem's composition and a previous text or texts which might have been.

2. D. L. Drew, "Virgil's Marble Temple: *Georgics* III.10-39," *CQ* 18 (1924) 195-202, is the first to my knowledge to have attempted to identify specific parallels between the description of Virgil's imaginary triumph in *Georgic* 3 and specific events from contemporary history. Although I do not subscribe to the conclusions, I have found the assemblage of data most useful. The best ancient account of the Triple Triumph is Dio Cassius 51.21.

various Illyrian, German, and Gallic tribes, these last being the Morini who lived on the coast of the English Channel and whose conquest may have inspired Virgil's anticipation of Caesar's defeat of the Britons in line 25. The second triumph commemorated Caesar's naval victory at Actium, a victory over Antony in fact but nominally over Cleopatra's navy, since Caesar hoped to belittle the internecine aspects of his rise to power through the fiction that Antony was no more than a cat's-paw of a sinister foreign power. The third and climactic triumph commemorated the actual capture of Egypt. Virgil alludes clearly enough to both Egypt and Actium in his references to scenes of the Nile surging with battle and to columns adorned with the bronze beaks of captured warships (28-29). The unchallenged supremacy of the new ruler and the spectacular wealth he had acquired with the capture of Egypt further contributed to making the Triple Triumph an event of unprecedented grandeur and a worthy inspiration for the florid style and extravagant expectations that characterize Virgil's tribute to Caesar in the introduction to *Georgic 3*.

The victories celebrated in the Triple Triumph, although the most decisive and politically significant, were not the only ones that may be reflected in *Georgic 3*. Also in 29 B.C. the dramatic news reached Rome that the Parthians, who in 53 B.C. had captured the standards of three Roman legions under the command of Marcus Licinius Crassus Dives, had become embroiled in a civil war and that Caesar had succeeded in establishing friendly relations with the leader of the victorious party and had brought his son to Rome, under the guise of friendship, as a virtual hostage.[3] The enthusiasm of the Roman people at this was overwhelming, and the Senate heaped extravagant honors upon their young leader—most of which he tactfully declined.[4] That hopeful beginning finds a parallel in *Georgic* 3.31, where Virgil anticipates the actual defeat of the Parthians. It is likewise possible that Virgil's reference to the conquest of Asia and Armenia, as well as his mention of *Idumaeas palmas* ("Palestinian palms"), was inspired by the successes of the Caesarean forces against those of Antony in the East prior to the fall of Egypt[5] and to Caesar's subsequent settlement of Asian affairs.[6] Yet another victory of this period may have influenced Virgil. That is

---

3. Dio 51.18.     4. Dio 51.20.
5. Dio 51.7.     6. Dio 51.18.

the victory of Marcus Crassus in 29 B.C. over the Basternae. Although Crassus was the actual general in the field, the victory belonged formally to Caesar as the superior officer with *imperium*. This victory on the shores of the Black Sea, without specific parallel in *Georgic* 3, may nonetheless, in combination with the victories of another Caesarian general on the English Channel,[7] have inspired Virgil's idea of double trophies for "victories on either shore" (32–33) and the further idea of universal dominion which that vague expression suggests.

That Virgil should include the dedication of a new temple in his imagined triumph is also consistent with events during the years immediately following the battle of Actium, for in that period Caesar dedicated numerous temples both at home and abroad. Two of them may have a particular relevance for our present discussion. Just as Virgil imagines dedicating his triumph to the divinized conqueror of the world, so, shortly after the celebration of his Triple Triumph, the young Caesar dedicated a shrine to his adoptive father, Divus Julius.[8] Parallels between the temple of *Georgic* 3 and subsequent descriptions in *Aeneid* 8.675–728 and in Propertius 2.31 of the Palatine Temple of Actian Apollo suggest that that temple, dedicated in 28 B.C. but well advanced in design and execution by 29 B.C., may also have influenced Virgil. Apollo's temple, like the young Caesar's, was notable for the lavish use of marble in its construction; Apollo, like Virgil's Caesar, was represented by a statue that was flanked by other statues of near relatives (mother and sister in the case of Apollo, Trojan ancestors in the case of Caesar). Apollo's great victories were apparently represented in magnificent ivory reliefs on the two leaves of the temple doors, just as victories over India, Egypt, and the nations of Asia will be depicted with gold and ivory on the doors of Caesar's temple.

Although the dedication of the Palatine Temple of Actian Apollo was not itself part of a formal triumph celebration, it was clearly planned in general recognition of Caesar's recent successes and of the hopeful prospects that lay before the new ruler of the civilized world. It was in keeping with the spirit of the times, or at least with

---

7. For Crassus' victories over the Bastarnae, Mysians, and Thracians, see Dio 51.23–26; for victories over the Morini and the Rhenish invaders of Belgium by Crassus' general, Carrinus, see Dio 51.21.

8. Dio 51.22.

the spirit Caesar wished to create, that there were numerous festivities of all sorts: triumphs and temple dedications, but also processions, sacrifices, games, and theatrical performances. Thus, just as Virgil mentions the unprecedented celebration of Greek games on Italian soil before he comes to the dedication of his temple to Caesar, so the actual dedication of the Palatine Temple of Actian Apollo on 9 October 28 B.C. was preceded by the celebration on 2 September 28 B.C. of the Actian games, which Caesar reorganized, subsidized, and set up in competition with the traditionally more prestigious Panhellenic games.[9] Likewise, Caesar's enthusiastic sponsorship of theatres, erected in every quarter of the City and offering performances in "all languages,"[10] provides a context for appreciation of the elaborate stage set and the richly embroidered stage curtain that will grace Virgil's own triumphant celebration.

Awareness of the intimate connections between Virgil's imagined triumph and contemporary events is essential to a full appreciation of the introduction to *Georgic* 3 and its potential impact on the poem's audience. Inasmuch as the terms in which Virgil describes his triumph call our attention to Caesar's recent celebrations and the successes they were intended to commemorate, our perception both of the actual present and of the poet's imagined future are influenced significantly. The triumphant celebration of *Georgic* 3 appears as a realization of the promise of a greater future which was implicit, or which Caesar at least encouraged his fellow Romans to see, in the events that confirmed his dramatic accession to world supremacy. On the other hand, by associating his own triumph with the heady atmosphere of the times, Virgil gives it the emotional intensity and the sense of immediacy of a historical reality; his triumph may seem the more plausible as the fulfillment of an extraordinary march of events that is already palpably under way.

Virgil's use of allusions to contemporary history has a second dimension as well. It demands not a simple but an ambivalent response from the poem's audience. As the virtual epitome of the numerous and varied events that characterized the first exultant years of Caesar's supremacy, Virgil's triumph conveys a degree of emotional intensity and of expectation that cannot be long sustained

---

9. Dio 53.1.
10. Suetonius, *Div. Aug.* 43.

but which threatens, like the floridity and extravagance of the style here, to encourage skepticism by its very excess. A further paradox is that allusions to contemporary history cannot contribute to the apparent substantiality and immediacy of the particular triumph that Virgil imagines without also repeatedly calling attention to the great distance separating a utopian future from the present—however hopeful that present may be. The details of Virgil's fantasy may well suggest comparison with the festivities of 29 and 28 B.C.; they do not celebrate the same achievements. The victories proclaimed in the Triple Triumph of 29 B.C. were real enough, but Virgil's prospective commemoration of victories over the Britons and the far-flung nations of the East—not the least of them being the Parthians—anticipates the successful conclusion of campaigns that had barely begun and in some cases were still little more than ideas in the minds of an elated new ruler and his hopeful subjects. Expansive suggestions of an entire world reduced to a harmonious order invite us to look still further beyond contemporary realities. Indeed, as I shall argue below, the achievement Virgil anticipates implies a transformation of human nature itself, which belongs more to the realm of myth than of history.

The extent to which Virgil is here contemplating an entirely new order of reality may perhaps be most clearly seen against the background of two earlier passages in the *Georgics*, each of which has very close affinities to the introduction of *Georgic* 3. On the one hand, Virgil's imagined triumph presents itself as a further development of the passage in praise of Italy in *Georgic* 2. There Virgil surveyed the growth of an Italian nation from its ancient beginnings to the present. Now he looks to the future. There he celebrated the Italians' success in defending themselves against their enemies. Now he looks ahead to Italian conquest of the world. There he emphasized the natural wealth of Italy: *Haec eadem [tellus] argenti riuos aerisque metalla / ostendit uenis atque auro plurima fluxit* ("The same land has revealed rivers of silver, bronze ore in veins and has flowed abundant with gold," 2.165-166). Now, that wealth is displayed in works of art that are as distinguished for the sophistication and fineness of their artistry as for the materials of which they are made. The refinement of man's *artes* has progressed beyond the massive and rough towns that were made by the Italians, *congesta manu praeruptis . . . saxis* ("heaped up by hand on sheer rock," 2.156). The art that will adorn Virgil's triumph expresses the ultimate control of man over nature: hard rock will be brought to life by the sculptor's skill; he will create *spirantia signa* ("breathing statues," 3.34). The poet himself, having claimed originality in the earlier passage, now looks forward to unchallenged supremacy.

The development from the conditions that called up the praise of Italy to those obtaining in the introduction to *Georgic 3* involves, however, considerably more than a simple realization of potentials or a growth of capacities. It assumes a fundamental transformation of the conditions that determine the character of civilization as they have been elaborated thus far in the *Georgics*. The praise of Italy was based on the idea that Italy offers not only wealth, as does the East, but also challenges, which become a focus for Italian energies. Italy became great because her people met the challenge of her rich, yet rugged countryside; they pitted themselves against the forces of nature and reached an accommodation with them. Because the work of building an Italian nation and of defending it is demanding but possible, the Italians find a continuing object for the very energies and toughness which that work encourages. The vision of complete mastery that Virgil presents in the introduction to *Georgic* 3, however, leaves Italian energies unopposed, with no challenges, no sense of limits by which to focus and thereby order themselves. It assumes an entirely different basis for an ordered existence than does the praise of Italy.

Contrast between the introduction of *Georgic* 3 and the praise of rustic life that concludes *Georgic* 2 is both more immediate and more pointed. The earlier passage emphasized the integrity that, ideally at least, characterizes rustic life, by contrasting life in the countryside with the corruption and disorders of the city. Now we find that the very activities and objects that seemed to epitomize the vices of urban life are evoked by Virgil to symbolize the ultimate triumph of Italian civilization. The farmer was contrasted approvingly with those who indulged a taste for *Assyrio . . . ueneno* ("Assyrian poison," 2.465); but Virgil plans to celebrate his triumph *Tyrio conspectus in ostro* ("conspicuous in Tyrian [purple] dye," 3.17). The rustic ideal was most fully realized in the mythical past *ante / impia quam caesis gens est epulata iuuencis* ("before the impious race [of man] fed on slaughtered bullocks," (2.536-537), but Virgil exclaims of his imagined triumph (3.23-25):

> . . . iuuat caesosque uidere iuuencos,
> uel scaena ut uersis discedat frontibus utque
> purpurea intexti tollant aulaea Britanni.

It is a delight to see bullocks slaughtered or to see how the stage set separates and reveals new scenes and how figures of Britons, embroidered into a stage curtain of purple [seem to] raise it up.

Virgil's delight in the sacrifice of bullocks has been combined, in fact, with a kind of awed admiration for the theatre which he had previously rejected as no more than an arena for manifestations of vanity and the fickleness of popular favor (2.508-510):

> . . . hunc plausus hiantem
> per cuneos geminatus enim plebisque patrumque
> corripuit.

The applause of the people and the elders doubling through the sections of the theatre has transported this one as he gapes.

Similarly, Virgil approved the farmers' indifference to the trappings of luxury (2.463-464):

> nec uarios inhiant pulchra testudine postis
> inlusasque auro uestis Ephyreiaque aera.

nor do they gape at doorposts variegated with beautiful tortoise shell, and at garments worked with golden thread and at Corinthian bronzes.

But his own triumph will be adorned with just such ostentatious display of wealth (3.26-29):

> in foribus pugnam ex auro solidoque elephanto
> . . . . . . . . . . . . . .
> . . . hic undantem bello magnumque fluentem
> Nilum ac nauali surgentis aere columnas.

On the doors I will show a battle in gold and solid ivory; . . . here the great Nile surging with war, and columns rising with the bronze of captured ships' beaks.

We may recall that in his praise of rustic life Virgil had condemned the kind of person who *stupet attonitus rostris* ("gapes, dumbfounded, at the bronze beaks of captured ships," 2.508). Even the statues of

Caesar's ancestors and of *Inuidia* reemphasize his change of perspective, for the farmer was praised as one who disdains *Ephyreia aera* ("Corinthian bronzes," 2.464) as much as he does inlaid door posts and gold-embroidered cloth. Those specific contrasts, sharpened by verbal parallels, help to point up a more fundamental reorientation away from the rejection and toward the acceptance of public life, the pursuit of power and glory, and the appreciation of the most refined arts. Virgil presents himself as inspired by the very objects, committed to the very pursuits, that he had characterized as vain and decadent in the immediately preceding passage. Yet he does this without apparent irony.

This change of perspective is supported by a vision of human nature that is the very antithesis of that implicit in the praise of Italy and in the farmer's life in *Georgic* 2. For underlying the praises of Italy and of rustic life is the assumption that the primary causes of disorder in society are human energies and passions. In his praise of Italy Virgil suggests that disorder can be avoided where there are suitable challenges for man's energies and objects for his loyalties. In his praise of rustic life he suggests that the countryside with the just discipline it imposes and even more with the simple pleasures it offers makes it possible for the farmer to renounce the disruptive passions that corrupt life in the city. In the introduction to *Georgic* 3, however, Virgil gives free rein to human energies and ambitions. He imagines them extended to their fullest, reaching out to embrace the entire world and the highest possible achievements of human skill. Yet he does not anticipate the kind of disorder that accompanied the chaotically aggressive extension of energies in the civil wars as evoked in *Georgic* 1 or in urban society as evoked in *Georgic* 2.

Rather, his imagined triumph conveys a sense of perfect order and stability. We have already noted in passing that Virgil sets his triumph against the background of the stately Mincius which meanders slowly (*tardis . . . flexibus*, 14) within its luxuriant banks. But it is also noteworthy that he imagines the celebration itself not in terms of activity or even of intense emotions—although triumphs were, in fact, occasions of great commotion and excitement—but, rather, almost exclusively in terms of static images, whether they are architectural forms, scenes elaborated in embroidery and inlays of precious materials, or statuary. We are invited to think of the conquest of Egypt, for example, not as a violent succession of acts but as a fixed scene, forever the same, unconnected with a past or a future. In a curious way the tremendously expansive energies and emotions Virgil looks forward to celebrating seem almost to lead to a world of contemplation rather than action, a world in which it is only the poet, the maker of images, who flys in irrepressible activity, whether on his four-horse chariot or on men's lips, while all others merely look on in admiration.

The great victories envisioned in the introduction to *Georgic* 3 lead not to chaos but to stability, because they will include the conquest of the impulses to violence and destruction within man himself. In a passage that looks forward to the great image in *Aeneid* 1.294-296 of *Furor impius*, bound and raging helplessly, Virgil concludes the list of trophies that will grace his triumph with the assertion that (37-39)

Inuidia infelix Furias amnemque seuerum
Cocyti metuet tortosque Ixionis anguis
immanemque rotam et non exsuperabile saxum.

Ill-fated Envy will fear the Furies, the severe river Cocytus, the twisting snakes of Ixion and his immense wheel, and [Sisyphus'] unconquerable rock.

The idea represents a natural continuation of the triumph theme. The triumph was the highest honor to which any Roman could aspire. Romans were aware of the jealousy that the triumphator might incur, especially in the competitive climate of Roman politics, and they traditionally provided him with a special ring to ward off its evil effects.[11] Virgil's celebration is complete because the triumphator need have no fear of envy.

In even that, its most restricted meaning, the assertion of *Inuidia*'s impotence has special significance for both Virgil and Caesar. On the one hand it recalls a tradition that can be traced back to the Hellenistic poets and, ultimately, to Pindar in the early fifth century B.C.[12] According to that tradition, the poet has become the object of envy because of his poetry, but by its very success he will silence the

11. See W. Ehlers, "Triumphus," *RE* II Reihe VII, pt. 1, 1939, col. 507.
12. The parallels are collected and surveyed clearly by L. P. Wilkinson, *The Georgics of Virgil* (Cambridge 1969, reprinted 1978) 170-171. For Callimachus see especially the prologue to his *Aetia* and his *Hymn to Apollo* 105-113; for Pindar see *Pythian* 1.5-28. Envy for any kind of excellence is a recurrent theme in Pindar's poetry.

carping of his rivals. Virgil presents himself as the actual triumphator here, and there are parallels between several details of his self-presentation and self-portraits of Pindar and Callimachus. But Caesar stands equally or even more in need of protection than the poet. No less to be glorified by the imagined triumph than Virgil himself, he must already contend with a legacy of envy and hostility from the civil wars. The *Inuidia* aroused by the success of this young upstart would be the major obstacle he would have to overcome in order to rule securely and effectively. It is, therefore, undoubtedly significant that Virgil's reference to *Inuidia* comes directly after his description of the statues of Caesar's glorious "ancestors."

But as I have already indicated, the conquest of *Inuidia* seems to apply more generally than just to Virgil or Caesar. The very fact that it is relevant to both figures alike urges us to see its significance in broad terms. The fact that Virgil looks forward to the actual conquest of *Inuidia* is also suggestive, for all that is required on the occasion of a triumph is the protection of the triumphator for the duration of the celebration. Association of *Inuidia* with Ixion, whose punishments she is to share, suggests a less specific sense of her role among men and a broader and more permanent curtailment of her powers than is required for the triumph alone. Such an interpretation is reinforced by the position of the description of *Inuidia* in the larger account of the projected triumph. It stands at the conclusion of the passage in striking isolation. It is not connected with the previous lines by any sign of continuation or transition such as the *atque*'s, *et*'s, or *addam* used to connect items earlier in the passage. The figure of *Inuidia* overcome, then, is like a pendant to the entire scene that precedes it, the symbol of a climactic achievement that embraces all the others and determines their significance.

The ideas both that destructive human passions could somehow be balanced by the harsh demands of the physical environment and that the rewards of rustic life could induce men to renounce those passions encouraged utopian visions of ordered and settled life in the previous *Georgics*, but both ideas proved to be impracticable. The challenge of the environment did not contain human energies and ambitions; its pleasures did not engender a philosophical serenity. Now, Virgil has introduced yet another utopian vision according to which Italian victories over the peoples of the world and the intractable elements of the environment will be perfect because they are accompanied by victory over the disruptive passions within the human breast. The conquest of *Inuidia*, then, adds to the worldly conquests of Caesar a whole new order of achievement. It takes us from the military and political struggles of historical reality to an archetypical conflict of purely mythic quality and scope. To suppress *Inuidia* is not to defeat this or that human enemy or even all human enemies, but rather to change fundamentally the nature of man and the conditions of human existence.

But Virgil refuses, finally, to commit himself to that vision. He concludes the passage with a statement of his intention to devote himself to more immediate goals (40-41, 46-48):

> interea Dryadum siluas saltusque sequamur
> intactos, tua, Maecenas, haud mollia iussa:
>
> . . . . . . . . . . . . . .
>
> mox tamen ardentis accingar dicere pugnas
> Caesaris et nomen fama tot ferre per annos,
> Tithoni prima quot abest ab origine Caesar.
>
> Meanwhile, let us pursue the virgin forests and untouched glades of the Dryads: the task, and no light one, that you, Maecenas, have set us. . . . Soon, nonetheless, I will gird myself to tell of the fiery battles of Caesar and to give his name a reputation that will last as many years as Caesar himself is distant from the very origins of the deathless Tithonus.

Such a refusal to celebrate subjects of epic scope, sometimes labeled a *recusatio*, belongs to a tradition that began with the influential Hellenistic poet, Callimachus.[13] Originally, the *recusatio* was a statement about the poet's aesthetic commitments. Callimachus regarded attempts to emulate the Homeric epics as misguided and trite. He justified his own refusal to join the bulging ranks of epic poets with the playful assertion that his muse was not up to the task. In the Augustan age such refusals were often addressed to a patron or to an important public figure and, thus, became a tactful way of declining, for whatever reason, to sing that individual's praises.[14] In

---

13. The nature of the Callimachaean *recusatio* and its appropriation by Augustan poets is the major concern of Walter Wimmel, *Kallimachos in Rom: Die Nachfolge seines apologetische Dichtens in der Augusteerzeit* (Wiesbaden 1960) = *Hermes* Einzelschriften Heft 16. On the proem to *Georgic* 3 as a *recusatio*, see Wimmel, esp. 167-187.

14. See the discussions of specific authors in Wimmel (above, n. 13). On the *recusatio* as a tactful device for expressing anti-Augustan sentiments, see J. P. Sullivan, *Propertius* (Cambridge 1976) 122-126.

the introduction to *Georgic* 3, Virgil asserts that he will attempt the ambitious task of celebrating Caesar's achievements only after he has completed his immediate project, the *Georgics*. The fact that he characterizes the *Georgics* as *haud mollia iussa* ("no easy task," 41) gives some indication of how very demanding he expects the subsequent effort to be. It calls our attention to the considerable gulf that separates the present and its immediate challenges from the promises of the future. The triumph Virgil has imagined for himself will follow the completion of an epic that he has not even begun, indeed that he cannot begin until he has finished his current difficult commission, which cannot be completed until Caesar has in his turn attained the goals which that future poem is to celebrate. We may well recall what Virgil had asserted at the beginning of his fantasy, that this is a triumph he hopes to celebrate *modo uita supersit* ("provided I live that long"). The prospect of fulfilling the utopian vision presented in the introduction to *Georgic* 3 recedes into an uncertain future, just as the utopian vision of rustic life that concluded *Georgic* 2 receded into an irretrievable past.

## II

Although Virgil concludes the introduction to *Georgic* 3 by postponing indefinitely the celebration of a utopia, he does not abandon altogether the idea of the perfectibility of energies that that vision implies. He does, however, consider that idea on a more modest scale, which is defined both by a return to the subject of husbandry and by a corresponding shift from the floridity of the last forty-eight lines to a more restrained expository style. The first lines of exposition in this book look to the possibility of victory (49–51):

Seu quis Olympiacae miratus praemia palmae
pascit equos, seu quis fortis ad aratra iuuencos,
corpora praecipue matrum legat.

Whether one nurtures horses, admiring the prizes of the Olympic palm, or bullocks, strong for plows, let him select the mothers' bodies in particular.

While both horses and plow animals are discussed in the first half of the book, Virgil devotes most of his attention to the breeding and training of horses that will excel in the harsh competitions of the battlefield or racecourse. In any case, he is concerned with raising animals that are outstanding of their kind and can best perform their various functions.

The farmer's work to achieve those goals is organized around two major themes, both of which have been important throughout the *Georgics* thus far. They are the elemental power of life and, paradoxically, its extreme precariousness. In *Georgic* 2, for example, we had impressed on us how delicate young plants are, how much like young people and animals, how in need of *indulgentia*. We also saw how irrepressible natural vitality is, how after a fire the domestic olive dies but the wild olive sprouts again from its charred trunk; we saw how man refused to accept limits, however salutary, abandoning rustic life to make Rome *pulcherrima rerum* and then abandoning Rome in search of "a new homeland under an alien sun." In *Georgic* 1 we saw the farmer swept downstream unable to save himself after the least remission in his work; we saw his efforts washed out by storms and saw man himself from a cosmic perspective as the puny beneficiary of a generous god's gift—the two temperate zones where alone out of the entire universe man can survive. But we also saw man energetically overcoming the degenerative forces of nature, succeeding in his hard struggle for survival, and we saw him, above all, as responsible for the Roman civil wars, throwing the whole world into disorder and implicating the entire cosmos in his violent destructiveness. In *Georgic* 3 the elemental power of life and its precariousness are presented as the primary conditions that determine the farmer's work. And it is in light of the poet's subsequent examination of those conditions that we must finally judge the vision of perfect mastery tentatively offered in the introduction to *Georgic* 3.

The first instruction to the farmer in this book describes the kind of cow to be selected for breeding. Elements of the description are clearly drawn from Varro (*RR* 2.5.7-8):

> Qui gregem armentorum emere vult, observare debet primum, ut sint eae pecudes aetate potius ad fructos ferendos integrae quam iam expartae; ut sint bene compositae, ut integris membris, oblongae, amplae, nigrantibus cornibus, latis frontibus, oculis magnis et nigris, pilosis auribus, compressis malis, subsimae, ne gibberae, spina leviter remissa, apertis naribus, labris subnigris, cervicibus crassis ac longis, a collo palearibus demis-

sis, corpore bene costato, latis umeris, bonis clunibus, codam profusam usque ad calces ut habeant, inferiorem partem frequentibus pilis subscrispam, cruribus potius minoribus rectis, . . . colore potissimum nigro, deinde robeo, tertio helvo, quarto albo; mollissimus enim hic, ut durissimus primus.

One who wishes to buy a herd of cattle ought to check first that these livestock be of an age for bearing offspring, still sound, rather than those which have given birth already, that they have good conformation, that they have sound limbs, that they are longish, large, have black horns, broad foreheads, large black eyes, hairy ears, snub noses, compact jaws, not humpbacked, their backbones slightly sunken, wide nostrils, blackish lips, their necks thick and long with dewlaps hanging down, good ribs on their bodies, broad shoulders, good haunches, a tail flowing down to the heels (the lower part with lots of hair in tight curls), their shanks on the other hand rather short and straight; . . . the best color is black, then reddish, third light bay, fourth white, for the latter is most delicate, the first is toughest.

Virgil's instructions are as follows (51–59):

. . . optima toruae
forma bouis cui turpe caput, cui plurima ceruix,
et crurum tenus a mento palearia pendent;
tum longo nullus lateri modus: omnia magna,
pes etiam, et camuris hirtae sub cornibus aures.
nec mihi displiceat maculis insignis et albo,
aut iuga detrectans interdumque aspera cornu
et faciem tauro propior, quaeque ardua tota
et gradiens ima uerrit uestigia cauda.

The best shape of a cow is that of a fierce one, one whose head is ugly, who has a great neck, and whose dewlaps hang down from her chin to her shanks. Then she should be long in the flank, immoderately long: everything about her should be big, even her foot and the hairy ears under her curved horns. I wouldn't be displeased at one with white blotches or one who balks at the yoke, who is sometimes aggressive with her horns, and has a face more appropriate to a bull, one who is tall all over and sweeps her tracks with the end of her tail as she walks.

Virgil's more compressed description, composed of the same elements as Varro's, is nonetheless infused with an entirely different spirit than its model. It is organized around a striking paradox: the cow's apparent defects are her virtues. Virgil insists on her ugliness, her hairy ears, drooping dewlaps, long tail, splotchy coloring. The very crudeness of her appearance reinforces our appreciation of the sheer massiveness of the animal's size and fierceness of spirit. Together, all three aspects of the cow combine to give an impression of overwhelming elemental vitality. The discussion of animals begins, then, with the presentation of a dramatic embodiment of the raw material with which the farmer must work. While the description suggests the magnitude of the farmer's task, it also conveys a promise of almost unbounded possibility.

That challenging and hopeful picture is immediately qualified (60-62, 66-71):

> aetas Lucinam iustosque pati hymenaeos
> desinit ante decem, post quattuor incipit annos;
> cetera nec feturae habilis nec fortis aratris.
>
> . . . . . . . . . . . . . . .
>
> optima quaeque dies miseris mortalibus aeui
> prima fugit; subeunt morbi tristisque senectus
> et labor, et durae rapit inclementia mortis.
> semper erunt quarum mutari corpora malis:
> semper enim refice ac, ne post amissa requiras,
> ante ueni et subolem armento sortire quotannis.

The age for enduring childbirth and suitable marriages ceases before ten years and begins after four. For the rest, an animal is neither useful for breeding nor strong for plowing. . . . All the best days of life are the first to flee wretched mortals; sickness, sorry old age, and hardship press upon them and the pitilessness of hard death snatches them away. Always there will be those whose bodies you would prefer to exchange for others; always, therefore, replace them and, so that you may not regret your loss when it is too late, be beforehand and choose the young for the herd each year.

Here we have impressed upon us the array of forces to which life is vulnerable and the narrowness of the limits within which even the most impressive energies can sustain their vitality. Virgil is not concerned, as he was in *Georgic* 2, with the toughening that age brings, but rather with the prospect of degeneration which inexorably overtakes all life. The final admonition to tend constantly (*semper, semper*) to the work of selection recalls to us the instructions in *Georgic* 1 never to slacken in sorting seeds and to the warning simile of the rower whose boat careers downstream helplessly once he has let up on his oars even for an instant.

The terms in which Virgil here expresses the fact of natural degeneration and the consequent necessity for constant vigilance are quite different, however, from the terms in which he expressed them in *Georgic* 1. There is nothing conditional about his reference to the forces of natural degeneration in *Georgic* 3. He is not issuing a warning of what will take place *if* one does not exercise vigilance. He is, rather, urging timeliness because of what must inevitably occur. His reference to old age, sickness, and death is not an exhortation to meet a challenge but the warning of an inevitable loss. There is no prospect here as in *Georgic* 1 of being able to meet or overcome the degenerative forces of nature. The initial image of raw vitality has been countered with the certainty of decay and the finality of death.

The juxtaposition of the two aspects of natural vitality is the more poignant because they both apply obviously to human as well as to animal life. In *Georgic* 1 the conditions of natural vitality and the forces of degeneration seemed comparatively remote from human beings themselves, if only because they were related then to the care of plants. In *Georgic* 3 Virgil deliberately exploits our greater sense of identity with animals in order to suggest that the conditions which define their natures define our own as well. He introduces his advice about the appropriate age for breed animals with metaphors drawn from human experience: he speaks of *hymenaeos*, "marriages," and invokes Lucina, the goddess of childbirth. Thus, we are prepared to see in the brief span of the animals' productive life a model for the briefness of our own. The analogy is made explicit in the subsequent generalization that the best days are the shortest for *all* mortals, and it is reinforced not only by the list of misfortunes that all too clearly afflict humans as well as beasts, but also by the characterization of old age as *tristis*, "sorrowful," a description that invites us to imagine old age for ourselves and thus to identify the more completely with the animals and their fate. Consequently, we have been prepared to see a commentary on our own natures in the poet's examinations of both the vitality of animals and its limitations.

## III

Although Virgil sustains his interest in both those themes throughout *Georgic* 3, broadly speaking the book falls into two halves, each of which is devoted primarily to one of them. In the first half of the book there are, to be sure, repeated reminders of the frailty and transience of animal vitality. We are instructed to drive out the sick and old because they are *frigidus in Venerem*, "cold for Love," ineffectual in work and war (95-100). We are warned of how much damage the mere gadfly can wreak (146-156). We are instructed to respect the tenderness of young animals and to treat them gently (157-189). But the main focus of the first half of the book, as we have already observed, is on the challenge and promise implicit in nature's great vitality.

That theme develops to a striking conclusion in reflections on the force and implications of animal passion, *amor* (209-283), and it is from the perspective of that conclusion that earlier remarks on breeding and training assume their full meaning.[15] For in that passage Virgil addresses an issue that is thematically central to the *Georgics* as a whole as well as being of immediate relevance to the farmer's task of breeding and training animals. That issue is the disparity between the necessity for control and order and man's ability to achieve such ideals. Juxtaposed to inspiring visions of the grace and fecundity of carefully trained animals, we are shown the violent behavior animal lust stimulates in them. The contrast leads to the disturbing conclusion that the potential for destruction is unavoidable precisely because it has its origins in the same vital energy that is necessary for creation. The explicit assertion that men, no less than animals, are vulnerable to *amor*'s disruptive influence argues for the inescapable ambiguity of human potential as well.

Virgil concludes his exposition of the breeding and training of animals with the paradoxical assertion that "Venus and the goads of blind love," the very impulses to procreation, are the chief obstacles

15. The following discussion of *amor* is taken almost verbatim from pp. 177-191 of my article, "*Georgics* 3.209-294: *Amor* and Civilization," *CSCA* 8 (1975) 177-197, and is reprinted here with the kind permission of the editors of *CSCA*.

to the husbandman's work (209-210). The examples by which he substantiates that claim, however, do not dramatize specific inconveniences to the farmer so much as the violence animals may do to each other and to themselves when sexually aroused. The passage begins with a brief narrative that has been remarked both for its own effectiveness and for the poet's later adaptation of it to the description of Aeneas' final struggle with Turnus (*Aeneid* 12.715-727). He sketches the setting in one line: *pascitur in magna Sila formosa iuuenca* ("there pastures on great Mount Sila a beautiful cow," 219). From that seemingly innocent beginning we are brought swiftly to the first bloody battle of two bulls for the cow, through the self-exile of the vanquished, his lonely and ascetic life, his single-minded and energetic preparations for revenge, to the moment of a second violent encounter (220-241). Even in bare outline the episode confronts the audience with disturbing questions about the interrelation of creative and destructive energies.

Extensive use of military metaphor contributes to a mock-heroic tone which helps to clarify the nature and implications of the bulls' behavior. In order to prevent wars among bulls, we are told, farmers "relegate" them to remote and lonely pasturage, just as states or totalitarian rulers "relegate" political subversives:[16] *atque ideo tauros procul atque in sola relegant / pascua* ("and thus they relegate bulls far off to isolated pastures," 212-213). Both the postponement of *relegant* to the end of its line and the enjambment of *pascua* in the next reemphasize the elaborate precautions the farmer must take. When bulls from the same herd do compete for a cow, they *multa ui proelia miscent* ("join battle with great force," 220), and suffer *uulneribus crebris* ("many wounds," 221).[17] They are *bellantes* (224). The defeated

---

16. *Relego* has a precise legal meaning in Latin. Festus, in his epitome of the Augustan Verrius Flaccus *De Significatu Verborum* 348, 18 (W. M. Lindsay, ed. [Leipzig 1913]), defines *relego: relegati dicuntur proprie quibus ignominiae aut poenae causa necesse est ab urbe Roma, aliove quo loco abesse* ("Those are properly said to have been relegated who are compelled as a punishment or sign of disgrace to stay away from the City of Rome or from any other place"). Likewise, *exsul* (*exulat*, 225) is a technical term designating one who is banished from his native land. Caesar, for example, *BC* 3.110.4, lumps together those "condemned to death and exiles," *capitis damnati exsulesque*.

17. Virgil's description of the battle of the bulls recalls, but often in a modified manner, the technical language of warfare. *Hostem* (236), of course, designates an enemy in battle or a foreign enemy, as opposed to an *inimicus*, a personal enemy. *Vulneribus crebris* (221) suggests the language of warfare, although it is attested only once in Caesar (*BC* 3.9.3), and there its syntactical relationship with the rest of its sentence is sufficiently strained to be noted in the

bull, *uictus* (225), goes off to exile worthy of an epic hero: *longeque ignotis exsulat oris* ("and far off he dwells in exile on unknown shores," 225). The pathos of his loss is acknowledged but undercut in a conspicuously well-balanced antithesis between the mundane reality and the bull's response to it: *et stabula aspectans // regnis excessit auitis* ("and looking back at the stables // he leaves his ancestral realms," 228). After rigorous training the defeated bull renews the conflict (235-236);

> Post ubi collectum robur uiresque refectae,
> signa mouet praecepsque oblitum fertur in hostem.
>
> But when he has gathered his strength and "replenished his forces," he "signals advance" and charges headlong against his oblivious "enemy."

Such mock-heroics invite the audience to reexamine their own attitudes toward human passions and conflicts—an aspect of the passage I will consider below.

But the use of military metaphor also reflects on the animals' own condition. Awareness of the fact that we can appreciate the absurdity of the bulls' actions and they cannot, helps both to reveal the magnitude of the disorder from which they suffer and also to point up the essential incongruity that makes their behavior at once pathetic and ridiculous: *amor*, the very cause of their battle, has been all but forgotten. The defeated bull actually imposes on himself the isolation Virgil had advised the farmer to impose. The bull's "exile," moreover, is the response to defeat, a time of anguish. He now suffers from a double burden: not only love, but disgrace. Even when he does recall his love, it is by no means certain whether it is

---

apparatus criticus by Alfred Klotz (*C. Juli Caesaris Commentarii*, 2 [Leipzig 1969]) as *neglegentius conscripta*. Other expressions in the description recall military language but with subtle changes that suggest poetic heightening. The expression *multa ui* (220) does not occur in Caesar (his equivalent is *magna ui*), but does occur, significantly, in *Aeneid* 12.720 in Virgil's comparison of the battle between Aeneas and Turnus to a fight between two bulls. Likewise, *proelia miscent* (v. 220) does not appear in Caesar (where the regular expressions are *proelia facio* and *proelia committo*), but does occur in *Aeneid* 10.23. Finally, *signa mouet* (236) makes sense only as an approximation of such regular military terms as *signa fero* or *signa infero*, but does not itself occur in Caesar's writings, where the other two expressions are frequent. On the other hand, *signa moueo* does occur in Livy (27.48.10 et passim), who we know made the use of poetic language a characteristic of his prose style.

the lost love or the fact that the loss is unavenged that is foremost in his mind. He goes (226-227)

> multa gemens ignominiam plagasque superbi
> uictoris, tum quos amisit inultus amores.
>
> greatly lamenting his disgrace and the blows of the haughty victor, then the love he lost, unavenged.

Virgil's insistence that *ignominia* has become the primary force motivating the bull's actions is clear. The word itself, a technical term for legal and, particularly, military disgrace,[18] is found rarely in poetry and only this once in Virgil's writings. It is made the more conspicuous here by its placement in the line: it is one of the few instances in Virgil where a single word bridges the main caesura; and while the word accents fall on the first and third syllables, the ictus of the verse falls on the second and last, creating a dissonance that further sets the word off from its context. We are urged to see that *amor* has initiated a self-generating process in which the passions aroused by violent conflict—anger, shame, vengefulness—themselves lead to renewed conflict. The object of future battles between the bulls will be at least as much to redeem the disgrace of previous defeats as to consummate the urge to procreation.

Significantly, then, Virgil does not even pause to glimpse the victor with his prize. Instead, after the initial battle, attention shifts immediately to the defeated bull and his anguish. Similarly, Virgil does not continue his narrative to the conclusion of the second encounter, although he could have done so easily enough. We can have no certainty, despite the poet's reference to the victor as *oblitum* ("forgetful"), that the defeated bull would have come any closer to victory and the consummation of his love on a second try than he did on the first. Nor can we be sure, even if he were successful, that that encounter would be the last. By focusing and concluding as it does, the narrative has emphasized the way in which the violent, uncontrolled energies released by *amor* may be self-perpetuating rather than fulfilling. The final result of the battle of the bulls, as Virgil

18. See, for example, Caesar, *BC* 3.74.1, *nonnullos signiferos ignominia notavit ac loco movit* ("some standard-bearers he stigmatized with *ignominia* and removed from their positions"), or Cicero, *Phil.* 7.9.23, *qui ignominia notandos censuerunt eos, si qui militiam subterfugissent* ("[they] decreed that draft dodgers should be stigmatized with *ignominia*").

presents it, is not consummation but injury, anguish, and continued violence.

In line 242 Virgil turns to a survey of *amor*'s effects on creatures more generally. The obvious danger of the lioness, of bears, or of the tigress in heat, for example, or the self-destructiveness and perversion of character implicit in *imbelles dant proelia cerui* ("unwarlike stags at war," 265) or in the lioness's neglect of her cubs reiterate themes that have already been developed in the battle of the bulls. In fact, this series of examples concludes with much the same abruptness as the introductory scene, and to the same effect. After he has described Glaucus' dreadful slaughter by his own frenzied mares, the mares' irresistible flight across all obstacles and their poisonous *hippomanes* (267-283), Virgil leaves the account of animal lust without warning and without any resolution of the chaotic forces he has revealed. Once again he has skillfully diverted the reader's attention, for the mares' violent behavior is, after all, the natural expression of the animals' inherent drive to procreation. But it is just that fact which the poet suppresses. His purpose has been, rather, to focus our attention on the destructive consequences of the energies released by *amor*.

The exposition of breeding and training earlier in *Georgic* 3, however, revealed that those same energies were indispensable raw material for the farmer. Under his strict and experienced discipline their creative possibilities were exemplified in the fecundity of mares and in the accomplishments of stallions. The prominence of specific contrasting scenes in the account of *amor*'s influence suggests a deliberate effort on Virgil's part to demonstrate that it is not natural vitality per se but rather the effectiveness of method and control that determines the character of animal behavior. Thus, the reaction of stallions to mares in heat dramatizes the awesome energies that make animals so dangerous when unchecked (250-254):

> nonne uides ut tota tremor pertemptet equorum
> corpora, si tantum notas odor attulit auras?
> ac neque eos iam frena uirum neque uerbera saeua,
> non scopuli rupesque cauae atque obiecta retardant
> flumina.

Don't you see how a trembling seizes the horses' entire bodies if the scent but brings familiar wisps, and neither men's reins nor their cruel lashes, nor crags and cavernous rocks and obstructing rivers slow them down.

But that vitality is precisely what Virgil recommends in a prospective war horse (77-85):

> primus et ire uiam et fluuios temptare minacis
> audet et ignoto sese committere ponti,
> nec uanos horret strepitus. . . .
> . . . tum, si qua sonum procul arma dedere,
> stare loco nescit, micat auribus et tremit artus,
> collectumque premens uoluit sub naribus ignem.

He first dares to set upon the road and to attempt threatening rivers and to entrust himself to an unknown bridge and does not bristle at empty racket. . . . Then, if weapons have made a sound in the distance he doesn't know how to stay in place, flicks his ears; his limbs tremble; he gathers his breath behind his nostrils, compresses it, and snorts out fire.

After the initial conflict in the battle of the bulls, Virgil describes the defeated animal's preparation for a second encounter (229-234):

> ergo omni cura uiris exercet et inter
> dura iacet pernox instrato saxa cubili
> frondibus hirsutis et carice pastus acuta,
> et temptat sese atque irasci in cornua discit
> arboris obnixus trunco, uentosque lacessit
> ictibus, et sparsa ad pugnam proludit harena.

Therefore, with every care he trains his forces and lies all night among hard rocks, his bed unmade, dines on shaggy greens and prickly sedge, tests himself and learns to put his anger into his horns, butts the trunk of a tree, slashes the breeze with thrusts and makes the sand fly with his war games.

Those lines recall the farmer's careful preparation of mares for breeding (130-137);

> atque, ubi concubitus primos iam nota uoluptas
> sollicitat, frondesque negant et fontibus arcent.
> saepe etiam cursu quatiunt et sole fatigant,
> cum grauiter tunsis gemit area frugibus, et cum

> surgentem ad Zephyrum paleae iactantur inanes.
> hoc faciunt, nimio ne luxu obtunsior usus
> sit genitali aruo et sulcos oblimet inertis,
> sed rapiat sitiens Venerem interiusque recondat.

And, when the already familiar desire urges the first unions, [farmers] deny the mares green foliage and keep them from springs. Often they even drive them hard on the race course and exhaust them under the sun, when grain crops are pounded and the threshing floor groans mightily, when the empty chaff is tossed to the rising west wind. They do this so that a usefulness somewhat dulled by too much luxury may not detract from the reproductive plowland and silt up the furrows, leaving them inert. Rather let a parched furrow snatch up Venus and bury her deep within.

Both the bull and the mares are isolated from the opposite sex—the bull must even forego the comfort of soft bedding. If the mares are denied food altogether, the bull is reduced to a meager and unpalatable diet of "bristly foliage" and "sharp reed grass." But his violent and futile gestures, as he thrashes at the wind and paws the sand, form a striking contrast to the promise of fertility that justifies the farmer's harsh regime.

Finally, an impressive simile describes the bull's enraged attack on his unsuspecting rival (235-241):

> post ubi collectum robur uiresque refectae,
> signa mouet praecepsque oblitum fertur in hostem:
> fluctus uti medio coepit cum albescere ponto,
> longius ex altoque sinum trahit, utque uolutus
> ad terras immane sonat per saxa neque ipso
> monte minor procumbit, at ima exaestuat unda
> uerticibus nigramque alte subiectat harenam.

Afterward, when he has gathered his strength and replenished his forces, he signals "advance" and charges headlong against his oblivious enemy: as when a swell begins to foam in mid-sea and away offshore draws up a trough and as it rolls toward land it makes a great sound amid the rocks and no less than a veritable mountain it crashes, but the wave seethes in eddies at its base and tosses up black sands from the depths.

We are reminded of the simile that expressed the grace and swiftness of a carefully trained horse (193-201):

> sitque laboranti similis; tum cursibus auras
> tum uocet, ac per aperta uolans ceu liber habenis
> aequora uix summa uestigia ponat harena:
> qualis Hyperboreis Aquilo cum densus ob oris
> incubuit, Scythiaeque hiemes atque arida differt
> nubila; tum segetes altae campique natantes
> lenibus horrescunt flabris, summaeque sonorem
> dant siluae, longique urgent ad litora fluctus;
> ille uolat simul arua fuga simul aequora uerrens.

> Let him be like one laboring; then, then, let him challenge the wind with his speed and, flying across open spaces as though with free rein, let him scarcely set his tracks on the surface of the sand: just as when a dense north wind from the shores of the Hyperboreans settles upon the land and scatters the storms of Scythia and dry clouds, then tall crops and fields are awash and bristle in gentle gusts; the treetops sing, and distant swells press to the shores. So that wind flies sweeping both field and sea in its flight.

The horse is only supposed to be *like* one who strains with effort: *sitque laboranti similis* (190). In fact, discipline culminates, paradoxically, in a kind of freedom: *ceu liber habenis* ("as though with free rein," 191). The north wind to which the horse is compared originates in the favored land of the Hyperboreans; it drives away storms and scatters clouds; it is swift, *densus* ("concentrated"), and yet gentle, *lenibus . . . flabris* ("with gentle . . . wisps"). In contrast, the bull's charge is described as *praeceps* ("headlong"), a word that conveys a sense of his energy and determination but implies disorder. The wave to which the charging bull is compared brings turbulence *albescere, exaestuat* ("foam, seethe"); the sound it makes, unlike the gentle *summaeque sonorem / dant siluae* ("the treetops sing") of the north wind, is both loud and awful, *immane*; it breaks with the thundering roar of a "collapsing mountain." The difference between the two similes and between the kinds of energy described in them can be sensed even in the contrasting sounds of the lines with which each simile concludes: the smooth, easy liquids and nasals of *ille uolat simul arua fuga, simul aequora uerrens*, and the rough, scraping sounds of *uerticibus nigramque alte subiectat harenam.*

If control is the measure by which Virgil judges *amor*, then it should not be surprising to find that his attitude toward *amor* is ambivalent. Not all of its expressions are undesirable—only those that exceed man's capacity for control or restraint. The first section of *Georgic* 3 contains a lengthy description of the conditions and care that make breeding fruitful. In the selection of a racer for breeding Virgil distinguished *amor laudum* ("love of praise") and eagerness for victory as the crowning qualities (112). Similarly, he advised that a war horse must learn to "love" the sound of his neck being patted: *et plausae sonitum ceruicis amare* (186). In each of those examples *amor* is subject to control or even, in the case of the war horse, a product of careful training. When Virgil introduces his condemnation of animal lust, he refers, significantly, to *amor caecus* ("blind love," 210). For it is not so much *amor* itself that leads to destruction as the blindness induced by it. Even that blindness may serve a useful end, but only when subject to some higher order of control.

The examples chosen to demonstrate the universality of *amor*'s influence, however, give rise to the disturbing suggestion that control and order are not always possible. We have seen that stallions, when they have scented mares in heat, are characterized by their unbounded energy (269–270, 276–279):

> illas ducit amor trans Gargara transque sonatem
> Ascanium; superant montis et flumina tranant.
> . . . . . . . . . . . . . . .
> saxa per et scopulos et depressas conuallis
> diffugiunt, non, Eure, tuos neque solis ad ortus,
> in Borean Caurumque, aut unde nigerrimus Auster
> nascitur et pluuio contristat frigore caelum.

> Love leads them across Gargara, the peaks of Mount Ida, across the roaring Ascanius River; they pass over mountains and swim across rivers. . . . Across rocks and crags and deep valleys they flee—not to your source, east wind, where the sun rises—they flee to the north wind and the Caurus in the northwest or to where the south wind, blackest of all, is born and veils the heavens in rainy cold.

Both passages are significantly reminiscent of Virgil's earlier account of the precautions farmers take to isolate their animals during mating season (212-214):

> atque ideo tauros procul atque in sola relegant
> pascua post montem oppositum et trans flumina lata,
> aut intus clausos satura ad praesepia seruant.

> And so [farmers] relegate bulls far off to isolated pastures, beyond an obstructing mountain and across broad rivers, or they keep them closed up at well-stocked mangers.

The intervention of mountains, rivers, and corrals may have seemed far-fetched when first introduced—charming examples of hyperbole chosen for poetic effect. Now it is clear that even they may be inadequate.

The impossibility of achieving complete control over animal vitality is epitomized in the description of the maniacal frenzy that brings the account of *amor* to its highest pitch of intensity (266-269):

> scilicet ante omnis furor est insignis equarum;
> et mentem Venus ipsa dedit, quo tempore Glauci
> Potniades malis membra absumpsere quadrigae.

> Surely the frenzy of mares stands out beyond all: Venus herself has determined their disposition ever since Glaucus' four-horse team from Potniae munched his limbs in their mouths.

The horses' munching and the crackle of Glaucus' bones are re-created in the assonance of *malis membra absumpsere quadrigae*. The gruesome vividness of the scene helps call attention to its almost symbolic character, for Glaucus is the horses' master and trainer, the one above all others who should be able to restrain them. In his last remarks on breeding and training, immediately before the passage on *amor*, Virgil summed up the value of control in a brief contrast between a fully trained horse and one as yet untrained (205-208):

> tum demum crassa magnum farragine corpus
> crescere iam domitis sinito; namque ante domandum
> ingentis tollent animos, prensique negabunt
> uerbera lenta pati et duris parere lupatis.

Then at last you must let their bodies grow big on fattening fodder, now that they have been tamed; before that they will raise their great spirits high, and once caught they will refuse to endure pliant reins and to obey hard-toothed bits.

Against that background Virgil's remarks on *amor* and his allusion to Glaucus achieve their full meaning.

Thus far our discussion has brought together several related themes that are central to the *Georgics*. Most directly, the passage is a reaffirmation of the need to work to control nature. The farmer's task of protecting his animals from *amor* is only one of innumerable examples which clearly demonstrate that an immediate plunge into destructive violence and chaos is the only alternative to productive effort. Controlled and ordered, the forces of nature are beneficent. Uncontrolled, they are destructive in their blindness. The husbandman who slips up, no less than the farmer in the yearly sorting and selecting of seeds, will inevitably and violently be swept away on the current of natural degeneration.

By demonstrating the value of the farmer's efforts to his subjects as well as to himself, the passage reaffirms another important argument in the poem. We have seen that there was implicit in the argument of *Georgic* 1 the assumption that man and nature are interdependent, that a necessary by-product of man's struggle with the land for a livelihood is the improvement of nature. The principle is manifest in all of man's dealings with nature. Whether it is the farmer with his crops, the vinekeeper with his vines, the farmer with his livestock, or, later, the beekeeper with his bees, the prosperity of man depends on the prosperity of nature, and nature prospers in proportion to man's control of it.

But, as we have already observed, control is not always possible. Tension between the obvious advantages, the absolute necessity of controlling nature and the great, sometimes insurmountable, challenges to man's capacity for control is not limited to instances of *amor*'s influence. It is repeated again and again in the *Georgics*. It is reflected in the obvious contrasts between the world of Jupiter's theodicy, where control is difficult (1.121–159), and the vision of a preeminently manageable environment in the praise of rustic life at the conclusion of *Georgic* 2 (458 ff.). It is felt still more strongly in the contrasts between Jupiter's purposeful arrangement of the cosmos in such a way as to encourage the development of human potential (1.121-159) and the meaningless chaos of the civil wars (1.465 ff.) or, later, of the plague (3.440 ff.). And it dominates the conclusion of the poem in the opposition of Orpheus' failure to Aristaeus' success (4.315 ff.). Throughout the poem there is a fine balance between a strong sense of man's responsibility, reflected in the continuous succession of instructions from the poet, and an equally strong sense of the inevitability of degeneration, reflected in recurrent scenes of disaster and man's helplessness.

By gathering those familiar themes together in a single passage, Virgil has created the context necessary for the introduction of a new and significant dimension to his argument: humans also have the elemental vitality that is the source of both creativity and destructiveness in animals. The assertion that *amor* is the same for all creatures expressly includes humans (242-244):

Omne adeo genus in terris hominumque ferarumque
et genus aequoreum, pecudes pictaeque uolucres,
in furias ignemque ruunt: amor omnibus idem.

Thus, every kind of man and beast on land and every kind of water creature, flocks, and painted birds rush to frenzy and fire: lust is the same for all.

A warning against the dangers of natural energies when they are not rigorously controlled comes home with particular force in the example of Hero and Leander, because they are human (258-263):

quid iuvenis, magnum cui uersat in ossibus ignem
durus amor? nempe abruptis turbata procellis
nocte natat caeca serus freta, quem super ingens
porta tonat caeli, et scopulis inlisa reclamant
aequora; nec miseri possunt reuocare parentes,
nec moritura super crudeli funere uirgo.

What shall I say of the youth in whose bones hard love stirs a great fire? Indeed late in blind night he swims straits churned by sudden storms. Above him the great gate of the heavens thunders and the seas breaking on crags roar back. His wretched parents cannot call him back, nor can the maiden, soon to die on the cruel funeral pyre.

The story of Hero and Leander shows unequivocally that both the problems of control and of self-control apply to people as well as to animals. Neither Hero nor Leander's parents can deter him from his rash course of action, and they pay for their failure with his death and their own suffering. Leander in his blindness is beyond both persuasion and self-control. His mad plunge into the Hellespont is self-destructive as well as a cause of suffering to others. The very anonymity of the figures in this vignette, although they are known to us from other versions of the story, generalizes their experience.[19] Man faces within himself the same problems he faces in nature. The need for self-control makes the same demands on man's abilities and reveals the same limitations as the need to control nature.

As if to insist that the reader see beyond the immediate concern with *amor* to the basic questions it raises, Virgil shapes the transition to his next subject around two calculated plays on the word's meaning. When he began his attack on *amor*, it was to Venus and to *amor caecus* that he referred: *Venerem et caeci stimulos auertere amoris* ("to avert Venus and the goads of blind love," 210). The semantic range of *amor* within the *Georgics* is broad and vague, but that of Venus is throughout limited to simple, physical lust.[20] The examples Virgil gives of Venus and *amor caecus* at work are confined to expressions of lust or passion. However, in his introduction to the discussion of small animals, the subject of the remainder of *Georgic* 3, Virgil uses *amor* in a new context, while continuing to make it a symbol of the problem of self-control. He turns away from the discussion of *amor* and its effects with an apology (284-286):

Sed fugit interea, fugit inreparabile tempus,
singula dum capti circumuectamur amore.
hoc satis armentis.

19. See Brooks Otis, *Virgil: A Study in Civilized Poetry* (Oxford 1964) 175. In fact, the explicit identification of Hero and Leander with the figures of this story is not attested outside of Virgil until Ovid (*Heroides* XVIII and XIX, *Amores* 2.16.31). Against Eduard Norden's hypothesis ("Orpheus und Eurydice," *Sitz. Berl. Akad.* [1934] 664, n. 5) that Virgil omitted their names because his version of the story was based on a general tale that was not associated with specific names or sites, see *Servius auctus* (ad loc.): *Leandri Nomen occultavit, quia cognita erat fabula* ("he suppressed the name of Leander because the story was well known"). See also the persuasive arguments of Willi Frentz, *Mythologisches in Vergils Georgica* (diss. Meisenheim Am Glan 1967) 124-129. In either case the absence of names in Virgil's account has the effect of generalizing the story.

20. See Herta Klepl, *Lucrez und Vergil in ihren Lehrgedichten* (diss. Leipzig 1940, reprinted Darmstadt 1967) 21, nn. 28 and 29.

But meantime it escapes us, time, never to be recaptured, escapes us while we linger over details, captivated by love. So much, then, for herds.

In saying that he has lingered over particulars, *capti amore* ("captivated by love"), of course, Virgil is punning. For the subject of the previous passage was, in fact, *amor*, and it was because of his interest in that subject that Virgil treated it at greater length than was appropriate. At the same time, *singula dum capti circumuectamur amore* quite naturally means that the poet has dwelt on particulars at too much length simply because they were in themselves fascinating. What Virgil says is that he had temporarily lost sight of his purpose, had lost perspective, and had lost control over his poem. By saying that, even playfully, and by saying it with the passage on Venus and *amor caecus* clearly in mind, Virgil has shown that his observations about the nature and value of control in that passage need not be confined exclusively to the operation of lust.

With greater seriousness, he turns to the next topic in his exposition of farming (286-292):

> . . . superat pars altera curae,
> lanigeros agitare greges hirtasque capellas;
> hic labor, hinc laudem fortes sperate coloni.
> nec sum animi dubius uerbis ea uincere magnum
> quam sit et angustis hunc addere rebus honorem;
> sed me Parnasi deserta per ardua dulcis
> raptat amor.

> There remains the other part of our concern, to manage fleece-bearing flocks and shaggy kids. Here is a labor. From this, brave farmers, expect praise. I am in no doubt about how great a task it is to master this subject in words and to add that distinction to such a confined topic. But through the deserted heights of Parnassus sweet, love carries me away.

Once again the use of *amor* is unexpected. Although Virgil had concluded a long discussion of *amor* as "lust" only eight lines before, "lust" (despite the proximity of *raptat*) is an inappropriate meaning for the term here. Nonetheless, in the context of his treatment of *amor caecus* and the questions it raised about self-control, the statement, *sed me Parnasi deserta per ardua dulcis / raptat amor*, points to the distinctive character of poetic inspiration: it induces a kind of madness, just as lust led *in furias*; it overwhelms the poet's self-control and compels him (*raptat*) to "bold undertakings," the *audacibus coeptis* with which he had identified his poem in the introduction (1.40). If the poet's *amor Parnasi* is not self-defeating and destructive, if it is *dulcis*, that is only because, like the *amor florum* ("love of flowers") of the bees in *Georgic* 4, it is the expression of a higher, divine purpose (4.205), just as the *amor* of the well-trained horse was a product of human design. *Amor* has lost the particular meaning it had in Virgil's discussion of the animals and has become, rather, a convenient term to designate anything that destroys or replaces self-control. We are urged to see that self-control is challenged in every sphere of human activity.

Through the use of metaphor, imagery, and verbal reminiscence, Virgil also recalls passages on the Roman civil wars and on urban corruption. I have already called attention to the conspicuous role of military and political metaphor in the description of the battle of the bulls (219–241). Within the context of the *Georgics* with its moving evocation of the Roman civil wars at the end of *Georgic* 1 and in the historical context of the *Georgics*' composition and publication during and immediately after those wars, the battle between the bulls would surely strike a responsive chord. The metaphors, then, work two ways. If the bulls' frenzied madness is like that of a civil war, civil war, in turn, is akin to the destructive and self-defeating violence unleashed by *amor*. What is true of *amor caecus* becomes true, also, of civil war. It is not warfare itself but blind, uncontrolled warfare that is criticized. It is, in fact, exactly the lack of orientation, the inability to distinguish right and wrong and the consequent utter helplessness which Virgil emphasized in his evocation of the civil wars (1.505–514):

> quippe ubi fas uersum atque nefas: tot bella per orbem,
> tam multae scelerum facies, non ullus aratro
> dignus honos . . .
> . . . . . . . . . . . . . . .
> uicinae ruptis inter se legibus urbes
> arma ferunt; saeuit toto Mars impius orbe,
> ut cum carceribus sese effudere quadrigae,
> addunt in spatia, et frustra retinacula tendens
> fertur equis auriga neque audit currus habenas.

inasmuch as right and wrong have been confounded: there are so many wars throughout the world, so many forms of wickedness; no suitable honor has been left to the plow. . . . Laws broken, neighboring cities bear arms against each other; Mars, impious, rages over the entire globe, as when four-horse chariots explode from the starting gates; they pick up speed on every length of the course and, uselessly pulling back on the bit, the charioteer is carried off by the horses; his chariot doesn't obey the reins.

The final simile is echoed in contrasting lines from Virgil's discussion of breeding and training horses in *Georgic* 3 (103–104):

nonne uides, cum praecipiti certamine campum
corripuere, ruuntque effusi carcere currus . . .

Don't you see when horses in all-out competition have burned up the field, when chariots explode from the starting gates and speed off . . .

and *per aperta uolens ceu liber habenis / aequora* ("flying across open spaces as though with free rein," 194–195). But these lines celebrate the marvelous culmination of careful breeding and training, and describe a freedom born of control. The contrast between them and the disorder expressed in the closing simile of *Georgic* 1 is picked up in the contrast between the creative and liberating discipline of the racehorse and the self-defeating, unchecked obsession of the bull. The chaos of the civil war and the frenzy of the bull are symptoms of a similar disorder.

Just as Virgil's description of impassioned animals in *Georgic* 3 was a criticism of *amor caecus* but not of *amor* per se, so his criticism of civil war does not preclude admiration for martial excellence and the great vitality it expresses. Just as well-bred and well-trained oxen or war horses exemplified the creative possibilities of animal energies in the exposition of husbandry, they helped also to epitomize the natural superiority of Italy over the sinister and degenerate nations of the East (2.140–148):

haec loca non tauri spirantes naribus ignem
inuertere satis immanis dentibus hydri,
. . . . . . . . . . . . . . .
hinc bellator equus campo sese arduus infert,

> hinc albi, Clitumne, greges et maxima taurus
> uictima, saepe tuo perfusi flumine sacro,
> Romanos ad templa deum duxere triumphos.
>
> These places are not plowed by bulls that breathe fire from their nostrils, nor are they sown with the teeth of a huge dragon. . . . From here the war horse strides tall to the field of battle; from here herds of white bulls, the greatest of sacrificial victims—often anointed with your sacred water, Clitumnus—have led Roman triumphs to the temples of the gods.

In that same passage Virgil went on to enumerate the great warriors and hardy peoples who have triumphed over Rome's enemies. His description of the Roman civil wars and his praise of Italy shortly thereafter are both impressive, then, because they present dramatic embodiments of seemingly irresistible forces. The essential difference between the two surveys of Roman civilization is that in the latter Virgil has focused on moments in history when Romans were secure in the world precisely because they were masters of themselves; in the former he has exposed the Romans at a time when they are helpless victims of their own energies. The recurrent images of animals help to preserve the continuity of Virgil's underlying concern at the same time as they accentuate significant contrasts in perspective.

The treatment of *amor caecus* recalls yet another notable passage of social criticism in the *Georgics*. At the conclusion of *Georgic* 2 Virgil celebrated rustic life. The force and effectiveness of his praise was heightened by explicit contrast with the corruption and chaos of contemporary Rome. The poet's condemnation of urban life concluded with a survey of the frantic, violent, and ultimately self-destructive activity that the pursuit of luxury and power encourages. In contrast to the farmer (2.503–512),

> sollicitant alii remis freta caeca, ruuntque
> in ferrum, penetrant aulas et limina regum;
> hic petit excidiis urbem miserosque penatis,
> ut gemma bibat et Sarrano dormiat ostro;
> condit opes alius defossoque incubat auro;
> hic stupet attonitus rostris, hunc plausus hiantem
> per cuneos geminatus enim plebisque patrumque
> corripuit; gaudent perfusi sanguine fratrum,

exsilioque domos et dulcia limina mutant
atque alio patriam quaerunt sub sole iacentem.

others stir up blind straits with their oars and rush to the sword, force their way across the thresholds into the courts of kings. This one brings destruction upon a city and wretched Penates that he might drink from a goblet encrusted with jewels and sleep on Tyrian purple. Another hides his wealth and sleeps on buried gold. This one gazes in astonishment at the rostra; the applause of the people and the elders, doubling through the sections of the theatre, has transported this one as he gapes. They take delight, soaked in their brothers' blood, exchange their own sweet thresholds for exile and seek a homeland under an alien sun.

Similarities with the destructive *amor* of the bulls should be clear enough: the perversion of goals, the self-defeating frenzy. But there are also parallels to Virgil's broader condemnation of *amor caecus*. The headlong rush of those aroused by *amor*, *in furias ignemque ruunt*[21] ("they rush to frenzy and fire"), is reminiscent of the city dwellers who *ruuntque / in ferrum* ("rush to the sword"). Leander's fatal plunge into the strait of the Hellespont in "blind night" (*nocte natat caeca serus freta*) is not unlike the merchants' frantic beating of the "blind straits" in pursuit of wealth (*sollicitant alii remis freta caeca*). But these verbal reminiscences only serve to point up a remarkable similarity in the general tone of the passages and in the kind of activity they describe.

The attack on contemporary vices achieved particular definition by contrast with the seemingly antithetical vision of rustic life against which it was set—a way of life in which the simpler virtues are honored and political ambitions have no place. Virgil's glorification of that rustic alternative, however, led to a disturbing glance at the origins of the Roman state and to the observation that the ultimate accomplishment of traditional rustic vitality was the founding and fortification of Rome! That accomplishment, moreover, was

---

21. The propensity to self-destruction implicit in the term *furiae* here is made explicit in 3.511–514: *mox erat hoc ipsum exitio, furiisque refecti / ardebant, ipsique suos iam morte sub aegra / (di meliora piis, erroremque hostibus illum!) / discissos nudis laniabant dentibus artus* ("soon even this was a cause of death; their frenzies renewed, they were burning at the very threshold of sickly death [may the gods grant better to the pious and reserve that delirium for enemies!]: they were ripping and tearing their own limbs with their naked teeth").

shown to be bound up with the same passions that led to the fratricidal civil wars of Virgil's own day.

The evocation of the civil wars, the attack on urban corruption, and the condemnation of *amor caecus* document the perversion of the energies that are the very source of creative achievement. All three passages share a strong sense of restlessness, of frantic and aimless or misdirected activity, of the utter inappropriateness of the use to which things and human energy are put. In each situation control and self-control are conspicuously absent, and each time the result is that action is both destructive and self-defeating.

The effect of such parallelism is to remove specific instances of violent disorder beyond immediate temporal and topical issues and to place them in a timeless, universal context. They appear as different consequences of a single tendency to disorder that is inherent in all creation. From this perspective mankind and civilization cannot be opposed to nature but must be considered within it. And inasmuch as the Roman civil wars or the corruption of urban society or Leander's fatal rashness are failures, like the farmer's, to contain a natural vitality that is boundless and irresistible, they must be seen as failures not of excess but of deficiency. Charges of willful violence or even of misguided temerity are insufficient to account for human destructiveness. *Amor caecus* is *amor* unseen by its victim as well as unseeing.[22] Human beings and their societies, like bulls and mares, are sometimes the unwitting agents of their own destruction.

Virgil's observations about *amor* have not, of course, denied altogether the prospect of achieving a civilized existence. The knowledge that human capacities are finite does not obviate the need for struggle—or the value of it. The certainties of failures do not negate the possibility for successes: appreciation of the disruptive effects of *amor* does not displace but rather intensifies admiration for the manifest accomplishments of well-bred and carefully trained animals. The very persistence of rustic life and the farmer's skill itself testify to the possibilities for renewal, even as the disruptive effects of *amor* exemplify the inevitability of decline. Juxtaposition of the discussion of breeding and training with that of *amor* calls attention to the fact

22. "Blind" in the sense of "unseeing" is an obvious and appropriate meaning for *caecus* in the context of Virgil's account of *amor*, for the behavior he describes is undeniably rash. But it is well, also, to acknowledge Servius' judgment (ad loc.): *Caeci Amoris latentis amoris* ("blind love, hidden love").

that decline and renewal are each implicit in the other. The boundless energy manifest in violent lust is the same as that which expresses itself in procreation, in the strength of the plow oxen, and in the spirit of the war horse. It is, in fact, the necessary basis for such excellence; it is the quality that the farmer selects in breeding and cultivates in training. Similarly, the civil wars manifest the very energies and ambitions that led to Roman greatness in the first place. What Virgil has done in the first half of *Georgic 3*, then, is not only to reaffirm that man's efforts to achieve a civilized existence sometimes result in uncontrollable disorder. He has also argued that such destructive outbreaks are inevitable for the simple reason that the elemental vitality that makes creative activity possible is itself also a source of disorder. By organizing his discussion of *amor* as he does, and by making it the culmination of his larger discussion of breeding and training and of his examination of the elemental vitality at the farmer's disposal, Virgil emphasizes the potential within man and nature for violent destruction rather than for orderly creation. The ideal of unrestrained mastery with which *Georgic 3* began has been decisively undercut.

## IV

In the second half of *Georgic 3*, Virgil attacks that ideal from a different perspective. Now he focuses on elemental vitality to emphasize not the potential for disorder implicit in it, but rather its inherent limitations. That change in emphasis is appropriately marked by a shift from the topic of the larger, more powerful animals to that of the smaller and more vulnerable, and by acknowledgment of the difficulty this new topic presents to the poet (289-392):

nec sum animi dubius uerbis ea uincere magnum
quam sit et angustis hunc addere rebus honorem;
sed me Parnasi deserta per ardua dulcis
raptat amor; iuuat ire iugis, qua nulla priorum
Castaliam molli deuertitur orbita cliuo.

I am in no doubt about how great a task it is to master this subject in words and to add that distinction to such a confined topic. But through the deserted heights of Parnassus sweet, love carries me away. It is a joy to pass from mountain ranges by a gentle descent where no one before me has wandered down to the Castalian spring.

Although those claims of originality and preeminence recall the ambitions expressed in the introduction to *Georgic* 3, they are less grandiose and confident. Virgil no longer anticipates bringing the Muses to Italy, nor does he even claim to tap new wellsprings of inspiration. More modestly, he now reflects on the pleasures of reaching the traditional sources of inspiration by a new path. His diminishing ambitions reflect his appreciation of the difficulty of investing his new and more limited topic with greatness. Implicit in the poet's relation to his material is a commentary on that of the farmer's. Just as the poet will find it difficult to give stature by words (*uerbis*) to the subject of small animals, so will the farmer find it difficult to lend stature by deed to the practice of keeping small animals. Nonetheless, the exposition, as in the first half of *Georgic* 3, begins hopefully. It leads, however, to a conclusion that is correspondingly more pessimistic as the poet's initial expectations are the more reserved.

The first discussions of the smaller animals reflect a guarded optimism, which is in keeping with the introduction to this half of *Georgic* 3. The fleece from Miletus fetches a high price—at least when it is colored with Tyrian dyes (306-307). Similarly, just as in *Georgic* 2 even comparatively barren land was found to have its uses (2.177-183), so here we are advised that the goat, although it offers nothing as glamorous as the sheep's fleece, nonetheless has its own value. In fact, we are reminded briefly of the sense of abundance and possibility that characterized nature in the most optimistic moments of *Georgic* 2. The goat is fruitful and provides milk in abundance (308-310). Soldiers and sailors find uses for its whiskers and shaggy hair (311-313), just as in *Georgic* 2 they found uses for different kinds of lumber (2.426-453). Like trees, goats require little care (315-317): of their own accord they come home with full udders, just as in the previous book nature was depicted as pouring out its fruits with virtual spontaneity.

The distinctive ambience of *Georgic* 2 is sustained also in the succeeding passage (295-338). There Virgil describes the routine of the Italian shepherd in grazing and watering his flock. The annual and, more especially, daily patterns of the herdsman's activities reflect the mildness and moderation of the Italian climate—partaking of all seasons but none to extreme. During the winter the herdsman keeps his flocks inside, protected from the cold, and provides them with fodder and bedding. But Italian winters are short, and the herdsman can look forward to the return of summer *mox* ("soon," 295-296). Once winter has passed, he drives his flocks to pasture. Early in the morning he grazes the sheep. As the day grows warmer, he waters them, and at midday, *aestibus mediis*, he retreats with them to shade (322-334). As the day cools, he waters them again and, finally, sets them to pasture with evening (335-338). The fecundity of the flocks attest to the wholesomeness of this climate. But Italy's moderate climate does more than make flocks fertile; it seems to offer a perfectly idyllic way of life. The herdsman's daily round of duties is a round of pleasures as well. Virgil goes out of his way to characterize each time of day by the attractions peculiar to it. The herdsman must drive his flocks to pasture (325-326):

> . . . dum mane nouum, dum gramina canent,
> et ros in tenera pecori gratissimus herba.

> while morning is new, while the blades of grass are white with frost and there is dew on the tender vegetation, most pleasing to the flock.

The time for the morning watering is signaled by the cicada's music as it fairly bursts from the trees (327-328). The heat of the day provides an occasion to seek out a shady valley (332-334),

> sicubi magna Iouis antiquo robore quercus
> ingentis tendat ramos, aut sicubi nigrum
> ilicibus crebris sacra nemus accubet umbra.

> where one of Jupiter's great oaks, ancient in its strength, extends its huge branches or where, black with dense ilex trees, a grove reclines in sacred shade.

Virgil has opposed the heat of the day to shade which is not only cooling but can offer the untroubled security of sacred inviolability. His description of a grove which "reclines" (*accubit*) in shade as a banqueter "reclines" for dinner brings together the sense of calm, almost solemn inviolability with a sense of festivity in a striking catachresis.

208    Virgil's *Georgics*

Just as the attractiveness of Italian moderation was enhanced by contrast with the degeneracy of the East in *Georgic* 2, so here the herdsman's pleasant round is contrasted with the lives of those who must endure extremes of cold and heat. There is, however, a significant difference in the nature of those two contrasts. In the former case the vices of the East were described only briefly and were the occasion for an extended appreciation of the virtues of Italy. In *Georgic* 3 the emphasis of the contrast is reversed. The pleasantness of the Italian herdsman's life now comes first and leads to a vivid and comparatively extended reflection on life at the fringes of the inhabited world. The result, then, is to qualify the idyllic image of the Italian herdsman with a reminder of the narrowness of the limits within which a civilized existence is possible. That shift of emphasis, in turn, acts as a pivotal point in the development of the argument of this book; it leads to a gradual and increasing emphasis on the limits of civilization within Italy itself.

Virgil first contrasts the life of Italian herdsmen with that of the pastoral nomads of Libya. The latter enjoy none of the varied pleasures that comprise the Italian herdsmen's day. The comparative simplicity of their life is offset by an oppressive lack of variety (341-343):

> saepe diem noctemque et totum ex ordine mensem
> pascitur itque pecus longa in deserta sine ullis
> hospitiis: tantum campi iacet.

> Often, day and night in succession, for an entire month their flock grazes and travels in long desert stretches without any refuge: so great a plain lies around them.

Lack of *hospitium* implies, in the lack of people to entertain strangers, a lack of the most fundamental amenities of civilization itself: society and the regular conventions of social intercourse. There is a particular aptness, consequently, in the following lines which compare the Libyan nomads to Roman soldiers on a forced march. The comparison draws attention to a quality of the Libyans' way of life that extends beyond its difficulty (343-348):

> . . . omnia secum
> armentarius Afer agit, tectumque laremque
> armaque Amyclaeumque canem Cressamque pharetram;

> non secus ac patriis acer Romanus in armis
> iniusto sub fasce uiam cum carpit, et hosti
> ante exspectatum positis stat in agmine castris.

The African herdsman takes with him everything, his house, household god, weapons, Spartan hound, and Cretan quiver, just as the fierce Roman soldier, when like his ancestors he makes a forced march with full pack and stands before the enemy, sooner than expected, in formation, camp already pitched.

The Libyans, like the Roman soldier, have acquired some of the terrifying fierceness engendered by a life of hardship and necessarily stern discipline. Their wanderings recall, perhaps, the restlessness that marked the final degradation of the ambitious city dwellers who (2.511–512)

> exsilioque domos et dulcia limina mutant
> atque alio patriam quaerunt sub sole iacentem.

> exchange their own sweet thresholds for exile and seek a fatherland under another sun.

But while their keenness and desperate energy might be appropriate for a Roman soldier in a difficult campaign, they seem more sinister than encouraging as an aspect of everyday life.

Like the shepherds of Libya, the Scythians lack the varied pleasures that the Italian climate offers. Their days, too, are characterized by a dreary sameness. Seasons and days alike are cold—never the invigorating crispness of an Italian morning but a sterile and forbidding cold (352–357, 367–370):

> illic clausa tenent stabulis armenta, neque ullae
> aut herbae campo apparent aut arbore frondes;
> sed iacet aggeribus niueis informis et alto
> terra gelu late septemque adsurgit in ulnas.
> semper hiems, semper spirantes frigora Cauri;
> tum Sol pallentis haud umquam discutit umbras,
> . . . . . . . . . . .
> interea toto . . . aëre ningit:
> intereunt pecudes, stant circumfusa pruinis
> corpora magna boum, confertoque agmine cerui
> torpent mole nova et summis vix cornibus exstant.

> There they keep their herds closed up in stables. No vegetation is to be seen in the field or foliage on trees, but the shapeless earth extends far and wide, piled with snow and thick ice seven ells deep. Always it is winter, always there are northeast winds breathing cold. Their sun never dispels the pall of shadows. . . . Meanwhile, . . . the sky is everywhere filled with snow. Flocks perish; the great bodies of cattle stand covered with frost, and stags, in close formation, grow numb under an unfamiliar burden; the tips of their antlers barely stick out.

The bleak harshness of the Scythians' environment is reflected in the quality of their life and in their character. Their method of hunting is dull and unimaginative (371-374):

> hos non immissis canibus, non cassibus ullis
> puniceaeue agitant pauidos formidine pennae,
> sed frustra oppositum trudentis pectore montem
> comminus obtruncant ferro. . . .

> They do not drive these [stags] by setting dogs on them or with nets or by frightening them with dyed feathers, but as the stags vainly force their breasts against the opposing mountain of snow, at close quarters they slaughter them with their swords.

That scene also introduces the brutishness of the Scythians themselves. The doomed stags raise cries so distorted by terror that Virgil describes them with a word used most frequently for the braying of donkeys: *grauiter rudentis* ("terribly the stags bray," 374). By contrast the Scythians' own joyful cries of success seem heartless, almost ghoulish: *caedunt et magno laeti clamore reportant* ("the men kill them and with great clamor joyfully carry them home," 375).

When the Scythians return home, it is to an enforced leisure which, like their hunt, also reveals both the harshness of their environment and the brutishness of their own character. Protracted winter makes the normal work of farming and herding impossible. Instead, the Scythians retreat underground to while away the time (376-378):

> ipsi in defossis specubus secura sub alta
> otia agunt terra, congestaque robora totasque
> aduoluere focis ulmos ignique dedere.

They themselves in dugout caves, carefree, deep beneath the earth spend their time in leisure. They roll heaped-up oaks and whole elm trees onto their hearths and give them up to the fire.

Their life is a grotesque parody of the homely relaxation that the Italian farmer enjoys in the winter. Even in its unusual location the scene might be idyllic. It might, for example, bring to mind a well-known drinking song of Alcaeus, which Horace (*Odes* 1.9) was later to put into Latin (Diehl, fr. 90):

Ύει μὲν ὁ Ζεύς, ἐκ δ' ὀράνω μέγας
χέιμων, πεπάγαισιν δ' ὑδάτων ῥόαι.
. . . . . . . . . . . . . . . .
κάββαλλε τὸν χέιμων· ἐπὶ μὲν τίθεις
πῦρ, ἐν δὲ κέρναις οἶνον ἀφειδέως
μέλιχρον, αὐταρ ἀμφὶ κόρσᾳ
μάλθακον ἀμφιβάλων γνόφαλλον.

Zeus rains and from the sky comes a great storm. The rivers are frozen. Strike down the storm; build up the fire; mix wine generously and round your temples put a soft woolen wreath.

But the Scythians' retreat from winter is the occasion for crude self-indulgence (379–380):

hic noctem ludo docunt, et pocula laeti
fermento atque acidis imitantur uitea sorbis.

Here they pass the night in revelry and joyfully copy draughts of wine with yeast and sour service berries.

Night-long carousal was a stock symbol of moral degeneracy—a characteristic of rebellious young men in Plautus' comedies, a favorite object of attack for social critics—and consider the length of the Scythian nights! Virgil sums up the character of the Scythians when he calls them a *gens effrena* ("an unbridled race," 283). The phrase comprehends both their brutal violence and their unrestrained revelry—and it is the more pointed because it recalls the emphasis on the value of control in the recent discussion of horses.

In *Georgic* 1 Virgil advanced one of the familiar Stoic arguments for divine beneficence, namely, that while two-fifths of the world were uninhabitable because of the cold and one-fifth because of the heat, the Stoic god in his goodness had made the remaining two-fifths, the temperate zones, suitable for man (1.231-251). The contrast between the temperate environment of the Italian herdsman and the extreme heat and cold that determine the barbaric existence of the Libyans and Scythians, respectively, recalls that argument, but with a significant shift of emphasis. A survey of life in the three climatic regions of the earth no longer encourages confidence in a beneficent deity or the sense that mankind enjoys a protected place in the universe. Rather, it expresses the contrasts between the temperate, arctic, and tropical zones in terms of human experience, not in large abstractions. As a consequence, it makes vivid mankind's dependence on the environment, gives to the regions where civilization is impossible an immediacy they did not have before, and leads to a sense of the limitations of civilization. Within the context of *Georgic* 3 those developments are important because they provide a clear standard against which we may gauge the progressive deterioration that Virgil records now within the boundaries of the civilized world itself.

Following the vignettes of life in Libya and Scythia, we are recalled pointedly to the more attractive life possible in Italy. But even amid comparatively encouraging scenes, signs of disorder begin to appear. While the Scythians clothe themselves in *fuluis . . . saetis* ("tawny bristles," 383), the Italian shepherd is instructed in how to breed and feed sheep for wool (384-390); we are reminded of the fecundity and usefulness of goats (394-403); a recommendation to breed dogs leads to the description of a hunt that is the very antithesis of the snow-cloaked butchery practiced by the Scythians (406-413). However, at the heart of those instructions to the shepherd is a warning to be on guard against the degenerative forces of nature. Just as the farmer of *Georgic* 1 had to keep up the work of selecting good seed without remission, so the shepherd must be careful to select for breeding only those sheep that are perfectly white. He must even be suspicious of a ram whose fleece is all white, for even if it has only a black spot under its tongue, its offspring will be tainted (386-390). The brief discussion of dogs introduces, if only in passing, the idea of conflict: dogs are useful in the first instance because they guard against theft, wolves, and Spanish brigands (404-408). The theme of degeneration and conflict is immediately picked up and developed more fully. Lines 414-449 (which I shall discuss further below) first advise the herdsman to fumigate his stables in order to drive out snakes, then go on to describe the danger, habits, and appearance of snakes in chilling detail. Here there can be no mistaking the destructive forces that are barely concealed even within Italy.

The final 126 lines of the book are devoted to the subject of disease, first generally and then in its most violent manifestation, plague. The agents of destruction are no longer hidden or restricted in their force. The effects of the plague are universal (480-482):

> et genus omne neci pecudum dedit, omne ferarum,
> corrupitque lacus, infecit pabula tabo.
> nec uia mortis erat simplex; . . .

> and [the plague] gave over every class of domestic animal to death, and every class of wild animal. It corrupted the water, infected the fodder with its putrification. Nor was there a single manner of death.

Even the *victor equus* (496-497), earlier the symbol of natural vitality at its most developed and refined, cannot escape the plague's destructive force. So likewise, its counterpart, the plow ox, perishes without dignity (515-517):

> ecce autem duro fumans sub uomere taurus
> concidit et mixtum spumis uomit ore cruorem
> extremosque ciet gemitus. . . .

> Behold, too, steaming under the hard plough, the ox falls, vomits from its mouth gore mingled with foam and raises its final groans.

At its height the plague throws the entire countryside, the sky and sea as well, into total confusion (537-549):

> non lupus insidias explorat ouilia circum
> nec gregibus nocturnus obambulat: acrior illum
> cura domat; timidi dammae ceruique fugaces
> nunc interque canes et circum tecta uagantur.
> iam maris immensi prolem et genus omne natantum
> litore in extremo ceu naufraga corpora fluctus
> proluit; insolitae fugiunt in flumina phocae.
> interit et curuis frustra defensa latebris

uipera et attoniti squamis astantibus hydri.
ipsis est aër auibus non aequus, et illae
praecipites alta uitam sub nube relinquunt.

No wolf attempts ambushes around the sheepfolds or stalks the flocks at night: a sharper care tames him. Timid does and stags, usually quick to flee, now wander among the dogs and around buildings. Now the huge sea's offspring, every kind of swimming creature, are washed up onto the edge of the shore, like shipwrecked bodies, washed up by the waves. Contrary to custom, seals flee to the rivers. The viper, too, perishes, protected in vain in his curved hiding places, as do water serpents, dumbfounded, their scales bristling. Even for birds the sky is no refuge and headlong beneath a high cloud they leave behind their lives.

The details of this scene reflect a literary tradition that goes back to a well-known poem by Archilochus (Diehl, fr. 74), who saw an eclipse of the sun as an event that challenged the very idea of an ordered cosmos. If the sun can be extinguished in midday, then all kinds of impossible things (ἀδύνατα) are possible: beasts of the fields and dolphins will exchange places and so forth. But there is an important distinction to be made between Archilochus' vision of a world turned topsy turvy and the use Virgil makes of that vision. For Archilochus the eclipse of the sun had a positive value: it confirmed Zeus' unlimited mastery over the cosmos, his ability to intervene in its workings at will. In Virgil's hands images of chaos lead to no transcendent order or purpose—an aspect of the representation of disorder in *Georgic* 3 that I shall discuss more fully below. We are confronted only with the stark reality of chaos.

The sense of loss which that experience elicits is emphasized in several ways. Not only does Virgil's description of it recall Archilochus' poem, it also recalls one of the conventional characteristics of the Golden Age, but to quite new effect. In the Golden Age domestic animals will not fear predators. As Virgil expressed it in *Eclogue* 4.22, *nec metuent armenta leones* ("nor will flocks fear lions"). Because of the plague, sheep and wolves will intermingle freely; stags will wander among the habitations of men: the hunted will no longer fear the hunters. The plague makes a mockery of our aspirations for an ideal existence; it even overshadows the almost unimaginably horrible and oppressive conditions that once seemed to exist only beyond the borders of the civilized world.

Just as the barbarism of the Libyans and Scythians reflected their environments, so increasing emphasis on conflict and disorder in the natural world is matched by a corresponding emphasis on the progressive brutalization of man. Thus, when a sheep is fevered, the shepherd should bleed the animal by locating a vein *salientem sanguine* ("pulsing with blood," 460) at the base of its foot and cutting it open (457-463). Although that remedy is required by the circumstances, it is, nonetheless, extreme, for in applying it, the shepherd is acting (461-463)

> Bisaltae quo more solent acerque Gelonus,
> cum fugit in Rhodopen atque in deserta Getarum,
> et lac concretum cum sanguine potat equino.
>
> just as the Bisaltae and the savage Geloni are accustomed to do when they flee to Mount Rhodope or to the deserted regions of the Getae and drink milk curdled with the blood of horses.

The Bisaltae, Geloni, and Getae all belong to the distant North. Mount Rhodope, in fact, was designated just a little more than one hundred lines earlier as the home of the Scythians (449-451), so that we are reminded of the very barbarism that recently seemed to exemplify the utter antithesis of life in Italy. While the comparison between the shepherd bleeding his sheep and the savage tribesmen drinking their unsavory mixture of milk and blood does not establish the identity of Italians and northern barbarians, it does suggest how precarious and vulnerable are man's efforts to be civilized—even in the most favorable of environments.

In the face of plague, moreover, man's skills are ineffectual and he finds himself helpless to retain even the minimal elements of a civilized existence. The most sophisticated arts are the first to fail. Virgil observes that there was only one remedy for the dying animals: to pour wine into their mouths through a horn funnel (508-509). But the remedy is useless to prevent death. All that it can do is to revive the animals enough so that they suffer renewed and protracted agonies (511-514):

> . . . furiisque refecti
> ardebant, ipsique suos iam morte sub aegra

(di meliora piis, erroremque hostibus illum!)
discissos nudis laniabant dentibus artus.

Their frenzies renewed, they were burning at the very threshold of sickly death (may the gods grant a better fate to the pious, and reserve that delirium for enemies!); they were ripping and tearing their own limbs with their naked teeth.

In the long and famous description of a plague that concludes the sixth book of his *De Rerum Natura*, and which surely influenced Virgil, Lucretius emphasized the helplessness of man to stem the plague's inexorable progress by mentioning a cure that worked for some victims (*DRN* 6.1229): *hoc aliis erat exitio letumque parabat* ("this [remedy] was the undoing for others and made death ready"). In describing the *uisa salus morientibus una* ("the one apparent salvation for the dying," 510), Virgil recalls Lucretius' phrase only to paint an even more uncompromising picture of man's utter helplessness (511): *mox erat hoc ipsum exitio* ("soon even this [remedy] was a cause of death"). "The dying animals' only salvation" does not cure some cases and exacerbate others; it only adds to the misery of the very animals whom it at first appears to help! Medicine proves to be worse than nothing. Virgil reasserts that idea even more directly a few lines later (549–550):

> quaesitaeque nocent artes; cessere magistri,
> Phillyrides Chiron Amythaoniusque Melampus.

> Sought-after skills do harm. The masters of medicine have abandoned the field: Chiron, son of Philyra, and Melampus, son of Amythaon.

The herdsmen's failures are not due to their imperfect skills. Even such paragons of myth and legend as Chiron and Melampus must yield to the plague.

The plague, however, does more than expose the limits of man's skills. As it kills off the farmer's animals it undermines his capacity to continue his cultivation of the earth, the very basis of all other civilized activity. The farmers themselves are reduced almost to the condition of animals (534–536):

> ergo aegre rastris terram rimantur, et ipsis
> unguibus infodiunt fruges, montisque per altos
> contenta ceruice trahunt stridentia plaustra.

Therefore, weakly, using rakes, they root about the earth, with their own nails dig holes for seed and along tall mountains they drag scraping plowshares on their straining necks.

The verb that describes the farmer's raking (*rimantur*, "root") is used only one other time in the *Georgics* (1.384), and then to describe the action of birds as they peck about in the marshy fields of Asia. In that context, the farmer's digging with his *unguibus*, "fingernails," might easily conjure up a picture of an animal pawing at the ground with its *unguibus*—"hooves" or "claws." Finally, the farmer actually takes the place of the oxen beneath the yoke. Even after they die, the farmer's animals are useless to him: the hides and fleece are infected and transmit the disease to any who touch them (559–562). Consequently, they cannot be used for clothing (563–566):

> uerum etiam inuisos si quis temptarat amictus,
> ardentes papulae atque immundus olentia sudor
> membra sequebatur, nec longo deinde moranti
> tempore contactos artus sacer ignis edebat.

> but if someone had touched even the hateful garments, burning pimples and an offensive sweating attacked their stinking limbs and not long afterward, as they died, *sacer ignis* devoured their infected limbs.

Those, the final words of the book, bring home the full extent of the plague's terrible consequences. Forced to do the work of an animal for his food, unable even to make new clothing for himself, the herdsman lives under the threat of a gruesome death. He has been reduced to a state even more bleak and desperate than that of the barbarians, with whose lives his own comparatively idyllic existence was contrasted earlier.

## V

The progressive collapse of civilization that occupies the final third of *Georgic* 3 is made to appear the more frightening by the recurrence of certain motifs from *Georgic* 2 and especially from *Georgic* 1. The snake lurking in the crannies of barns and threatening the herdsmen's flocks (414–439) is an example of the pest that attacks the farmer's crops when once he has seen to the immediate tasks of cultivation. In *Georgic* 2 this was represented by the goat whose bite was thought to poison the vine (2.371-396). The danger of goats attacking the vine even after it was growing healthily required additional precautions, which included the propitiatory offering of a goat to Bacchus. That sacrifice became an occasion for merriment and celebration which led ultimately to the development of the traditional theatres of the Greeks and the Romans. In *Georgic* 1 warning against the attacks of geese and cranes on cereal crops led to reflection on the value of struggle and the divine beneficence that made the difficult but rewarding work of cultivation necessary.

While the warning in *Georgic* 3 to be on guard against snakes recalls those earlier passages, it contrasts sharply with them in that it offers no consolation for the existence of danger and the necessity for conflict. Instead of reminding us that the rise of the civilized *artes* is stimulated by conflict and the necessity of work, the warning in *Georgic* 3 is gradually displaced by a kind of mesmerized fascination with the snake's repulsive deadliness (420-424):

> . . . cape saxa manu, cape robora, pastor,
> tollentemque minas et sibila colla tumentem
> deice! iamque fuga timidum caput abdidit alte,
> cum medii nexus extremaeque agmina caudae
> soluuntur, tardosque trahit sinus ultimus orbis.

> Take rocks in your hand, take sticks, shepherd, and as the snake rises threateningly and its hissing neck swells up, strike it down. Now in flight it has hidden its fearful head deep, while its coiling mid-section and the column of its tail's end are loosened; its last fold draws in its slow coils.

That picture leads to a description of the awful Calabrian water snake which, like the geese and cranes of *Georgic* 1, is *improbus* ("ruinous") in its pursuit of its natural prey during the wet seasons of the year. The brief discussion of snakes ends simply with a grim warning that, when the weather is dry and hot, the water snake becomes vicious and attacks even men (435-439):

> ne mihi tum mollis sub diuo carpere somnos
> neu dorso nemoris libeat iacuisse per herbas,
> cum positis nouus exuuiis nitidusque iuuenta

uoluitur, aut catulos tectis aut oua relinquens,
arduus ad solem et linguis micat ore trisulcis.

Then I would take no pleasure in gentle naps under an open sky or in stretching out on my back in the grass of a grove when the new snake, his slough cast, shining with youth, coils along, leaving at home its young—or its eggs. It rises up toward the sun and its tongue flicks from its mouth, forked.

It is, then, with a sense that the serenity of the countryside has been fundamentally compromised and that man must live on his guard that Virgil concludes his discussion of snakes.

That warning against going abroad at certain times anticipates the repetition of another motif from *Georgic* 1 by which we are made more aware of the bleakness of the perspective that controls the latter half of *Georgic* 3. It recalls lines late in *Georgic* 1 that warn of the terrible storms signaled by changes in the sun's appearance (1.455-457):

omnia tum pariter uento nimbisque uidebis
feruere: non illa quisquam me nocte per altum
ire neque a terra moneat conuellere funem.

Then you will see everything with wind and clouds alike seething. Let no one advise me on that night to voyage across the deep and to cast off from land.

The echo of that passage in *Georgic* 3, as faint as it may be, looks ahead to the fact that the discussion of diseases that follows is presented in such a way as to recall the discussion of weather signs in *Georgic* 1. The two topics occupy similar positions in their respective books. In both cases Virgil presents a succession of natural disasters and arranges them in an order of increasing intensity leading to a final and climactic disaster: in *Georgic* 1 the storms described tend on the whole to be each more violent and destructive than the last, and culminate in the metaphorical storm of the Roman civil wars when the entire world is thrown into disorder; in *Georgic* 3 a survey of various ailments that attack livestock leads to a discussion of a plague which, like the civil wars, disrupts the normal order of the world. Virgil, in fact, explicitly compares the multitude of diseases that attack the shepherd's flocks to the rush of winter storms (470-471):

non tam creber agens hiemem ruit aequore turbo
quam multae pecudum pestes.

The gusts of a whirlwind that drives a storm when it rushes off
the sea are not so numerous as are the diseases of flocks.

The plague itself is likened (478–480) to a storm or to the kind of
seasonal change signaled by the signs described in *Georgic* 1:

Hic quondam morbo caeli miseranda coorta est
tempestas totoque autumni incanduit aestu
et genus omne neci pecudum dedit, omne ferarum.

Here once because of a sickness in the sky there gathered a grim
storm. It burned with all the autumn's heat and gave up to death
every kind of wild beast.

Finally, diseases, like storms, are presented as, paradoxically, being
part of or having an order of their own, despite the chaos to which
they reduce the world. Real storms and the metaphorical storms of
the civil wars in *Georgic* 1 were presented within the larger discussion
of weather signs. In *Georgic* 3 Virgil introduces the sections on disease with the heading, *Morborum quoque te causas et signa docebo* ("The
causes and signs of disease I will also teach you," 440). The progress
of the plague in particular is marked by clear signs (503): *haec ante
exitium primis dant signa diebus* ("These are the signs which [the infected animals] show before death, in the first days [of the sickness]").

The effect of such parallels with the discussion of weather signs
in *Georgic* 1 is manifold. In the first place, it continues the contrast,
begun in the section on snakes, between the complex perspective of
*Georgic* 1 and the unqualified sense of futility dominating the conclusion of *Georgic* 3. In the earlier book a sense of alienation from the
beneficent order of the Stoic universe came late. The natural disorders Virgil recorded were either revealed, like the depredation of
the geese and cranes, to have a purpose or were preceded by warning signs, which attested to the generous concern of the gods for men
and recalled the divine beneficence that shapes the universe (1.351–354):

Atque haec ut certis possemus discere signis,
aestusque pluuiasque et agentis frigora uentos,
ipse pater statuit quid menstrua luna moneret,
quo signo caderent Austri.

And that we might know these things—heat spells, rain, winds that drive cold before them—by reliable signs, the father himself decreed what in its monthly cycle the moon would warn, under what star the south winds would subside.

Comparisons between the presentations of storms and of the plague help to emphasize how utterly the destructiveness of the latter is unrelieved by any sense of a higher order or a redeeming purpose. Far from pointing to a benevolent divinity, the plague cuts men off from their gods. During the plague, sacrifices to the gods were flawed and unpropitious, with the sacrificial animal sometimes dropping dead just before it was to be slaughtered (486-493). Sometimes, too, it was even impossible to find the kinds of animals required by ritual: bears instead of cows had to pull processional chariots to the temple of Minerva (531-533). The gods themselves were notably unresponsive to human needs. Virgil notes caustically that disease simply worsens when the shepherd refuses to treat sores and, instead, *meliora deos sedet omina poscens* ("sits asking the gods for better omens," 456).

Because the plague seems to be a disaster without any redeeming purpose, without any meaning, the loss and suffering it causes are accompanied by a growing pathos. This is nowhere more clear than in a passage that reflects on the death of a plow ox (517-530):

> . . . it tristis arator
> maerentem abiungens fraterna morte iuuencum,
> atque opere in medio defixa reliquit aratra.
> non umbrae altorum nemorum, non mollia possunt
> prata mouere animum, non qui per saxa uolutus
> purior electro campum petit amnis; at ima
> soluuntur latera, atque oculos stupor urget inertis
> ad terramque fluit deuexo pondere ceruix.
> quid labor aut benefacta iuuant? quid uomere terras
> inuertisse grauis? atqui non Massica Bacchi
> munera, non illis epulae nocuere repostae:
> frondibus et uictu pascuntur simplicis herbae,
> pocula sunt fontes liquidi atque exercita cursu
> flumina, nec somnos abrumpit cura salubris.

The plowman goes sadly, unhitching the bullock who grieves for his fallen brother. He has left the plow thrust motionless in the midst of his work. Neither the shade of tall groves nor soft fields can rouse the bullock's spirit, nor a river that curls through the rocks, more translucent than amber, and seeks the plain, but his sides slacken completely; stupor presses upon his dull eyes, and his neck droops to the earth bending under its own weight. What pleasure do his work or his services do him? What good is it that with a plow he turned the heavy earth? And yet neither Bacchus' gift of Massic wine nor endless banqueting ever harmed those animals. They graze on foliage and a diet of simple grass; their drinks are flowing fountains and rivers tumbling in their course; no care breaks their healthful sleep.

To appreciate the impact of those lines it is helpful not only to recall the contrasting perspective on natural disasters in *Georgic* 1, but also to look briefly at the literary antecedents of Virgil's account of the plague. The sixth and final book of Lucretius' *De Rerum Natura* concludes with the description of a plague that was undoubtedly inspired, in turn, by Thucydides' famous description of the plague that swept Athens in 429 and again in 427 B.C. For Lucretius the plague serves as vivid, climactic proof that the universe is governed by mechanistic processes totally indifferent to mankind. Within the larger context of his argument in *De Rerum Natura*, the plague has a hortatory function as well: since the gods do not concern themselves with men either in this life or afterward and since death or, worse, such suffering as the plague brings may come at any time, we should strive to realize while we can the good life that Epicurus advocates. Virgil offers no such exhortation. Rather than being a call to the good life, he suggests that whatever benefits might once have been derived from a life of mental serenity and simple pleasures are rendered of no account by the experience of the plague. It is true, of course, that Virgil is, strictly speaking, talking about animals; but we are strongly encouraged to apply his comments to the human condition as well: the animals are described as suffering in very human sorts of ways; their virtues and the vices they avoid are among the virtues and vices that occupied moral philosophers and social critics; the two well-known models for Virgil's description of the plague—the accounts of Lucretius and Thucydides—were both primarily concerned with people; finally, Virgil has prepared us from the very opening of the exposition in *Georgic* 3 to view the condition of animals as analogous to the condition of humans. If, then, the plague can have no positive meaning for animals, it has none for humans either.

Besides intensifying the futility of Virgil's perspective in *Georgic* 3, the parallels with *Georgic* 1 serve another important function. They suggest that disease and plague, despite the fact that they bring disorder, are nonetheless natural phenomena. We have seen that diseases, no less than changes in the weather, have causes and can be recognized by specific signs. They even follow definite, recognizable sequences. Virgil can describe their courses just as he can describe the seasonal pattern of changes in the weather or the course of a particular kind of storm. Again, awareness of Virgil's literary predecessors reinforces his own argument. I have already observed that Lucretius saw the plague as an expression of a universe governed according to strictly mechanistic principles. While Thucydides was not confident that the causes of plague could be found, he perceived it as a natural phenomenon and reported it on the assumption that, if it occurred again, it would produce the same symptoms and follow the same course (*Peloponnesian War* 2.48). Throughout his description of the plague, he stressed the specific order of symptoms and the regular course of the disease (2.49-57). For Virgil, as for Lucretius and Thucydides, disease and plague, however disruptive they may be, however meaningless in terms of human experience, are nonetheless not anomalous intrusions into the workings of the universe but are a part of them. As a consequence they offer a vivid warning of man's limited ability to impose his own order on nature.

The application of that warning is broadened because of the parallels I have noted between the final sections of *Georgics* 1 and 3. The cumulative effect of those parallels not only calls attention to differences of perspective in the two books, it also reveals a fundamental similarity between the Roman civil wars and plague. The two passages occupy comparable positions in the overall organization of their respective books. Both, as I have already observed, are presented as the last and greatest in a series of natural disasters; both are viewed as a reduction of order to chaos; both stand at the conclusions of their books as complete antitheses of hopeful introductions addressed to the young Caesar. Because the plague is presented as a parallel to the Roman civil wars, it suggests a reinterpretation of Virgil's earlier description of that historical event. In *Georgic* 1 Virgil introduced his description of the civil wars within the context of a

Stoic conception of the universe. Appropriately, then, he presented them as a punishment that the Romans brought on themselves by their own crimes—most importantly, although not exclusively, the murder of Julius Caesar. That punishment was accompanied by all sorts of terrible portents, which further suggested that it was an expression of divine anger. Virgil himself appealed to the gods not to deny the world Caesar's help any longer (1.498–501). The experience of plague suggests a quite different interpretation of the civil wars. Insofar as they are analogous to the plague, we must regard them neither as a consequence of human failing, nor as retribution for wickedness, nor as an expression of divine disfavor. They must be seen, rather, as a natural phenomenon, neither more nor less than an aspect of the workings of nature. Civil disorder, like the plague, is inevitable and inescapable; its destructiveness is beyond human power to check or ameliorate.

Virgil's account of the plague suggests a different perspective on the Roman civil wars from that offered in his discussion of *amor*. But even though the two perspectives are different, they are complementary rather than mutually exclusive. The evocation of the civil wars at the conclusion of *Georgic* 1 itself combined two perspectives. On the one hand, the civil wars were seen as an expression of human energies, human wickedness. But they were also felt, like storms, to involve disorder on a greater than human scale: the entire world is in disorder; the gods are inflicting their vengeance. The first half of *Georgic* 3 speaks to the former perspective; the second half speaks to the latter. Man's capacity to create and sustain an ordered existence is imperfect first of all because his ability to control the vital energies of nature, including his own, is limited and, secondly, because the capacity of those vital energies to survive the degenerative forces of nature is itself limited.

Looking back to the first *Georgic* as we are encouraged to do by parallels between the passages on the civil wars, *amor*, and the plague, we may be struck by a notable feature of Virgil's organization. The passages that most clearly record the failures of civilization occur in those books that are dedicated to Caesar and begin with hopeful visions of his mastery. The effect of that organization is twofold. Most specifically it undercuts the optimism of the introductions and warns both us and Caesar himself against utopian expectations. More generally, the effect of that organization is to call our attention to the fact that human limitations, and therefore failures of civilization, are inescapable. Indeed, the conclusion of *Georgic* 3, like the conclusion of the passage on *amor*, stops abruptly with a vision of disorder at its height. It leads nowhere except back to the scene of the desolate pastures with which the description of the plague began. Had Virgil concluded his poem at the end of *Georgic* 3, the effect would have been to suggest that civilization is at best precarious and its achievements vulnerable, and that at worst it may not be possible at all. But he does not conclude his poem there. Rather, he incorporates that awareness of limitation and failure within a larger and more complex vision of the human condition in the fourth and final *Georgic*.

CHAPTER V

# *Georgic* 4

## I

Thus far in the *Georgics* successive idealized visions of rustic life and of Roman civilization have been found inadequate for one of two reasons. Either they provide no true alternative to the violent disorder of contemporary Roman society, or they are inconsistent with certain inescapable and irreducible realities: the necessity for constant selection, care, and hard work; the inevitability of disorder and degeneration nonetheless; the narrowness of the limits, both physical and spiritual, within which a civilized existence is possible; and the fact that the elemental vitality of man and nature may itself be a source of disorder inasmuch as it exceeds man's capacity to control and direct. Such are the major themes I have identified in my discussion of the first three *Georgics*. They come to our attention as the expression of fixed truths through their persistent recurrence in contexts that are otherwise widely diverse or even inconsistent with one another. They emerge as the essential realities that must, after all, be included in any account of the labor required to secure a livelihood from the natural environment. If the necessity for work and the dangers of natural degeneration or human excess were removed, one might be able to write about a Golden Age; but one could not write about rustic life or the difficulties facing the new leader of the Roman world.

In *Georgic* 4 Virgil continues, at least for the first half of the book, to make rustic life a vehicle for identifying the fundamental conditions of human existence. Exploiting still further the suggestive comparison of human and animal existence that characterized the exposition of *Georgic* 3, he finds in bees animals that seem to exemplify a desirable alternative to the disorder of Roman society. To take bees as an example is the more promising because their own struggle for survival seems to epitomize much of what we have learned about the human condition. Moreover, because of their complex social organization, bees alone of the animal world seem to provide a suitable model for the highly developed society of contemporary Rome. But just as previous visions of rustic life offered only imperfect and partial insights into the human condition, so too the example of the bees proves to be inadequate. Because bees seem so analogous to Roman society, their inadequacies as a model for Roman society or, more generally, human societies suggest the inadequacies of the georgic mode itself. When Virgil concludes his discussion of bees, he also changes radically both the substance and the style of his poem. He gives up his didactic exposition of the rustic *artes* for mythical narrative. It is only when he examines human experience directly in the stories of Aristaeus and Orpheus that he presents a fully developed interpretation of what it means to be human.

It is perhaps significant that *Georgic* 4 is not introduced as a radical break from what precedes it. In this, the fourth *Georgic* differs from the second and third. The opening word of the book, *protinus* ("forward," "continuously," "immediately," however translated), looks ahead, to be sure, but suggests also that the new topic is related to the old, that it will somehow be a continuation rather than a rejection of what has gone before. That initial suggestion of continuity and development is supported by the first lines of the book. The perspective they announce, in contrast to those announced in the introductions to the earlier *Georgics*, is complex and tentative, inclusive of attitudes that have preceded rather than exclusive (1–7):

Protinus aërii mellis caelestia dona
exsequar: hanc etiam, Maecenas, aspice partem.
admiranda tibi leuium spectacula rerum
magnanimosque duces totiusque ordine gentis
mores et studia et populos et proelia dicam.
in tenui labor; at tenuis non gloria, si quem
numina laeua sinunt auditque uocatus Apollo.

> Forthwith airy honey's celestial gifts will be my subject: have regard, Maecenas, even for this part. You will marvel at the spectacle of slight matters, and I will relate in succession the courageous leaders of an entire race, its mores, pursuits, peoples, and battles. In a slight subject I labor, but not slight is the glory—if hostile gods allow and Apollo answers prayer.

The conspicuously paradoxical union of frailty and of greatness of spirit indicates that in this *Georgic* Virgil will attempt to join within a single perspective both the precariousness and the miraculous vitality of man and nature, characteristics that tended to be separated or contrasted in the previous *Georgics*.

That we must, in fact, think here in broad terms and not just of the bees is indicated at once by the metaphor and personification in those lines. References to the bees' "courageous leaders," their "mores," "pursuits," "peoples," and "battles" suggest that they share many distinctive characteristics with humans: spirit, consciousness, a sense of purpose, and a complex social order. We are prepared from the outset, then, to find in the bees' existence insights into our own. That implicit suggestion is confirmed in the very next lines when the poet reflects briefly on his own relationship to his subject. If the exposition of beekeeping offers the possibility for glory, it is precisely because it is an apparently slight topic, a difficult subject for the poet to invest with importance and dignity, and, therefore, a real measure of his abilities. It is precisely the prospect of that challenge, in turn, that makes the poet aware of his own human limitations, his dependence on the goodwill of the gods. It is, then, with a sense of the pervasive tension between possibility and limitation, from the hives of bees to the activity of the poet, that *Georgic* 4 begins.

## II

We learn first of the bees' great vulnerability. The exposition begins (8–17) with an impressive list of conditions from which bees must be protected. The cereal farmer of *Georgic* 1 had to beware of geese and cranes; the viticulturist of *Georgic* 2 had to guard against goats; the stock breeder of *Georgic* 3 had to steel himself against repulsive and fearsome snakes. The bees of *Georgic* 4 turn out to be besieged by a veritable army of predators. A sense of the progressive narrowing of the limits within which an ordered and fruitful existence is possible is further elaborated in the following lines (18-19):

> . . . liquidi fontes et stagna uirentia musco
> adsint et tenuis fugiens per gramina riuus.
>
> Let there be flowing springs and still ponds with moss, and a fine stream, fleeing through the grass.

The beekeeper must do more than isolate the bees from their enemies; he must provide them with an environment that is as fine and delicate as the bees themselves. Even though some parts of the garden, such as fresh streams or herbs, are clearly designed to satisfy basic needs for drink and food, others serve to protect bees from the elements. Just as the farmer of *Georgic* 1 had to look out for violent storms, so the bees require stones to sun themselves on (25-28) in case they get caught in the rain, a disaster of almost Odysseyan proportions (29-30): *si forte morantis / sparserit aut praeceps Neptuno immerserit Eurus* ("if by chance as they linger the east wind should sprinkle them or plunge them into Neptune").

Above all, the bees must be protected from climatic extremes of heat and cold. They are creatures of the springtime; they hibernate in the winter. Even so, the entrance to their hive must be shaded (20); when they first emerge in the early spring, they must have cooling waters and shade to protect them from the heat (21-23). We may recall that the first three *Georgics* presented a progressive narrowing of the regions within which the environment allowed a civilized existence. In *Georgic* 1 the tropic and arctic zones were excluded; in *Georgic* 2, the East; in *Georgic* 3, the northern and southern fringes of the civilized world where excessive heat and cold reduced men to barbarism. In *Georgic* 4 the beekeeper is instructed to see that the entrances to hives are narrow (35-37),

> . . . nam frigore mella
> cogit hiems, eademque calor liquefacta remittit.
> utraque uis apibus pariter metuenda.
>
> for with cold, winter solidifies honey; the same honey is liquified by heat. Each force is equally to be feared for the bees.

The range of conditions in which life and cultivation are possible is reduced to its finest and most precarious limits in the case of the bees, and in them we see epitomized the frailty of all life.

Paradoxically, it is only because we appreciate the bees' slightness that we acknowledge their remarkable vitality. Those two characteristics complement each other in a kind of fine balance. The more the bees are threatened by heat and cold, the more heroic are their efforts to protect themselves (37-44):

> . . . neque illae
> nequiquam in tectis certatim tenuia cera
> spiramenta linunt, fucoque et floribus oras
> explent, collectumque haec ipsa ad munera gluten
> et uisco et Phrygiae seruant pice lentius Idae.
> saepe etiam effossis, si uera est fama, latebris
> sub terra fouere larem, penitusque repertae
> pumicibusque cauis exesaeque arboris antro.

> and it is not without purpose that at home they zealously line openings with wax, fill doors with honeycomb and flowers. They keep a glue, gathered for this very purpose, stickier than birdlime and pitch of Phrygian Ida. Indeed, often, if the story is true, in dugout hideaways beneath the earth they cherish their Lar, and they have been found deep in hollow pumice and in a cave that has been eaten out of a tree.

Even so, the beekeeper should look after their hives, avoid placing them near yew trees and avoid making smells or noises that will frighten his small charges (45-50).

Those instructions are balanced in turn by renewed acknowledgment of the bees' spirit and resourcefulness: the bees leave their hives at the very first opportunity in spring (51-53); of their own accord they seek out flowers and water (54-55, 58-62). Like the spontaneous fruits of *Georgic* 2, they generate instinctively; but more than that, like humans they are creatures of skill who seek to order and control their environment (55-57):

> . . . hinc nescio qua dulcedine laetae
> progeniem nidosque fouent, hinc arte recentis
> excudunt ceras et mella tenacia fingunt.

> Thus by some sweetness of joy they cherish their progeny, their nestlings; thus, with skill they beat out fresh wax and fashion sticky honey.

The use of the verb *excudo*, "to beat out," as of iron on an anvil may seem particularly inapposite to describe the manufacture of something so soft as wax. But precisely because the word stands out so sharply in its context, it emphasizes not only the slightness of the bees, to whom even wax presents the hard intractability of iron, but also the extraordinary humanness of their characters. In *Georgic* 1 Virgil presented the "beating out" of fire from the veins of flint (*excuderet ignem*) as a specific example of the difficult "beating out" of the arts (*extundere artes*) that characterized the rise of civilization under the impetus of Jupiter's harsh innovations (1.135, 133).[1] Likewise, *fingere* (57) is the regular verb for an artist working in wax or clay, so that the bees' efforts mirror the characteristic skills and technology of mankind. The beekeeper, then, may have recourse to special scents and sounds to attract bees (62–66), but that is not to deny the bees' own remarkable powers and qualities.

In fact, our growing appreciation of the extent to which it is the bees' own energetic determination that compensates for their slightness prepares us to think of them in almost heroic terms. Heroism from that perspective is not absolute but relative. The mock-heroic description of a conflict among the bees, therefore, expresses a complex attitude toward the bees and the notion of heroism itself (67–76):

> Sin autem ad pugnam exierint—nam saepe duobus
> regibus incessit magno discordia motu,
> continuoque animos uulgi et trepidantia bello
> corda licet longe praesciscere; namque morantis
> Martius ille aeris rauci canor increpat, et uox
> auditur fractos sonitus imitata tubarum.
> tum trepidae inter se coeunt pennisque coruscant
> spiculaque exacuunt rostris aptantque lacertos
> et circa regem atque ipsa ad praetoria densae
> miscentur magnisque uocant clamoribus hostem.

> But if, however, they should go out to battle—for often two kings become involved in discord and there is a great tumult— straightaway you can sense the spirit of the mob and hearts

---

[1]. Compare also the famous lines from the *Aeneid* that characterize the martial and political Romans by contrast (6.847–848): *Excudent alii spirantia mollius aera / credo equidem, uiuos ducent de marmore uultus* ("Others will hammer bronze into more supple forms, I am sure, and will draw living features from marble").

beating for war, even from a distance; for as the bees delay, that martial blare of raucus bronze chides them on and a cry is heard like the broken sounds of trumpets. Then, again, they gather; then wings flash; they sharpen their stickers on their beaks and arm themselves. They mingle densely about the king before his very tent and with great outcry challenge the enemy.

To be sure, images like that of bees busily rubbing their faces with their legs ("sharpening their stickers on their beaks") do not allow us to ignore the humorous disproportion between the tiny bees and the grandiose metaphors used to describe their preparations for battle.

Nonetheless, the bees are no less determined or courageous because of their smallness. Within the dimensions of their own experience the battle for which they prepare is of great consequence (79-83):

> . . . magnum mixtae glomerantur in orbem
> praecipitesque cadunt; non densior aëre grando,
> nec de concussa tantum pluit ilice glandis.
> . . . . . . . . . . . . . . .
> ingentis animos angusto in pectore uersant.

Mingling, they gather into a great ball and fall headlong. No more thickly from the air does hail rain down or, from a shaken oak, acorns; . . . great spirits are contained within their narrow breasts.

As in all such mock-heroic scenes, the metaphors encourage us to see both elements of the comparison from a new perspective. The grandiose vocabulary of warfare reinforces our awareness of the bees' slightness and frailty. At the same time, their behavior may still suggest new insights into the nature of human warfare.

That is particularly true in the present instance for two reasons. First, the fact that the mock-heroic is tempered with genuine respect for the bees—that the application of military language to their conflicts is felt to be in some sense appropriate despite their tiny size—reduces the apparent disparity between them and humans. Second, the particular character of their conflict would have struck a responsive chord in a contemporary Roman audience, for the bees' battle is presented as a civil war. The term Virgil uses to describe it, *discordia*, referred especially to civil conflict. And although that was not its exclusive meaning, the distinction between *discordia* ("civil war") and *bellum* ("foreign war") became increasingly marked in Roman usage from the end of the Republic.[2] In the present context it would have been natural for a Roman to assume that the two bee kings to which Virgil refers (67–68) come from the same hive, a fact that in any event is confirmed in lines 88–102. The terrible losses the two armies of bees inflict on each other, consequently, bring to mind the losses the Romans had themselves suffered in their recent civil wars. As a model for the Roman civil wars the conflict of the bees reiterates a suggestion made earlier in the poem, that civil war is a kind of natural phenomenon. However costly it might be in terms of human experience, it may be viewed as being, like the civil strife of the bees, neither unusual nor of great moment in the larger order of things.

The heroism of the bees, however, and with it their effectiveness as models for Roman society, is undercut in the two lines that conclude the description of their battle (86–87):

hi motus animorum atque haec certamina tanta
pulueris exigui iactu compressa quiescent.

These disturbances of their spirits, these conflicts, as great as they are, by the toss of a little dust are checked and quieted.

That brief observation epitomizes all the earlier evidence of the bees' distinctive slightness and insubstantiality, and makes clear a single decisive difference between them and Romans: the bees' well-being and prosperity are assured above all by the efforts of the beekeeper. That important point is emphasized at precisely the moment when the poet confronts the most pressing issue of his day, how to control the forces of disorder within Roman society. Henceforth, similarities between the bees and Romans are qualified by the knowledge that the bees offer only an imperfect model for Rome.

In the lines that follow that dramatic reversal it becomes increasingly clear that the causes of disorder among bees and what the beekeeper does to control them simply do not apply to the Romans. The bees' conflict, we are told, is the result of a split within their community that reflects the now-familiar pattern of all things to degenerate (88–95):

---

2. This development is traced by Pierre Jal in two articles, "Pax Civilis-Concordia," *REL* 39 (1961) 210–231; "Bellum civile . . . bellum externum dans la Rome de la fin de la république," *LEC* 30 (1962) 257–267, 384–390 and, more fully, in his book *La guerre civile à Rome* (Paris 1963).

Verum ubi ductores acie reuocaueris ambo,
deterior qui uisus, eum, ne prodigus obsit,
dede neci; melior uacua sine regnet in aula.
alter erit maculis auro squalentibus ardens—
nam duo sunt genera: hic melior insignis et ore
et rutilis clarus squamis; ille horridus alter
desidia latamque trahens inglorius aluum.
ut binae regum facies, ita corpora plebis.

But when you've called back both leaders from the line of battle, you must kill the one who seems inferior so that he not be a wasteful parasite. Let the better one rule by himself in his court. The one will be mottled with golden spots, burning bright—for there are two classes. This one is better, of distinguished countenance and conspicuous with its auburn scales. The other is shaggy from slothfulness and ingloriously drags a broad belly. As the kings have different appearances, so do the bodies of their plebs.

Even if we could believe that Virgil is capable of such a schematic division of Roman factions into noble and degenerate or of such a simplistic explanation for the Roman civil wars, an interpretation of the present passage as an allegory for Rome cannot be sustained. For one thing, the two classes of bees are distinguished from one another by clear physiological signs. Can any division of Romans be as self-evident and objective?

But more important than that is the fact that it is the beekeeper who not only stops the conflict, but also identifies the inferior faction and by expelling it protects the future prosperity of the bees. In *Georgic* 1 the farmer was instructed to sort through his seeds continually, selecting out the bad, lest they quickly predominate and threaten to undermine all his hard-won progress. *Georgic* 2 recommended the cultivation of the domestic olive and avoidance of the wild for similar reasons. In *Georgic* 3 that pattern received a paradoxical variation: cows that were too old or young were to be rejected for breeding; the desirable cow was distinguished by its ugliness. That same book contains the closest parallel to the passage in *Georgic* 4: the herdsman is advised to weed out sheep with the least trace of black on them lest the entire flock become tainted. The beekeeper's task of selection simply extends that familiar pattern. He is as foreign to the bees as the farmer to his crops or the herdsman to his sheep. Insofar as their conflicts are resolved by their human keeper, the bees offer no guidance for Romans. Humans do not have a keeper. Their rulers are themselves human.

That truth is brought home even more emphatically in the final lines devoted to the control of the bees' disruptive impulses. The bees, we are told, have *instabilis animos* ("unstable spirits,") and are given sometimes to neglecting vital responsibilities (103-105):

> At cum incerta uolant caeloque examina ludunt
> contemnuntque fauos et frigida tecta relinquunt,
> instabilis animos ludo prohibebis inani.

> But when swarms fly without direction, play in the sky and disdain their honeycombs and leave their chilly homes, you will constrain their unstable spirits from empty play.

We may believe that humans, too, have "unstable spirits" which demand constraint; the idea has become a familiar one in the *Georgics* already.[3] But we cannot find in the beekeeper's solution to that problem a solution for ourselves (106-108):

> nec magnus prohibere labor: tu regibus alas
> eripe; non illis quisquam cunctantibus altum
> ire iter aut castris audebit uellere signa.

> Nor is it a great labor to constrain them: you must rip off the kings' wings. As long as they hold back, no one will dare to take a journey on high or to remove their standards from camp.

The ruthlessness required of the beekeeper is not without precedent in the *Georgics*, but it is not easy to see exactly how it might apply to the control of human leaders, just as it is difficult to guess who could take the beekeeper's place in relation to human society.

If, therefore, the common people are utterly subservient to their rulers, as the bees are to their kings, and the leaders go astray, then the community must look outside itself for salvation. Insofar as the bees are regarded as a model for Roman society, their example suggests the particular dilemma of a people who can destroy themselves but cannot save themselves. Virgil's discussion of bees thus far has,

---

3. Most notably in the passages of political and social commentary that conclude the first two *Georgics*.

after all, been focused on bee*keeping*. It concludes, accordingly, with emphatic reiteration of the keeper's role (112-115):

> ipse thymum tinosque ferens de montibus altis
> tecta serat late circum, cui talia curae;
> ipse labore manum duro terat, ipse feracis
> figat humo plantas et amicos inriget imbris.

> He himself, the one who is concerned with such matters, must bring thyme and laurel shrubs from tall mountains and plant them all around the bees' shelters. He himself must wear his hands with work, with hard work. He himself must set fertile cuttings in the soil and guide in the friendly rains.

That final emphasis on the beekeeper's virtually all-encompassing care for his bees leads directly to the exploration of an alternative to the model suggested by the bees. Perhaps the human dilemma suggested by the example of the bees is not really valid: even if bees cannot be self-sufficient, perhaps humans, who guard the bees' welfare so effectively, can be. Virgil turns, briefly, from his discussion of bees to consider the example of the beekeeper himself.

### III

The notion of individual self-sufficiency is not a new one in the *Georgics*. The traditional Roman ideal of the self-sufficient small farmer has provided the implicit context for virtually all Virgil's instructions on farming in the poem. But that ideal has also been repeatedly shown to be unrealistic: the farmer's independence has been compromised by the relentless spread of Roman political conflict, by the higher ambitions of Roman farmers themselves, and by the destructive forces within nature.

It is significant, therefore, that the ideal of self-sufficiency is presented here in *Georgic* 4 as an elaborate *praeteritio*, something for which, despite its apparent promise, the poet does not really have time (116-121):

> Atque equidem, extremo ni iam sub fine laborum
> uela traham et terris festinem aduertere proram,
> forsitan et pinguis hortos quae cura colendi
> ornaret canerem biferique rosaria Paesti,

quoque modo potis guaderent intiba riuis
et uirides apio ripae.

And, indeed, if I were not already at the very end of my labors, about to draw in my sails and hastening to turn my prow toward land, perhaps I would also celebrate rich gardens, what care in cultivation enhances them, and I would celebrate the rose gardens of that place that blossoms twice a year, Paestum, and how endives delight in streams to drink, how green riverbanks delight in parsley.

The nautical metaphors recall the introductory passages of *Georgic* 2, where Virgil urged the value of restraint and containment in the face of superabundant possibilities (2.35-46). In principle that method of composition is admirable; and indeed, within the context of the argument of *Georgic* 2 it seemed fully justified. Its application in the present context, however, must seem puzzling. Why is it that such an important and promising possibility cannot be treated fully? Why must it be treated as a digression, something irrelevant to the poet's essential purpose?

These questions become more puzzling before they are finally answered. First, we are reminded of the attractive variety of plants and vegetables that gardening produces (119-124). Even more appealing is the example of the gardener himself. He combines two cardinal virtues that heretofore had seemed to be mutually exclusive or were, at least, treated as separate and distinct. The first of these virtues is his untiring capacity for hard work: any suggestion of natural abundance or of ease that was encouraged by the initial survey of the garden's varied fruits is rudely undercut. For the garden Virgil chooses to celebrate began as (127-129)

. . . pauca relicti
iugera ruris erant, nec fertilis illa iuuencis
nec pecori opportuna seges nec commoda Baccho.

a few acres of countryside, left over, neither good grazing for cattle nor good fodder for livestock nor suitable for Bacchus.

Such unpromising beginnings make it clear that the garden's fruitfulness is the result of the gardener's own efforts. The fact that he is an old man only further emphasizes his unusual capacity for hard work. Indeed, he is the *first* to harvest each season's fruits (134, 140-141); his plants are the most prolific (141); he overcomes nature's tendency to degenerate (142-143):

> quotque in flore nouo pomis se fertilis arbos
> induerat, totidem autumno matura tenebat.

> And with as many fruits as a fertile tree clothed itself when it was first in bloom, so many did it hold in autumn when it had reached maturity.

Virgil's gardener is even impatient with nature's own limits to fruitfulness (135-138):

> et cum tristis hiems etiamnum frigore saxa
> rumperet et glacie cursus frenaret aquarum,
> ille comam molis iam tondebat hyacinthi
> aestatem increpitans seram Zephyrosque morantis.

> And when sad winter was still breaking rocks with its cold and was reining in water courses with ice, *he* was already pruning the foliage of the soft hyacinth, chiding summer for being late, the west wind for delaying.

That capacity to wrest a livelihood from a hard and unyielding environment marks the old gardener as a paragon of the ideal presented in the first *Georgic*.

But he also embodies the cardinal virtue of *Georgic* 2, the capacity for restraint and the containment of desires (132-133):

> regum aequabat opes animis, seraque reuertens
> nocte domum dapibus mensas onerabat inemptis.

> He used to equal kings' riches with his spirit, and when he returned home late at night, he used to load his table with feasts unbought.

Even though he must work into the evening, the old gardener can look forward to a generous meal. And as satisfying as the abundance of his produce is the knowledge that it is the fruit of his own labor, that he is beholden to no one. The fact that his feasts are unbought is emphasized by the position of the adjective *inemptis* at the end both of its metrical line and of its period. The gardener's enviable self-sufficiency, then, is shown to result from the convergence of two virtues. One is the capacity for hard work: he returns from his work only late in the evening. The other virtue is his restraint: he enjoys the wealth of kings not because his possessions are as numerous or as costly as a king's but rather because he has enough and is satisfied with what he has. He equals the wealth of kings not in his possessions but in his *animis*, his spirit.

Paradoxically, the very qualities that win our admiration for the gardener implicitly suggest his inappropriateness as a model for Virgil's contemporaries. His character and accomplishments are, after all, extraordinary. From the first he is presented as atypical, even unique. Virgil recalls him as a specific individual from a specific place (125-127). He is not even an Italian but a kind of displaced person, a Corycian from mainland Greece, or perhaps from Cilicia, who now lives in a Spartan colony of southern Italy.[4] The examples of his energy, moreover, finally become so exaggerated as to make him appear almost superhuman (144-146):

ille etiam seras in uersum distulit ulmos
eduramque pirum et spinos iam pruna ferentis
iamque ministrantem platanum potantibus umbras.

He even arranged elms into rows after the usual time, likewise the hardened pear tree and blackthorns which were already bearing sloes and the plane tree when it was already providing shade for drinkers.

In that final description, the gardener almost assumes the stature of Silvanus, the Italian god of trees who made his entrance in the introduction to the *Georgics*, *teneram ab radice ferens . . . cupressum* ("carrying a tender cypress, roots and all," 1.20).

The gardener is set off from Virgil's contemporaries in yet another way. He is only a memory for Virgil (*memini*), and even when Virgil saw him he was already an old man (125-127). Indeed,

---

4. The adjective *Corycius* may refer either to a famous cave on Mount Parnassus (Statius, *Th.* 7.347) or to the community of Corycus (also the home of a cave) in the kingdom of Cilicia on the coast of Asia Minor (Livy 37, 12, 10; 36, 43, 13). Servius in his commentary on *G.* 4.127 assumes the latter although in terms that suggest the possibility of confusion on his part: *Corycos enim, civitas est Ciliciae, in qua antrum illud famosum est, paene ab omnibus celebratum.* He also raises the possibility that the old gardener to whom Virgil refers may have been one of the Cilician pirates whom Pompey was reported to have resettled after he had defeated them in 67 B.C.

like all such ideals of self-sufficiency or heroic achievement, he belongs to the past rather than the present. There is a special point in emphasizing the obsolescence of the gardener's example for Virgil's audience. For, as we have already observed, the Roman civil wars had made it clear that such individual self-sufficiency was not secure against the disorder that emanated from the Roman state. Virgil himself acknowledged that reality explicitly in his commentary on the civil wars at the conclusion of *Georgic* 1: *non ullus aratro / dignus honos, squalent abductis arua colonis* ("there is no fitting honor given to the plow; the fields are in the tatters of mourning; the farmers have been driven off," 1.507-508). We should not be surprised, then, that Virgil dismisses the old man and his accomplishments, attractive as they are, as irrelevant to his own most urgent concerns (147-148):

> uerum haec ipse equidem spatiis exclusus iniquis
> praetereo atque aliis post me memoranda relinquo.

> But as to these things, I for my own part am compelled by the unfair constraints of space to pass them over. I leave them to be recalled by others after me.

The example of the old gardener was, indeed, attractive. The statement *iniquis exclusis spatiis* ("compelled by the unfair constraints of space") is a convincing expression of regret at having to pass on to other topics. But from the *ipse quidem* to the final *relinquo* the author's own clear finality of purpose demands our understanding and acquiescence.

## IV

Although Virgil dismisses the gardener and returns to beekeeping at line 149, the ideal of self-sufficiency continues to be, at least implicitly, the central concern of the exposition. Now, however, it is the possibility of collective rather than individual self-sufficiency that is explored. That the bees can provide a model for the examination of that ideal is possible only because Virgil presents quite a different view of them here than he presented in the opening passages of this book (149-152):

> Nunc age, naturas apibus quas Iuppiter ipse
> addidit expediam, pro qua mercede canoros

> Curetum sonitus crepitantiaque aera secutae
> Dictaeo caeli regem pauere sub antro.

> Now come, I will explain the natures of bees, the natures that Jupiter himself gave to them. That was the reward for which they followed the ringing sounds of the Curetes and their clashing bronze and nourished the sky god in a cave at Mount Dictē.

The abruptness of that explanation, its reminiscence of epic style, the focus on Jupiter's direct agency, and the reference to the god's own origins combine to heighten our expectations and signal a new beginning. In fact, the initial passage of exposition reveals a significant divergence from the original description of bees and their social organization (153-157):

> solae communis natos, consortia tecta
> urbis habent magnisque agitant sub legibus aeuum,
> et patriam solae et certos nouere penatis;
> uenturaeque hiemis memores aestate laborem
> experiuntur et in medium quaesita reponunt.

> They alone hold their children and the buildings of their city in common, and regulate their lives with mighty laws. They alone have an unchanging fatherland and household gods. Mindful of coming winter, they labor diligently in summer and store up grain for the common use.

The stability and prosperity of these bees are linked at the very outset with a thoroughgoing communality which seems quite inconsistent with the description of internecine strife that concluded the first passage on bees.

Jupiter's bees do share characteristics that were included in the earlier descriptions of bees and the gardener, but those characteristics are now clearly subordinated to the bees' communality. Although Jupiter's bees exhibit great restless energy, it is no longer an expression of "unstable spirits." Disorder is only apparent. The bees' bustling diversity of activity is controlled by an elaborate division of labor. Each act, however random it may appear, is shown to contribute to the common welfare (158-168). Bees and the Cyclopes who work for Vulcan can legitimately be compared despite their laughable disparity in size, for the aura of energy and business that surrounds the Cyclopes' work is a consequence not so much of their massive strength as of their own division of labor (170–178):

> ac ueluti lentis Cyclopes fulmina massis
> cum properant, alii taurinis follibus auras
> accipiunt redduntque, alii stridentia tingunt
> aera lacu; gemit impositis incudibus Aetna;
> illi inter sese magna ui bracchia tollunt
> in numerum, uersantque tenaci forcipe ferrum:
> non aliter, si parua licet componere magnis,
> Cecropias innatus apes amor urget habendi
> munere quamque suo.

> and just as when the Cyclopes hasten lightning bolts from resistant ore, some with ox-hide bellows take in the air and force it out; others wet shrilling bronze in water. Beneath the weight of their anvils Aetna groans. With great might the Cyclopes raise their arms together in rhythm and with gripping forceps turn the iron. No differently, if small things may be compared with great, are the Cecropian bees urged on by an innate love of possessing, each one according to his own function.

By attributing the origin of the bees' extraordinary communality to their *amor habendi*, their "love of possessing," this passage looks ahead to a subsequent identification of the bees' distinctive passions as a basis for their unique natures and for their fundamental difference from human beings (197–209). For the present, differences in size between the bees and the Cyclopes are shown ultimately to be less important than the special divinity of natures that is revealed in a shared capacity for the complex division of labor.

Virtues that the bees share with the old gardener are likewise transformed by the bees' communality. Like the gardener, they are tired at the end of their long day's work but able, nonetheless, to look forward to the enjoyment of an abundant harvest reaped by their own efforts (180–183):

> at fessae multa referunt se nocte minores,
> crura thymo plenae; pascuntur et arbuta passim
> et glaucas salices casiamque crocumque rubentem
> et pinguem tiliam et ferrugineos hyacinthos.

But tired, they return homeward late at night, the younger ones do, their legs heavy with thyme. And they feed on arbute trees all about and on grey willows and the wild cinnamon tree and the ruddy crocus and the rich linden tree and dusky hyacinths.

In addition, the bees' enjoyment of rest is colored by their distinctive communality (184, 189-190):

> omnibus una quies operum, labor omnibus unus.
> . . . . . . . . . . . . . . . .
> post, ubi iam thalamis se composuere, siletur
> in noctem, fessosque sopor suus occupat artus.

> For them all, there is one repose from their work, one time of work for all. . . . Afterward, when they have already settled themselves in their chambers, there is silence into the night and one by one drowsiness overtakes their tired limbs.

The normal satisfactions of a job well done and of repose after hard work are enhanced by the sense of peace, security, and fellowship that can only come from an orderly existence whose routines are shared.

What follows immediately after that last explicit description of the bees' communality recalls a different and apparently unrelated aspect of the bees' natures (191-192):

> nec uero a stabulis pluuia impendente recedunt
> longius, aut credunt caelo aduentantibus Euris.

> Nor, indeed, when rain threatens do they withdraw from their stables—not very far, at least—nor do they trust the sky when the east wind is on its way.

Those lines return us to the slightness and vulnerability that were dominant themes in Virgil's first description of bees. Familiar characteristics, however, take on a different value in the description of Jupiter's bees (193-196):

> sed circum tutae sub moenibus urbis aquantur
> excursusque breuis temptant, et saepe lapillos,
> ut cumbae instabiles fluctu iactante saburram,
> tollunt, his sese per inania nubila librant.

But around about beneath the walls of their secure city they gather water and try brief excursions. Often they carry pebbles, just as unstable boats tossed on a current carry a ballast of sand. With these pebbles they balance themselves among the harmless clouds.

The mention of rain in the initial description of bees was limited to warning against its dangers and directions to the beekeeper to provide protective covering, rocks for the bees to dry themselves on, and the like. That part of the exposition contributed to the overriding concern for the responsibilities of the beekeeper and the bees' dependence on him. Contrast with that earlier passage illuminates the distinctive emphasis of the new account of how bees are affected by rain. Although lightness continues to be a significant characteristic of bees, it is no longer presented as evidence for their dependence on the beekeeper. He is not mentioned at all in the second passage. Instead our attention is directed toward the bees' own determination and resourcefulness as the basis for self-sufficiency.

There is no apparent logical connection between that testament to the bees' independence and the previous discussion of their natural communality. The discussion of their behavior in rainy weather seems rather to emerge through a loose process of association: bees rest indoors at night (189-190); they don't go out much in the rain either (191-192); but when they do, they manage surprisingly well on their own (193-196). Although that final emphasis on the bees' independence may not be logically related to the preceding description of their special natures, it is, by necessity, related dramatically. It may help to call attention to the fact that Jupiter's bees have been presented throughout as self-sufficient and that their description has included no mention of a beekeeper at all. Simply by being at the end of a fairly protracted and admiring description of the bees' special natures, the testament to their self-sufficiency implies a connection between it and the major topic of the exposition. In short, the bees' self-sufficiency is made to appear to be the consequence and culminating virtue of their divinely granted instinct for communality.

At this point in the exposition, then, the account of Jupiter's bees might seem to offer their kind of thoroughgoing mutual cooperation as a promising solution to the particular disorders that had been plaguing Rome. The example of the bees' communality, moreover, seems to overcome the specific shortcomings of the two models first presented in *Georgic* 4: the dependent bees and the vulnerable individual. For, strict communality of values, division of labor, and sharing of goods not only acknowledge that welfare must be sought on the societal rather than individual level, they seem also—in the bees' case, at least—to assure a stable order without reliance on some external agency.

Nonetheless, very early in the description of Jupiter's bees there are muted warnings against uncritical acceptance of their example as a model for Roman society. To begin with, the bees' nature is extraordinary, a unique reward from the father of men and gods for a special service to him; their way of life recalls conditions that previously have been associated with the Golden Age. The bees, for example, surrender their acquisitions to the common use: *in medium quaesita reponunt* (157). In *Georgic* 1 the prosperous and easy, albeit enervating, life before Jupiter's reign was characterized by just such selfless sharing and communality of property: in that age men *in medium quaerebant* (1.127). The verbal echo of that phrase in the fourth *Georgic* might help readers to recall what in any event had become a familiar attribute of the Golden Age.[5] Jupiter's special gift to the bees was to restore them to the condition that all life enjoyed before his reign. Insofar as we sense that the bees' essential virtue is an extraordinary, divinely granted reversion to the conditions of a mythical past, we must view their example with some reserve.

In fact, having presented bees in the most hopeful light, Virgil turns to consider two underlying components of their special excellence that reveal the utter inappropriateness of Jupiter's bees as models for humans; in the process he also brings to light two related and fundamental aspects of what it means to be human. Lines 149-157 introduced the bees' communality as the basis for their admirable, indeed unique, social stability: they alone have a fixed

---

5. For references to this idea in pre-Virgilian literature, see Kirby Flower Smith, *The Elegies of Albius Tibullus* (New York 1913, reprinted Darmstadt 1971), the commentary on Tibullus 1.3.43-44, p. 249. Smith does not mention *de Off.* 1.22, where Cicero presents it as a matter of Stoic doctrine that nature's produce is all intended for man's use, so that *in hoc naturam debemus ducem sequi, communes utilitates* **in medium afferre** *mutatione officiorum* ("in this matter we ought to follow nature's lead, to contribute general profits to the common good by the exchange of services").

household and fatherland (155). Lines 197-209 comment further on the enviable permanence of the bees' race and society:

> Illum adeo placuisse apibus mirabere morem,
> quod neque concubitu indulgent, nec corpora segnes
> in Venerem soluunt aut fetus nixibus edunt;
> uerum ipsae e foliis natos, e suauibus herbis
> ore legunt, ipsae regem paruosque Quirites
> sufficiunt, aulasque et cerea regna refingunt.
> saepe etiam duris errando in cotibus alas
> attriuere, ultroque animam sub fasce dedere:
> tantus amor florum et generandi gloria mellis.
> ergo ipsas quamuis angusti terminus aeui
> excipiat (neque enim plus septima ducitur aestas),
> at genus immortale manet, multosque per annos
> stat fortuna domus, et aui numerantur auorum.

You will marvel that the bees are so satisfied with the following practice, that they never go to bed together, do no lazily relax their bodies for Venus or bear their young with birth pangs. Rather, they themselves gather their children from leaves and sweet grasses with their mouths; they themselves furnish the king and the tiny Quirites and repair the court and their waxen kingdoms. Often, indeed, by straying onto hard stone they have worn away their wings and they have willingly given their lives under their burdens. Such is their love of flowers and the glory of making honey. Therefore, however short the term of life that overtakes them individually—for their lives do not extend beyond the seventh summer—still their race remains immortal; for many years the fortune of their house continues, and they count their grandfathers' grandfathers.

The curious manner in which bees are here reported to propagate their species is an essential aspect of that special nature which assures the stability and permanence of their society. It is not just that the means of generation is simple, easy, and readily available to all members of the community. More important, it releases the bees from the disruptive effects of *amor* which were revealed to us in *Georgic* 3. Instead of wasting their energies in sexual intercourse, bees alone can devote themselves untiringly to the maintenance of their community: the gathering of babies, the restoration of their public works, the replenishing of their stores. It should be recalled, too, that in the earlier discussion of *amor* Virgil treated physical exhaustion as much less dangerous than the violently destructive passions associated with animal lust. In the case of Jupiter's bees those passions are replaced by the *amor habendi* noted above (177-178), by the *amor florum* and the *generandi gloria mellis* that underlie both the bees' unanimity of spirit and their dedication to the most important task of preserving the race.

From the present perspective certain details in the initial account of bees in *Georgic* 4 assume a new importance. That earlier passage, as we have observed, concluded with the description of a regular civil war in which two factions of bees warred for supremacy and the destiny of the hive. But then Virgil did not seem to be thinking of bees as embodiments of a uniquely unpassionate nature; he might even be accused of deliberate misdirection when he refers to the obscure *dulcedo* (55) which induces bees like other animals to care for their *progeniem nidosque* (56) in the spring. Such a statement is not necessarily inconsistent with the later account of the bees' sexless generation of their species; but the use of *progenies*, with its obvious parallel in human experience, and use of the metaphor *nidos* ("nestlings") suggest that bees are motivated by the same instinctive drives as other animals. In retrospect we can see why Virgil had to suppress any notion of the bees' asexuality in his discussion of their internal conflicts. To acknowledge it would have been to undermine both the association of passion with social violence in *Georgic* 3 and the association of social stability with asexuality that was to follow.

Repeated presentation of evidence for the mutual exclusion of sexual passion and social order argues for the inevitability of disorder in human affairs. Thus, comparison with Roman society in the description of Jupiter's bees has a complex nature. Reference to the bees as *Quirites*, the formal title of Roman citizens, encourages us to consider the human application of the bees' example. To do so, however, is also to be compelled to recognize the actual differences between bees and Romans, and, indeed, all humans. Not only do bees embody an ideal of social order to which Romans have only aspired, Romans can never enjoy the unanimity of purpose on which the realization of that ideal depends, for it is a patent truth that Romans simply do not collect their babies off of leaves. Virgil, in fact, introduced this section of the poem with the assertion that what he was about to relate is quite alien to our experience. *Mirabere* —"you will marvel"—he said, at what I am about to tell you. By asking us to consider the unique nature of bees Virgil has, indirectly, reminded us of an essential aspect of human nature and of its important implications for an understanding of the human condition.

Lines 210–218 take up a second and equally illuminating constituent of the bees' special unanimity of spirit, their elaborate devotion to their leader:

> Praeterea regem non sic Aegyptus et ingens
> Lydia nec populi Parthorum aut Medus Hydaspes
> obseruant. rege incolumi mens omnibus una est;
> amisso rupere fidem, constructaque mella
> diripuere ipsae et cratis soluere fauorum.
> ille operum custos, illum admirantur et omnes
> circumstant fremitu denso stipantque frequentes,
> et saepe attollunt umeris et corpora bello
> obiectant pulchramque petunt per uulnera mortem.

Moreover, as for their king, no Egyptian, not great Lydia, not the Parthian populace, nor the River Hydaspes of Media so look to him. When the king is safe, all are of one mind. The minute he is lost, they have broken faith. As for the honey they accumulated, they have looted it themselves and smashed the wicker cells of the honeycombs. He is the guardian of their work; he is the one they admire. They all stand round him with a dense murmur and press upon him in mobs. Often they raise him on their shoulders, thrust their bodies forward in battle and through wounds seek a beautiful death.

The first description of the bees noted their loyalty to their leaders and exposed the particular vulnerability that such unqualified dependence involves. There, however, Virgil raised the further possibility of divided loyalties which might undermine the welfare of the swarm. Here he ignores that danger and emphasizes more the unity of purpose that such loyalty fosters and its value for the defense against outsiders. This aspect of the bees' nature would have had, of course, a particular relevance for Virgil's contemporaries. Even before Caesar's decisive triumph over his rivals in 31 B.C., there must have been many Romans who were inclined to think that Republican institutions had been discredited and that the time had come when the concentration of power and loyalties around a single ruler was the only reasonable safeguard against renewed factionalism and civil strife. Julius Caesar had proclaimed as much in his ridicule of Republican institutions and his fateful assumption of the Perpetual Dictatorship in 44 B.C.[6] The new Caesar himself took an important step in that direction when, in 32 B.C., he asked for and received an oath of allegiance to his person from individuals throughout Italy.

The manner in which the bees' allegiance to their leader is presented, however, makes it clear from the outset that their example must be virtually unthinkable for Romans. Opposition to monarchy —especially among the ruling aristocracy—dated from the expulsion of the last Etruscan king and the establishment of Republican government and had gained renewed currency with the political conflicts of the Late Republican period. From the time of Tiberius Gracchus, the charge of *regnum* had been a major weapon in the arsenal of political propaganda.[7] The fate of Julius Caesar and his successor's elaborate constitutional maneuvers to avoid the charge of *regnum* against himself are sufficient evidence that the idea (if not the practice) of despotism continued to be unacceptable to many Romans throughout Virgil's lifetime.[8]

The description in *Georgic* 4.210-218 of the bees' allegiance to their king clearly exploits traditional Roman prejudices. It begins with a comparison between the bees and the peoples of the East. We have already noted that Romans regarded Eastern mores with suspicion at best and feared them as destructive influences on Roman society at worst. Moreover, ever since the great Persian disasters at

---

6. Examples of Caesar's cavalier behavior toward Republican institutions are conveniently summarized in Lilly Ross Taylor, *Party Politics in the Age of Caesar* (Berkeley 1949, reprinted 1971) 172-174.

7. On *regnum* as a term of political invective in the Late Republic, see Ch. Wirzubski, *Libertas as a Political Idea at Rome* (Cambridge 1950, reprinted 1968) 62-64.

8. The most relentless attempt to demonstrate that Augustus deliberately sought to mask complete power with a façade of Republican constitutionality is that of Sir Ronald Syme, *The Roman Revolution* (Oxford 1939, reprinted with corrections 1967). P. B. Brunt and J. M. Moore, *Res Gestae Divi Augusti* (Oxford 1967, reprinted with corrections 1970) 8-18, provide an excellent brief summary of the view that Augustus assumed powers that were individually precedented in the Republican constitution but which in combination amounted to totalitarian control of the state.

Marathon and the Bay of Salamis, despotism had been singled out as a signal defect in Eastern civilizations. Greeks, particularly those sympathetic to Athens, pictured the Persian Wars as conflicts between free men and slaves, in which Greek victories confirmed the strength of democracy and the essential weakness of Oriental despotism. The latter was attributed to two separate but closely related circumstances. One was that being totally bound to their leader, Persians lacked the individual resourcefulness and determination of free men: they were unwilling to give their all because they fought for their king, not for themselves.[9] A corollary was that their entire social and political order was especially precarious, dependent as it was on a single individual.[10] Those criticisms are recalled in lines 213–214, where the self-destructive frenzy of the bees when their leader is lost is presented as one measure of their loyalty to him. The next lines (215–216) emphasize the moblike behavior of the bees as they look up to their king in a body (*omnes*) and gather around him in a dense, undifferentiated mass.[11] The bees' totally selfless dedication to their leader—their eagerness to make the ultimate sacrifice for him—gives the impression that they live only to die for him, an impression that is encouraged by the final climactic position of *mortem* in line 218. We may admire the bees' selflessness because it seems to express a degree of social coherence and political loyalty that is quite unexpected in animals, but this admiration vanishes when we read of the chaos and riotous pillaging following the king's death. So our admiration for their loyalty yields to the reflection that the importance of the individual is an essentially human value, and one to which Romans, with their highly developed sense of personal dignity, attached particular importance.

The passages on the bees' unique asexuality and on their un-Roman spirit of political loyalty form the immediate context for

---

9. This idea is central to the argument of both Aeschylus' *Persae* and Herodotus' *Histories*. Note especially *Persae* vv. 242–244 and Herodotus 7.101–104, 135; 5.78; and see also Xenophon, *Anabasis* 3.2.13. A. S. F. Gow, "Notes on the *Persae* of Aeschylus," *JHS* 48 (1928) 133–158, argues on the basis of epigraphical evidence (p. 134) that the depiction of the Persian king's subjects as slaves was not confined to literature.

10. See again Aeschylus, *Persae* esp. vv. 584–593 and 852–857. In his representation of the Persian debate on Xerxes' plan to bridge the Hellespont and invade Greece, Herodotus (7.8–18) emphasizes how the constraints on open discussion make the Persians' disastrous expedition against Greece a consequence of the king's personal misjudgments.

11. It may not be simple coincidence that Aeschylus compares Xerxes' followers to a swarm of bees (*Persae* 126–132).

renewed speculation in the following lines (219-227) about the Stoic concept of pervasive divinity. In brief, Virgil notes that some people have seen, in the remarkable behavior he has just described, confirmation of the idea that all creatures partake of a single divine spirit from which they themselves derive their being. Further, that divine essence of life is supposed to be concentrated in the fiery matter of stars to which individual spirits return when they leave their mortal bodies. Those beliefs would have been immediately recognized by Virgil's contemporaries as Stoic. Cicero, for example, had made them the basis for the famous "Dream of Scipio" which crowned his plea for responsible Roman leadership in *De Republica*. For Virgil to remark on the elevated thoughts that the contemplation of bees inspired in some people is, of course, for him to acknowledge once again how truly unusual and demanding of admiration the bees really are. Nonetheless, by associating the bees with the most rarefied and ethereal aspects of the universe, Virgil's remarks here tend to remove the bees still further from the mundane practicality of human experience.

Virgil himself, moreover, introduces the whole question of the significance of the bees' behavior with an explicit indication of his own personal reserve. He ascribes Stoic interpretation of the bees' example to other unnamed "certain people" (*quidam*, 210), and presents their views in the accusative-infinitive construction of indirect discourse, only as a report of what those vague "certain people" say. In withholding judgment Virgil does more than indicate the speculative nature of such interpretations. He suggests that those speculations are essentially irrelevant to his interests, that they require no decision of assent or denial, because they have no important bearing on the very concrete and worldly concerns his poem addresses. The reference to Stoic doctrine performs much the same function here as it did in the final sections of *Georgic* 1. To believe, as "certain people" do (226-227), that

> omnia, nec morti esse locum, sed uiua uolare
> sideris in numerum atque alto succedere caelo
>
> there is no room for death, but all creatures still alive fly to the stars and mount to the high heavens

may inspire awe. It does little, however, to guide the farmer in his struggle for a livelihood or the Roman statesman in his search for an alternative to civil strife. That belief, in fact, offers no more encouragement than the assurance in *Georgic* 1 that disorder in the human microcosm is subsumed under a larger cosmic design.

Although bees continue to be the subject of the next eighty-six lines, there is no further mention of their special nature or of their extraordinary capacity for cooperation and complex social organization; nor are there any further suggestions of their self-sufficiency. Instead, reminders of their industriousness (231-235), their fiery spirit (236-238), and their determined response to adversity (248-250) give way to increasingly dramatic and protracted evidence of their vulnerability to natural predators (242-247) and disease (251-263), and to a corresponding reemphasis on the responsibilities of the beekeeper (239-240, 264-280). That pattern reaches its fullest development with the dramatic revelation that a beekeeper may generate a new swarm of bees if his original swarm is wiped out by disease.

V

Up to the point of that final revelation, the organization of *Georgic* 4 may be seen, very broadly, to recapitulate the argument of the first three books of the poem. The first account of the bees, stressing their difficult struggle for survival, recalls the description of the harsh and demanding conditions of rustic life in *Georgic* 1. Like that book, this passage concludes with productive energies released chaotically in civil strife. The description of the old gardener recalls the second *Georgic*'s attractive vision of an idyllic rustic existence safely removed from the turbulence of contemporary Rome. Like *Georgic* 2, the description of the gardener concludes by assigning that vision to a remote and inaccessible past. The second discussion of the bees parallels the dispiriting development of *Georgic* 3 from the initial prospect of absolute mastery to the final scenes of helpless failure and death.

The announcement that the destruction of even an entire swarm of bees is not irremediable marks an important turning point in *Georgic* 4 and in the poem as a whole for several reasons. For one, it places the elaboration thus far in the poem of an increasingly bleak assessment of man and nature in a more hopeful perspective. Although the new information does not constitute a simple reversal or denial of what has preceded, it does complement the earlier pessimism and contribute to the elaboration of the more complex point of view that was promised in the introduction to this book. New bees may be generated, but they do not just appear from nowhere. In lines 284–314 Virgil describes in some detail the *bugonia*, the procedure by which a new swarm of bees may be generated.[12] In early spring the orifices of a young bull are stopped up; as the animal struggles he is beaten violently, but in such a way that his skin remains unbroken while his entrails are smashed; thereafter the body is left to rot on a bed of fragrant herbs in a small, semienclosed cell; after a suitable interval the beekeeper returns (308–314):

> interea teneris tepefactus in ossibus umor
> aestuat, et uisenda modis animalia miris,
> trunca pedum primo, mox et stridentia pennis,
> miscentur, tenuemque magis magis aëra carpunt,
> donec ut aestiuis effusus nubibus imber
> erupere, aut ut neruo pulsante sagittae,
> prima leues ineunt si quando proelia Parthi.

> Meanwhile, the liquid in the soft bones has warmed and cooks. Then, you ought to see how the animals in their remarkable forms, at first without feet, then their wings buzzing, mingle and, more and more, try the fine air until they have burst forth like rain pouring down from summer clouds or like arrows from a pulsing bowstring whenever the light-armed Parthians begin an engagement.

Those final images of bees bursting from the putrid carcass of a dead bullock are fraught with meaning. They invite specific contrast with the images in *Georgic* 3 of plague-stricken livestock that symbolized the ultimate powerlessness of man against the degenerative forces of nature.

This hopeful scene in *Georgic* 4, however, does not simply deny the fact of death or its horror. The discussion of *amor* in *Georgic* 3 implied that creation and destruction are unavoidably interrelated, because both emanate from the same elemental vitality. The introduction of *Georgic* 4 likewise insisted on the paradoxical interrelation

---

12. Virgil does not himself use the term *bugonia*. We learn that it is the technical term for the procedure he describes from Varro, *RR* 2.5.5.

of smallness and greatness, frailty and vitality. The *bugonia* extends those ideas further with the paradox that destruction is actually a necessary condition for creation, that life is impossible without death. In the *bugonia* that paradox is expressed precisely and vividly: in order to achieve his end the beekeeper must perform a particularly brutal and repugnant sacrifice. If the emergent swarm of bees symbolizes the unquenchable powers of human resourcefulness and of natural vitality, the repellent images of the suffocating bullock in the paroxysms of death and of his rotten carcass do not allow us to ignore or easily dismiss the awful conditions that the creation of new bees requires. The complex meaning of the *bugonia* is pointedly reemphasized in the two similes that conclude its description. On the one hand, the new bees are compared to summer rains. The superficial basis for the comparison is visual, but a further effect of it is to suggest that the bees, like the fructifying rains of summer, are expressions of nature's essential fertility. On the other hand, the bees are compared to the arrows released by Parthians in their attacks. Again, the superficial basis of the comparison is visual. But the fearsome deadliness of the Parthians' archery was notorious.[13] Reference to it here is a reminder that the vitality embodied in the new bees cannot be entirely dissociated from violence and death.

As evidence for the hopeful possibility of radical renewal, the bees' example has particular relevance to the condition of Virgil's contemporaries. The discussion of bees has throughout called attention to the striking similarities between their social organization and behavior, and those of humans. Their society, like human society, is complex and hierarchical: they employ a systematic division of labor and have "leaders" to whom they are intensely loyal. More specifically, their swarm has been compared to the Roman state. The members of the swarm are "Quirites," and they engage in civil wars. Virgil's contemporaries, and especially readers of the *Georgics*, would have been prepared to see the destruction of the bees' swarm as a restatement of the parallel already established in *Georgic* 3 between natural and civic disaster. The bees' fate would be the more pointed inasmuch as they, unlike the livestock of *Georgic* 3, have been presented as a microcosm, however imperfect, of Rome. Just as their annihilation confirms the idea that the collapse of the Roman

13. See Horace, for example, *C.* 2.13.17; 1.18.12.

Republic is in some sense natural and therefore unavoidable, like its parallels in the animal world, so the revelation that a new swarm of bees can be generated to replace the old offers hope that a new Roman state can also be created. The consequences of the Roman civil wars, as all-encompassing as they were, need not be any more final than the seemingly irremediable destruction of an entire swarm of bees.

As the initial description of the *bugonia* has shown, however, the process of renewal, of regeneration, is not a simple one: it is inseparably bound up with violence and destruction; not simply a matter of attacking barren fields to make them fruitful, it requires the destruction of life in its prime. Generalization of the principles underlying the *bugonia* to include people and societies must inevitably raise far-reaching and difficult questions. Although the description of the farmer's techniques and the conditions of his struggle for a livelihood has revealed the basic principle of regeneration, the example of the bees has shown that the georgic mode has its limits: even the most nearly human of all animals are not fully human; descriptions of the farmer's activities can only begin to suggest the meaning of the interrelations between life and death, creation and destruction, as they apply directly to humans. Thus, the repeated and increasing emphasis on the beekeeper in the latter sections of the passages on bees prepares for a shift from a georgic to a mythical perspective, from a didactic to a narrative style, from the techniques and responsibilities of the anonymous farmer to the heroic agency of Aristaeus, the semidivine discoverer of the *bugonia*.

That shift in perspective involves another of equal importance. Thus far in the *Georgics*, the focus of Virgil's interest has been aggressively Roman. Contrasted with the rest of the world, Rome and Italy have been presented as the only places where true civilization is possible. Virgil's farmer has been the Roman farmer; the techniques and conditions Virgil has described, those of Roman farming. The poem's different visions of rustic life have been measured against the ills of contemporary Rome, and they have been informed by the Romans' idealization of their own past. Virgil has addressed the collapse of his society in distinctively Roman terms. He has, in an important sense, been trying to find a solution to a contemporary Roman crisis in Roman history, to find a Roman future in the Roman past—or, rather, he has been assessing others' efforts to do so.

256    Virgil's *Georgics*

The introduction to the discovery of the *bugonia* shifts the perspective radically away from Rome. The hero of the discovery is Aristaeus, a Greek not a Roman. He brings us back to the very origins of civilization, to those divinities of invention and discovery whom the poet invoked in the opening lines of the poem (1.7-20). But that return does not signal a recapitulation of the poem's argument; we have already had that in the discussion of bees. Rather, it reflects a new, non-Roman beginning. Virgil emphasizes the remote and exotic origins of the *bugonia* from his first mention of it (287-294):

> nam qua Pellaei gens fortunata Canopi
> accolit effuso stagnantem flumine Nilum
> et circum pictis uehitur sua rura phaselis,
> quaque pharetratae uicinia Persidis urget,
> et diuersa ruens septem discurrit in ora
> usque coloratis amnis deuexus ab Indis,
> et uiridem Aegyptum nigra fecundat harena,
> omnis in hac certam regio iacit arte salutem.

> Where the fortunate race of Pellaean Canopus cultivates the stagnant waters of the Nile when it has overflowed its banks and rides about their lands in painted boats; where the neighborhood of the quivered Persian presses and the river runs out into seven mouths, sweeping down all the way from the colored Indians and makes green Egypt fertile with black silt, the entire region makes this art the foundation for certain well-being.

Egypt was regarded as perhaps the oldest of all civilizations. By identifying the *bugonia* as an established, indeed basic, custom of the Egyptians, Virgil places it at the beginning and heart of all civlization.

His decision to abandon the georgic mode and the familiar world of Roman tradition is a tacit assertion that Romans must look beyond their own experience, that the Roman past can no longer be an adequate guide to a Roman future—if indeed it ever was. The *Georgics* have examined different versions of traditional ways of Roman life and have shown that they lead nowhere but to civil war, to a never-never land of escapist fantasy, or to despair. Romans must free themselves of their preoccupation with their past if they are realistically to confront the present and discover a future: they must look to Egypt, to Greece, to Aristaeus, to the universal realm of myth. As one aspect of its commentary on the human condition, Virgil's story of the *bugonia*'s discovery reconfirms the necessity of giving up the past.

## VI

The narrative of the myth is organized around the contrast between two related but different worlds of experience, that of the semidivine hero who is able to transcend nature's limits and that of the mortal who is bound by them. The story begins when Aristaeus, whose bees have perished, complains bitterly to his mother, the nymph Cyrene, and she comes to his aid. It ends when she finally reveals the technique of the *bugonia* to him. Between those two episodes, each colored by the beneficent influence of his divine mother, Aristaeus must forcibly subdue the sea god, Proteus, and demand instruction from him. Proteus, in turn, reminds Aristaeus that in his attempt to rape the nymph Eurydice he had inadvertently caused her death: she had run into the path of a poisonous snake in her headlong rush to escape Aristaeus. In addition, Proteus reveals the terrible suffering that Eurydice's death brought to her lover, Orpheus, and explains that Orpheus' anger is the reason for the death of Aristaeus' bees. From that contrast between the comparatively serene world Aristaeus shares with his divine mother and the wholly human world of toil, mortality, passion, and suffering that he must encounter before the *bugonia* is revealed to him, there emerges a fully developed vision of the human condition and of the hero's special relation to it.

The discovery of the *bugonia* is introduced as an epic event: *Quis deus, hanc, Musae, quis nobis extudit artem?* ("Which god, Muses, which one forged for us this art?" 315). Those words announce the discoverer as a hero of the traditional epic mold. He combines divinity and human qualities: he is a god, yet he toiled; like man he "beat out" (*extudit*) his art. Likewise, the telling of his story, like the telling of Achilles' or Odysseus', demands the direct assistance of the Muses. When we eventually learn that our hero is *pastor Aristaeus* (317), we are well prepared to see him as no ordinary shepherd. In fact, Aristaeus was already known before Virgil as the originator of many important agricultural practices.[14] His name itself has epic associations. It is cognate with the Greek heroic title *aristos* ("noble") and with the specific term that came to designate the hero's moment of unique excellence, his *aristeia*. The distinctive feature of Virgil's introduction is that it emphasizes the specifically heroic association of his name and assures that we will regard him not simply as yet another homely deity of the countryside, but rather as a prototypical hero.

Although emphasis on Aristaeus' special stature persists throughout the story of his achievement, it is especially pronounced in the initial sections where the hero's character is defined. Aristaeus is not quite like any other hero. The divine element of his being does not manifest itself primarily in the extraordinary might or resourcefulness of the epic warrior or adventurer. Nor does it, in combination with his mortality, lead to a heightened perception by the hero of the tragic circumstances of human existence. In Aristaeus it seems, rather, to lead both to impatience with those limitations and dilemmas that might be regarded as characteristically human and then to a unique exemption from them. The narrative begins with Aristaeus' indignant response to the death of his bees (317–332):

> pastor Aristaeus fugiens Peneia Tempe,
> amissis, ut fama, apibus morboque fameque,
> tristis ad extremi sacrum caput astitit amnis
> multa querens, atque hac adfatus uoce parentem:
> "mater, Cyrene mater, quae gurgitis huius
> ima tenes, quid me praeclara stirpe deorum
> (si modo, quem perhibes, pater est Thymbraeus Apollo)
> inuisum fatis genuisti? aut quo tibi nostri
> pulsus amor? quid me caelum sperare iubebas?
> en etiam hunc ipsum uitae mortalis honorem,
> quem mihi vix frugum et pecudum custodia sollers
> omnia temptanti extuderat, te matre relinquo.
> quin age et ipsa manu felicis erue siluas,
> fer stabulis inimicum ignem atque interfice messis,
> ure sata et ualidam in uitis molire bipennem,
> tanta meae si te ceperunt taedia laudis."

---

14. See Schirmer, "Aristaios," *Roscher* vol. 1, cols. 547–551; and also Willi Frentz, *Mythologisches in Vergils Georgica* (diss., Meisenheim am Glan 1967) 5–6, 21, 25.

The shepherd Aristaeus, fleeing from Peneus' Tempe, since he had lost his bees, according to report through sickness and famine, sadly stopped at the very edge of the river, at its sacred head, and with much lamentation, he addressed his mother as follows: "Mother, Cyrene, Mother, you who occupy the depths of this pool, why did you bear me from the famous stock of the gods (supposing, of course, that my father is, as you claim, Thymbraeus Apollo), since I am hateful to the fates? Or where has your love for me been driven? Why did you use to command me to hope for the heavens? Look! Even this very honor of a mortal life which I scarcely beat out for myself with resourceful overseeing of my plants and flocks, leaving nothing untried, with you for a mother I lose it. Come, then, with your own hand level my fruitful trees; set destructive fire to my stables and destroy my harvests; parch my crops in the field and wield a mighty axe among my vines, if you have been taken with such disdain for my reputation."

The curious tone of Aristaeus' complaint may perhaps be best gauged by comparison with two earlier passages from which it appears to be a kind of composite. The first is Achilles' famous lament to his mother in *Iliad* 1.348–356:

... αὐτὰρ Ἀχιλλεὺς
δακρύσας ἑτάρων ἄφαρ ἕζετο νόσφι λιασθεὶς
θῖν' ἐφ' ἁλὸς πολιῆς, ὁρόων ἐπὶ οἴνοπα πόντον·
πολλὰ δὲ μητρὶ φίλῃ ἠρήσατο χεῖρας ὀρεγνύς·
"μῆτερ, ἐπεί μ' ἔτεκές γε μινυνθάδιόν περ ἐόντα,
τιμήν πέρ μοι ὄφελλεν Ὀλύμπιος ἐγγυαλίξαι
Ζεὺς ὑψιβρεμέτης· νῦν δ' οὐδέ με τυτθὸν ἔτισεν.
ἦ γάρ μ' Ἀτρεΐδης εὐρὺ κρείων Ἀγαμέμνων
ἠτίμησεν· ἑλὼν γὰρ ἔχει γέρας, αὐτὸς ἀπούρας."

But, crying, Achilles sat apart from his companions, going far off to the shore of the grey salt water, looking out over the wine-dark sea and repeatedly he appealed to his mother, stretching out his hands: "Mother, since you bore me to be short-lived, Olympian Zeus who thunders on high ought to grant me honor. But now not even a little has he honored me, for, indeed, the son of Atreus, wide-ruling Agamemnon, has dishonored me. He has taken away my prize and keeps it. He took it away himself."

The obvious parallels between that passage and Aristaeus' lament to his own divine mother clearly help to reconfirm Aristaeus' status as a hero. At the same time, the tone of the two passages and our sense of the larger context of events to which they belong combine to create quite different impressions. The important symbolic value attached to Agamemnon's taking of Achilles' Briseis is clearly established, for example, before Achilles' lament is reported to us. Aristaeus' efforts to demonstrate the importance of his bees suggest rather a childish lack of perspective. His list of accomplishments, which his mother may as well destroy if he cannot have his bees, reduces to relative insignificance virtually all the agricultural topics that Virgil has discussed in his poem and that he has identified as the very foundations of civilization.

The petulance of Aristaeus' tone seems to owe something to another model, the Cyclops, Polyphemus, of Theocritus' eleventh *Idyll*. Like Aristaeus and Achilles he is the child of a god (Poseidon) and a nymph (Thoos), and like his counterpart he turns to his mother when things go wrong. When he fails to win the affections of the sea nymph, Galatea, he complains bitterly (*Idyll* 11.67-71):

> ἁ μάτηρ ἀδικεῖ με μόνα, καὶ μέμφομαι αὐτᾷ·
> οὐδὲν πήποχ' ὅλως ποτὶ τὶν φίλον εἶπεν ὑπέρ μευ,
> καὶ ταῦτ' ἆμαρ ἐπ' ἆμαρ ὁρεῦσά με λεπτύνοντα.
> φασῶ τὰν κεφαλὰν καὶ τὼς πόδας ἀμφοτέρως μευ
> σφύσδειν, ὡς ἀνιαθῇ ἐπεὶ κἠγὼν ἀνιῶμαι.

> My mother alone does me wrong; I hold her responsible. She has never said anything at all good to you on my behalf, and that, even though she sees me growing thinner day by day. I will say that my head aches and my feet, both of them; so let her suffer, since I suffer.

Although the comic Polyphemus' petulance is more exaggerated than Aristaeus', the speeches of the two characters reveal much in common. Both are spiteful. Polyphemus will complain to his mother of aching feet and head, since it is only right that she suffer if he does. Aristaeus is more subtle, but not by much. His expressed doubt about her version of his parentage is an insult calculated to hurt.

In both cases, moreover, the characters' spitefulness is motivated by a refusal to accept any responsibility for their misfortune and by a corresponding desire to shift the blame onto someone else. Polyphemus cannot accept the possibility that Galatea's aversion to him may be due to his own ugliness and boorishness. In shifting the blame for his failure onto his mother, he makes the further assumption that it is the mother's role to act as advocate for her son in his courtships. Although Aristaeus does not actually come out and say that his mother is responsible for his bees' death, he clearly means to imply as much. When he says that his honor has been ruined, *te matre* ("with you as mother," 528), the phrase is ambiguous at best. It might mean "even though you are my mother," but it could just as well mean "*since* you are my mother." That second possibility is reinforced in the immediately following lines where Aristaeus challenges his mother to destroy the rest of his accomplishments, as though she is already to blame for having allowed his bees to perish. Like Polyphemus, he assumes that his mother has more than the usual maternal responsibilities toward her adult son. Aristaeus implies that if he really is of divine stock he should never have suffered his present misfortune.

Aristaeus' sense of his own privileged status is confirmed explicitly and vividly in the subsequent description of his mother's world and of his visit to it. Immediately after the report of his complaint the scene shifts to Cyrene and her exotic household (333-344):

> At mater sonitum thalamo sub fluminis alti
> sensit. eam circum Milesia uellera Nymphae
> carpebant hyali saturo fucata colore,
> Drymoque Xanthoque Ligeaque Phyllodoceque,
> caesariem effusae nitidam per candida colla,
> Cydippe et flaua Lycorias, altera uirgo,
> altera tum primos Lucinae experta labores,
> Clioque et Beroe soror, Oceanitides ambae,
> ambae auro, pictis incinctae pellibus ambae,
> atque Ephyre atque Opis et Asia Deiopea
> et tandem positis uelox Arethusa sagittis.

> But his mother in her chamber deep beneath the river heard the sound [of Aristaeus' lament]. Around her, nymphs plucked

Milesian wool that had been dyed a deep glassy green: Drymo, Zantho, Ligea, and Phyllodoce, their shining hair flowing over their white necks, Cydippe and tawny Lycorias, the one a virgin, the other then experiencing the first labors of Lucina, and Clio and her sister Beroe, both daughters of Ocean, both girt with gold-embroidered pelts, and also Ephyre and Opis and Asian Deiopea and, finally, swift Arethusa, her arrows set aside.

The luxuriant beauty of Cyrene's home with its fine wools, embroidered fleeces, rich colors, and gleaming maidens is immediately apparent. Equally conspicuous is its otherworldliness. From the first two lines of the passage with the aqueous succession of liquids and nasals through the list of Cyrene's companions, with their abundance of distinctively Greek consonants and vowels, we are immersed, as it were, in a sea of exotic sounds, which offer a sensation of strangeness in place of a precise depiction of the setting.

Those superficial manifestations of otherworldliness are complemented by the aura of serene detachment that seems to characterize Cyrene's household. Here, Arethusa lays aside her arrows and joins the other nymphs in spinning, the timeless emblem of the well-ordered home. Meanwhile (345-347),

> inter quas curam Clymene narrabat inanem
> Volcani, Martisque dolos et dulcia furta,
> aque Chao densos diuum numerabat amores.

> Among them Clymene related the empty cares of Vulcan, Mars' deceit, his sweet thefts, and, beginning with Chaos, enumerated the gods' endless succession of *amours*.

Among mortals, erotic passion has been shown to release violently destructive energies, and *amor* has been presented as a metaphor for all of the most self-destructive potentialities in man. Clymene's songs reveal that love is a universal affliction of the gods as well—but with an important difference. Its influence among them is merely comic—at least that is the impression created by the one specific example that Virgil selects to characterize Clymene's songs. Vulcan's "empty cares" and Mars' "sweet thefts" allude to a story that was assured a prominent place in ancient literary tradition when Homer put it in the mouth of Demodocus, the archetypical bard (*Odyssey* 8.266-366). According to his song, Hephaestus discovered that his wife, Aphrodite, was secretly having an affair with Ares. Determined to get revenge, he rigged a net of fine chain to fall upon and trap the lovers as they embraced in bed. Once they were caught, the other gods and goddesses stood around the embarrassed couple, ogling, laughing, and making risqué jokes at their expense. The story ends when the two gods are released: Ares flees to Thrace and Aphrodite to her island of Cyprus, where the Graces bathe, anoint her, and clothe her in lovely garments that were θάμα θεάσθαι, "marvelous to behold." The tone of the entire episode is implicit in Virgil's brief introductory summary of it: this is the story of Vulcan's *inanes curas*, his "empty cares." They are empty in that Vulcan, despite his efforts and his desire, cannot win Aphrodite's affection. They are also "empty" in the larger sense that they are of no real consequence at all. They are simply an amusement for the gods, an entertaining diversion.

Just as Hephaestus' useless ingenuity and the plight of Ares and Aphrodite amused the Olympian gods who witnessed them, so Clymene's story about them helps Cyrene and her companions to pass the time: *carmine quo captae . . . fusis mollia pensa / deuoluunt* ("captivated by this song, [the nymphs] unravel their soft measures of wool from their spindles," 349-350). Indeed, the story of Hephaestus and Ares epitomizes the essential inconsequentiality of divine existence as it is portrayed in the Homeric epics and typifies the contrast there between the divine comedy and the tragedy of human conflict: in the *Odyssey* Demodocus' song of Hephaestus and Ares is juxtaposed to the songs he sings of the Trojan war, songs that recall human suffering and loss and bring tears to Odysseus' eyes. In the *Georgics* as in Homeric epic the important conflicts originate in the human world, not the divine: it is the muffled sound of Aristaeus' complaints that strikes terror into his mother's heart and throws her household into momentary confusion; it is not Clymene's song of *amor*.

The significance of that evocation of the traditional epic contrast between the divine and human realms is that it prepares us to gauge the full distance that separates the divine aspect of Aristaeus from the world of human experience. Cyrene observes of her son that *fas illi limina diuum / tangere* ("it is permitted for him to touch the thresholds of the gods," 358-359), and she sends one of her companions to escort Aristaeus to her. There follows a fantastic journey as Aristaeus descends through the waters to his mother's household. The scene is not altogether without precedent in the exploits of earlier heroes. Theseus proved his divine parentage by descending beneath the sea to the home of his mother, the nymph Amphitrite.[15] But nothing in the extant versions of that journey equals the description of Aristaeus' experience (359–373):

> . . . simul alta iubet discedere late
> flumina, qua iuuenis gressus inferret. at illum
> curuata in montis faciem circumstetit unda
> accepitque sinu uasto misitque sub amnem.
> iamque domum mirans genetricis et umida regna
> speluncisque lacus clausos lucosque sonantis
> ibat, et ingenti motu stupefactus aquarum
> omnia sub magna labentia flumina terra
> spectabat diuersa locis, Phasimque Lycumque,
> et caput unde altus primum se erumpit Enipeus,
> unde pater Tiberinus et unde Aniena fluenta
> saxosusque sonans Hypanis Mysusque Caicus
> et gemina auratus taurino cornua uultu
> Eridanus, quo non alius per pinguia culta
> in mare purpureum uiolentior effluit amnis.

Immediately [Cyrene] commands the deep rivers to separate far apart where the youth might make his way. The water curved into the likeness of a mountain around him, received him in its vast fold, and carried him beneath the river. And now, marveling at his mother's home and her watery realm, he passed by lakes enclosed in caves and resounding groves; struck dumb by the great movement of the waters, he observed all the different rivers flowing beneath the earth to different lands, the Phasis and the Lycus and the source whence the deep Enipeus first breaks forth, whence father Tiber, whence Anio's waters and the rocky-sounding Hypanis, whence Mysian Caicus and, its twin horns gilded on its bullish forehead, the Eridanus—no other river flows through rich crops toward the dark blue sea more powerfully.

As the impressive scene develops, it gradually overshadows Aristaeus and his plight. His role in the first half of the passage is chiefly that of

---

15. The story survives in Bacchylides fr. 16.

spectator (*mirans, stupefactus, spectabat*); there is no clear picture of Aristaeus himself. In the final six and one half lines, there is not even any mention of Aristaeus. Our attention is directed rather to the dramatic and deafening outpouring of the rivers from their common source. Transition from the imperfect tense to describe Aristeaus' reactions (*spectabat*) to the present tense for the rivers (*erumpit, effluit*) further increases the vivid immediacy of the scene until it effectively removes us, as well as Aristaeus, from the world of mortals.

When at last Aristaeus arrives in his mother's cavernous chambers, she sees that his tears are, like Vulcan's cares, *inanis* (375)—profitless and also of no consequence. She and her companions prepare to comfort him (376-381):

> . . . manibus liquidos dant ordine fontis
> germanae, tonsisque ferunt mantelia uillis;
> pars epulis onerant mensas et plena reponunt
> pocula, Panchaeis adolescunt ignibus arae.
> et mater "cape Maeonii carchesia Bacchi:
> Oceano libemus" ait.

> With their hands the sisters offer fresh water in sequence, and bring napkins of shorn wool; some set tables with food, fill the cups and set them back in place; Panchaean incense glows upon the altars, and his mother says, "Take up goblets of Maeonian Bacchus; let us pour a libation to Ocean."

The regular processes of Cyrene's household assert themselves. The parallelisms and balanced rhythms of her prayers mark the final assimilation of Aristaeus' disruptive presence into the order of her divine world (381-386):

> . . . simul ipsa precatur
> Oceanumque patrem rerum Nymphasque sorores,
> centum quae siluas, centum quae flumina seruant.
> ter liquido ardentem perfundit nectare Vestam,
> ter flamma ad summum tecti subiecta reluxit.
> omine quo firmans animum sic incipit ipsa. . . .

> At once she herself prays to Ocean, the father of things, and to the Nymphs, her sisters who preserve a hundred forests, who preserve a hundred rivers. Three times with liquid nectar she sprinkles burning Vesta; three times a flame shoots up to the

very roof and instantly flashes bright again. With this omen buoying her spirits she begins as follows. . . .

The calmness of Cyrene's household, her orderly enactment of ritual, have overcome Aristaeus' petulance and prepared him to hear his mother's advice.

From the extreme perspective of Cyrene's world and Aristaeus' gentle reception there, we can see clearly that Aristaeus' subsequent adventures involve an encounter with the harsh realities that distinguish human from divine existence. That encounter is partially anticipated in Cyrene's initial instructions to Aristaeus. She explains to him that he must subdue the sea god, Proteus, compel him to reveal the cause of the bees' death, and exact the promise of a favorable outcome to Aristaeus' efforts. Once again Aristaeus' story places him among the traditional epic heroes. The narrative both of Cyrene's instructions and of Aristaeus' subsequent encounter is modeled very closely on the description in *Odyssey* 4.351–575 of Menelaus' efforts to command Proteus' assistance. In both cases a hero has suffered a serious setback and is at a loss how to proceed; a sea nymph tells him that he must subdue Proteus, who will take on many forms in his efforts to escape, but he must force the sea god to reveal the reason for the hero's misfortune and its remedy; the nymph helps the hero to catch Proteus unawares; the hero finally overpowers Proteus, who conveys the required information grudgingly and then abruptly dives back into the sea.

## VII

Within the context of the *Georgics*, Aristaeus' struggle with Proteus acquires a particular significance that the story of Menelaus' conflict with the sea god does not have. Like Menelaus, Aristaeus must grapple with a god who changes shape, taking on the forms of wild animals and the vital elements of nature. Cyrene tells Aristaeus what to expect (405–410):

uerum ubi correptum manibus uinclisque tenebis,
tum uarie eludent species atque ora ferarum.
fiet enim subito sus horridus atraque tigris
squamosusque draco et fulua cervice leaena,
aut acrem flammae sonitum dabit atque ita uinclis
excidet, aut in aquas tenuis dilapsus abibit.

But after you've caught him with your hands and you have him in chains, then in various ways the appearance and forms of wild beasts will trick you. He will suddenly become a bristling boar, a foul tigress, a scaly dragon, a tawny-necked lioness, or he will give the sharp sound of flame and so escape his bonds, or slipping into trickling water, he will go off.

That warning is later summarized in Virgil's description of the actual conflict (440-442):

> . . . ille suae contra non immemor artis
> omnia transformat sese in miracula rerum,
> ignemque horribilemque feram fluuiumque liquentem.

> He, on his side, not unmindful of his own arts, transforms himself into all kinds of miraculous things: fire, a horrible wild beast, a running stream.

The struggle to subdue Proteus in all his varied forms might be interpreted in almost any context as symbolic of mankind's efforts to subdue the forces of disorder and destruction in nature. In the *Georgics* such a symbolic conflict effectively epitomizes in a single scene one of the major themes of the entire poem. This is especially clear since the description of the struggle with Proteus recalls the terms in which that theme has been presented in the poet's reflections on the farmer's struggle for a livelihood. Already, as in *Georgic* 3, for example, the violence of wild boars, tigresses, and lionesses and the sinister viciousness of scaly snakes have dramatized the destructive forces that the farmer must strive to control. Elsewhere we have been warned of the danger of fire and shown the indiscriminate raging of floods. In fact, our attention is directed specifically toward the implicit parallel between Aristaeus' struggle with Proteus and the farmer's struggle with his environment. Virgil describes how Proteus arrives at his cave at noon and then proceeds to count his flocks of seals (433-436),

> . . . uelut stabuli custos in montibus olim,
> Vesper ubi e pastu uitulos ad tecta reducit
> auditisque lupos acuunt balatibus agni,
> consedit scopulo medius, numerumque recenset.

> just as in the mountains at times, when Vesper brings calves back from pasture to their barns and wolves grow alert at the

sound of bleating sheep, a herdsman sits on a crag among his livestock and rechecks their number.

Although Proteus is also compared to a shepherd counting his flocks in the *Odyssey*, Homer makes no mention of dangerous predators. Virgil's simile, occurring as it does between Cyrene's description of the struggle that Aristaeus must expect and Virgil's subsequent summary of it, points clearly to the essential similarity between the kinds of struggle in which both Aristaeus and the farmer must engage.

Emphasis on the sheer physical demands made of the hero is the controlling focus of the narrative up through the actual combat with Proteus. In the *Odyssey*, for example, Menelaus' helpful nymph dabs ambrosia under his nose to protect him from the awful stench of the seal skins that he must hide under while he awaits Proteus' arrival (*Od.* 4.441–446). In the *Georgics*, Cyrene anoints her son's entire body, so that his limbs are suffused with *uigor* (418). Likewise, Virgil elaborates minimal references in Homer to the time of day when the hero must encounter Proteus. Homer seems to specify the noon hour primarily because that is the time when Proteus would come ashore to rest, presumably as shepherds typically did, during the heat of the day. Cyrene characterizes noon as the time (401–402)

. . . medios cum sol accenderit aestus,
cum sitiunt herbae et pecori iam gratior umbra est.

when the sun kindles the midday heat, when grasses thirst and the flocks take more pleasure in shade.

Later, in his narrative of Aristaeus' actual ambush Virgil expands his description of the dryness and fiery heat that the hero must endure (425–430):

iam rapidus torrens sitientis Sirius Indos
ardebat caelo et medium sol igneus orbem
hauserat, arebant herbae et caua flumina siccis
faucibus ad limum radii tepefacta coquebant,
cum Proteus consueta petens e fluctibus antra
ibat.

Now at full force, parching the thirsty Indians, Sirius burned in the sky and the fiery sun had consumed half its course; the grasses burned, and hollow rivers, their mouths dry, were warmed to mud by the sun's rays and cooked, when Proteus came out of the waves in search of his usual caverns.

Aristaeus, who must toil in that fiery heat, when all other life withdraws to the comfort of shade, recalls the relentless farmer of *Georgic* 1 who stripped to plow and sow under the full heat of the sun (1.299). As Cyrene warns (398-400),

> nam sine ui non ulla dabit praecepta, neque illum
> orando flectes; uim duram et uincula capto
> tende; doli circum haec demum frangentur inanes.

> without force [Proteus] will give no precepts nor will you move him by prayer. You must apply hard force and bonds (once you have captured him). On them his stratagems will break at last, empty.

Force (*uis*) and hardness (*duritia*) have repeatedly been shown to be essential to mankind's efforts to impose a fruitful order on the environment. In sending Aristaeus to do battle with Proteus, Cyrene sends her son out of her own protected world to encounter an aspect of mankind's struggle for civilized existence. If she extends her protection to Aristaeus even in this encounter, it is because he is still more god than man and must encounter the destructive forces of nature in a particularly stark and elemental form.

That summary of the external realities of the human condition is preparatory to Proteus' revelations about human nature itself. It is here that Virgil departs most radically from his Homeric model. In the *Odyssey* Proteus' unwillingness to share his knowledge is presented simply as an inherent aspect of the crotchety old god's character. It lacks any specific motivation and is important only because of its consequences: it explains why Proteus resists Menelaus and why the hero must subdue him forcibly. The recalcitrance of Virgil's Proteus is an expression of anger directed specifically against Aristaeus' past behavior (445-446, 453-459):[16]

---

16. In line 455 I have diverged from the text of Mynors, which I have otherwise followed without exception. I prefer the reading *ad meritum* to *ob meritum*. The manuscript tradition is ambiguous: most manuscripts read *ob*, but the Palatine, generally quite reliable, reads *ad. Haudquaquam ad meritum*, "not at all according to or up to what is deserved," as a commentary on the price Aristaeus must pay seems more appropriate to the situation and the

nam quis te, iuuenum confidentissime, nostras
iussit adire domos? . . .
    Non te nullius exercent numinis irae;
magna luis commissa: tibi has miserabilis Orpheus
haudquaquam ad meritum poenas, ni fata resistant,
suscitat, et rapta grauiter pro coniuge saeuit.
illa quidem, dum te fugeret per flumina praeceps,
immanem ante pedes hydrum moritura puella
seruantem ripas alta non uidit in herba.

Who, most brazen of youths, ordered you to enter my house? . . . Divine anger—no lesser thing—pursues you. You pay the price for great offenses. Against you pitiable Orpheus stirs punishment—not at all undeserved (if the fates should not resist him) and because of his stolen wife he is in a deep rage. When she was running from you along a river in headlong flight —she who was about to die although just a girl—she did not see at her feet a huge snake which kept to the river bank in deep grass.

Proteus' words reveal that Aristaeus has, after all, brought misfortune on himself and that he has done so, moreover, by committing a reprehensible act, one for which (in Proteus' eyes at least) punishment is well deserved.

Even more important than those specific revelations, dramatic as they are, is the insight they give into Aristaeus' character: he not only caused Eurydice's death, he seems actually to be utterly oblivious both to her loss and to his responsibility for it. More striking, from this new perspective, than the petulance of Aristaeus' complaint to his mother is the complete absence of any reference in it to Eurydice. By most standards of human behavior it should be Eurydice's loss that mattered to Aristaeus, not the loss of his bees; Eurydice, after all, was human. But Aristaeus has not the least thought for her. When he reviews the things that once were but are no longer of value to him since the death of his bees and the blow to his reputation, he does not include Eurydice anywhere on his list: she is beneath his notice. Aristaeus' petulance on that occasion, therefore,

---

tone of Proteus' remarks than does *haudquaquam ob meritum*, "not at all on account of what is deserved," which could only make sense as a reference back to Orpheus' characterization as *miserabilis*.

has been shown to be but the superficial expression of a more profound and disturbing amorality. Aristaeus seems to be completely self-centered: he thinks only of what he wants for himself and is indifferent to the consequences for others. When his bees die he thinks only of his own reputation whose paramount importance to him is signaled by the final and climactic position of the term *laus* in his complaint to Cyrene (332). Deprived, as he thinks, of his good reputation, he not only strikes out spitefully at his mother, but is also prepared to see destroyed all of those accomplishments of his on which human civilization depends. Just so, he pursued Eurydice against her will; and when she died, he quite simply erased her from his mind.

Proteus' anger is compounded by an implicit fear that Aristaeus may not, in fact, get the punishment he deserves—that he can, as a god, act without regard for the concerns of justice. The story of Aristaeus' pursuit of Eurydice places him among the number of those gods who pursued the unwilling objects of their lust to tragic fates. Stories of such exploits were already well established in Hellenistic literature and were soon to become dominant motifs in the Latin epic of Virgil's younger contemporary, Ovid.[17] When Proteus expressed the opinion that Orpheus was calling down a well-deserved punishment on Aristaeus, he added a pointed qualification: *ni fata resistant* ("unless the fates oppose," 455). If Aristaeus does not reflect on the consequences of his actions, it is because he has no need to. Aristaeus' selfishness and his awareness of his privileged status are summed up in Proteus' initial description of him as *confidentissime*. The word means "confident" or "self-assured," but it also often has a strong pejorative connotation: "bold," "audacious," "brazen."

Proteus' response to Aristaeus is an assault on the hero's brazenness. It is notable that Proteus does not, in fact, tell Aristaeus, as he does Menelaus in the *Odyssey*, how to resolve his difficulties. Nor is it certain that his explanation for the bees' death is accurate: he attributes it to Orpheus' desire for revenge; Cyrene later will attribute it to the anger of Eurydice's fellow nymphs (532-534). What Proteus does instead is to confront Aristaeus with the human consequences of his behavior and to emphasize the grief of those who

---

17. For a brief summary and references to the literature, see Karl Galinsky, *Ovid's Metamorphoses: An Introduction to the Basic Aspects* (Berkeley 1975) 1-2.

cared for Eurydice. He begins by describing the grief of Eurydice's fellow Dryads (460-463) and, then, introduces that of her lover, Orpheus (464-466):

> ipse caua solans aegrum testudine amorem
> te, dulcis coniunx, te solo in litore secum,
> te ueniente die, te decedente canebat.

> He himself soothing his sorrowful love with his hollow lyre, sweet wife, sang of you, of you by himself on the lonely shore, of you when the day was new, of you as the day grew dim.

The repetition of the pronoun *te* and of similar sounds conveys a sense of great emotional intensity and of immediacy, so that Proteus seems almost to speak to Eurydice in Orpheus' own words and to take the lover's place before us.

That repeated emphasis on the pronoun *te* also conveys Orpheus' single-minded concentration on his lost Eurydice and her unique individuality. Unlike Aristaeus, who thinks only of his own reputation, Orpheus devotes his thoughts to another. Aristaeus' lost bees are for him only a means to an end; they are of no value to him in and of themselves. He can and will be satisfied by a new swarm to replace the old. Any healthy swarm of bees will attest equally to his prowess; he does not require a specific bee or a specific swarm, for, of course, bees, as we have seen, lack individuality and are therefore interchangeable. Orpheus' lament reveals how far removed such insignificance of the individual is from human experience. There can be no substitute for his Eurydice; he sings of her and of her alone.

Like Aristaeus, Orpheus attempts to redeem his loss, to overcome death and create life anew. But there is a world of difference in the two characters' approach to that task. Everything that Aristaeus attempts is, as we have seen, colored by his divinity. It is his divine mother who comforts him, secures good omens for him, directs him to Proteus, anoints him with invigorating ambrosia; and it is she who, finally, will explain to her son the actual technique of the *bugonia*. Of course, Orpheus by tradition was a heroic figure in his own right. By some accounts he was the child of the Muse, Calliope, and of Apollo, the god of prophecy and song. He was the legendary founder and priest of some or perhaps all mysteries; and he was a poet who had the power to move all nature with his song.[18]

18. The ancient testimonia on Orpheus and Orphica are collected in O. Kern,

Orpheus' semidivine heroic stature is minimized in the *Georgics*, however. When Virgil refers, in passing, to Orpheus' father, he chooses a variant of the Orpheus myths that designates Oeagrius, a legendary king and river god of Thessaly rather than Apollo. Virgil says nothing of Orpheus' special relation to the mysteries. Rather, in the *Georgics*, Orpheus is presented as an archetypical human lover. In contrast to the harmless infatuations of Venus, Vulcan, and Mars, his love is fraught with the gravest dangers for himself and the object of his desire. The energy and determination inspired in him by his love are themselves the bases for his extraordinary accomplishments. Just as *amor* led animals to swim raging rivers and to cross steep mountains, so it leads Orpheus to do the impossible, to enter the Underworld in search of Eurydice.

Likewise Orpheus' love is sufficient explanation for the power of his songs to charm. When he entered the Underworld (469–480),

. . . Manisque adiit regemque tremendum
nesciaque humanis precibus mansuescere corda.
at cantu commotae Erebi de sedibus imis
umbrae ibant tenues simulacraque luce carentum,
quam multa in foliis auium se milia condunt,
Vesper ubi aut hibernus agit de montibus imber,
matres atque uiri defunctaque corpora uita
magnanimum heroum, pueri innuptaeque puellae,
impositique rogis iuuenes ante ora parentum,
quos circum limus niger et deformis harundo
Cocyti tardaque palus inamabilis unda
alligat et nouies Styx interfusa coercet.

he approached the dead and the awesome king and hearts that do not know how to be softened by human prayers. But stirred by his song, the insubstantial shades came from Erebus' deepest recesses, images of those denied light, as many as the thousands of birds that settle themselves on leaves when the evening star or winter rain from the mountains drives them: mothers, husbands, bodies devoid of life, the bodies of high-spirited heroes,

---

*Orphicorum Fragmenta* (Berlin 1922); I. M. Linforth, *The Arts of Orpheus* (Berkeley 1941), offers the standard conservative assessment of that evidence. On Virgil's relation to earlier literary treatments of Orpheus, see Eduard Norden, "Orpheus und Eurydice," *Sitz. Berl. Akad.* (1934) 626–683 = *Kleine Schriften zum klassischen Altertum* (Berlin 1966) 468–532. See also J. Heurgon, "Orphée et Eurydice avant Virgile," *Mélanges d'archéologie et d'histoire* (1932) 6–66.

boys and unwed girls, youths placed on funeral biers before their parents' eyes. The black mud and shapeless marsh of Cocytus, a hateful swamp with sluggish water, binds them round, and the Styx, flowing around in nine circles, keeps them in.

Contrast between the responses of the immortal ruler of the Underworld and that of the captive shades makes clear the basis of Orpheus' appeal. While the king of the Underworld is characterized as unpitying, the shades of the dead gather to hear Orpheus.

Those who comprise that gathering of shades are designated, for the most part, by their relationship to those they loved and were loved by before death took them away: mothers, husbands, children. Each category—even that of heroes, once vital and inspiring, now empty bodies—invites us to reflect on the grief death brings to both the living and the spirits of the dead when it separates those who had been joined in life by bonds of affection. The sense of loss is the more profound because the separation is final. Between the living and the dead lie dank swamps, stagnant waters, and the River Styx itself. Orpheus' very personal song expresses emotions that the dead share. So universal is the experience of separation and longing in the Underworld that the entire region—its chambers, its guardian spirits, even the winds that pass through—seem to join the rustling shades as they settle into rapt attention (481-484).

Although *amor* is the source of both Orpheus' determination and his song's power to charm the Underworld, it is, equally, the source of his undoing. In *Georgic* 3 we saw that the potentials for creation and destruction are both joined in that natural vitality whose most elemental form is sexual passion. In Proteus' story of Orpheus we see that truth elaborated in its particularly human application and with tragic meaning. On the one hand, Orpheus' all-too-human love for Eurydice leads him to join those few heroes like Heracles and Odysseus, who braved the Underworld before their time. Through songs that are informed by his love he achieves the impossible: he wins permission to bring the dead back to the living. But that same love undermines all his heroic accomplishments and condemns himself and Eurydice to eternal separation (485-498):

> iamque pedem referens casus euaserat omnis,
> redditaque Eurydice superas ueniebat ad auras
> pone sequens (namque hanc dederat Proserpina legem),

cum subita incautum dementia cepit amantem,
ignoscenda quidem, scirent si ignoscere Manes:
restitit, Eurydicenque suam iam luce sub ipsa
immemor heu! uictusque animi respexit. ibi omnis
effusus labor atque immitis rupta tyranni
foedera, terque fragor stagnis auditus Auernis.
illa "quis et me" inquit "miseram et te perdidit, Orpheu,
quis tantus furor? en iterum crudelia retro
fata uocant, conditque natantia lumina somnus.
iamque uale: feror ingenti circumdata nocte
inualidasque tibi tendens, heu non tua, palmas."

And now as he retraced his steps, he had avoided every pitfall; Eurydice, restored to him, was approaching the breezes above, right behind him, following (for Proserpina had set this law) when a sudden madness took the incautious lover, a madness surely to be forgiven—if the dead knew how to forgive. He stopped and even though Eurydice was his own, already about to enter the light itself, he forgot, alas; and, his reason overcome, he looked back. Then all of his labor poured away and the harsh tyrant's conditions were broken. Three times a crashing was heard over the stagnant waters of Avernus. She said, "Who has destroyed both me, unhappy one, and you, Orpheus? What madness can be so great? Behold, a second time the cruel fates call me back, and my swimming eyes are covered by sleep. And now, farewell; I am carried off, surrounded by an immense night, even as I hold out my weak hands to you, alas, yours no longer."

The specific terms of Proteus' account indicate that Orpheus' disastrous lapse is due neither to some inexplicable quirk of fate nor to a particular character deficiency. Proteus' depiction of Orpheus as a lover who is overcome by madness (*dementia*) suggests an analogy between Orpheus' fateful error and the kinds of helpless self-destruction that, in *Georgic* 3, was ascribed to the influence of *amor*.

It also evokes the conventional representation of love, which can be traced as far back in Latin literature as Plautus' comedies; which had exponents as varied as Lucretius, Cato the Elder, and Cicero; and which were receiving new and forceful expression in the erotic elegies of Virgil's contemporaries.[19] A. W. Allen has said of its representation in Roman elegy that "love is a violent passion, a fault that destroys the vision and perverts the will, but a power that the lover is helpless to control and from which there is no release. This kind of love is the subject matter of elegy. It is common material, which may be found anywhere in literature dealing with love . . . love as it is normally and traditionally regarded in classical thought."[20] As a measure of his helplessness, the lover may be described as "sick" and suffering *aegritudo* or *perturbatio animi* ("mental sickness or disorder").[21] There are a number of specific terms that are so frequently used to characterize the lover and his plight as to acquire a quasi-technical status in erotic literature. Some of them occur in the description of *amor* in *Georgic* 3: *furiae, furor, miser*. The conditions of *dementia* and *furor* were commonly contrasted with *constantia* and *sanitas* as manifestations of the lover's abject helplessness. In Proteus' story Eurydice shows her assumption of conventional attitudes by calling herself *miseram* (494) and by attributing Orpheus' error to *furor* (495). Proteus himself reflects the same point of view in his use of *dementia*. Orpheus *is* "incautious," *incautum*, to be sure. But the whole thrust of the conventional interpretation that controls Proteus' narrative is that such incaution as Orpheus' is an inevitable consequence of his condition as a lover.

That certainty of failure inherent in Orpheus' efforts points to another distinctive condition of human existence: unlike Aristaeus who enjoys the special protection of his divine mother, Orpheus can expect neither the gods nor fate to make any concessions to his human frailties. Proteus characterized Pluto and his consort as *regem tremendum / nesciaque humanis precibus mansuescere corda* ("the awesome king and hearts which do not know how to be softened by human prayers," 469-470). The full extent of their heartlessness is revealed in their swift punishment of Orpheus' momentary lapse, a lapse

---

19. For documentation see A. W. Allen, "Elegy and the Classical Attitude Toward Love: Propertius 1.1," *YCS* 11 (1950) 255-277, esp. 258-264. The argument of this paragraph follows closely that on pp. 192-193 of my article "*Georgics* 3.209-294: *Amor* and Civilization," *CSCA* 8 (1975) 177-197, and is presented here with the kind permission of the editors of that journal.

20. Allen 264.

21. For this and the discussion of Roman erotic language that follows, see Allen 258-264.

that, according to the conventional views of love in Roman antiquity, Orpheus was helpless to prevent. Proteus himself observed of Orpheus' sudden madness that *ignoscenda quidem, scirent si ignoscere Manes* ("it is certainly to be forgiven, if the dead knew how to forgive," 489). Implicit in that exclamation is the idea that, if the dead cannot forgive Orpheus' error, an error that deserves forgiveness if any does, then they will forgive no human failing.

The significance of Orpheus' loss of Eurydice pertains to more than the specific operation of *amor* and the gods of the Underworld. It confirms earlier suggestions in the *Georgics* that humans can expect no concessions from any of the suprahuman forces, whether the fates or the gods, who control the world. Proteus, we have observed, claimed that Orpheus would bring disaster on Aristaeus, *ni fata resistant* ("unless the fates resist," 455). But we knew even at the time that the fates *would* resist, that Aristaeus' fortunes and reputation would be restored. The significance of Orpheus' particular relationship to the gods is generalized still further by parallels with the poet himself. Virgil introduced this *Georgic* with an expression of uncertainty about his own relationship to the divine patrons of poetry. He said that no small glory might be won by his exposition of beekeeping, *si quem / numina laeua sinunt auditque uocatus Apollo* ("if hostile gods allow and Apollo answers prayer," 6-7). At the conclusion of the *Georgics* Virgil contrasts his poem, the product of *ignobilis oti* ("ignoble leisure," 564) with Caesar's triumphant progress into the East. Of course, we must allow for various rhetorical functions of such statements, and I will consider them below. But whatever ulterior purpose Virgil's expressed uncertainty about the goodwill of the gods may have, it functions like similar statements of poetic intent in previous *Georgics*. It fits the poet's own activity into the general pattern of the poem's argument so that this argument is shown to apply, however specific the terms in which it is expressed, to a wide range of human experience.

The specific terms in which Proteus describes Orpheus' fate also help to generalize its significance, since they often recall previous statements about the impersonal workings of nature. The turning point in Orpheus' heroic effort to bring Eurydice back to life came when he paused (*restitit*) and looked back at her. That momentary lapse was followed by an abrupt reversal of Orpheus' fortunes: *ibi omnes / effusus labor* ("then all his labor poured away," 491-492). That description is reminiscent of the simile in *Georgic* 1 of the rower who, once he lets up the least bit at his oars, is carried off headlong downstream (1.199-203). Similarly, the language of Proteus' narrative recalls Virgil's description in *Georgic* 1 of the inflexible laws that govern nature (1.60-61):

> Continuo has leges aeternaque foedera certis
> imposuit natura locis.

> At the very outset nature imposed these laws and eternal conditions on specific places.

Proserpina's condition that Orpheus not look back at Eurydice is described as a *legem* ("law," 487), and Orpheus' violation of it is a violation of the *foedera* ("conditions" or "pacts") of a harsh tyrant, (492). His punishment confirms the inevitability of man's failures to arrest the natural process of degeneration and the stern inflexibility of nature's laws.

Orpheus' loss must be irrevocable and can lead only to despair. Proteus asks (504-505),

> quid faceret? quo se rapta bis coniuge ferret?
> quo fletu Manis, quae numina uoce moueret?

> What was he to do? Where, now that his wife had been torn away a second time, where was he to turn? With what tears might he move the dead, with what appeal, the divine spirits?

His questions are, of course, rhetorical. There *was* nothing for Orpheus to do; there are no prayers that can move the gods or alter fate: *illa quidem Stygia nabat iam frigida cumba* ("she, indeed, was crossing, already cold, in the Stygian boat," 506).

It is the nature of human passion, however, that the knowledge of hopelessness provides no consolation. Orpheus pours out his grief in song, even though he must know that he does so to no avail. And just as in the Underworld, so now his song has extraordinary power (507-510):

> septem illum totos perhibent ex ordine mensis
> rupe sub aëria deserti ad Strymonis undam
> flesse sibi, et gelidis haec euoluisse sub antris
> mulcentem tigris et agentem carmine quercus.

They say that for seven months in a row at the foot of an airy crag, at the deserted Strymon's waters, he mourned to himself and that he pondered these things in chill caves, calming tigresses and moving oak trees with his song.

Once again, the effects of Orpheus' song may be ascribed not to any superhuman power, but rather to the universality of its appeal. He laments in song (511-515),

> qualis populea maerens philomela sub umbra
> amissos queritur fetus, quos durus arator
> obseruans nido implumis detraxit; at illa
> flet noctem, ramoque sedens miserabile carmen
> integrat, et maestis late loca questibus implet.

> just as a nightingale, lamenting beneath a poplar's shade, complains of its lost offspring whom a hard plowman saw and took, unfledged, from their nest; but she cries the night long and sitting on a branch renews her pitiable song, and with her sad plaints fills the countryside far and wide.

The example of the nightingale demonstrates that Orpheus' sense of loss is but the personal manifestation of an experience that is shared by all creatures.

It also points to the indifference of the larger world to such grief as Orpheus and the nightingale share. The nightingale's fate is presented merely as tangential to the larger creative process of cultivation and civilization. Her loss is the farmer's gain. His ruthless destruction of her young echoes the description in *Georgic* 2 of how the farmer, in his efforts to clear the land for plowing, must uproot trees and drive birds from their "ancestral homes" (2.207-211). More generally, it recalls Virgil's repeated exhortations to the farmer to steel himself for the harsh acts that the work of cultivation necessitates. The nightingale's fate is parallel to Orpheus' own. Just as cultivation proceeds at the expense of individual loss and suffering, so also the vital processes of nature are shown to continue unaffected by Orpheus' personal tragedy. For Orpheus, Eurydice's death is an all-consuming event. Like the nightingale, he gives himself over completely to his grief. He retreats to a barren wasteland that reflects his own sense of desolation and his total lack of interest in life (516-520):

> nulla Venus, non ulli animum flexere hymenaei:
> solus Hyperboreas glacies Tanaimque niualem
> aruaque Riphaeis numquam uiduata pruinis
> lustrabat, raptam Eurydicen atque inrita Ditis
> dona querens.

> No Venus, no wedding hymns moved him. Alone he wandered the Hyperborean ice floes and snowy Tanais and fields never free from Riphaean frost, as he complained that his Eurydice had been stolen and that Dis' gifts were useless.

Even though Orpheus' grief exemplified an experience that is universal, his loss, still, is only personal. The elemental forces of life and creation in nature go on unabated. They display the same indifference to Orpheus' suffering as the farmer does to that of the nightingale. Virgil symbolizes their inexorable progress in the orgiastic violence of Bacchantes who assert their power here, as in Euripides' *Bacchae*, with utter ruthlessness (520-522):

> . . . spretae Ciconum quo munere matres
> inter sacra deum nocturnique orgia Bacchi
> discerptum latos iuuenem sparsere per agros.

> Angered by his devotion to the dead, the Ciconian mothers, during their worship of the gods and the orgies of nocturnal Bacchus, tore the young man apart and scattered him over the broad fields.

The *sparagmos*, the Bacchantes' dismemberment and scattering of their victim, was not simply spiteful destruction. It was an acknowledged ritual of creation.[22] The pieces of their victim (regarded as an embodiment of Dionysus himself) were intended to impart fertility to the fields where they fell. In calling the Bacchantes *matres*, Virgil explicitly designates them in their role as agents of life and fertility. Their murder of Orpheus, therefore, incorporates his death and that of Eurydice into the regenerative processes of nature. It reconfirms Virgil's earlier argument that death and birth, destruction and creation, are interdependent.

---

22. For the ancient evidence on the *sparagmos* and its interpretation, see Linforth, (above, n. 18) esp. ch. V, "Myth of the Dismemberment of Dionysus," 307-364.

If Orpheus is a victim of the inexorable processes of nature rather than an active agent or a beneficiary of them, it is because he does not perceive them or does not acknowledge them. He is aware only of his own personal loss (523–527):

> tum quoque marmorea caput a cervice reuulsum
> gurgite cum medio portans Oeagrius Hebrus
> uolueret, Eurydicen uox ipsa et frigida lingua,
> a miseram Eurydicen! anima fugiente uocabat:
> Eurydicen toto referebant flumine ripae.

Then, even as his head, torn from its marble neck, was carried off, tossed in mid-current by Oeagrian Hebrus, of its own accord his voice and his cold tongue—even as his spirit fled, called Eurydice, o wretched Eurydice; all along the river the banks echoed back, Eurydice.

Orpheus denies himself a place among the living because he will not or cannot reconcile himself to his losses, because he cannot give up what is irretrievably gone. His example is a dramatic warning to Aristaeus and to us all that we must not attempt to live in the past, that we must accept loss, even of the most personal and tragic kind, as the natural complement of growth and new life. That does not mean that we must simply reject the past or strive for an attitude of detached indifference toward it. Proteus' story of Orpheus and Eurydice does not allow indifference. It demands that we respect the human suffering that loss and change entail, for it is only by acceptance of them and their place in the natural order of things that we can hope to confront the future honestly. Both relationships to the past, acceptance and freedom, are formalized, as I shall demonstrate, in the ritual regeneration of bees that concludes the narrative of Aristaeus' achievement.

The story of Orpheus' suffering and fate concluded, our attention is shifted abruptly back to Aristaeus and his privileged existence. Without a further word Proteus dives into the waters, leaving Cyrene to reassert her calming influence (528–547). As in the opening scene of Aristaeus' story, she finds her son in a state of agitation. His encounter with Proteus has left him *timentem* ("terrified," 530). She immediately reassures him: *nate, licet tristis animo deponere curas* ("child, you may put these sad concerns out of your mind," 531). She tells him that the anger of Eurydice's companions is the "whole cause" (*omnis causa*) of his misfortune (532–534). Although she instructs Aristaeus to make a propitiatory sacrifice to the nymphs, she adds that they are *faciles* ("easy [to appease]," 535), that they will respond favorably to his offerings, and that they will give up their anger (536).

As in her previous encounter with Aristaeus in her subaqueous chambers, she counters his turbulent emotions with the orderly demands of ritual (537–542, 544–545, 548–553):

> sed modus orandi qui sit prius ordine dicam:
> quattuor eximios praestanti corpore tauros,
> qui tibi nunc uiridis depascunt summa Lycaei,
> delige, et intacta totidem ceruice iuuencas.
> quattuor his aras alta ad delubra dearum
> constitue, et sacrum iugulis demitte cruorem,
> post, ubi nona suos Aurora ostenderit ortus,
> inferias Orphei Lethaea papauera mittes
> . . . . . . . . . . . . .
> haud mora, continuo matris praecepta facessit:
> ad delubra uenit, monstratas excitat aras,
> quattuor eximios praestanti corpore tauros
> ducit et intacta totidem ceruice iuuencas.
> post, ubi nona suos Aurora induxerat ortus,
> inferias Orphei mittit.

"But as to the manner of prayer and its orderly sequence, I will tell you: select four excellent bulls with outstanding bodies which you now have grazing on the peaks of green Lycaeus, and an equal number of heifers whose necks have not yet touched the yoke. Set up for them four altars at the high shrines of the goddesses and draw the sacred blood from their throats. . . . Afterward, when for the ninth time Dawn has made her appearance, send death offerings of the Lethean poppy to Orpheus. . . ." No delay. Right away he follows his mother's precepts. He goes to the shrines as instructed, erects the altars, leads four excellent bulls with outstanding bodies and an equal number of heifers whose necks have not yet touched the yoke. Afterward, when for the ninth time Dawn had made her appearance, he sends death offerings to Orpheus.

With apparent effortlessness Cyrene has once again replaced confusion with order, distress with serenity. One effect of that final encounter between Cyrene and her son, coming as it does immediately after the report of Orpheus' helpless cries to Eurydice, is to reestablish the contrast between Orpheus and Aristaeus, between the mortal and the hero. At the beginning of Virgil's story, that contrast was softened by the account of Aristaeus' struggle with Proteus which came between the initial characterization of the petulant hero and Proteus' subsequent story of Orpheus. Now, in the direct juxtaposition of the two figures and their characteristic experiences, we are reminded of how different the hero's circumstances are from those of other mortals.

One of the most striking aspects of the scene is how much it seems to minimize Aristaeus' own role in his success. The *bugonia* was first announced as a heroic achievement of such magnitude as to warrant calling its discoverer a god. After Aristaeus' story has been told, the role of the hero and his art seem curiously restricted and passive. It is Cyrene who brings order from confusion, serenity from distress, not her son. She directs Aristaeus' actions from beginning to end. It is she who reveals the *bugonia*; Aristaeus merely follows her instructions. Even the assertion that he does so *haud mora* ("without delay," 548) attests as much to his subservience as to his eagerness. Insofar as his success depends on his divine mother, his example suggests that heroic achievement must always be beyond the reach of ordinary mortals. It is not simply a matter of effort or will or even of an extraordinary character. It is a gift of the gods. We cannot match Aristaeus' achievements by knowing more or trying harder. In the last analysis heroes are the agents of a fate that is exceptional, unpredictable, and uncontrollable. We can never count on them to avert the tragedies of human existence. In fact, Cyrene's final instructions to Aristaeus reveal that the hero himself can only succeed by recognizing and adapting to nature.

Our attention is called to the precise terms of those instructions by the very fact that they are inconsistent with the description of the *bugonia* that introduced the myth of Aristaeus. For example, Virgil reported that a single calf should be selected, that its orifices be blocked, and that it should be beaten in such a manner that its entrails are smashed while its skin remains unbroken (295-314). Cyrene specifies, rather, eight animals, four bulls and four heifers. While she says nothing about blocking their orifices or beating them, she does order that their throats be cut (542). Such inconsistencies help to isolate the essential underlying conception that is common to both sacrifices, namely, that destruction and death are the necessary conditions for creation and life. In a sense, Cyrene does exactly what Aristaeus first spitefully challenged her to do. In demanding sacrifice of eight of his best cattle, she extends her son's loss to include other claims to glory in addition to his bees. But her demand is now seen not as an expression of malice but, rather, as the condition for a new swarm. Aristaeus willingly accepts it, because he has been shown that destruction and loss are integral parts of the creative process.

The specific details of Cyrene's instructions also have a significance in their own right. In particular, they make the technical procedures for generating new bees into a ritual acknowledgment of the important truths that were expressed in the story of Orpheus. Indeed, what Cyrene requires of Aristaeus is not so much a technical procedure as a ritual appeasement of the dead, which is organized around the two major themes of the Orpheus story: respect for human mortality and suffering, and acceptance of loss as the means to freedom from the past. Cyrene begins by telling Aristaeus that he must perform *munera* (534), a regular term for funeral rites.[23] She presents her instructions on the selection and sacrifice of animals as a *modus orandi* ("manner of praying," 537). Details of the ritual that Cyrene dictates are drawn specifically from conventional Roman worship of the dead. The beating of a suffocating animal—the procedure Virgil ascribed to the Egyptians—seems to be unparalleled in Rome as a sacrificial act, but the cutting of a victim's throat was a normal means of sacrifice, especially to the dead: they received their nourishment from the blood that poured into the earth from the victim's body.

Likewise, in the initial description of the *bugonia* we were told simply that new bees would appear *mox* ("soon," 310) after the dead bull had been left to rot. Cyrene, on the other hand, tells Aristaeus to return to the scene of the sacrifice in nine days (545, 552). At

---

23. As in Catullus 101.3; *Aeneid* 4.624; 6.886 et passim.

Rome the ninth day was traditionally the time for the conclusion of funeral rites, burial of the dead, and a final offering: the *novendiale sacrum*.[24] In addition, the *parentalia*, an official state holiday for worship of the dead, lasted nine days. The first eight were occupied with the private worship of the family dead. The ninth day was reserved for the *feralia*, public sacrifices to all the dead.[25] Cyrene's requirement that Aristaeus sacrifice a black sheep to Orpheus also suggests that her model is the *parentalia*. Victims intended for sacrifice to the dead usually had to be black, and the offerings of the *parentalia* might include the blood of a black sheep.[26] Insofar as Aristaeus' sacrifice is modeled on the *parentalia*, his generation of new bees is made to be contingent on his formal expression of respect for Orpheus and Eurydice and for human mortality in general.

There remain some other aspects of the rites prescribed by Cyrene that are unconventional and, therefore, the more notable. Underlying worship of the dead was respect for their powers over the living. Offerings were made not only to ensure the dead a peaceful existence, but also to win their active help and, equally important, to avert their anger.[27] In Cyrene's instructions to Aristaeus, acts of atonement and appeasement, which we might expect to be addressed to the dead, are transferred, rather, to Eurydice's living

---

24. See *Servius auctus* on *Aeneid* 5.64, and see Porphyrion's commentary on Horace, *Epode* 17.48.

25. The most complete ancient source for the *parentalia* and *feralia* is Ovid's *Fasti* 2.533-570; cf. *Frazer's* commentary on those lines (vol. 2, pp. 431-446).

26. Will Richter, ed. and comm., *Vergil: Georgica* (Munich 1957), in his commentary on *G.* 4.544ff. asserts that inclusion of black sheep in this context is an anomalous borrowing from Greek cult. In his description of the celebration in the *Fasti*, Ovid specifies votive garlands, grain, salt, bread soaked in wine, and violets as the necessary offerings (2.535-540). However, he does go on to say that other larger sacrifices, while not necessary, are acceptable (2.541). Ovid traces the origin of the *parentalia* with its customary offerings to Aeneas' sacrifices to his father, Anchises. Virgil's account of that original celebration (*Aeneid* 5.42-108) is not completely consistent with Ovid's description of subsequent practice. While Virgil omits offerings of grain and salt, he emphasizes sacrifices of animals, including *bidentes* (sheep of an appropriate age), which are described as black (5.96-97). Lucretius, *DRN* 3.51-53, specifically associates the *parentalia* with the sacrifice of black animals: *et quocumque tamen miseri venere, parentant / et nigras mactant pecudes et manibu' divis / inferias mittunt* ("and wherever those wretches have gone, they sacrifice to their ancestors; they sacrifice black cattle and dispatch funeral offerings to the holy shades"). C. Bailey has collected further evidence in *Religion in Virgil* (Oxford 1935, reprinted 1969) 284. See also the commentary of Franz Bömer, *P. Ovidius Naso: Die Fasten* (Heidelberg 1957) vol. 2 ad *Fasti* 2.534ff., p. 121.

27. See *Frazer's* discussion of the *Lemuria* in his commentary on *Fasti* 5.421 (vol. 4, pp. 36-46, esp. p. 40).

companions, the Napaeae. It is they whom Aristaeus must approach as *supplex* ("suppliant," 534)—they whose "peace" he must seek, whom he must "venerate," and whose "anger" he must avert with offerings (535-536). Cyrene's emphasis on the anger of the nymphs —her identification of them, not Orpheus, as the source of Aristaeus' misfortune—is the more striking because it is in apparent contradiction to Proteus' opening assertion that it was Orpheus' anger that caused the loss of Aristaeus' bees. In so conspicuously transferring the desire and power for revenge from Orpheus to the living nymphs, Cyrene denies, or at least modifies, the conventional reasons for worshipping the dead.

Her own reasons for such worship, on the other hand, are implicit in the offerings she requires Aristaeus to give to Orpheus (545-546):

inferias Orphei Lethaea papauera mittes
et nigram mactabis ouem.

You will offer Orpheus funeral rites, Lethean poppies, and you will sacrifice a black sheep.

The sacrifice of the black sheep was, as I have already observed, a regular, if not absolutely necessary, part of rites for the dead. But Cyrene's instructions subordinate that offering to a prior one, that of Lethean poppies. The organization of line 545 actually presents poppies as parallel syntactically to *inferias* ("funeral rites") and object of the same verb, so that poppies might be regarded as standing in apposition to *inferias*—that is, they are presented as being by themselves the virtual equivalent of funeral rites. The sacrifice of a sheep, then, is added on almost as an afterthought, certainly as a matter of secondary importance. The offering of forgetfulness to Orpheus is the essential part of the ritual that Aristaeus must perform. When, subsequently, he comes to honor Eurydice, he will find, according to Cyrene, that she has *already* been appeased (547): *placatam Eurydicen uitula uenerabere caesa* ("Eurydice, who has already been placated, you will worship with a slaughtered calf").

The critical role of the poppy in Cyrene's instructions is unexpected inasmuch as that flower is nowhere attested in ritual offerings to the dead. In fact, when any particular kinds of flowers are specified in ancient literature, they are the rose and, less frequently, the violet.[28] Cyrene's choice of the poppy, then, is striking. But it is not unintelligible. Against the background of Proteus' story the singular appropriateness of the poppy as an offering is clearly indicated by its description as Lethean. Lethe, of course, was the Underworld river whose waters induced forgetfulness in all those who drank them and thereby relieved the dead from fruitless desire for return to the world of the living. The epithet "Lethean" is further explained by the narcotic effect of the poppy, which was well known in antiquity. It is not uncommon in ancient literature for poppies to be noted for their soporific effect and to be presented, consequently, as a source of comfort for the suffering to whom they brought the relief of forgetfulness.[29] For Orpheus, Lethean forgetfulness will have a special value. It may help him, as it does all the dead, to forget the world of the living; but it is not the loss of life for which Orpheus grieves. More important, Lethean poppies will enable him to forget that prior loss that made life itself not worth living, his separation from Eurydice. Forgetfulness will free Orpheus from a past he cannot reclaim.

Cyrene's intermingling of elements from agricultural technology and from traditional Roman worship of the dead is significant in several ways. I have already observed that it transforms the nature and meaning of the *bugonia*. By returning the focus of the poem from a general to a specifically Roman context, it also establishes a connection between the universal truths expressed in the Aristaeus myth and the Romans' own experience. In particular, it seeks to reinterpret Roman worship of the dead as a ritual acknowledgment of the universal truth that human loss is inevitable and irredeemable. For Romans to worship the dead as Cyrene directs is to express respect for human mortality and to affirm that there can never be a return to the way things were. It is to lay the past to rest, as Aristaeus does for both Orpheus and himself when he makes his offering of Lethean poppies. The value of the rite that Aristaeus must perform, therefore, lies not so much in its power to transform nature as in its demand that man recognize and conform to nature.

28. The evidence is collected and discussed by Frazer in his commentaries on *Fasti* 2.533 (vol. 2, pp. 433-434) and on 2.539 (vol. 2, pp. 436-437).

29. Alluded to in *Servius* on *G.* 4.544 and more explicitly on *G.* 1.78, 212. Other references to the ancient evidence are to be found in *Frazer* on *Fasti* 4.531 (vol. 3, p. 292) and on *Fasti* 4.661 (vol. 3, p. 322). Virgil himself calls the poppy *soporiferum* in *Aeneid* 4.486.

That insistence on the subordination of man to nature is confirmed in the sudden appearance of Aristaeus' new bees (554–558):

> hic uero subitum ac dictu mirabile monstrum
> aspiciunt, liquefacta boum per uiscera toto
> stridere apes utero et ruptis efferuere costis,
> immensasque trahi nubes, iamque arbore summa
> confluere et lentis uuam demittere ramis.

But hereupon, suddenly and marvelous to tell, they see a prodigy throughout the liquified entrails of the cattle: bees buzzing everywhere in their womb. They burst from the animals' sides and seethe; huge clouds are formed and now at the top of a tree they gather and hang in a cluster from the swaying branches.

The transition from the bees' sudden violent outburst of energy to calm repose parallels the pattern of Cyrene's healing influence on her son. The clustered bees suggest an intense vitality that is yet contained—not straining to break out, but ordered and concentrated within itself. Like Cyrene's easy control, so the spontaneity and self-sufficiency of the bees seem to undercut Aristaeus' heroic stature. Their birth is like the seasonal appearance of new grapes to whose cluster (*uuam*) they are compared—or, indeed, like all birth in nature. It is a prodigy (*monstrum*), a miracle (*dictu mirabile*) that attests more to the inherent vitality of nature than to the extraordinary powers of the hero. He has acted, to be sure, but the bees' dramatic birth makes it clear once again how limited his role has been. He has not wrested his new bees from nature. His art, the ritual he performs—as bloody and ruthless as it is—does not violate nature or change it. Rather, it conforms to nature's own complex processes. In his story of Aristaeus Virgil has redefined the role of the hero. Aristaeus' art, as announced from the outset, is that of discovery; his accomplishments are *inuenta* (not "creations" but "findings," 283). And what he has discovered is that heroic achievement, whatever mastery of the world is possible, requires an understanding of nature's workings and a respect for the limitations they impose on humans.

The knowledge Aristaeus acquires through his encounter with Proteus is only partially realized in the literal generation of new bees. Why Aristaeus must understand the impersonal laws of nature and the interrelation of creation and destruction that they dictate, is clear enough. But why Proteus' insistence that Aristaeus learn to respect the tragic circumstances of human existence? The answer, of course, is that it was Aristaeus' insensitivity to human loss and suffering that cost him his bees in the first place. He must atone for his ruthlessness, and the best way to do that is to come genuinely to understand the human condition. Inasmuch as we have been encouraged to regard the bees' swarm as analogous to human society, and Aristaeus, to the Roman statesman or founder, then Virgil's dramatic emphasis on human experience is also relevant to larger thematic concerns of the poem. Just as the farmer must understand the demands of nature and her inviolable laws, so equally must the statesman understand human nature and respect the essential tragedy of human life.

## VIII

Appropriately, it is to the statesman that Virgil returns in the final lines of his poem. He recalls our attention to the political realities expressed in his first appeal to Caesar in the introduction to the *Georgics* (4.559–567):

> Haec super aruorum cultu pecorumque canebam
> et super arboribus, Caesar dum magnus ad altum
> fulminat Euphraten bello uictorque uolentis
> per populos dat iura uiamque adfectat Olympo.
> illo Vergilium me tempore dulcis alebat
> Parthenope studiis florentem ignobilis oti,
> carmina qui lusi pastorum audaxque iuuenta,
> Tityre, te patulae cecini sub tegmine fagi.

So much have I sung about the cultivation of fields and about trees while the great Caesar wields his lightning by the deep Euphrates in war and, victorious, gives laws to willing peoples and makes his way to Olympus. At that same time sweet Parthenope was nurturing me, Virgil, as I flourished in the pursuits of my inglorious leisure, I who played shepherds' songs and, as an audacious youth, sang of you, Tityrus, beneath the shade of the spreading beech tree.

That brief address preserves the distinction between the (heroic, soon-to-be divine) statesman and the (humble) poet, which defined the relationship of Virgil to the young Caesar in the introduction to *Georgic* 1. Caesar's metaphorical thundering suggests comparison with Jupiter, king of the gods and wielder of lightning, and, thus, not only attests to Caesar's current prowess but also recalls previous intimations of his deification. Now, we find, he has already embarked on that glorious progress toward divinity that Virgil foresaw at the beginning of his poem.

The poet, likewise, is revealed as a beneficiary already of the indulgence he requested in his first appeal to the statesman. He identifies himself as the same person who once "played" (*lusi*) at pastoral verse with youthful audacity. By a nice ambiguity in the last line of the poem, Virgil actually makes himself a kind of pastoral figure. That line repeats the first line of the first *Eclogue*. There, it is addressed as here, to Tityrus whose ease beneath the protective shade of the beech tree looks forward symbolically to his revelation that he has been spared the confiscation of his property and his displacement by the benevolent intervention of a godlike young man at Rome. In the transposition of that line to the *Georgics*, there is an important change: Virgil replaces Tityrus as the subject of the sentence. Instead of Tityrus reclining beneath the beech tree, we now have Virgil singing beneath it. Virgil has taken Tityrus' place or, at least, has joined the shepherd; he now partakes of that very leisure which Tityrus owes to his young patron at Rome. We are thus informed that Virgil's own *ignobile otium*, his "inglorious leisure," and the poetry that it makes possible are owed to Caesar's heroic actions.

In the light of what has taken place since the poet's first address to the statesman, however, their relationship has become more complex and ambiguous than it first seemed to be. Even though Virgil admits that his pursuits are inglorious by traditional Roman standards and even though he acknowledges his very real indebtedness to the statesman-soldier, this does not mean that we are to regard the contemplative life as a mere luxury. Nor does it mean that we are to see the active and contemplative lives as mutually exclusive and opposed. Throughout his poem Virgil has shown, to the contrary, that the two are necessary complements to each other. If it is action that provides the opportunity for contemplation, we have also been instructed repeatedly, from the very first passage of exposition onward, that observation, reflection, and understanding are necessary prerequisites to action.

Although agriculture has provided the most concrete examples of this truth in the *Georgics*, the poem has demonstrated its relevance to more general human concerns as well. It has shown that there are no utopias. Whether inspired by the venerable tradition of the farmer-soldier, by the longing for return to an essentially apolitical rustic life, by the hopeful prospect of universal Roman *imperium*, or by despair, simple alternatives to the complex realities of contemporary Rome have been exposed as illusory. The statesman can no more create a new Rome by simple reliance on past ideals or present fantasies than the farmer can produce fruitful crops without first looking to the disposition and character of his land and adapting to the inviolable laws of nature. While the story of Aristaeus demonstrates the gulf that separates the hero from lesser mortals, it also argues that the hero must, paradoxically, bridge that gulf, that he must learn to work within the bounds set by nature's laws and with a respect for human experience. Symbolically, he must submit to the instruction of Proteus, the personification of nature, and he must learn the fate of Orpheus, the poet, before he can achieve his goal. Consequently, even though Virgil's address to Caesar explicitly affirms his indebtedness to the statesman, that affirmation must be read in the context of a poem that assumes a quite different relationship between the poet and the man of action.

Most immediately, inescapable parallels with the story of Aristaeus suggest a complex interpretation of the poem's final lines. Aristaeus and Caesar are both heroes who either have demonstrated or will demonstrate their godlike superiority to ordinary men by performing the seemingly impossible task of replacing a ruined society with a new one. Although no parallel is actually drawn between the character and behavior of the young Caesar and the initial ruthlessness of Aristaeus, that *iuuenum confidentissimus* (445), the possibility of such a parallel would not need to have been spelled out for Virgil's contemporaries. If anyone of Virgil's era deserved that title in its fullest sense of ruthless and insensitive as well as self-assured, above all others it would have to be the young man who entered Roman politics at nineteen, who within a year joined a triumvirate that controlled Rome and was responsible for wholesale proscriptions, and who in less than thirteen years made himself undisputed master of the entire civilized world. In fact, by recalling his own *audax iuuenta*, "audacious youth," and the first *Eclogue*, set as it was during the

Second Triumvirate's initial reign of terror, Virgil invites his audience to recall the recent period of Roman history which saw the young Caesar's excesses as well as the poet's own and thus, perhaps, to reflect that rashness in two such disparate characters expresses a universal condition of youth itself.

Given persistent emphasis throughout the *Georgics* on the value of reflection and given, at the same time, the obvious possibility for significant parallelism between the young Caesar and the impetuous Aristaeus, it is notable that Virgil emphasizes the statesman's active virtues almost exclusively, if not altogether so. As singlemindedly as Aristaeus pursued his own kind of glory, the young Caesar pursues the traditional Roman ideal of the statesman-general, seeking glory through the giving of laws and the winning of battles. Aristaeus' aggressive demand for glory was related to his awareness of divine parentage and to his consequent impatience with the normal vicissitudes of human existence. The final description of Caesar's triumphant progress likewise expresses, although only implicitly, a criticism of the statesman's aloofness from his people. While the poet has contemplated, however ingloriously, the state of Italy and the needs of her people, Caesar is pictured at the Euphrates, fighting and giving laws among a people who are geographically, politically, and morally alien.[30]

Just as our understanding of the young Caesar and his role is colored by the depiction of Aristaeus, so our perception of Virgil's own role is influenced by the story of Aristaeus' encounters with Proteus and Cyrene. While they direct Aristaeus' attention to the necessity for harsh toil, to the irresistible force of the passions, to the finality of death, and to the uncompromising operation of fate in human affairs, so, by telling the story of Aristaeus, Virgil brings those same concerns to the attention of the Roman statesman to

---

30. The implicit meaning of this address to Caesar is in much the same spirit as the beginning of Horace's *C*. 4.5 published some nine years later (1–5):

Divis orte bonis, optume Romulae
custos gentis, abes iam nimium diu:
maturum reditum pollicitus patrum
   sancto concilio, redi.
lucem redde tuae, dux bone, patriae.

Born under kind gods, excellent guardian of Romulus' nation, you have stayed away too long. Grant that return, now due, which you promised to the august body of the senate. Kind leader, bring back the light to your fatherland.

whom his poem is dedicated. Virgil's role as expositor of the human condition is confirmed by the naming of his Muse in the last lines of the poem. Parthenope, who nurtured the poet as he composed the *Georgics*, was the tutelary divinity of Naples.[31] But she was also a Siren, one of those enchantresses who not only lured men to their deaths at sea, but also were supposed to accompany the dead to the Underworld and to mourn for them with songs of lamentation.[32] Parthenope herself perished tragically. According to one version of her story she, along with her sisters, threw herself into the sea in despair when she failed to overcome Odysseus. Her body was washed ashore at Naples.[33] A later version of her story, apparently well established during the Hellenistic Age, presented Parthenope as a maiden who fell in love with a Phrygian, Metiochos, and gave herself to him despite her determination to resist Aphrodite's power. Furious with herself, she cut off her hair and fled from Phrygia to Campania, where an enraged Aphrodite turned her into a bird.[34] The second century A.D. author, Lucian, identified her with Phaedra and Rhodope as a classic example of the "erotic woman."[35] By naming Parthenope as his Muse, Virgil does more than simply identify the city in which he composed his poem. In Parthenope the experience of human mortality and of passion is epitomized. When Virgil acknowledges his indebtedness to her, he asserts his own particular appreciation of those realities and their consequences for mortals. However deferential Virgil may appear, he has put himself in the same relation to the young Caesar that Proteus and Cyrene hold to Aristaeus.

Virgil's closing statements in the *Georgics*, therefore, are hardly to be taken as simple self-depreciation. His reference to the humbleness of his own contemplative efforts does not conceal a persistent commitment to them and betrays their essential daring. In looking

---

31. This is how *Servius* identifies her in his commentary on *G.* 4.563. Parthenope's identification with Naples was widespread in antiquity, and the ancient citations are listed both by J. Ilberg, "Parthenope" in *Roscher*, vol. 3.1, cols. 1653–1655, and in the unsigned "Parthenope," *RE*, Reihe 1, vol. 18, pt. 4, cols. 1934–1935.

32. For the Sirens as mourners of the dead, see Dositheus 8 in Hyginus, *Fabulae*, ed. H. J. Rose (Leiden 1934); and Euripides, *Helen* 167–179. On the general attributes of the Sirens, I have followed Weicker, "Seirenen," in *Roscher*, vol. 4, cols. 601–639.

33. Dionysius, *Periegesis* 359, and Eustathius in his commentary on *Odyssey* 12.167.

34. Dionysius, *Periegesis* 358; Eustathius and the Scholia to Dionysius ad loc. in C. Müller, *Geographici Graeci Minores*, vol. 2 (Paris 1855–1961), pp. 280, 445.

35. Lucian, *de Saltat.* 2.

back to the origins of his poetry in his "audacious youth," Virgil recalls his first description of the *Georgics* as *audacibus coeptis*—"an ambitious undertaking" (1.41)—in the introduction to the poem. He thereby implies a contrast between the audacious youth he shared with the young Caesar and a different, more mature audacity which informs his present work. Addressed as it is to the statesman as he pursues a traditional ideal of glory, the *Georgics* is more than an invitation to spend some time in the sheltered environment of ease and reflective play, which the statesman has himself made possible. It is also a challenge to come to terms with the facts that the Roman past and contemporary idealizations of it are not satisfactory models for the future and that there are no simple solutions to the complex problems of human existence. The poem is, in short, a challenge to efforts of contemplation and understanding that are as ambitious, daring, and important in their own way as Caesar's pursuit of glory in the East. The *Georgics* is also a plea—a plea to respect the human loss and suffering that must inevitably accompany even the most high-minded efforts to establish a new Roman order.

# A Bibliographical Note

In the concluding section of chapter 1, pp. 59–63, I identified and commented on works that have had an important influence on the course of *Georgics* scholarship and, also, works that exemplify particular approaches to criticism of the poem. The following short bibliography is more personal. I have singled out these works not because they are seminal or especially representative in the history of *Georgics* scholarship, but because they have been particularly helpful to me in developing and elaborating my own interpretation. I have not attempted a full bibliography of modern work on the *Georgics* because, as I pointed out in chapter 1, note 78, such bibliographies are numerous and easily accessible. I have followed throughout the text of R. A. B. Mynors, *P. Vergili Maronis Opera* (Oxford 1969).

Among commentaries on the *Georgics* I have referred most often to J. Conington, H. Nettleship, and F. Haverfield, *The Works of Virgil, with a Commentary* (London 1898, reprinted Darmstadt 1963), which is consistently helpful on points of grammar and, even more so, for citations of parallels to the *Georgics* in earlier Greek and Roman literature. Although I disagree regularly with the interpretations of Will Richter, *Vergil: Georgica* (Munich 1957), his clear surveys of the controversies surrounding the interpretation of specific passages and themes in the poem provide a most helpful, quick access to the relevant modern scholarship up to 1957 and to the kinds of interpretative questions the poem raises. L. P. Wilkinson's *The Georgics of Virgil: A Critical Survey* (Cambridge 1969, reprinted 1978) views the poem from a greater variety of perspectives than attempted here and offers an abundance of valuable information. It is, and should long remain, the standard work that students of the *Georgics* will consult first for a basic introduction to the poem and its place in literary history.

Three works that treat the *Georgics* in the context of a larger discussion deserve particular notice. Jean-Marie André, *L'otium dans la vie morale et intellectuelle romaine* (Paris 1966), has provided an important context for locating the *Georgics* in Roman thought. Likewise, I am much indebted to Michael J. K. O'Loughlin's *The Garlands of Repose: Studies in the Literary Representation of Civic and Retired Leisure* (diss. New Haven 1966), not only for its provocative study of the *Georgics* but even more for introducing me to interpretative categories and concepts that became central to my own efforts: contrasts between civic and retired leisure, between a "contracted" and an "expanded" focus, and between human energy perceived as "centripetal" and as "centrifugal." O'Loughlin's dissertation has been published with revisions by the University of Chicago Press, 1978. In general, Raymond Williams's *The Country and the City* (New York 1973) offers perhaps the most far-reaching and provocative discussions of his announced topic in contemporary criticism. Although Williams' particular concern is the relation of country and city in English thought and literature, much of what he has to say provides helpful perspectives for the study of classical Greek and Latin literature as well. Although Herta Klepl, *Lucrez und Vergil in ihren Lehrgedichten* (diss. Leipzig 1940, reprinted Darmstadt 1967), does not attempt a systematic analysis of the entire *Georgics*, her contrasts of specific passages in the *Georgics* and in Lucretius' *De Rerum Natura* are models of concise lucidity which invariably lead to a precise understanding of importantly distinctive aspects of each author.

Of articles and monographs relating specifically to the *Georgics*, H. Altevogt's "Labor Improbus," *Orbis Antiquus* 7 (1952), makes interpretation of *Georgic* 1.145-146 the focal point for a far-ranging discussion of the entire first book and is excellent on the relation of man and nature as it is elaborated there. L. P. Wilkinson's "Virgil's Theodicy," *CQ*, n.s. 23 (1963) 75-84, helped me out of the morass of controversy that surrounds the interpretation of Jupiter's theodicy in *Georgic* 1.121-159. Friedrich Klingner's "Über das Lob des

Landlebens in Virgils Georgica," *Hermes* 66 (1931) 159-189, is particularly suggestive on the relation of philosophy and country life in the concluding passages of *Georgic* 2. Adam Parry's "The Idea of Art in Virgil's *Georgics*," *Arethusa* 5 (1972) 35-52, is an eloquent appreciation of the tragic dimension to Virgil's perspective in the *Georgics*. C. P. Segal's "Orpheus and the Fourth *Georgic*: Vergil on Nature and Civilization," *AJPh* 87 (1966) 307-325, is a very ambitious and perceptive attempt to demonstrate the interrelationships between the *Georgics*' concern for art, nature, and politics as they are epitomized in the Aristaeus epyllion.

| | |
|---|---|
| Compositor: | Freedmen's Organization |
| Printer: | Braun-Brumfield |
| Binder: | Braun-Brumfield |
| Text: | Compugraphic Baskerville |
| Display: | Compugraphic Baskerville |
| Cloth: | Holliston Roxite B 51565 |
| Paper: | 50 lb. P&S offset |

873 V587 DM594vc1
Miles, Gary B.
Virgil's Georgics : a new inte